Taxing Wages in Latin America and the Caribbean

Please cite this publication as:
OECD/CIAT/IDB (2016), *Taxing Wages in Latin America and the Caribbean*, OECD Publishing, Paris.
http://dx.doi.org/10.1787/9789264262607-en

ISBN 978-92-64-26256-0 (print)
ISBN 978-92-64-26260-7 (PDF)

Corrigenda to OECD publications may be found on line at: *www.oecd.org/about/publishing/corrigenda.htm*.

Foreword

This new publication is jointly undertaken by the OECD Development Centre and the OECD Centre for Tax Policy and Administration, the Inter-American Center of Tax Administrations (CIAT) and the Inter-American Development Bank (IDB). It provides details of taxes paid on wages in 20 economies in Latin America and the Caribbean. The information contained in the Report covers the personal income tax and social security contributions paid by employees, the social security contributions and payroll taxes paid by their employers and cash benefits received by families. The objective of the Report is to illustrate how personal income taxes, social security contributions and payroll taxes are calculated and to examine how these levies and cash family benefits impact on net household incomes. The results also allow quantitative cross-country comparisons of labour cost levels and of the overall tax and benefit position of single persons and families.

The Report shows the amounts of taxes, social security contributions, payroll taxes and cash benefits for eight family-types, which differ by income level and household composition. It also presents the resulting average and marginal tax rates. Average tax rates show that part of gross wage earnings or total labour costs which are taken in personal income taxes (before and after cash benefits), social security contributions and payroll taxes. Marginal tax rates show the part of an increase of gross earnings or total labour costs that is paid in these levies. The average and marginal tax rates are also measured by income decile across the whole of the distribution of labour income for two types of family and in US dollar equivalents for a single person without children.

The focus of the Report is the presentation of new data on the tax/benefit position of employees in 2013. It uses household income survey data for each country to estimate the average wage of workers who reported being full-time employees within the formal sector of the economy. These data sources also enable the estimation of the labour income distribution by deciles for all the countries included in this publication.

The Report is structured as follows:

- *Chapter 1 contains an overview of the main results for 2013.*
- *Chapter 2 is a special feature entitled 'A view on taxes, social protection and informality in Latin America using Taxing Wages modelling'. It includes an analysis of the costs of formalisation for informal workers.*
- *Part I (International Comparisons) reviews the main results for 2013 and is divided into 2 chapters (Nos. 3 and 4). Chapter 3 reviews the main results for 2013, which are summarised in comparative tables and figures included at the end of that section. Chapter 4 presents a graphical exposition of the estimated tax burden on labour income in 2013 by income deciles across the whole of the distribution of labour income.*
- *Part II contains individual country tables specifying the wage levels considered and the associated tax burdens for eight separate family types, together with descriptions of each tax/benefit system.*
- *The Annex describes the methodology and its limitations.*

Acknowledgements

Taxing wages in Latin America and the Caribbean has been jointly produced by the Organisation for Economic Co-operation and Development (OECD) Centre for Tax Policy and Administration, the OECD Development Centre, the Inter-American Development Bank (IDB) and the Inter-American Center of Tax Administrations (CIAT). The staff from these organisations with responsibility for producing the publication were: Juan Carlos Benítez and René Orozco of the OECD Development Centre under the supervision of the Director Mario Pezzini and the Head of the Latin American and Caribbean Unit Angel Melguizo; Maurice Nettley and Dominique Paturot of the OECD Centre for Tax Policy and Administration under the Director Pascal Saint-Amans, Deputy Director Grace Pérez-Navarro and the Head of the Tax Policy and Tax Statistics Division David Bradbury; Agnes Rojas under the supervision of Principal Technical Leader in Fiscal Economics, Alberto Barreix from the IDB, and Miguel Eduardo Pecho from the CIAT.

The authors would like to thank other staff at the OECD Development Centre, the OECD Centre for Tax Policy and Administration and the IDB for their invaluable help in completing this first edition of the publication. We are especially grateful to Santiago Levy, Carmen Pagés and Martin Bès from the IDB who supported this project from the beginning and gave insights to an earlier version of this work. Veronica Alaimo, Mariano Bosch, Melany Alejandra Gualavisi and Maria Laura Oliveri from the IDB provided substantial technical insights, support and data for the elaboration of this publication and the special feature herein. Bert Brys from the OECD Centre for Tax Policy and Administration also provided valuable insights on the special feature. Agustina Vierheller from the Development Centre provided invaluable support in the edition of the chapters. Elizabeth Nash and Delphine Grandrieux from the OECD Development Centre's Communications and Publications team and Meral Gedik and Gabriella Scaduto from OECD Public Affairs and Communications ensured the production of the publication, in both paper and electronic form.

Finally, the IDB, the OECD Development Centre and the Centre for Tax Policy and Administration are also very grateful to our colleagues Daniel Artana from the Fundación de Investigaciones Económicas Latinoamericanas (FIEL), Marcela Meléndez from Econ Estudio, Héctor Villareal from the Centro de Investigación Económica y Presupuestaria (CIEP), Jonathan Menkos, Abelardo Medina and Ricardo Barrientos from the Instituto Centroamericano de Estudios Fiscales (ICEFI) and Raynata Wiggins for the comments provided on earlier versions of the country models.

Table of contents

Tables

Figures

Follow OECD Publications on:

http://twitter.com/OECD_Pubs

http://www.facebook.com/OECDPublications

http://www.linkedin.com/groups/OECD-Publications-4645871

http://www.youtube.com/oecdilibrary

OECD Alerts http://www.oecd.org/oecddirect/

This book has...

StatLinks
A service that delivers Excel® files from the printed page!

Look for the *StatLinks* at the bottom of the tables or graphs in this book. To download the matching Excel® spreadsheet, just type the link into your Internet browser, starting with the *http://dx.doi.org* prefix, or click on the link from the e-book edition.

Executive summary

The estimated amounts of tax and social security contributions (SSCs) paid on labour income by the average worker in Latin American and Caribbean (LAC) countries in 2013 was 21.7%. These payments are measured by the tax wedge which takes the total taxes and compulsory SSCs paid by employees and employers, less family benefits received as a proportion of the total labour costs for employers. This measure provides an analysis of the combined impact of these levies on net household income.

There are wide national variations in the tax wedge across LAC countries. The LAC countries covered by the Report range from 34.6% in Argentina and 32.2% in Brazil to 11% in Trinidad and Tobago and 10% in Honduras. Two other countries, Colombia and Uruguay had measures of 30% or more and one other, Guatemala had a tax wedge of less than 15%.

The average tax wedge in OECD countries was around two-thirds greater than in LAC countries (35.9% compared with 21.7%). This is mainly because the vast majority of the working population in the LAC region do not have to pay personal income tax (PIT) as their incomes are below the minimum PIT thresholds. Of the group of 20 LAC countries, it was only in Mexico that the average worker was liable for PIT. The LAC average tax wedge (21.7%) is comprised of the following components: PIT 0.3%; employee SSCs 7.7%; and employer SSCs 13.6%. The corresponding breakdown for the OECD average (35.9%) is: PIT 13.3%; employee SSCs 8.3%; and employee SSCs 14.3%.

LAC countries do not offer generous tax reductions or cash transfers for households with children at the average earnings level, which results in only small variations between the tax wedges of workers with children as compared to workers without children. The tax wedge for the average one-earner married couple with two children in the LAC group was only 0.3% percentage points less than for the single worker at 21.4%. The corresponding difference for OECD countries where such benefits are substantially higher was 9.5 percentage points. Family allowance schemes existed in only 5 of the 20 LAC countries – Argentina, Brazil, Chile, Colombia and Uruguay – and these are not available at the average wage level in Chile.

This new Report provides, for the first time, internationally comparable data on taxes and SSCs paid on labour income for the group of 20 LAC countries. It is a joint publication by the Inter-American Development Bank (IDB), the Inter-American Center of Tax Administrations (CIAT), and the OECD. Using a similar methodology to the OECD Taxing Wages database, it presents cross-country comparisons between LAC economies and OECD economies. The LAC countries covered are Argentina, Bolivia, Brazil, Chile, Colombia, Costa Rica, the Dominican Republic, Ecuador, El Salvador, Guatemala, Honduras, Jamaica, Mexico, Nicaragua, Panama, Paraguay, Peru, Trinidad and Tobago, Uruguay and Venezuela. The tax wedge figures for Chile and Mexico in this Report are different from the figures presented in the corresponding OECD Taxing Wages publication as they include the impact of all compulsory SSCs paid by employees and employers – both to the public and private sector – whereas OECD Taxing Wages only counts those contributions paid to the public sector as taxes.

The Report also contains a special feature which explores some of the relationships existing in LAC countries between taxes on wages (specifically SSCs), characteristics of labour markets and levels of labour informality. The analysis makes estimates of the formalisation costs – proxied by social contributions – that workers across the whole of the income distribution would have to pay to join or remain in the formal sector. There is some evidence that high rates of informality are correlated with high theoretical formalisation costs, especially for those at the lower end and in the low-middle range of the income distribution. This adds to the many other non-tax factors that explain decisions to work or remain in the informal labour market. The interaction between lower earnings thresholds of SSCs (generally minimum wages) and social security program contribution rates increases the costs of adhering to social programs for those with earnings in the lower and middle-income deciles while the cost of formal labour market participation as a percentage of earnings decreases for those in the upper half of the earnings distribution.

Other key findings:

- The estimated average personal tax rate in LAC countries was 9.3% of gross wage earnings in 2013. The great majority, 8.9%, of earnings comprised payments of employee SSCs with the remaining 0.4% being PIT. The corresponding figures for OECD economies were a personal tax rate of 25.4% of gross wage earnings, 9.9% being employee SSCs and 15.5% being PIT. This highlights the difference in the capacity of PIT to generate tax revenues from labour earnings in the OECD compared with LAC countries.
- The average tax wedge for the single worker without children ranged from 10.8% of total labour costs in the first income decile to 25.9% in the tenth decile. The corresponding figures for a one-earner married couple with two children were 7.1% and 25.7%.
- In the first income decile, a single individual without children paid an average of 3.9% of gross earnings in PIT and employee SSCs compared with 15.0% in the tenth decile. A one-earner married couple with two children, on average received 0.5% of gross earnings at the first income decile and paid 14.8% at the tenth decile.
- Total average annual labour costs including employer SSCs in the region expressed in USD in Purchasing Power Parities totalled USD 16 125 in 2013, the corresponding figures for the average wage and the net income after taxes that workers take home after PIT and SSCs being USD 13 771 and USD 12 347 respectively.
- Measures of the after-tax income elasticity show that on average tax systems on labour for average earners in LAC countries tend to be proportional, in contrast with OECD tax systems which tend to be much more progressive. For a single worker without children, LAC tax systems start to exhibit slight progressivity around the eighth income decile as workers in some countries start to pay PIT. Whereas for a one-earner married couple with two children, the average tax system is slightly progressive at lower levels of income, then becomes proportional in the middle-income deciles before matching the single worker without children at the upper deciles of the income distribution.

Chapter 1

Overview

This chapter presents the main results of the analysis of the taxation of labour income for twenty economies in Latin America and the Caribbean in 2013. Most emphasis is given to the tax wedge – a measure of the difference between labour costs to the employer and the corresponding net take-home pay of the employee – which is calculated by expressing the sum of personal income tax, employee plus employer contributions together with any payroll tax minus benefits as a percentage of labour costs. The calculations also focus on the net personal average tax rate. This is the term used when the percentage income tax and employee social security contributions net of cash benefits are expressed as a percentage of gross wage earnings. In this Report, the methodology used to estimate the tax wedges is based on the compulsory payments methodology;

- *The deductions from labour income (referred to in this Report as taxes) are defined as personal income tax, employee and employer social security contributions (paid either to general government or privately managed funds) and payroll taxes less cash transfers.*
- *Labour costs are defined as the sum of gross wage earnings, employers social security contributions (paid either to general government or privately managed funds) and payroll taxes.*

A more detailed description of the methodology is set out in the Annex. The key results focus on the single worker with no children on average earnings and include a comparison with the single married couple earner with two children. The analysis includes a review of how tax wedges vary across the income distribution.

1. Introduction

This Report provides unique information for each of twenty Latin American and Caribbean (LAC) countries on the income taxes paid by workers, their social security contributions, the family benefits they receive in the form of cash transfers as well as the social security contributions and payroll taxes paid by their employers.

The Report focuses on full-time employees in the formal sector assuming that their only source of income is derived from wage earnings. Additional assumptions are made regarding the personal circumstances of individuals to estimate their tax/benefit position. The results focus solely on taxes applied to wage earnings. Other forms of taxation due on non-wage income as well as taxes on consumption or net wealth are not taken into account. The cash benefits included are paid by general government as cash transfers, usually in respect of children in the household.

The Report presents several measures of taxation on labour. Most emphasis is given to the tax wedge – a measure of the difference between the total labour cost to the employer and the corresponding take-home-pay of the employee. The tax wedge is calculated by expressing the sum of personal income taxes, all compulsory social security contributions paid by employee and employers – both to the public and private sector – and payroll taxes, minus cash benefits as a percentage of the total labour cost. Employer social security contributions and – in some cases – payroll taxes are added to the wage earnings[1] to determine the amount of the total labour cost. The average tax wedge identifies the percentage of the labour cost which encompasses all compulsory taxes and social security contributions, net of cash benefits. Similarly, the marginal tax wedge measure identifies the share of these levies on an additional unit of labour cost.

The Report models the resulting tax wedge on different percentages of the average wage earnings, income distributions ordered by decile and annual fixed sums expressed in USD of full-time employed adults. The estimated earnings figures, which cover all industries within the productive sectors of Latin American and Caribbean economies, are derived from responses to representative national household income surveys. It should be recognised that the associated measures of total labour cost may, in some cases, be less that the actual labour costs incurred by employers as they can also willingly provide other monetary incentives and in-kind benefits to their employees.

The analysis also focuses on net personal average tax rates. This is the term used when the personal income tax and employee social security contributions net of cash benefits is expressed as a percentage of the annual gross wage earnings. The net personal marginal tax rate shows the share of an additional unit of income that is paid on taxes and employee social security contributions net of cash benefits.

The tax data and tax calculations relate to the calendar year of 2013. In Chile, the model is based on the Budget Law 2014 (voted in December 2013 and applied on income earned in 2013).

2. Review of results for 2013

2.1. *Tax wedge*

Table 1.1 describes the composition of the tax wedge between the total labour costs to the employer and the corresponding net take-home pay for a single individual without children earning the average wage. It also shows the estimated labour costs in both USD and dollars with equivalent purchasing power.

Argentina has the highest tax wedge at 34.6% of labour costs. Brazil, Uruguay and Colombia also have figures of 30% or more. Honduras had the lowest tax wedge at 10% with Guatemala and Trinidad and Tobago also having figures below 15%. The average tax wedge in the LAC countries was 21.7%. Mexico was the only country where workers pay personal income tax at the average wage level.

Compulsory social security contributions paid by the employee as a percentage of labour costs were highest in Chile at 18.2% followed by Uruguay (15.3%) and Argentina (13.4%). The lowest percentages were in Mexico (2.0%) and Honduras (3.4%).

Table 1.1. **Composition of the total tax wedge, 2013**

As % of labour costs

Country[1]	Total Tax Wedge[2]	Income Tax	Social Security Contributions		Labour Costs	
			Employee	Employer	USD	PPP[3]
Argentina	34.6	0.0	13.4	21.2	26 155	40 380
Brazil	32.2	0.0	6.7	25.5	14 125	18 992
Uruguay	30.5	0.0	15.3	15.2	14 877	17 188
Colombia	30.0	0.0	5.3	24.7	9 915	15 774
Costa Rica	28.0	0.0	7.3	20.7	14 419	19 468
Mexico	26.9	7.0	2.0	17.9	9 438	15 477
Panama	22.9	0.0	9.9	13.0	10 573	18 615
Chile	22.6	0.0	18.2	4.4	13 949	20 009
Bolivia	21.6	0.0	9.3	12.3	6 599	14 257
Paraguay	20.9	0.0	7.8	13.0	9 322	17 943
El Salvador	20.5	0.0	7.7	12.8	6 084	12 341
Nicaragua	19.2	0.0	4.9	14.3	3 739	9 613
Dominican Republic	19.2	0.0	5.1	14.1	6 291	13 049
Ecuador	18.5	0.0	8.5	10.0	8 893	16 169
Peru	17.5	0.0	10.1	7.4	6 771	12 085
Venezuela	17.4	0.0	4.8	12.6	9 925	15 682
Jamaica	16.6	0.0	6.0	10.7	4 088	6 639
Guatemala	13.2	0.0	3.6	9.6	6 552	13 761
Trinidad and Tobago	11.0	0.0	4.2	6.8	8 283	12 778
Honduras	10.0	0.0	3.4	6.6	6 264	12 290
Unweighted averages						
LAC	**21.7**	**0.3**	**7.7**	**13.6**	**9 848**	**16 125**
OECD[4]	**35.9**	**13.3**	**8.3**	**14.3**	**50 616**	**47 082**

Note: Single individual without children at the income level of the average worker.

1. Countries ranked by decreasing total tax wedge.
2. Includes payroll taxes where applicable.
3. Expressed in dollars with equal purchasing power.
4. The OECD averages are based on results published in OECD (2014) Taxing Wages – Table 0.2. The OECD figures shown for social security contributions are not directly comparable with the LAC country figures as they exclude contributions paid to privately managed funds.

StatLink http://dx.doi.org/10.1787/888933410070

Figure 1.1. **Income tax plus employee and employer social security contributions, 2013**

As % of labour costs

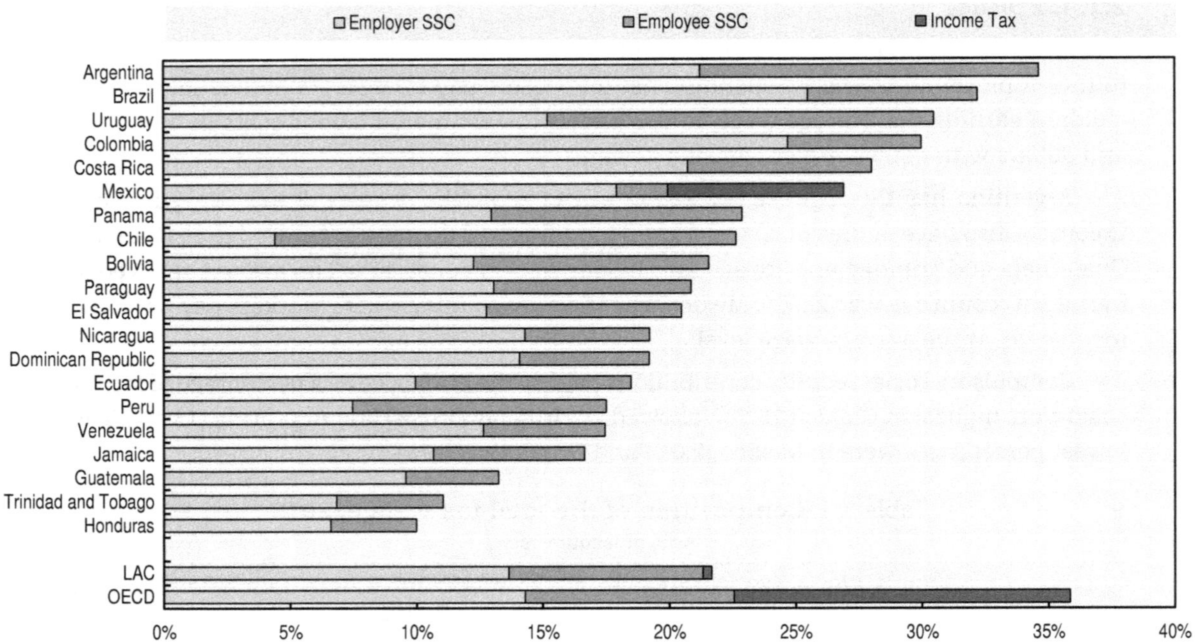

Notes: Single individual without children at the income level of the average worker.
Payroll taxes are included with employer SSCs where applicable.

StatLink http://dx.doi.org/10.1787/888933407321

The percentage of labour costs paid in employer social security contributions also varies widely across the countries in the Report. The highest levels were in Brazil (25.5%) and Colombia (24.7%). The lowest levels were in Chile (4.4%), Honduras (6.6%), Trinidad and Tobago (6.8%) and Peru (7.4%).

2.1.1. Personal average tax rates

The personal average rate is defined as income tax plus mandatory social security contributions paid by workers to both general government and privately managed funds as a share of gross wage earnings. Table 1.2 and Figure 1.2 show the personal average tax rates in 2013 for a single individual without children at the average earnings level decomposed into income tax and employee social security contributions. Table 1.2 also shows the gross annual average wages expressed in both in USD and in dollars with equivalent purchasing power.

Chile (19.1% of gross wage earnings) had the highest personal average tax rate in the region followed by Uruguay (18.0%) and Argentina (17.0%). The lowest rates were in Honduras (3.6%), Guatemala (4.0%) and Trinidad and Tobago (4.5%). The average amongst the LAC countries was 9.3%.

Table 1.2 and Figure 1.2 show that, with the exception of Mexico, workers in Latin America and the Caribbean countries do not pay any personal income tax at the average wage level. This is a very different situation to the OECD average in which the share of the income tax is higher than that of the employee social security contributions. This illustrates the weakness of the personal income tax as an instrument for collecting revenue from wages in Latin America and the Caribbean.[2] High levels of exempt income, prevalent informality and high levels of tax expenditures arising from personal deductions and basic reliefs are important contributory factors. It should be noted that this analysis only takes account of standard deductions and reliefs. There can be other non-standard deductions dependent on specific behaviours by taxpayers that serve to further reduce the average personal income tax rate.

Table 1.2. **Income tax plus employee social security contributions, 2013**

As % of gross wage earnings

Country[1]	Total payments	Income Tax	Social Security Contributions	Average wage	
				USD	PPP[2]
Chile	19.1	0.0	19.1	13 334	19 127
Uruguay	18.0	0.0	18.0	12 616	14 576
Argentina	17.0	0.0	17.0	21 155	31 808
Panama	11.4	0.0	11.4	9 202	16 202
Mexico	11.0	8.5	2.5	7 748	12 705
Peru	10.9	0.0	10.9	6 267	11 185
Bolivia	10.6	0.0	10.6	5 791	12 510
Ecuador	9.5	0.0	9.5	8 007	14 559
Costa Rica	9.2	0.0	9.2	11 428	15 430
Brazil	9.0	0.0	9.0	10 525	14 152
Paraguay	9.0	0.0	9.0	8 106	15 602
El Salvador	8.9	0.0	8.9	5 308	10 766
Colombia	7.0	0.0	7.0	7 466	11 878
Jamaica	6.7	0.0	6.7	3 653	5 932
Dominican Republic	6.0	0.0	6.0	5 405	11 212
Nicaragua	5.7	0.0	5.7	3 205	8 239
Venezuela	5.5	0.0	5.5	8 671	13 701
Trinidad and Tobago	4.5	0.0	4.5	7 718	11 906
Guatemala	4.0	0.0	4.0	5 925	12 443
Honduras	3.6	0.0	3.6	5 851	11 480
Unweighted averages					
LAC	**9.3**	**0.4**	**8.9**	**8 369**	**13 771**
OECD[3]	**25.4**	**15.5**	**9.9**	**43 631**	**40 292**

Note: Single individual without children at the level of income of the average worker.

1. Countries ranked by decreasing total payments.
2. Expressed in dollars with equal purchasing power.
3. The OECD averages are based on results published in OECD (2014) Taxing Wages, Table 0.3. The OECD figures shown for social security contributions are not directly comparable with the LAC country figures as they exclude social security contributions paid to privately managed funds.

StatLink http://dx.doi.org/10.1787/888933410080

Conversely, in all the Latin American and Caribbean countries, the share of employee payments to social security systems is highly important. These payments are contributions made to old age, disability, sickness, maternity, work injury, and unemployment schemes that are mandated by legislation.[3] Each country in the analysis requires their workforce to contribute to some kind of social security program. In Table 1.2 and Figure 1.2, the payments have been aggregated to calculate a single rate covering all the social security contributions paid by the employee. In some cases, countries have established lower thresholds and upper ceilings to the payments. In the region, the lower thresholds are generally set at the national minimum wage. In practice, given that an individual working in the formal sector should not earn less than the minimum wage, no worker is exempt from contributing to these schemes. If individuals were to earn less than the minimum wage, then they would be exempt.

Figure 1.2. **Percentage of gross wage earnings paid in income tax and employee social security contributions, 2013**

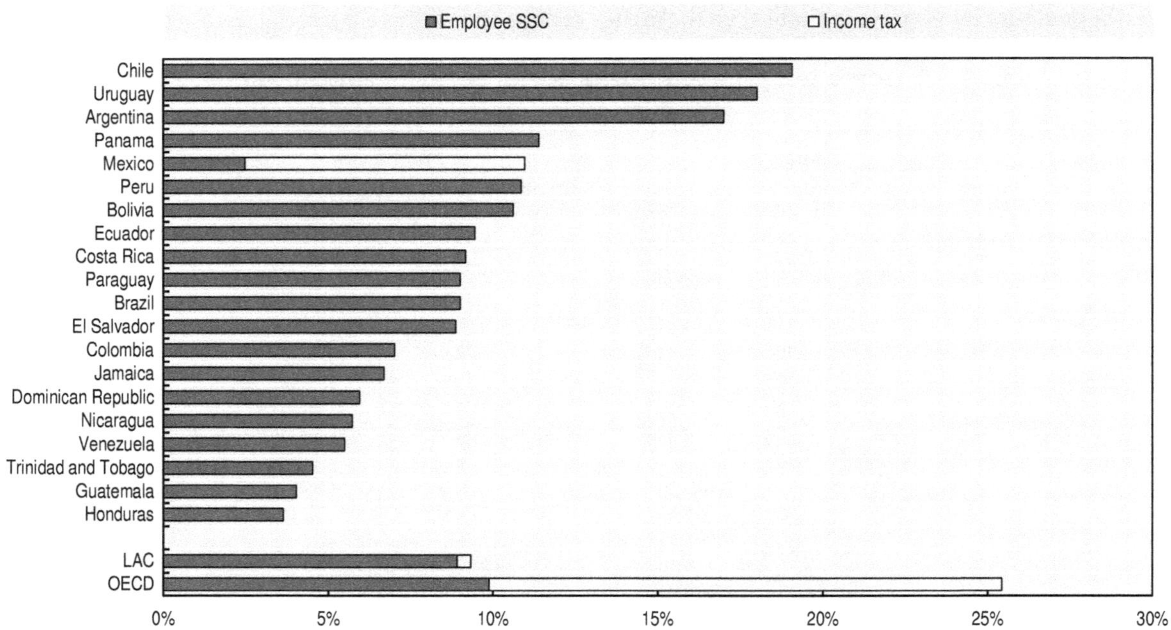

Notes: Countries ranked by decreasing tax burden.
Single worker without children at income level of the average wage.

StatLink http://dx.doi.org/10.1787/888933407331

2.1.2. *Family tax rates*

Table 1.3 and Figure 1.3 compare the tax wedges of a single worker with no children and a one-earner married couple with two children, both at the average wage level. The tax wedges of the married couple are either the same or lower than the corresponding figure for the single worker. Any differences between the two figures represent savings for the family compared with the single worker.

In the LAC region, these savings are small. The average tax wedge for the one-earner married couple with two children is only 0.3 percentage points lower than that for the single worker. In contrast, the corresponding comparison for OECD countries shows that the average saving for the family reduces the tax wedge by 9.5 percentage points of the total labour costs.

Table 1.3 and Figure 1.3 show that only 4 countries in the LAC region; Argentina, Colombia, Costa Rica and Uruguay have differences in the tax wedge due to family benefits at the average earnings level. In Argentina, Colombia and Uruguay, the differences are attributed to cash transfers and in Costa Rica they arise from full payment of the non-wastable tax credit for the head of the family and child tax credits. The size of these differences range from 1.6 percentage points of labour costs in Argentina to 0.6 percentage points in Uruguay.

This contrast between Latin American and Caribbean countries and their OECD counterparts in this respect is because the former do not offer generous fiscal benefits or cash transfers for households with children whereas these are commonplace in the OECD. In fact, only 5 of the 20 countries: Argentina, Brazil, Chile, Colombia and Uruguay offer family allowance schemes and only those in Brazil and Chile impact on earners below the average wage. In the same way, several Latin American and Caribbean countries offer special tax deductions in respect of the spouse and children, which do not have any impact at the average wage level.

Table 1.3. **Comparison of total tax wedge by family type, 2013**

As % of labour costs

Country	Single worker[1]	Married couple[2]	Difference
Argentina	34.6	33.0	1.6
Bolivia	21.6	21.6	0.0
Brazil	32.2	32.2	0.0
Chile	22.6	22.6	0.0
Colombia	30.0	27.0	3.0
Costa Rica	28.0	27.2	0.8
Dominican Republic	19.2	19.2	0.0
Ecuador	18.5	18.5	0.0
El Salvador	20.5	20.5	0.0
Guatemala	13.2	13.2	0.0
Honduras	10.0	10.0	0.0
Jamaica	16.6	16.6	0.0
Mexico	26.9	26.9	0.0
Nicaragua	19.2	19.2	0.0
Panama	22.9	22.9	0.0
Paraguay	20.9	20.9	0.0
Peru	17.5	17.5	0.0
Trinidad and Tobago	11.0	11.0	0.0
Uruguay	30.5	29.8	0.6
Venezuela	17.4	17.4	0.0
Unweighted averages			
LAC	**21.7**	**21.4**	**0.3**
OECD[3]	**35.9**	**26.4**	**9.5**

1. Single individual without children and earnings at the income level of the average wage.
2. One-earner married couple with two children at the income level of the average wage.
3. The OECD averages are based on results from OECD (2014) Taxing Wages, Table I.3. The OECD figures shown for social security contributions are not directly comparable with the LAC country figures as they exclude contributions paid to privately managed funds.

StatLink http://dx.doi.org/10.1787/888933410093

2.1.3. *Tax wedges by income deciles*

Tables 1.4 and 1.5 describe how average tax wedges vary across the income distribution for a single worker and a one-earner married couple with two children. On average, the trends are progressive. Table 1.4 shows that while single workers without children in the first decile of earnings have a tax wedge of 10.8% of total labour costs, this percentage increases as incomes rise to reach 25.9% of total labour costs in the tenth decile. In Table 1.5, the corresponding figures for the one-earner married couple with two children have a tax wedge of 7.1% of total labour costs in the first decile of income and 25.7% in the tenth decile.

Figures 1.4 and 1.5 present the decompositions of the total tax wedges over the income distributions for each of the two family types. These graphs show that couples with children have relatively lower tax wedges at the lowest levels of income. The gap between the average tax wedges for the average single worker and the one-earner married couple with children is 3.7 percentage points at the first income decile. This gap diminishes as income increases until it is only around 0.2 to 0.4 percentage points at income deciles 7 to 10. It is also noticeable that social security contributions paid by both employees and employers start to diminish as a percentage of total labour costs at income deciles 9 and 10.

Figure 1.3. **Income tax plus employee and employer social security contributions less cash benefits, 2013**

As % of labour costs, by family-type

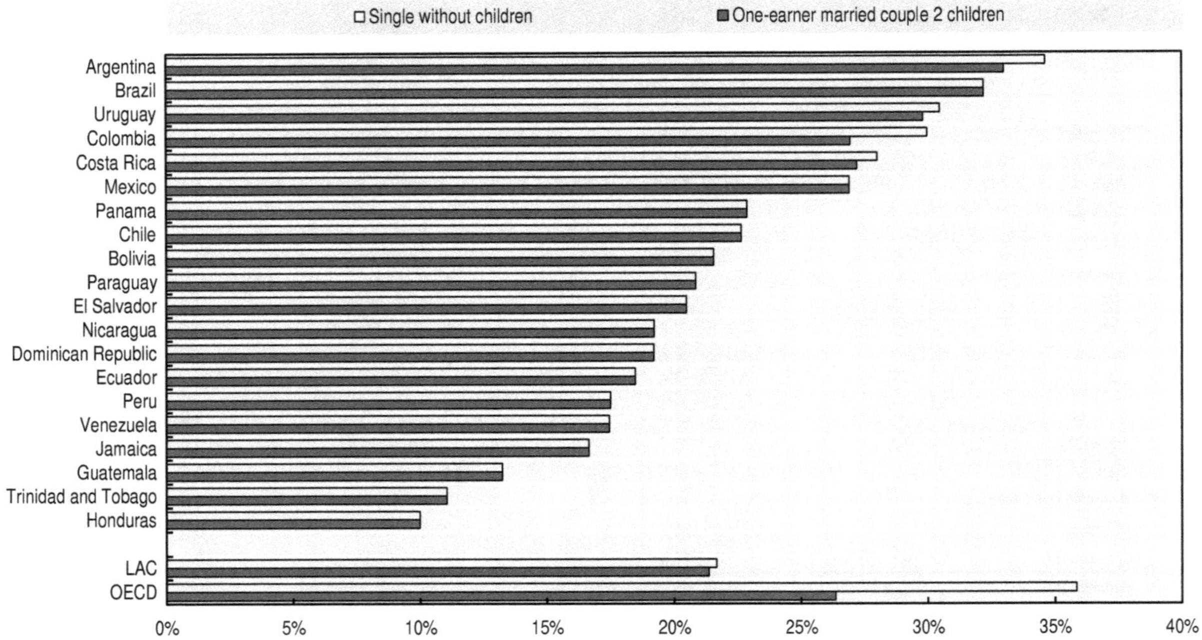

Notes: Countries are ranked by decreasing tax wedge of the single worker.

Family types: Single individual without children at the average wage level and a one-earner married couple with two children at the average wage level.

StatLink http://dx.doi.org/10.1787/888933407340

Table 1.4. **Tax wedges for a single earner without children by income decile, 2013**

As % of labour costs

Country	Decile 1	Decile 2	Decile 3	Decile 4	Decile 5	Decile 6	Decile 7	Decile 8	Decile 9	Decile 10
Argentina	36.4	36.4	36.4	36.4	36.4	36.4	36.4	36.4	36.4	36.4
Bolivia	0.0	21.6	21.6	21.6	21.6	21.6	21.6	21.6	21.6	24.0
Brazil	31.4	31.4	31.4	31.4	31.4	31.4	32.2	32.2	34.5	32.1
Chile	22.6	22.6	22.6	22.6	22.6	22.6	22.6	22.6	22.6	24.6
Colombia	0.0	30.0	30.0	30.0	30.0	30.0	30.2	30.2	30.2	31.1
Costa Rica	0.0	0.0	0.0	0.0	28.0	28.0	28.0	28.0	28.0	32.0
Dominican Republic	1.2	1.2	1.2	19.2	19.2	19.2	19.2	19.2	19.2	25.6
Ecuador	0.0	18.1	18.1	18.5	18.5	18.5	18.5	18.5	18.5	20.7
El Salvador	0.9	20.5	20.5	20.5	20.5	20.5	20.5	23.5	24.5	26.3
Guatemala	4.8	4.8	4.8	13.2	13.2	13.2	13.2	13.2	13.3	14.9
Honduras	0.0	0.0	0.0	0.0	0.0	0.0	10.2	8.4	6.7	9.1
Jamaica	16.6	16.6	16.6	16.6	16.6	16.6	16.6	16.6	21.5	30.9
Mexico	16.7	18.8	19.8	20.9	22.4	23.5	26.8	27.8	29.6	33.1
Nicaragua	0.0	0.0	2.0	19.2	19.2	19.2	19.2	19.2	20.8	25.6
Panama	22.9	22.9	22.9	22.9	22.9	22.9	22.9	22.9	24.8	31.0
Paraguay	1.0	1.0	20.9	20.9	20.9	20.9	20.9	20.9	20.9	20.9
Peru	0.0	0.0	0.0	17.5	17.5	17.5	17.5	17.5	17.5	23.9
Trinidad & Tobago	16.1	14.0	13.2	12.8	12.6	12.4	12.0	11.3	15.9	20.7
Uruguay	29.3	30.5	30.5	30.5	30.5	30.5	30.5	31.3	33.4	37.2
Venezuela	17.4	17.4	17.4	17.4	17.4	17.4	17.4	17.4	17.4	18.7
Unweighted average										
LAC	**10.8**	**15.3**	**16.4**	**19.5**	**21.0**	**21.1**	**21.7**	**21.8**	**22.8**	**25.9**

StatLink http://dx.doi.org/10.1787/888933410109

Table 1.5. **Tax wedges for a one-earner married couple with two children by income decile, 2013**

As % of labour costs

Country	Decile 1	Decile 2	Decile 3	Decile 4	Decile 5	Decile 6	Decile 7	Decile 8	Decile 9	Decile 10
Argentina	1.6	14.8	18.6	20.6	25.6	26.9	30.5	32.6	32.9	33.6
Bolivia	0.0	21.6	21.6	21.6	21.6	21.6	21.6	21.6	21.6	24.0
Brazil	26.1	26.5	27.0	27.6	31.4	31.4	32.2	32.2	33.9	32.1
Chile	11.5	15.1	17.9	18.3	18.8	19.3	21.8	22.0	22.6	24.6
Colombia	(8.2)	24.9	25.2	25.5	26.0	26.6	27.4	27.9	28.6	31.1
Costa Rica	(4.1)	(2.4)	(2.0)	(1.8)	26.8	27.0	27.1	27.3	27.5	31.7
Dominican Republic	1.2	1.2	1.2	19.2	19.2	19.2	19.2	19.2	19.2	25.6
Ecuador	0.0	18.1	18.1	18.5	18.5	18.5	18.5	18.5	18.5	20.7
El Salvador	0.9	20.5	20.5	20.5	20.5	20.5	20.5	23.5	24.5	26.3
Guatemala	4.8	4.8	4.8	13.2	13.2	13.2	13.2	13.2	13.3	14.9
Honduras	0.0	0.0	0.0	0.0	0.0	0.0	10.2	8.4	6.7	9.1
Jamaica	16.6	16.6	16.6	16.6	16.6	16.6	16.6	16.6	21.5	30.9
Mexico	16.7	18.8	19.8	20.9	22.4	23.5	26.8	27.8	29.6	33.1
Nicaragua	0.0	0.0	2.0	19.2	19.2	19.2	19.2	19.2	20.8	25.6
Panama	22.9	22.9	22.9	22.9	22.9	22.9	22.9	22.9	24.0	30.7
Paraguay	1.0	1.0	20.9	20.9	20.9	20.9	20.9	20.9	20.9	20.9
Peru	0.0	0.0	0.0	17.5	17.5	17.5	17.5	17.5	17.5	23.9
Trinidad & Tobago	16.1	14.0	13.2	12.8	12.6	12.4	12.0	11.3	15.9	20.7
Uruguay	16.7	23.5	25.0	25.9	26.6	29.5	29.8	30.1	32.5	37.0
Venezuela	17.4	17.4	17.4	17.4	17.4	17.4	17.4	17.4	17.4	17.4
Unweighted average										
LAC	**7.1**	**13.0**	**14.5**	**17.9**	**19.9**	**20.2**	**21.3**	**21.5**	**22.5**	**25.7**

StatLink http://dx.doi.org/10.1787/888933410111

Figure 1.4. **Average LAC country wedge decomposition for a single earner with no children**

As a % of total labour costs

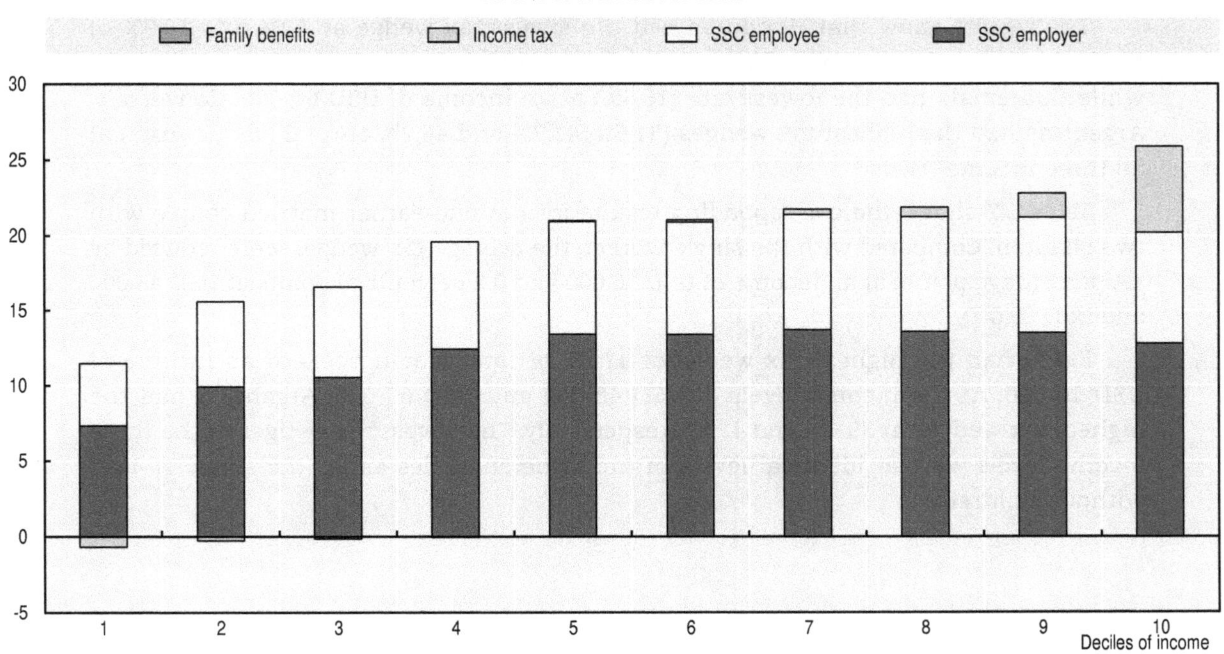

StatLink http://dx.doi.org/10.1787/888933407353

Figure 1.5. **Average LAC country tax wedge decomposition for one-earner married couple with two children**

As % of total labour costs

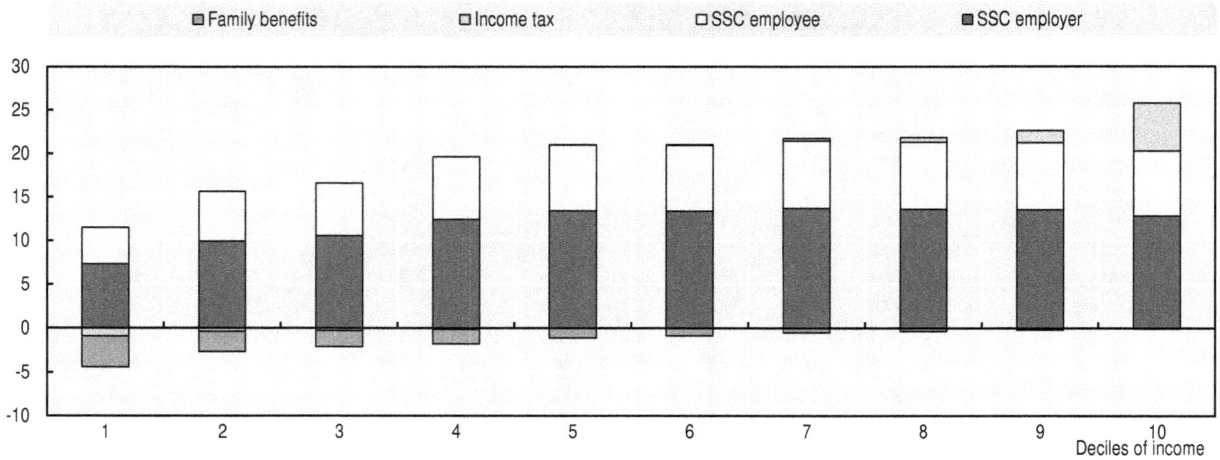

StatLink http://dx.doi.org/10.1787/888933407366

2.1.4. Tax wedges for earned income in USD.

Tables 1.6 and 1.7 compare tax wedges in the region for earnings in USD equivalents showing results for workers earning an annual gross wage of USD 10 000, USD 48 000 and USD 60 000.

Table 1.6 shows that at the level of annual income of USD 10 000, the average tax wedge for the single worker without children in the 20 Latin American and Caribbean countries was 22.8% of the total labour costs. The average tax wedge rose with increasing income to 29.0% of labour costs for an income of USD 48 000 and to 30.1% for workers whose wages are USD 60 000.

The results show that Honduras had the lowest tax wedge at 7.1% and 15.9% of total labour costs at the annual income level of USD 10 000 and USD 48 000 respectively, while Guatemala had the lowest rate (16.5%) at an income of USD 60 000. Conversely, Argentina had the highest tax wedges (34.6%, 43.7% and 46.2% of total labour costs) at all three income levels.

Table 1.7 shows the corresponding results for the one-earner married couple with two children. Compared with the single worker, the average tax wedges were reduced by 1.1 percentage points at an income of USD 10 000 and 0.2 percentage points at USD 48 000 and USD 60 000.

Brazil had the highest tax wedge of 32.2% of total labour costs at an income of USD 10 000. At the income levels of USD 48 000 and USD 60 000, Argentina had the highest tax wedges at 39.6% and 42.8% respectively. The lowest tax wedges at the three income levels were at identical levels in the same countries as for the single worker without children.

Table 1.6. **Total tax wedges for a single worker without children**

As % for labour costs

Country	USD 10 000	USD 48 000	USD 60 000
Argentina	34.6	43.7	46.2
Bolivia	21.6	28.6	31.8
Brazil	32.2	31.0	30.4
Chile	22.6	22.4	20.5
Colombia	30.2	35.7	37.5
Costa Rica	28.0	33.9	34.9
Dominican Republic	19.4	30.5	29.6
Ecuador	18.5	24.6	25.8
El Salvador	25.1	32.8	34.0
Guatemala	14.1	16.2	16.5
Honduras	7.1	15.9	17.3
Jamaica	26.9	33.9	34.2
Mexico	28.1	36.6	35.5
Nicaragua	26.2	27.4	26.9
Panama	22.9	32.9	35.0
Paraguay	20.9	21.2	22.7
Peru	18.2	28.8	30.4
Trinidad and Tobago	11.5	23.0	23.4
Uruguay	30.5	36.7	36.4
Venezuela	17.4	26.5	33.9
Unweighted average			
LAC	**22.8**	**29.1**	**30.1**

Note: Results are based on 2013 average exchange rates.

StatLink http://dx.doi.org/10.1787/888933410128

Table 1.7. **Total tax wedges for a one-earner married couple with two children, 2013**

As % of labour costs

Country	USD 10 000	USD 48 000	USD 60 000
Argentina	20.9	39.6	42.8
Bolivia	21.6	28.6	31.8
Brazil	32.2	31.0	30.4
Chile	21.9	22.4	20.5
Colombia	27.9	35.7	37.5
Costa Rica	27.1	33.7	34.7
Dominican Republic	19.4	30.5	29.6
Ecuador	18.5	24.6	25.8
El Salvador	25.1	32.8	34.0
Guatemala	14.1	16.2	16.5
Honduras	7.1	15.9	17.3
Jamaica	26.9	33.9	34.2
Mexico	28.1	36.6	35.5
Nicaragua	26.2	27.4	26.9
Panama	22.9	32.7	34.7
Paraguay	20.9	21.2	22.7
Peru	18.2	28.8	30.4
Trinidad and Tobago	11.5	23.0	23.4
Uruguay	27.0	36.8	36.7
Venezuela	17.4	25.5	33.1
Unweighted average			
LAC	**21.7**	**28.9**	**29.9**

Note: Results are based on 2013 average exchange rates.

StatLink http://dx.doi.org/10.1787/888933410136

2.1.5. *Wages*

Table 1.8 presents a comparison of the average wages in 2013 in local currency, their equivalent value in USD (at 2013 average annual exchange rates), their equivalent in dollars with equal purchasing power and the number of minimum wage levels contained in the average wage. The figures represent the average incomes reported by workers within the formal economy in each country's income survey. The exceptions were Argentina, Brazil, Chile, Colombia and Mexico where estimates of the average wage are available from the Ministry of Labour. For Bolivia, the results from the 2011 national survey were adjusted to 2013 using the national real wage index.[4] The average income distribution by deciles was calculated by first ordering from lowest to highest the reported income for each worker in the formal economy, dividing them into ten equal groups and calculating an average wage for each group.

Table 1.8. **Comparison of average wage levels**

Country	Value in local currency	Value in USD[1]	Value in PPP[2]	AW[3] ratio to the minimum wage
Argentina	116 352	21 155	31 808	3.3
Bolivia	40 420	5 791	12 510	2.8
Brazil	22 686	10 525	14 152	2.8
Chile	6 604 419	13 334	19 127	2.8
Colombia	13 954 218	7 466	11 878	2.0
Costa Rica	5 607 303	11 428	15 430	1.6
Dominican Republic	225 961	5 405	11 212	2.2
Ecuador	8 007	8 007	14 559	2.1
El Salvador	5 308	5 308	10 766	2.3
Guatemala	46 563	5 925	12 443	1.6
Honduras	115 465	5 851	11 480	1.4
Jamaica	358 993	3 653	5 932	1.3
Mexico	98 922	7 748	12 705	4.2
Nicaragua	79 231	3 205	8 239	1.7
Panama	9 202	9 202	16 202	1.7
Paraguay	35 322 396	8 106	15 602	1.8
Peru	17 034	6 267	11 185	1.9
Trinidad and Tobago	49 305	7 718	11 906	1.9
Uruguay	252 060	12 616	14 576	2.7
Venezuela	54 490	8 671	13 701	1.7
Unweighted averages				
LAC	-	**8 369**	**13 771**	**2.2**
OECD[4]	-	**43 631**	**40 292**	-

1. Exchange rate data was attained from central banks of each country. The average exchange rate is for the entire year 2013.
2. Exchange rates of dollars per local currency is an average for the year 2013. The implied conversion rate for international dollars in parity of purchasing power was obtained from the IMF World Economic Outlook dataset (2015).
3. Minimum wages for the year 2013 according to the legislation of each country.
4. The source for OECD averages is OECD (2014) Taxing Wages, Table 0.3. It should be noted that averages are not directly comparable since OECD average of the tax wedge are those estimated under the compulsory tax payments model.

StatLink http://dx.doi.org/10.1787/888933410140

Notes

1. Payroll taxes are aggregated with employer social security contributions in the calculation of the tax rates.
2. Further analysis on tax revenue collection is provided in OECD/ECLAC/CIAT/IDB (2016).
3. Details of the programs available for each country are provided in Part II Country details.
4. Labour statistics published by the central bank.

References

OECD/ECLAC/CIAT/IDB (2016), *Revenue Statistics in Latin America and the Caribbean 2016*, OECD Publishing, Paris. *http://dx.doi.org/10.1787/rev_lat_car-2016-en-fr*

OECD (2015), *Taxing Wages 2015*, OECD Publishing, Paris. *http://dx.doi.org/10.1787/tax_wages-2015-en*

OECD (2014), *Taxing Wages 2014*, OECD Publishing. *http://dx.doi.org/10.1787/tax_wages-2014-en*

OECD/IDB/The World Bank (2014), *Pensions at a Glance: Latin America and the Caribbean*, OECD Publishing. *http://dx.doi.org/10.1787/pension_glance-2014-en*

Chapter 2

A view on taxes, social protection and informality in Latin America using Taxing Wages modelling[1]

1. Introduction

This special feature explores some of the relationships existing in Latin American (LAC) countries between taxes on wages (specifically social security contributions), characteristics of labour markets and levels of informality and identifies some of the outcomes of the interaction between tax policy and labour markets. Section 2 considers the structure of tax revenues in LAC countries and in particular the weight that personal income tax (PIT), social security contributions (SSCs) and payroll taxes have in the region's total tax revenues. Section 3 describes the main labour market outcomes in the region during the last decade. Section 4 reviews one the most important characteristics of labour markets in LAC countries: informality. The Taxing Wages models developed for the LAC countries have been used to estimate a theoretical cost for workers to move from the informal to the formal economy (a proxy of the formalisation cost). This is defined as the amount of SSCs workers would have to pay, given the labour income they declare to earn, if they decided to register and comply with tax and labour regulations. Section 5 sets out some conclusions.

The gains attained during the last decade from increased fiscal revenues and improved labour market outcomes are being jeopardized by the current lacklustre economic growth in LAC countries. The commodity super cycle that propelled much of the economic growth over the period has come to an end. Low commodity prices coupled with weak global growth prospects and tight financing conditions are undermining the region's growth prospects. On average, gross domestic product (GDP) levels are expected to fall in 2016 for the second year in a row, before recovering slightly in the following year (OECD/CAF/ECLAC, forthcoming).

The downturn in economic activity is having a negative impact on the labour markets in the region, enhancing the risks of long term detrimental effects on workers in the lower halves of the labour income distributions. On average, unemployment is increasing and job quality is diminishing. In addition, wages are stagnant and informal sectors continue to represent a large portion of economic activity (OECD/ECLAC/CAF, forthcoming; Alaimo et al., 2015). Within this framework, the role of taxes and their implications for labour markets are becoming increasingly relevant.

Tax systems in LAC countries rely heavily on consumption taxes while taxes on labour income have a more limited share. In 2013, consumption taxes accounted for almost half of tax revenues in LAC countries whereas the share of taxes on labour income was about one quarter. Of the latter the major share is accounted for by SSCs at around 16% of the total with less than 10% from personal income tax (PITs). However, despite their relatively low share of total revenues, PITs and SSCs do impact on the levels of total labour costs and the gaps between gross and net wages for workers.

There is evidence of a correlation between the cost of becoming formal and the levels of informality particularly at the lower end and middle range of earnings distribution. High theoretical formalisation costs are correlated with high levels of informality. In Latin America, some authors have highlighted the negative effects that high tax burdens might have on the incentives for transition between informality and formality (Loayza, et al., 2005; De Soto, 1989;

Melguizo and González-Páramo, 2012). Similarly, others have illustrated the positive impact that reductions in tax rates and labour costs could have on economic formality (Levy, 2008; Pagés, 2010). This chapter uses the new data on taxes on labour income for the countries in this Report to explore in further detail the relationship between informality levels and formalisation costs, as proxied by the SSCs workers would have to pay to become or remain formal.

2. Taxation in Latin America: A *work in progress*

LAC economies are characterised by relatively low tax revenues, with heterogeneity across countries. Tax revenues as a share of GDP in LAC countries averaged 21.7% in 2014, considerably lower than the OECD average of 34.4% of GDP. Tax revenues diverge considerably across the region. In 2014, the tax to GDP ratios ranged from 33.4% in Brazil and 32.2% in Argentina to 12.6% in Guatemala and 14.1% in the Dominican Republic (Figure 2.1).

Figure 2.1. **Total tax revenues as a percentage of GDP in Latin America and the OECD, 2014[1]**

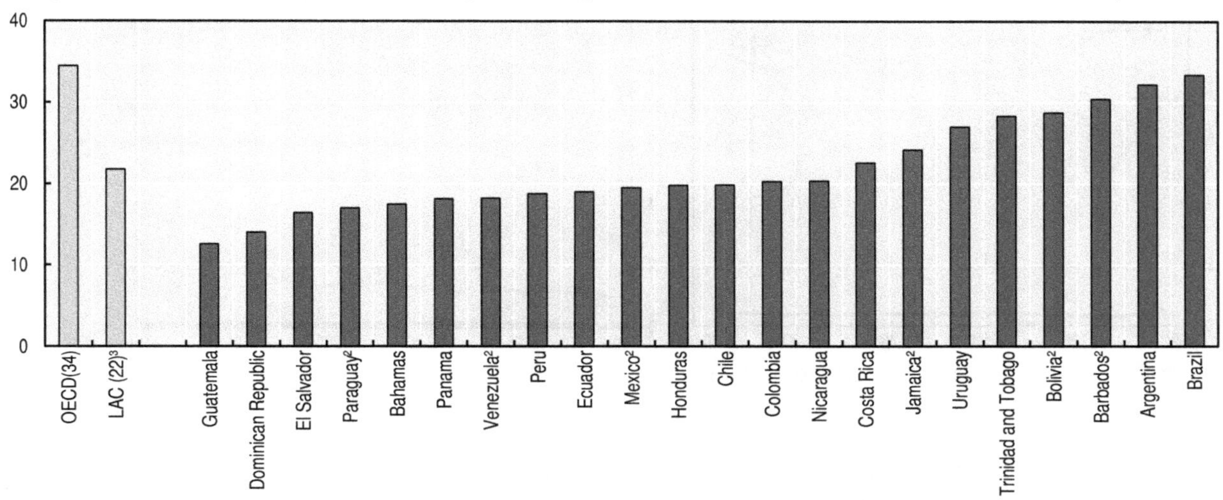

1. Countries have been ranked by their total tax revenue to GDP ratios.
2. The data are estimated.
3. Represents the unweighted average for a group of 22 Latin American and Caribbean countries. Chile and Mexico are also part of the OECD (34) group.
4. Represents the unweighted average for OECD member countries.

Source: OECD/ECLAC/CIAT/IDB (2016).

StatLink http://dx.doi.org/10.1787/888933407374

The gap between the LAC region and the OECD economies is mostly explained by the region's relatively low direct-tax take (especially PIT and SSCs). OECD PIT revenues are higher than in the LAC region (8.8% compared with an estimated 2% of GDP, respectively in 2013). SSCs, on average across the OECD, account for 9.1% of GDP while the LAC average is only 3.7%. Payroll tax yields are relatively small for both groups (0.1% of GDP in LAC and 0.4% in OECD economies).

The relatively low levels of revenues from PIT can be explained by a range of factors, from differing economic characteristics in LAC countries compared with the OECD, to tax design, and even tax avoidance and evasion. First, the share of labour income in GDP is substantially lower in LAC countries (Daude, Melguizo and Neut, 2010). Secondly, PIT minimum thresholds are relatively high compared with average wages resulting in the vast majority of the working population having taxable incomes below these thresholds.

Thirdly, tax expenditures tend to be relatively high in the region, as many economies have generous allowances for a range of items such as mortgage interest deductions, education and health expenses in addition to other justified allowances such as employee SSCs. Fourthly, the PIT base is eroded by high levels of tax avoidance and evasion that combined with high levels of informality decimate the ability of the tax to raise revenue. Some authors argue that about half of the potential revenue from PIT is lost through evasion (IDB, 2013). Finally, high PIT privileges are granted on capital income to encourage investment.

Figure 2.2. **Taxes on labour income in OECD and Latin American and Caribbean countries, 1990-2014**

(As a percentage of GDP)

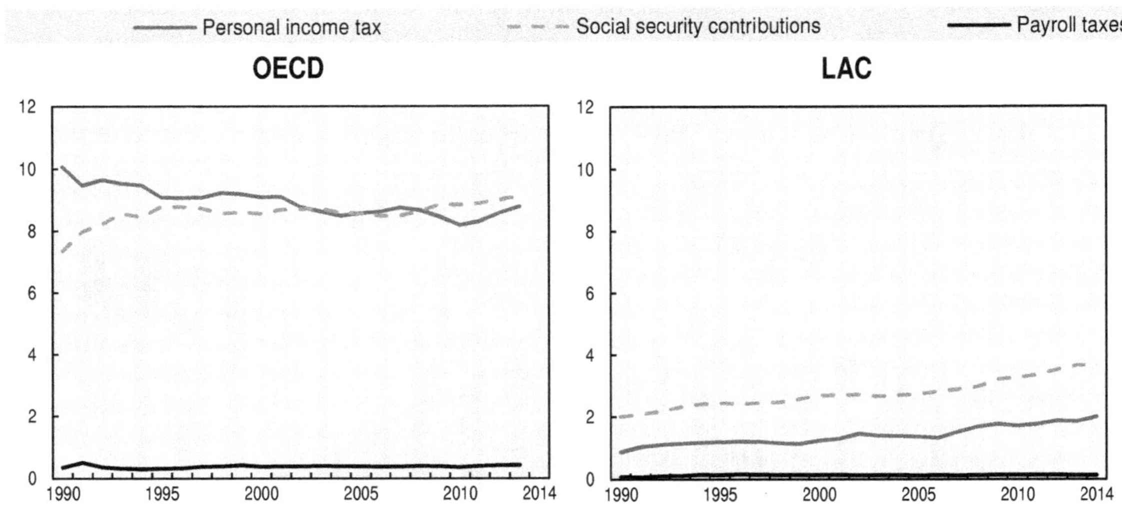

Source: Data from tables in OECD/ECLAC/CIAT/IDB (2016) and OECD (2015).

StatLink http://dx.doi.org/10.1787/888933407382

The relatively low levels of SSCs stem both from low levels of social insurance coverage and the more significant role of the private sector as a social protection provider. In many LAC countries, social security systems did not aim to cover all households but were only targeted at employed salaried workers (Bosch, Melguizo and Pagés, 2013). From the 1980s onwards, many LAC countries reformed their social security systems and introduced fully capitalized accounts for pension plans and privatised healthcare. Chile, El Salvador and Mexico for example have shifted their public pension programmes to fully privately funded pension systems. In Colombia and Peru, the private and public programmes co-exist and employees opt for either one or the other (OECD/ECLAC/CIAT/IDB, 2015). Argentina, Brazil and Uruguay also follow a model where the public and private systems are complementary and substantial reforms have been undertaken in these countries to extend the coverage of social security systems to those previously excluded (ECLAC, 2014). Across the OECD, SSCs to privately managed funds exist in several countries, but the main emphasis is on the public provision of these services which requires higher revenue receipts, particularly in Europe.

In summary, as shown in Chapter 3 of this report, while PIT is only paid at very high levels of income, the fact that SSCs are only levied on salaried workers results in a difference between gross and net wages that might provide an incentive towards informality for these workers, thus affecting the outcomes on labour markets.

3. Labour markets in Latin America: Informal is normal

The last ten years have seen several positive developments in Latin American labour markets, although these could be challenged or even reversed in the current macroeconomic context. Between 2003 and 2013 there have been substantial job creation, real wage increases and reductions in unemployment and informality. In this period, the region's economies were able to employ a larger number of workers, with the employed population increasing by 4 percentage points on average. At the same time, real wages increased by an average of 2% per year, unemployment fell from 9% to 6.1% and informality decreased to 55%. Nevertheless, the current economic slowdown could reverse some of these achievements. For example, in 2015, the rate of unemployment increased for the first time since 2009 (ECLAC/ILO, 2016).

LAC averages hide wide disparities across countries, and also within countries by income level. In 2013, unemployment rates for Bolivia, Ecuador, El Salvador and Guatemala were below 4%. At the other end of the distribution, Barbados, Costa Rica, Colombia and Jamaica faced unemployment rates above 8%, with the Caribbean countries experiencing the highest rates, at 11.3% and 14.7%, respectively of the total labour force. Unemployment rates are higher among workers in the first quintile of the income distribution, except in Honduras, where the first quintile has an unemployment rate of 4% compared with 5% for the fifth quintile. In Argentina, Brazil, Colombia, the Dominican Republic, Uruguay and Venezuela, the unemployment rate among the lowest income groups varied between 14% and 19%, while it exceeded 20% in Chile, Costa Rica and Jamaica (Alaimo et al., 2015).

Despite the gains in formality in the past decade, the bulk of employment in Latin America remains informal. In 2013, on average, approximately 55% of the workers in the region were informal. Although, this represented a 7 percentage point decrease from the 2003 level (Alaimo et al., 2015), it still meant that more than half of the working population did not contribute to social security programmes, a common feature in many emerging economies (Jütting and de Laiglesia, 2009).

Informality rates also vary significantly across countries and by income within countries, affecting the poor and low-middle income workers the most. Figure 2.3 describes formality rates across the region. Compared with the whole labour force, three Central American countries (Honduras, Guatemala and Nicaragua) have the lowest formality rates in 2013 (implying informality rates of over 80%). At the other end of the distribution, Chile, Costa Rica and Uruguay have formality rates of more than 70% and informality rates below 30%.

There is a strong variation in informality rates by income within countries. They are highest in all countries for workers in the poorest quintile, and tend to fall as income rises. In Guatemala and Honduras, the informality rate for the first quintile is close to 100% falling to below 60% in the fifth quintile. On the other hand, Uruguay, Costa Rica and Chile present the lowest informality rates among the first quintile workers (56%, 52% and 41%, respectively). The results show that informality is high among middle-income workers (middle-class proxy, according to Easterly, 2001) at 64% over quintiles 2-4, and still prevalent for the highest income workers in the fifth quintile (42%) (Figure 2.4).

Figure 2.3. **Formality rate in Latin American and Caribbean countries**

(Percentage of workers contributing to social security- aged 15-64 years)

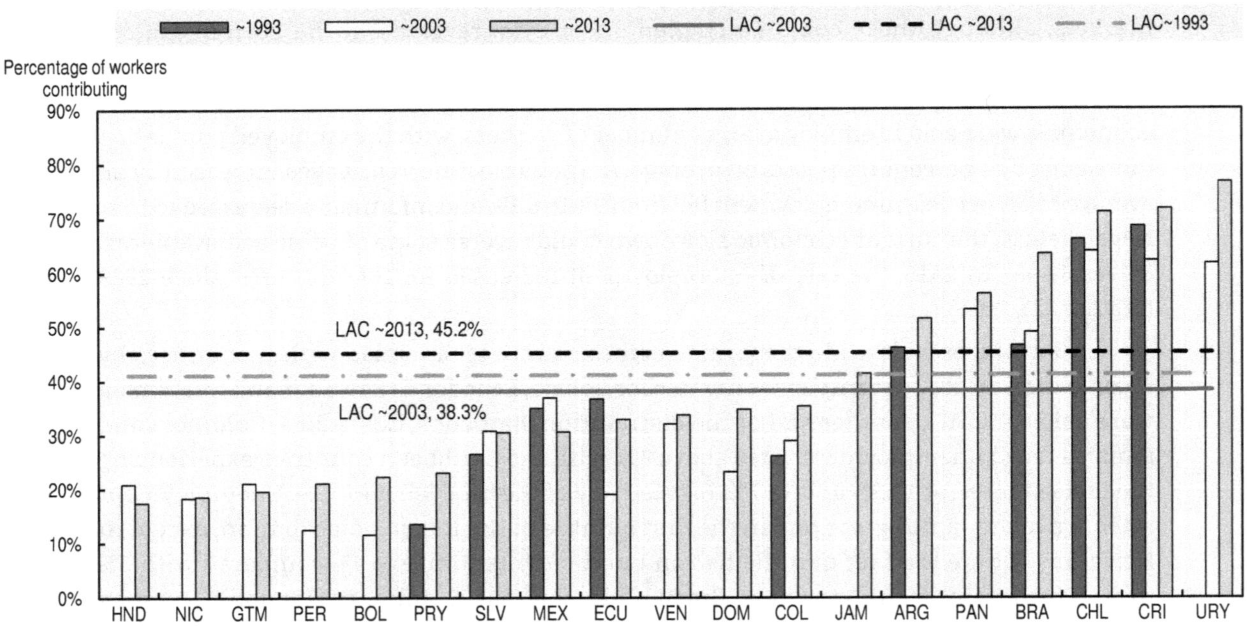

Note: The formality rate is computed for all employed workers (not only salaried workers) aged 15-64 years.
Source: IDB (2015). Sistema de Indicadores de Mercado Laboral y Seguridad Social (SIMS).

StatLink http://dx.doi.org/10.1787/888933407394

Figure 2.4. **Informality rates in Latin American countries, by quintile of per capita family income, 2013**

(Percentage of workers not contributing to social security programmes- aged 15-64 years)

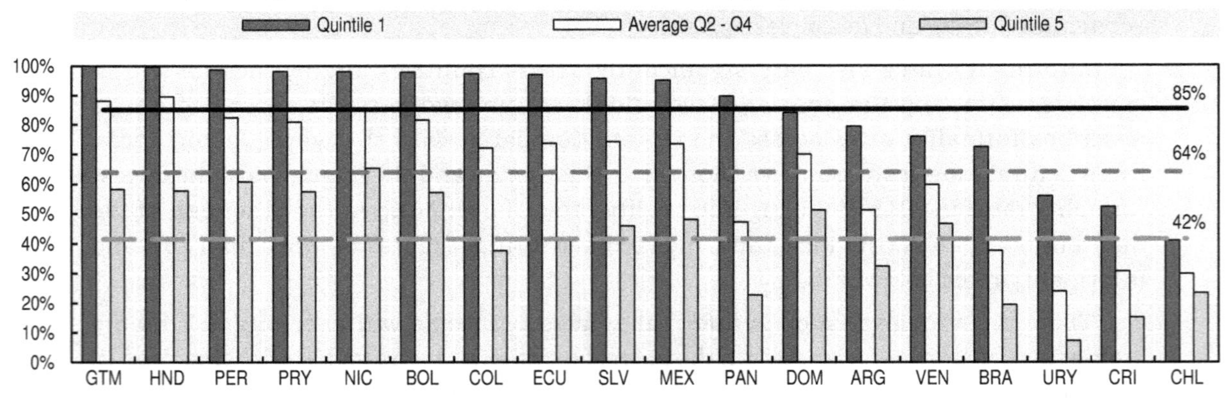

Note: 'Average Q2 – Q4' denotes the average of quintiles 2 – 4.
Source: Based on data from Alaimo et al. (2015) and IDB (2015). Sistema de Indicadores de Mercado Laboral y Seguridad Social (SIMS).

StatLink http://dx.doi.org/10.1787/888933407401

Informality tends to more prevalent among the self-employed than employees in Latin American countries. Figure 2.5.a shows a breakdown of individuals by category of labour relationship in 2013. On average, 60.8% of the workforce are employees, 27.9% self-employed, 4.86% employers and 6.48% unpaid family workers. There is a substantial rate of informality among the self-employed (88.3 %). Informality is also important among paid employees, accounting for 46.5 % of this group.

Figure 2.5. **Occupational status in the labour market and informality among employees and the self-employed, 2013.**

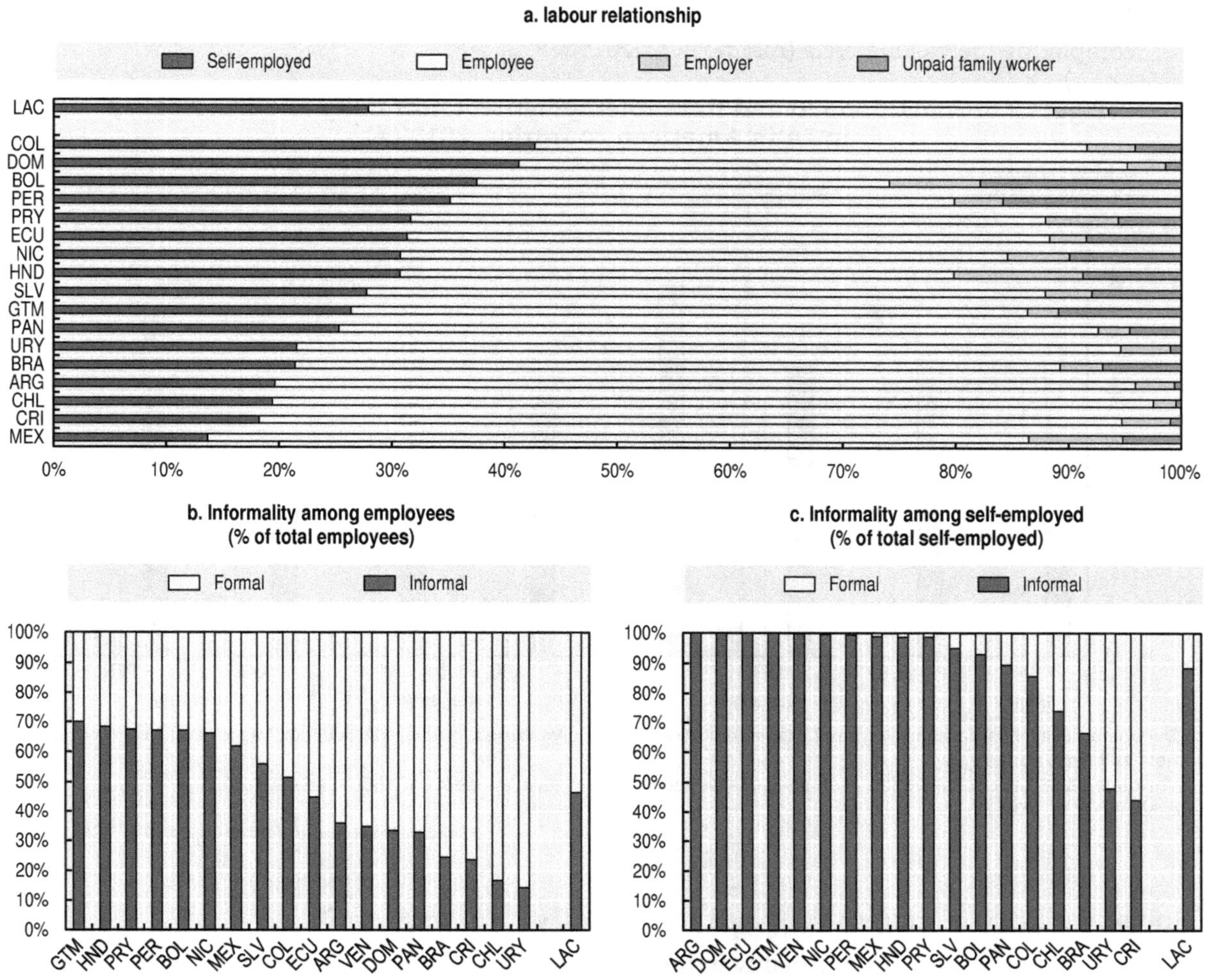

Source: Based on IDB (2015). Sistema de Indicadores de Mercado Laboral y Seguridad Social (SIMS).

StatLink http://dx.doi.org/10.1787/888933407418

There are relatively high turnover rates of workers in jobs in the region and many jobs are only temporary. At least one in four workers in the major part of their working life (i.e. aged between 24 and 54) has been in their current job for one year or less. And many of the transitions between jobs or from unemployment to a job imply becoming an informal worker (Figure 2.6). So even for the 45% of workers with formal jobs at a point in time, many of them have experienced a period of informality in the past and will do so in the future.

The region is trapped in a 'vicious cycle' of high employment turnover, low productivity, high labour costs and high informality. High employment turnover discourages workers from seeking more on-job education and training, which could otherwise result in employment relationships that generate increases in productivity. In turn, low labour productivity relative to the costs of formality, including taxes and SSCs, contributes to a high level of informality. Alongside the high levels of job turnover and high informality, most workers lack safety nets (e.g. unemployment insurance) to withstand a period of unemployment while looking for a good job that is suited to their skills and training, leading to inefficient job matches. These inefficient matches in turn tend to break up quickly, continuing high turnover and completing the vicious cycle (Alaimo et al.,2015).

Figure 2.6. **Transitions to and from unemployment, formality and informality in Latin American countries, 2013 (%)**

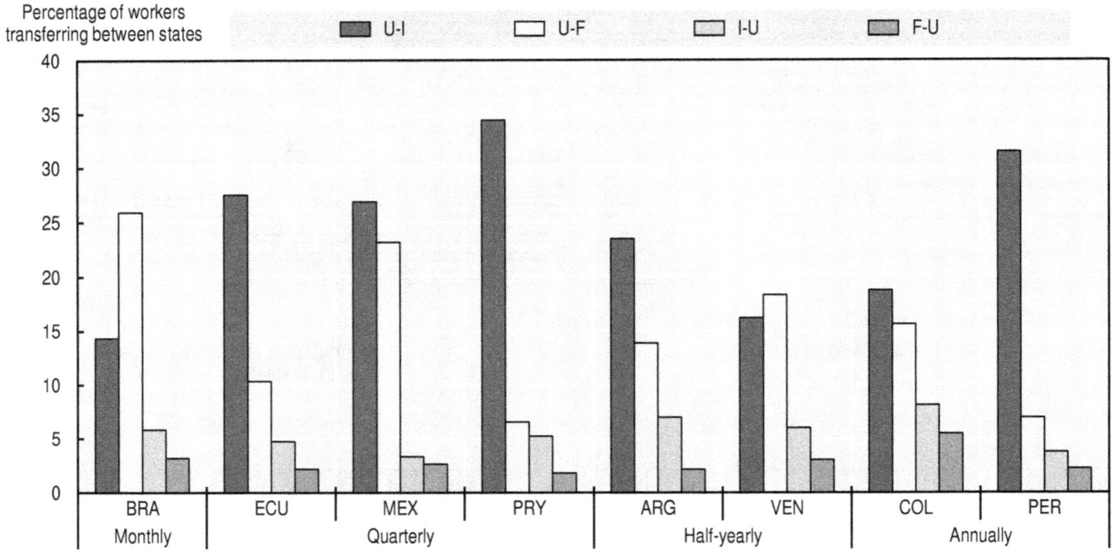

Note: U = unemployed, I = informal, F = formal. Transitions: Argentina and Venezuela, half-yearly; Ecuador, Mexico and Paraguay, quarterly; Colombia and Peru, annually.
For information about the construction and panels please see methodological appendix of Alaimo et al. (2015).
Source: Alaimo et al. (2015)

StatLink http://dx.doi.org/10.1787/888933407426

4. Social security contributions and informality: *In it together?*

The high levels of informality in the region have a very diverse set of roots. There are several factors that can influence an individual's decision between formality and informality, such as: tax burdens, wage levels, job security, excessive labour regulations, the valuation a person places on the programme or services, expectations of receiving future benefits, and a component of myopic behaviour from the individual, not to mention the role of institutions in performing inspections and setting up enforcement mechanisms. However, there are cases in which the decision of the individual is purely based on the price of social security programmes and taxes. In such scenarios, the cost of becoming part of the formal sector is judged to be too large when compared with the level of earned income, thus effectively preventing any possibility of participating in these social schemes (Bosch, Melguizo and Pagés, 2013; and Melguizo, 2015 for a focus on middle class).

This section identifies the informality rates among dependent workers over the whole of the income distribution and makes corresponding estimates of the theoretical costs of becoming formal. Figure 2.7 shows the rates of informality (measured on the left axis) by income decile for 18 countries drawing on data from the household income surveys in the region.[2] Harmonised data from these sources is used to estimate the annual labour earnings distributions of all dependent workers[3] and to calculate informality rates by deciles of income. The analyses identify the approximate location of the minimum wage in each country with a white bar. The figure also shows estimates of the theoretical costs of becoming formal (measured on the right axis) expressed as the proportion of their wages that workers should pay in social security contributions to become or remain formal. This measure can be taken as a lower bound, given that formalisation generally entails other monetary and non-monetary costs stemming from various legislations. For workers earning the minimum wage or above, this cost is defined as the amount of employee SSCs payable on the wages. However, many workers are excluded from social security programmes because their earnings are below the minimum wage which commonly acts as a lower income threshold for these schemes. For these workers, the cost of becoming formal is the amount of SSCs payable at the minimum wage or at the lower earnings threshold if that is different. As a result, the larger the shortfall between a worker's income and the established minimum threshold/wage, the higher is the theoretical cost of formalisation that this individual faces. These costs are expressed as a percentage of the workers actual wages in the charts.

The theoretical cost of becoming formal, even when only considering social security contributions, is relatively high in some countries of the region, especially in the lower and middle income deciles although there are significant variations among countries. On average, most countries show relatively high formalisation costs, as a percentage of their labour income, in the first two income deciles. In Mexico, the theoretical formalisation costs for the first decile exceeds the workers' income, implying that the earnings are less than the minimum payments of social security contributions, while in Panama and Venezuela, it is around 20% of the workers income. As incomes rise, the costs of formalisation steadily fall till they become flat or proportional. This is always the case at earnings deciles above the minimum wage except where there are declines due to the existence of upper earnings ceilings to the SSCs.

High costs of adhering to social security programs as a percentage of earned income are associated with higher levels of informality. Figure 2.7 shows the relationship between theoretical formalisation costs and informality rates and how these costs and rates vary over the income distribution. In most countries the informal workers at the lower end of the income distribution (deciles 1-2) have higher formalisation costs that the remainder. Similarly, in most countries, informality tends to be largest in the first two deciles of the income distribution, although in some economies informality is also substantial in higher income groups. In Argentina, Brazil, Chile, Costa Rica, Dominican Republic, Panama, Uruguay, Venezuela, informality impacts mainly those on the lowest incomes (deciles 1-2). In Ecuador and Colombia, it additionally impacts on a so called 'vulnerable middle class' (deciles 1-5) (as proxied by Easterly, 2001). Finally, relatively high informality is present even at middle income levels in Bolivia, El Salvador, Guatemala, Honduras, Mexico, Nicaragua and Peru.

Figure 2.7. **Theoretical formality costs and informality rates for dependent workers in Latin American countries, 2013**

By labour income decile for workers aged 15-64 years

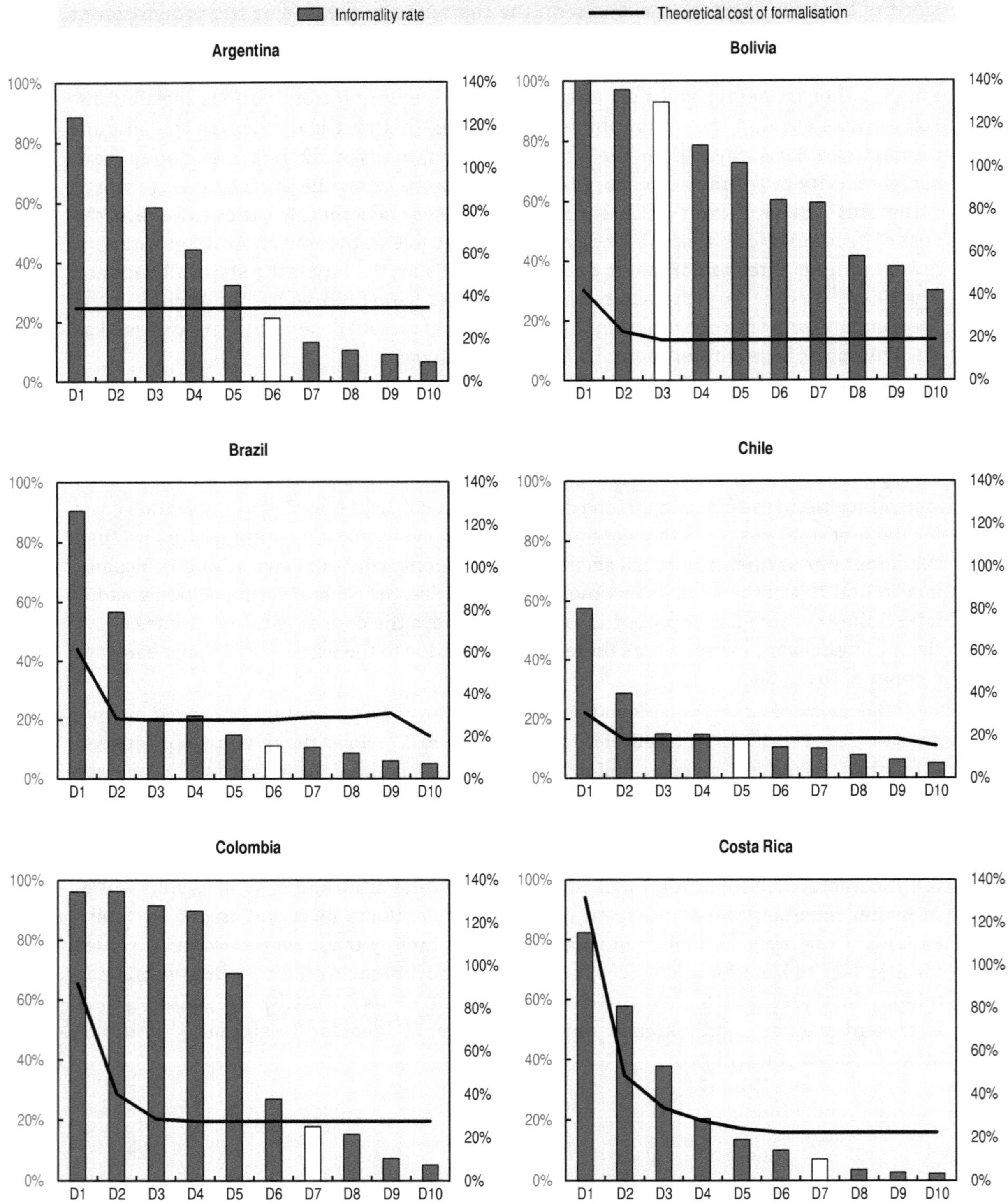

Figure 2.7. **Theoretical formality costs and informality rates for dependent workers in Latin American countries, 2013** *(cont.)*

By labour income decile for workers aged 15-64 years

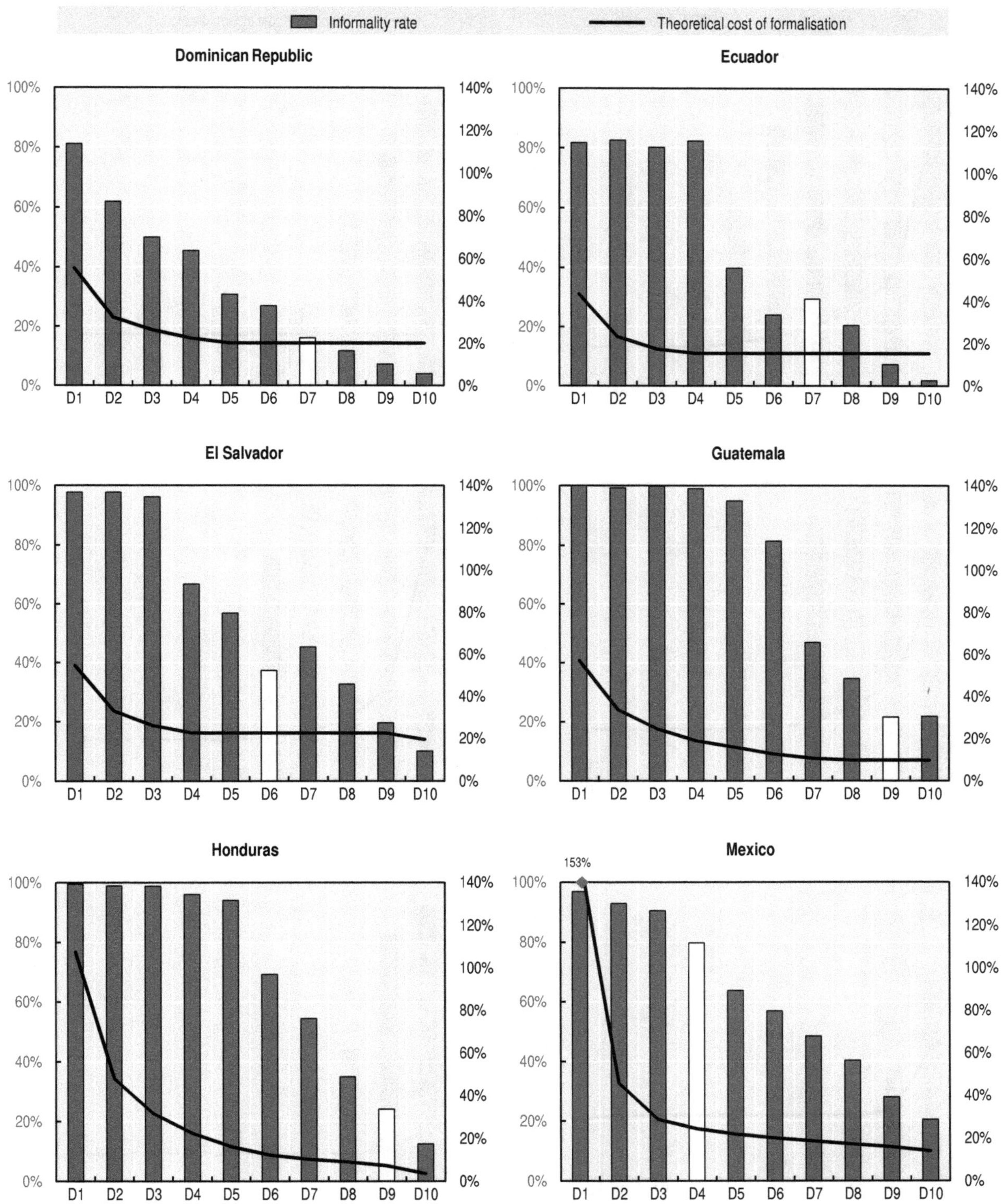

Figure 2.7. **Theoretical formality costs and informality rates for dependent workers in Latin American countries, 2013** *(cont.)*

By labour income decile for workers aged 15-64 years

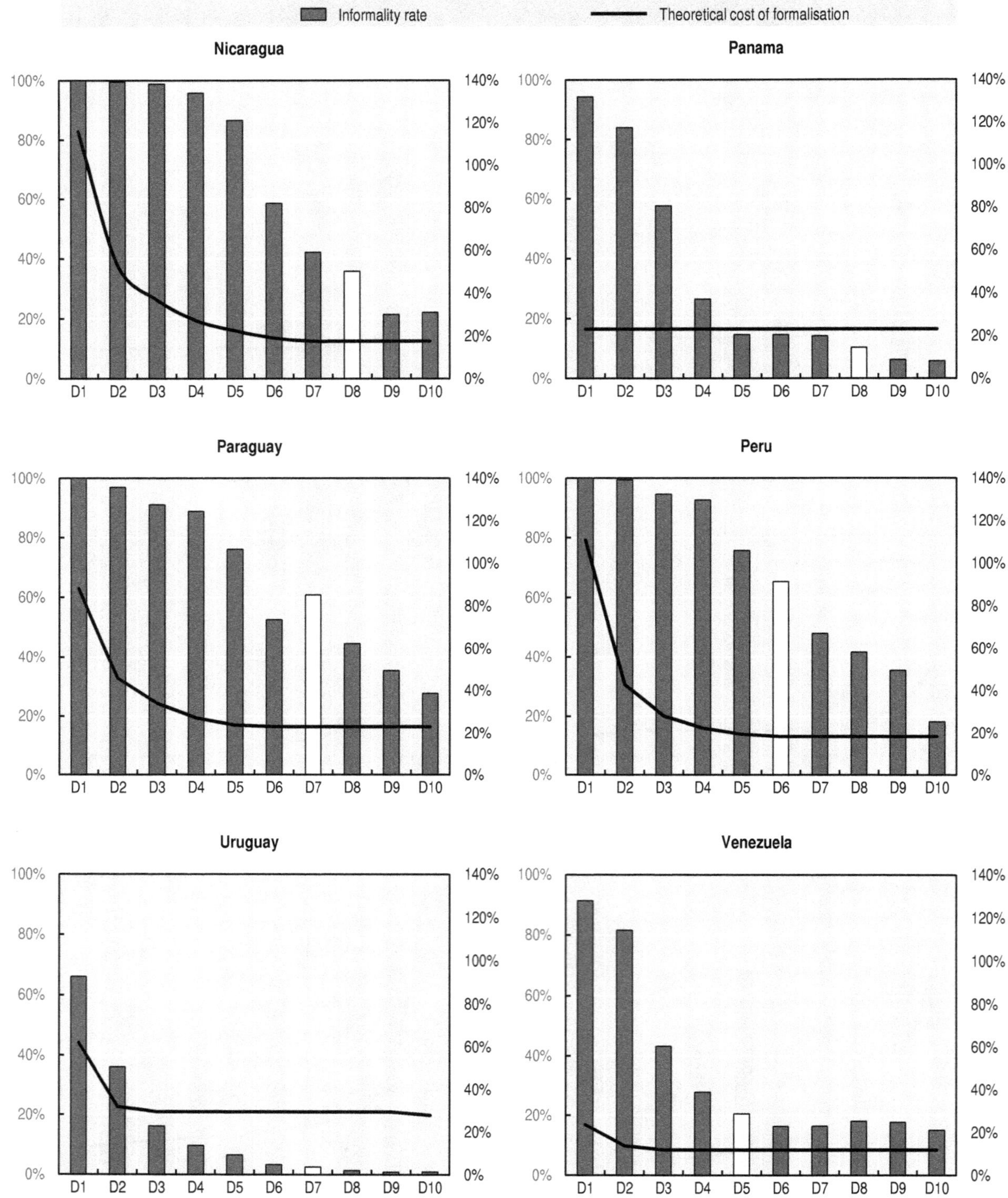

Source: Based on data from Sistema de Indicadores de Mercado Laboral y Seguridad Social (SIMS) and harmonized household surveys, circa 2013.

StatLink http://dx.doi.org/10.1787/888933407436

For the workers at the lower end of the income distribution (deciles 1-2), there are relatively high levels of both the costs of formalisation and informality rates in the majority of countries, implying that higher costs are associated with higher levels of informality (Figure 2.8, Panel A).

Figure 2.8. **The relationship between formalisation costs and informality**

A cross country approach by income decile

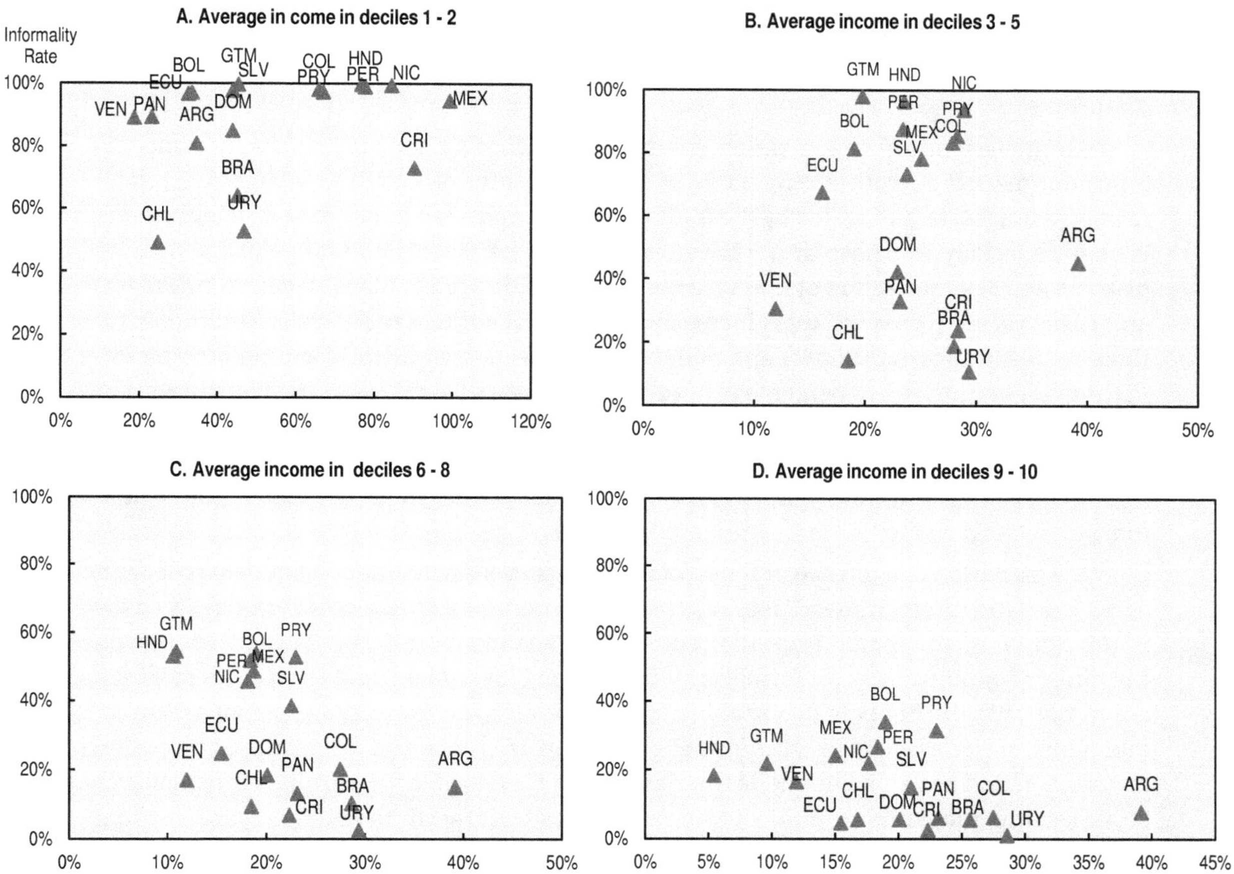

Source: Based on data from Sistema de Indicadores de Mercado Laboral y Seguridad Social (SIMS).

StatLink http://dx.doi.org/10.1787/888933407441

As levels of income rise, (deciles 3-5 in Figure 2.8, Panel B), two groups of countries can be identified, one with relatively high levels of informality (above 60%) and the other with lower levels (around 40% or less). In both groups of countries, the positive relationship between formalisation costs and rates is still evident. But in each group, both the level of dispersion and the formalisation costs are lower than in the corresponding analysis for deciles 1 and 2.

In income deciles 6-8 (Figure 2.8, Panel C), the distinction between the two groups of countries fades. However, in contrast with the two analyses covering the lower half of the income distribution, they show a negative relationship between formalisation costs and informality rates. This means the informality rates are falling while the costs of formalisation are rising. This implies that at these levels of income, formalisation costs may not be the main determinant in worker decisions with respect to formality. There are two other notable features of this group. First, countries with the larger proportion of informally employed workers also have lower formalisation costs relative to the other group of countries, and secondly the range of the levels of informality covered by the two groups is smaller than in the income deciles 3-5.

At the upper level of the income distribution (deciles 9-10 in Figure 2.8, Panel D), informality rates also tend to fall as the cost of formalisation rises. The correlation between formalisation costs and informality rates remains negative as in Figure 2.8 Panel C. As in the latter case, this points to the existence of other factors, apart from the cost of formalisation, explaining levels of informality.

5. Conclusions

The analysis shows that taxation, specifically social security contributions, has impacts on labour market outcomes. High rates of informality are correlated with high theoretical formalisation costs, as proxied by the SSCs workers would have to pay to remain or become formal, especially for those at the lower end and in the low-middle range of the income distribution. The interaction of lower earnings thresholds of SSCs (usually minimum wages) and social security program rates increases the costs of adhering to social programmes for those with earnings in the lower and middle income deciles, while the costs of participation in these programmes as a percentage of earnings decreases for those at the higher levels of the income distribution. From the employer's perspective, high non-labour costs (i.e. holiday pay, severance costs and other labour regulations) might affect also play a detrimental role in the supply of formal jobs. This adds to the many other non-tax factors that explain individual decisions to become or remain informal.

This situation is evidence of a need for new policies on taxation, labour markets and social insurance programmes. Ensuring a proper environment for the creation of quality jobs in the formal sector should be at the centre of the agenda for inclusive growth. Improving the range of opportunities for formal employment so that workers and companies can fully enjoy, not only the benefits of social insurance, but also the capacity for personal growth and added value associated with formal economies is critical to LAC countries. Focusing on taxation and social insurance, an appraisal of the levels of lower earnings thresholds of social security programs is required. Also, progressive social security schedules, and pension schemes where governments or employers match the individual's contributions would increase the returns from becoming formal would be good avenues to achieve these aims. Promoting productive job stability to lay the foundation for longer lasting and productive employment relationships is key to ensuring growth in long-term and consolidating a stronger and more vibrant middle class.

Notes

1. The authors of the special feature are Veronica Alaimo, Juan Carlos Benítez, Angel Melguizo and René Orozco. The authors thank Maurice Nettley, Bert Brys and Dominique Paturot for their contributions to this special feature and Melany Gualavisi and Maria Laura Oliveri for providing the data that enabled the analysis. The opinions expressed and arguments employed herein are the views of the authors and do not necessarily represent the official views of the Inter-American Development Bank (IDB), the Inter-American Centre of Tax Administrations (CIAT), the Organisation for Economic Co-operation and Development (OECD) and the OECD Development Centre or the governments of its member countries.
2. Details on the household income surveys are presented in the methodological appendix.
3. Self-employed and independent workers are not included in this simulation exercise as many special regimes and provisions may apply to these cases.

References

Alaimo, V., M. Bosch, D. Kaplan, C. Pages and L. Ripani (2015), *Jobs for Growth*, Inter-American Development Bank, Washington, D.C.

Bosch, M., A. Melguizo and C. Pages (2013), *Better pensions, better jobs. Towards universal coverage in Latin America and the Caribbean*, Inter-American Development Bank, Washington DC.

De Soto, H. (1989), *The other path: the invisible revolution in the third world*, HarperCollins, New York.

Daude, C., A. Melguizo and A. Neut (2010), "Fiscal Policy in Latin America: Countercyclical and Sustainable at Last?", *OECD Development Centre Working Paper* No. 291, OECD, Paris.

Easterly, W. (2001), "The Middle Class Consensus and Economic Development", *Journal of Economic Growth* 6(4), 317-335.

ECLAC (2014), *Tax policy in Latin America. Assessment and guidelines for a second generation of reforms*, ECLAC, Santiago de Chile.

ECLAC/ILO (2016), Employment Situation in Latin America and the Caribbean. ECLAC-ILO Bulletin No.14, Santiago de Chile.

Ferreira, F. H. G., J. Messina, J. Rigolini, L. F. López-Calva, M. A. Lugo, and R. Vakis (2013), *Economic Mobility and the Rise of the Latin American Middle Class*, World Bank, Washington, D.C.

IDB (2015), *Base de datos Sociómetro-BID: Sistema de Indicadores Sociales de América Latina y el Caribe*, Inter-American Development Bank, Washington, D.C., *http://www.iadb.org/en/research-and-data//sociometro-bid,6981.html*.

IDB (2013), *More than revenues, Taxation as a development tool*, Inter-American Development Bank, Washington, DC.

Jütting, J. and J. de Laiglesia (2009), *Is Informal Normal ?: Towards More and Better Jobs in Developing Countries*, OECD Publishing, Paris, *http://dx.doi.org/10.1787/9789264059245-en*

Loayza, N., A.M. Oviedo and L. Serven (2005), "The Impact of Regulation on Growth and Informality – Cross-Country Evidence", *World Bank Policy Research Working Paper* 3263, World Bank, Washington, DC.

Melguizo, A. (2015), "Pensions, informality, and the emerging middle class". IZA World of Labor, pp. 1-10, Institute for the Study of Labor.

Melguizo, A. and J. González-Páramo (2012), "Who bears labour taxes and social contributions? A meta-analysis approach", *Journal of the Spanish Economic Association*, 4(3), 247-271.

OECD/CAF/ECLAC (forthcoming), *Latin American Economic Outlook, 2017: Youth, Entrepreneurship and Skills for Development*, OECD publishing, Paris.

OECD/CAF/ECLAC (2015), *Latin American Economic Outlook 2016: Towards a New Partnership with China*, OECD Publishing, Paris, *http://dx.doi.org/10.1787/9789264246218-en*.

OECD/ECLAC/CIAT/IDB (2016), *Revenue Statistics in Latin America and the Caribbean 1990-2014*, OECD Publishing, Paris, *http://dx.doi.org/10.1787/rev_lat-2016-en-fr*.

OECD (2015), *Revenue Statistics 2015*, OECD Publishing, Paris, *http://dx.doi.org/10.1787/rev_stats-2015-en-fr*.

OECD/ECLAC/CIAT/IDB (2015), *Revenue Statistics in Latin America and the Caribbean 1990-2013*, OECD Publishing, Paris, *http://dx.doi.org/10.1787/rev_lat-2015-en-fr*.

OECD/IDB/WB (2014), *Pensions at a glance in Latin American and the Caribbean 2014*, OECD Publishing, Paris, *http://dx.doi.org/10.1787/pension_glance-2014-en*.

World Bank (2015), "Working to End Poverty in Latin America and the Caribbean: Workers, Jobs, and Wages", *LAC Poverty and Labor Brief*, World Bank, Washington, D.C.

PART I

International comparisons

This section provides unique information for each of 20 Latin American and Caribbean countries on the income taxes paid by workers, their social security contributions, the family benefits they receive in the form of cash transfers as well as the social security contributions and payroll taxes paid by their employers. It provides detailed results for 2013; which include the marginal and average tax burdens for eight different family types based on a combination of marital status, number of children and annual gross wage income. The same results are also presented for a single person without children and for a one-earner married couple with two children by income deciles and for three levels of USD income with equal purchasing power.

In this Report, the methodology used to estimate the tax wedges is based on the compulsory payments methodology:

- *The deductions from labour income (referred to in this Report as taxes) are defined as personal income tax, employee and employer social security contributions (paid either to general government or privately managed funds) and payroll taxes less cash transfers.*
- *Labour costs are defined as the sum of gross wage earnings, employer social security contributions (paid either to general government or privately managed funds) and payroll taxes.*

PART I

Chapter 3

2013 tax burdens

The 2013 tax burden estimates are presented in Tables 3.1 to 3.10 and Figures 3.1 to 3.8. There are eight model family types varying by marital status, number of children and level of earnings: single taxpayers without children earning 67%, 100% and 167% of the average wage (AW); a single parent with two children earning 67% of the AW; a one earner couple at the AW level with two children; two-earner couples with two children at 133% and 167% of the AW and a two-earner couple without children at 133% of the AW. The results are also presented for a single worker without children and a married couple with two children for each decile of the income distribution. There is a third set of results for these two family types earning an annual gross wage equivalent to USD 10 000, USD 48 000 and USD 60 000.

The chapter presents different measures for the average tax burdens (tax wedge, net personal tax rate, personal income tax rate and employee social security contribution rate) and marginal rates (tax wedge and net personal tax rate). The results for two measures of tax progressivity are also considered: tax elasticity on gross earnings and labour costs.

Average tax burdens, 2013 estimates

This section comments on Tables 3.1.a-3.4.d and Figures 3.1.a-3.4.d. These summary tables and charts show results for 8 family types, characterised by different family status (single/married, no children or 2 children), household income composition (one earner-two earner) and wage level (33%, 67%, 100% and 167% of annual gross wage earnings for an average worker). They also show results by income deciles of formal workers for the single person without children and the one-earner married couple with 2 children and in USD equivalents for the single worker without children and one-earner married couple with 2 children.

Table 3.1.a and Figure 3.1.a show the average tax wedge (the combined burden of income tax and all compulsory employee and employer social security contributions) taking into account the cash benefits each of 8 specific family-types is entitled to receive. Total levies due minus cash transfers received are expressed as a percentage of total labour costs, defined as gross wage plus employer social security contributions (including payroll taxes). In the case of a single individual without children at the average wage level, the wedges range from 10.0% (Honduras) and 11.0% (Trinidad and Tobago) to 32.2% (Brazil) and 34.6% (Argentina). For the one-earner married couple with 2 children at the average wage level, the results follow a similar pattern. The lowest are still 10.0% (Honduras) and 11.0% (Trinidad and Tobago) and the highest 33.0% (Argentina) and 32.2% (Brazil). As noted in Section 1.3, Family Rates in Chapter 1, the wedge is lower for a married couple with 2 children due to the receipt of cash benefits and/or more advantageous tax treatment in 5 countries in the region. It is also notable that the presence of children reduces the tax wedge of a single individual at 67% of the average wage by an average of 0.7 percentage points. The largest reductions in the tax wedge were 4.5 percentage points in Colombia, 4.4 percentage points in Argentina and 4.3 percentage points in Uruguay.

Tables 3.1.b and 3.1.c present the average tax wedge over the whole of the labour income distributions of formal wage earners in each country. These data are derived from the household surveys. Figures 3.1.b and 3.1.c compare for the tax wedges for these two family types in both the fifth and the tenth income deciles.

Table 3.1.b shows a zero tax wedge for a single person without children in the first decile of labour income for seven countries (Bolivia, Colombia, Costa Rica, Ecuador, Honduras, Nicaragua and Peru). This is due to the existence of lower earnings thresholds that are in place for the contributions to the social security programmes. In the case of the one-earner married couple with 2 children, the family benefits or preferential tax treatments reduce the tax wedge in the first decile of the income distribution for some countries, turning it negative in the cases of Colombia (-8.2%) and Costa Rica (-4.1%). In the cases of Argentina, Chile and Uruguay, the tax wedge is significantly reduced (33.0, 11.1 and 12.6 percentage points respectively). The average reduction is 3.7 percentage points. The sizes of these benefits decrease as labour incomes rise. In the tenth income decile (Figure 3.1.c), the difference between the regional averages for the two family profiles narrows to only 0.2 percentage points in favour of the married couple with two children profile. Finally, Table 3.1.d and Figure 3.1.d compare the tax wedges for employees earning an annual wage of USD 10 000, USD 48 000 and USD 60 000. At these levels of earnings, the average tax wedges for a single earner without children are 22.8%, 29.1% and 30.1% of total labour costs respectively. For the one-earner married couple with 2 children, the corresponding figures are 21.7%, 28.9% and 29.9% of total labour costs.

Tables 3.2.a-d and Figures 3.2.a-d present the combined burden of the income tax and employee social security contributions after cash benefits, expressed as a percentage of gross wage earnings (the corresponding separate measures for income tax and social security contributions are shown separately in Tables 3.3.a-d, and 3.4.a-d). The average tax and contributions rate for a single person at the average wage level without children across the region is 9.3% of annual gross wage earnings. This worker is liable to a 19.1% tax burden in Chile[1] and 18% in Uruguay. The countries with the lowest average rates were Honduras, Guatemala and Trinidad and Tobago (3.6%, 4.0% and 4.5% of annual average gross wage earnings respectively).

The regional average for the one-earner married couple 2 children at the average wage was 8.9% of gross wage earnings, 0.4 percentage points below the corresponding single individual without children. The highest average rates for this family profile were also in Chile (19.1%) and Uruguay (17.2%), while the lowest burdens were the same as for the single without children family profile.

In contrast, there is a much larger gap between the measures for the two family types in OECD countries[2] (11.2 percentage points compared with 0.4 in Latin America and the Caribbean). Furthermore, the average tax rate that a single taxpayer without children in Latin American and the Caribbean faces is only slightly less (0.9 percentage points) than a single individual with 2 children when both earn a 67% of the average wage. The corresponding gap in the OECD averages is 17.4 percentage points.

The number of sources of income that comprise the total amount of the wage earnings in the household also affects the size of the tax burden. Consider the case of a single individual without children earning 167% of the average wage compared with the two-earner married couple whose combined income totals 167% of the average wage. In this situation, the tax burden faced by the former is 2.5 percentage points higher in the LAC region and 10.9 percentage points larger in OECD countries.

Tables 3.2.b and 3.2.c show how the net tax rates after cash benefits change across the income distribution. Single individuals without children in the first income decile have a zero tax rate in 10 countries (Bolivia, Colombia, Costa Rica, Dominican Republic, Ecuador, El Salvador, Honduras, Nicaragua, Paraguay and Peru). The tax rate at this income level is negative in Mexico due to the annual employment subsidy, through which a worker receives an additional 17.0% of the average wage. On the other hand, the corresponding workers in Chile, Argentina and Uruguay face the highest tax rates (19.1%, 17.0% and 16.6% of the average wage respectively). One-earner married couples with 2 children in the first income decile face lower tax rates compared with the single worker without children in 5 countries. In Argentina, the tax rate in the first income decile for a single individual without children is reduced from a liability of 17.0% of gross wage earnings to a benefit or credit of 24.9% for the one-earner married couple with two children family profile. One-earner married couples also receive tax benefits in Colombia and Costa Rica, (8.2% and 4.1% of gross earnings respectively), compared with zero liability for the single worker without children. In

Uruguay, the tax rate is reduced by 14.9 percentage points to 1.7% of average wage earnings. The tables show that the tax rates for the two family types in these 5 countries tend to converge as incomes rise. In the tenth income decile, the highest tax rates for both family profiles are in Uruguay (26.0% and 25.7% respectively) while the lowest rates are 5.9% for both in Guatemala.

Table 3.3.a shows that workers in the 8 family types receiving the average wage are not liable for personal income tax in any of the countries except in Mexico. For the single individual without children at 167% of the average wage, the picture changes and workers in 7 of the 20 countries pay no income tax, while the other 13 countries have average income tax rates that vary from 0.8% of gross wage earnings (Chile) to 13% (Mexico). The average for the region is 2.2%, substantially less than the OECD average (21.7%). For the married couple family types, there is a zero income tax rate in each country except for Mexico and Costa Rica, where it is negative because of tax credits granted in respect of spouses and children in the household. Tables 3.3.b and 3.3.c show that even in the seventh income decile, it is only in Mexico that workers pay income tax. The pattern starts to alter in the eighth and ninth deciles where single workers pay income tax in 3 countries and 9 countries respectively. But even at the higher levels of wage earnings, the average income tax rates are relatively low, averaging 6.4% of wage earnings for a single individual without children and 6.2% for the one-earner married couple with 2 children in the tenth income decile. Also, in the ninth income decile, the average income tax rates range from zero in 11 countries to 12.8% in Mexico for both family profiles. Table 3.3.d shows an average income tax rate across the region of 2.0% paid on annual wage earnings of USD 10 000. These tables also highlight an important feature of personal income tax systems in Latin American and Caribbean countries; although they are designed to be very progressive, they raise relatively little revenue because of the high levels of exempt income, which erode the redistributive power of the tax.

Table and Figures 3.4.a-d present figures for employee social security contribution rates. The payments vary from 2.5% (Mexico) to 19.1% (Chile) of gross wage earnings for a single individual without children on the average wage. The average for the region is 8.9%. In comparison, the average worker across the OECD pays 9.9% of gross wage earnings. The situation is very similar for a one-earner married couple with 2 children at the average wage level where the average rate is also 9.0% with payments ranging from 2.5% (Mexico) to 19.4% (Uruguay).

Tables 3.4.b and 3.4.c show that the rates of mandatory social security contributions vary at the different deciles of labour income. Some countries do no impose social security payments on their citizens at the lowest income levels because of lower earnings thresholds associated with social security contribution programmes. These thresholds are generally linked to the minimum wage. After the contributions commence, the contribution rates are in most cases stable as income rises. In most countries, this stability is attained by the fifth income decile of income. Honduras is an exception where payments start at the seventh income decile. In some countries the contribution rates start to decline in the higher income deciles as upper earnings ceilings on payments, usually in old-age and health insurance programmes, start to take effect. For the single person without children, employee social security contributions are an average of 8.5% of gross wage earnings across the region at the tenth decile of labour income being highest at 19.1% in Chile and lowest at 1.4% in Honduras. For the one-earner married couple with 2 children at the same income decile, the average rate contribution rate is 8.6% with the same highest and lowest examples.

A comparison between the regional averages paid at the fifth income decile and the tenth income decile shows a reduction of 0.2 percentage points for the higher decile group for both family profiles.

Table 3.4.d provides a clearer illustration of the decline of average employee social security contribution rates as income rises from USD 10 000 to USD 60 000; the average contribution rate across the region for the single worker declines by 1.6 percentage points of gross wage earnings between the two earnings levels. The rates are reduced in 12 countries and unchanged in 6 others. Bolivia and Colombia are the exceptions which exhibit an increase in the employee social security contribution rate as income increases. The results for the one-earner married couple with 2 children show a similar pattern.

Marginal tax burdens, 2013 estimates

Table 3.5.a and Figure 3.5.a show the percentage of a one unit increase of labour costs of a worker that is deducted through the personal income tax and both employee and employer contributions after changes in cash benefits. This is known as the marginal tax wedge. The difference between the marginal tax wedge and the increase in wages provides a measure of how much of a marginal increase in labour costs adds to net take-home pay. In most of the countries in the region, the marginal wedge absorbed between 13% and 35% of the rise in one unit of the labour costs for a single individual without children on the average wage. Honduras and Trinidad are exceptions where these workers have a zero marginal tax wedge at the average income level. The average marginal tax wedge for the region is 20.8% compared with the OECD equivalent of 45.0%. The figures for a one-earner married couple with 2 children present a similar picture.

Tables 3.5.b and 3.5.c show the marginal tax wedge over the whole of the income distribution. For a single individual without children and wages in the first income decile, the average marginal tax wedge for the region is 10.2% of total labour costs. At this level of income, the highest marginal tax wedge is 34.6% (Argentina), while there is a zero marginal wedge in Bolivia, Colombia, Costa Rica, Ecuador, Honduras, Nicaragua, Peru and Trinidad and Tobago. At the tenth income decile, the average marginal tax wedge for the region rises to 29.3% of total labour costs with a range of 16% to 39%.

Tables 3.6.a-d and Figures 3.6.a-d show the marginal rates of personal income taxes, employee social security contributions and cash benefits of a unit increase in annual gross earnings. Across the region, a single person without children on average earnings faced an average marginal rate of 9.3% with different countries ranging from zero to 19.1% compared with the OECD average of 36.1%. There is a similar picture for the one-earner married couple with 2 children.

Tables 3.6.b and 3.6.c show the estimates of the marginal rate of income tax and employee social security contributions minus cash benefits over the whole of the labour income distribution. The figures show that the marginal rate increases as incomes rise. For a single individual without children, the average marginal rate across the region is 4.7% at the first income decile increasing to 20.2% at the tenth decile. At the tenth decile, the marginal rates range from 7.9% in Colombia to 29.2% in Jamaica. For the one-earner married couple with 2 children, the variation in the average rate across the income distribution is slightly smaller, ranging from 4.7% to 20.0%. It is notable that over the whole of the labour income distribution, Trinidad and Tobago has a zero marginal rate until the ninth decile of income and Honduras until the tenth decile of income for both family profiles.

Tables 3.7a-d present the percentage increases in net income when gross wage earnings rise by 1 currency unit (the elasticity of after-tax income).[3] Under a proportional tax system, net income would increase in the same proportion as the increase in gross wage earnings, in which case the elasticity is equal to 1. The more progressive the system is – at the earnings level considered – the lower the elasticity will be. In contrast, higher elasticities imply that a percentage increase in gross payment leads to an increase in net income in excess of the percentage increase in gross wage earnings and thus a regressive tax system. For a single earner without children on the average wage, the most progressive system, on this measure, is Mexico (0.91). The remainder of the countries exhibit proportional tax systems (elasticity of 1), with the exception of Honduras (1.04) and Trinidad and Tobago (1.05). The average for the region displays a proportional tax system (elasticity of 1) in which net income increases at the same percentage of gross earnings (1.0). In comparison, the corresponding OECD average is 0.85. These results are very similar for the one-earner married couple with 2 children, except for Argentina (0.98), Colombia (0.96), Costa Rica (0.99) and Uruguay (0.97). For the other countries, the elasticity of the after-tax income equals 1. The regional average was 0.99 well above the corresponding OECD average of 0.73.

Figure 3.7 shows that the average elasticity coefficients of a single individual without children in the region vary across the labour income distribution from 0.94 to 1.00. At the lower and middle levels of income the tax systems tend to be proportional on average becoming slightly more progressive at the higher levels (income deciles 8 to 10). For the one-earner married couple with two children, the elasticity coefficients range from 0.94 to 0.99. In this case, the average elasticity coefficient is slightly progressive at the lowest income deciles. As income rises, the average coefficient tends to become more proportional until the eigth income decile where it starts to become more progressive.

Tables 3.8.a-d provide a related but different form of elasticity measure: the percentage increase in net income when labour costs (i.e. gross wage earnings plus employer social security contributions and payroll taxes) rise by 1 currency unit.[4] In this case, taxes and social security payments made by employers are also part of the analysis. For a single individual without children on the average wage, the most common value of the elasticity across the region is 1.0, the exceptions being Mexico (0.94), Honduras (1.11) and Trinidad and Tobago (1.12). The average elasticity for the region as a whole is 1.01, 0.16 percentage points higher than the OECD average of 0.85. At 167% of the average wage, the average elasticity for the region is reduced to 0.94 compared with 0.86 for OECD countries. The most progressive systems are Jamaica (0.77), Peru (0.84) and Panama (0.87), while the only regressive, on this measure, is El Salvador (1.05).

For the one-earner married couple with 2 children the regional average is 1.0 compared with 0.73 for the OECD. The lowest elasticities were 0.94 (Mexico), 0.96 (Colombia), 0.97 (Uruguay) and 0.98 (Argentina); whereas the highest elasticities were 1.11 (Honduras) and 1.12 (Trinidad and Tobago).

Figure 3.8 compares the regional averages for the single worker without children and the one-earner married couple with 2 children. For a single individual the elasticity tends to be either 1.0 or slightly higher until the ninth income decile when it reduces to 0.96. In contrast, the one-earner married couple with 2 children shows more progressivity at the lower income deciles, becoming proportional in the middle income deciles and then progressive at the higher levels of income. It should be noted that that the two family profiles shown in Figure 3.8 converge at the higher income deciles.

Tables 3.9.a and 3.9.b show the annual gross wage and net income, in USD equivalents using purchasing power parities (PPP), for the 8 family-types. At the average wage, total earnings before taxes varied from USD 5 932 (Jamaica) to USD 31 808 (Argentina). The average for the region is USD 13 771 which is about one-third of the USD 40 292 equivalent for OECD countries. Once taxes are taken into account, the net income for the average single worker in the region varied from USD 5 535 (Jamaica) to USD 26 400 (Argentina). The average for the region was USD 12 347, about 41% of the OECD average (USD 29 592).

Tables 3.9.c-f show the corresponding figures for two family profiles over the whole of the labour income distribution. Gross labour income in the region varied from an average of USD 4 542 in the first income decile to USD 38 947 in the tenth decile. In the first decile, it varied from USD 973 (Jamaica) to USD 7 365 (Venezuela). In the tenth decile, the range was USD 24 795 (Jamaica) to USD 55 960 (Chile). Once taxes are accounted for, the net income of a single individual without children in the first income decile ranged from USD 908 (Jamaica) to USD 6 959 (Venezuela). The corresponding range for the tenth decile was USD 19 188 (Jamaica) to USD 46 231 (Colombia). The situation is very similar for the married one-earner married couple with 2 children.

Finally, Tables 3.10.a-f present a similar analysis comparing total labour costs with net incomes. At the average wage, the average labour cost for the region was USD 16 125 ranging from USD 6 639 (Jamaica) to USD 40 380 (Argentina). The corresponding net income figures are the same as in Tables 3.9.a-f.

Notes

1. This figure is in contrast to corresponding result of 7% shown in the Taxing Wages model (OECD, 2014) which does not take account of social security payments paid to privately managed funds.
2. The figures are not directly comparable (see endnote 1 above) but they demonstrate the relatively generous more treatment of family with children in the income tax/ benefit systems of OECD countries compared with Latin America and the Caribbean.
3. The reported elasticities in Tables 3.7 are calculated as (100 – METR)/(100 – AETR), where METR is the marginal rate of income tax plus employee social security contributions less cash benefits reported in Tables 3.6 and AETR is the average rate plus employee social security contributions less cash benefits reported in Tables 3.2.
4. The reported elasticities in Tables 3.8 are calculated as (100 – METR)/(100 – AETR), where METR is the marginal rate of income tax plus employee and employer social security contributions less cash benefits reported in Tables 3.5 and AETR is the average rate plus employee and employer social security contributions less cash benefits reported in Table 3.1.

References

OECD (2014), *Taxing Wages 2014*, OECD Publishing. *http://dx.doi.org/10.1787/tax_wages-2014-en*

Table 3.1.a. **Income tax plus employee and employer contributions less cash benefits, family profiles, 2013**

As % of labour costs, by family-type and wage level

Country	Single no ch 67 (% AW)	Single no ch 100 (% AW)	Single no ch 167 (% AW)	Single 2 ch 67 (% AW)	Married 2 ch 100 - 0 (% AW)	Married 2 ch 100 -33 (% AW)	Married 2 ch 100 - 67 (% AW)	Married no ch 100 - 33 (% AW)
Argentina	34.6	34.6	34.6	30.3	33.0	33.4	33.6	34.6
Bolivia	21.6	21.6	21.6	21.6	21.6	16.7	21.6	16.7
Brazil	32.2	32.2	35.1	32.2	32.2	30.0	32.2	32.0
Chile	22.6	22.6	23.5	21.8	22.6	20.5	22.3	22.6
Colombia	30.0	30.0	30.2	25.5	27.0	19.2	26.4	24.0
Costa Rica	28.0	28.0	28.0	27.3	27.2	21.6	27.4	21.9
Dominican Republic	19.2	19.2	19.2	19.2	19.2	15.2	19.2	15.2
Ecuador	18.5	18.5	18.5	18.5	18.5	14.2	18.5	14.2
El Salvador	20.5	20.5	24.7	20.5	20.5	16.1	20.5	16.1
Guatemala	4.8	13.2	14.0	4.8	13.2	11.2	10.0	11.2
Honduras	0.0	10.0	7.0	0.0	10.0	7.6	6.1	7.6
Jamaica	16.6	16.6	19.5	16.6	16.6	16.6	16.6	16.6
Mexico	22.3	26.9	29.7	22.3	26.9	24.7	25.0	24.7
Nicaragua	19.2	19.2	22.2	19.2	19.2	15.0	19.2	15.0
Panama	22.9	22.9	26.6	22.9	22.9	22.9	22.9	22.9
Paraguay	20.9	20.9	20.9	20.9	20.9	16.4	20.9	16.4
Peru	17.5	17.5	18.7	17.5	17.5	13.4	17.5	13.4
Trinidad and Tobago	11.8	11.0	17.1	11.8	11.0	11.4	11.4	11.4
Uruguay	30.5	30.5	34.1	26.2	29.8	29.7	30.6	30.2
Venezuela	17.4	17.4	17.4	17.4	17.4	17.4	17.4	17.4
Unweighted average								
LAC[1]	**20.6**	**21.7**	**23.1**	**19.8**	**21.4**	**18.7**	**21.0**	**19.2**
OECD[2]	**32.2**	**36.0**	**40.4**	**17.9**	**26.9**	**28.5**	**31.3**	**32.9**

Note: ch denotes children and AW denotes the average wage.

1. Represents the average for the group of 20 Latin American and Caribbean countries. Chile and Mexico are also part of the OECD group.
2. The source for OECD averages is OECD (2014) Taxing Wages, Table I.1. It should be noted that the OECD figures are not directly comparable with the other figures in the table as they do not include social security contributions paid to privately managed funds which are not classified as taxes in the OECD methodology.

StatLink http://dx.doi.org/10.1787/888933410156

Figure 3.1.a. **Income tax plus employee and employer contributions less cash benefits, 2013**

As % of labour costs, by family-type

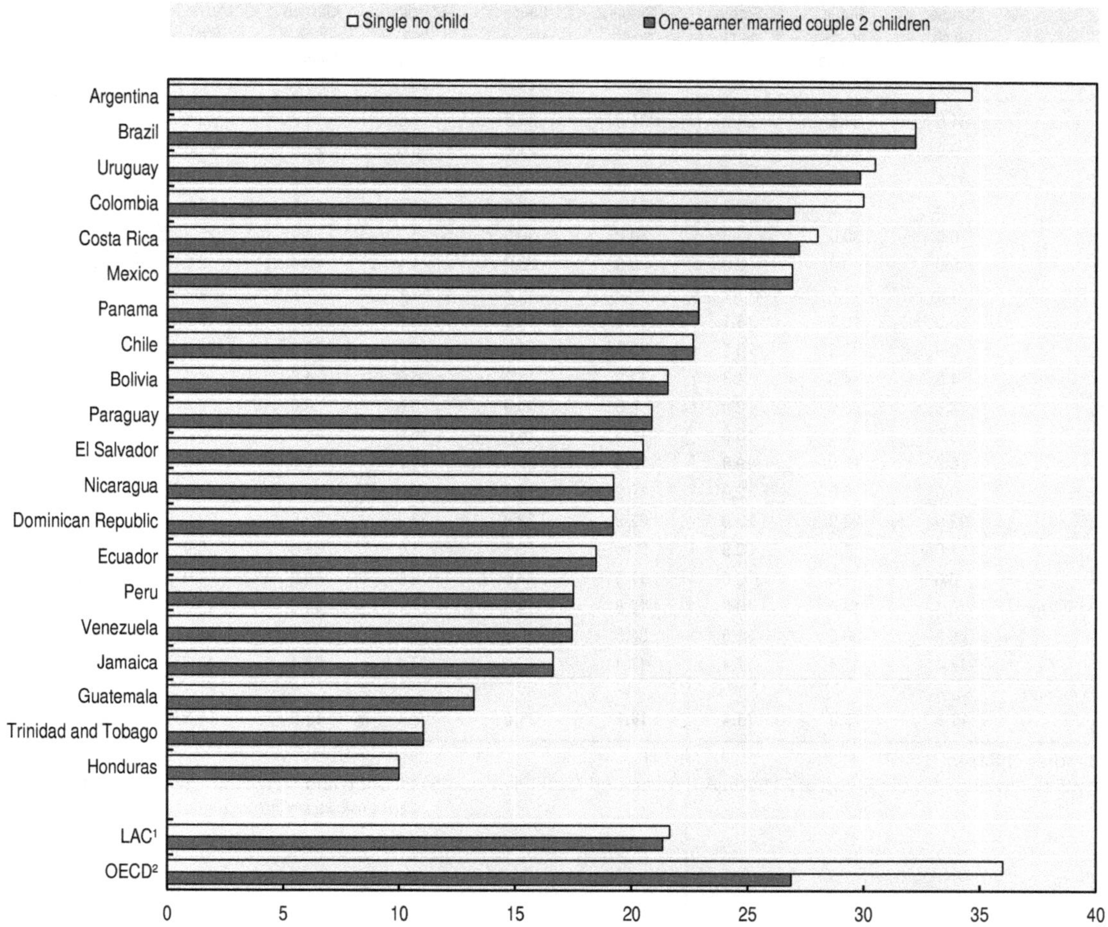

Note: Both the single worker without children and the one-earner married couple with 2 children are assumed to earn the average wage.

1. Represents the unweighted average for the group of 20 Latin American and Caribbean countries. Chile and Mexico are also part of the OECD group.
2. The source for OECD averages is OECD (2014) Taxing Wages, Table I.1. It should be noted that the OECD figures are not directly comparable with the other figures in the table as they do not include social security contributions paid to privately managed funds which are not classified as taxes in the OECD methodology.

StatLink http://dx.doi.org/10.1787/888933407452

Table 3.1.b. Income tax plus employee and employer contributions less cash benefits, income deciles 1-5, 2013

As % of labour costs, by family-type and income decile

Country	Single no ch Income decile1	Single no ch Income decile 2	Single no ch Income decile 3	Single no ch Income decile 4	Single no ch Income decile 5	Married 2 ch Income decile1	Married 2 ch Income decile 2	Married 2 ch Income decile 3	Married 2 ch Income decile 4	Married 2 ch Income decile 5
Argentina	34.6	34.6	34.6	34.6	34.6	1.6	14.8	18.6	20.6	25.6
Bolivia	0.0	21.6	21.6	21.6	21.6	0.0	21.6	21.6	21.6	21.6
Brazil	31.4	31.4	31.4	31.4	31.4	26.1	26.5	27.0	27.6	31.4
Chile	22.6	22.6	22.6	22.6	22.6	11.5	15.1	17.9	18.3	18.8
Colombia	0.0	30.0	30.0	30.0	30.0	-8.2	24.9	25.2	25.5	26.0
Costa Rica	0.0	0.0	0.0	0.0	28.0	-4.1	-2.4	-2.0	-1.8	26.8
Dominican Republic	1.2	1.2	1.2	19.2	19.2	1.2	1.2	1.2	19.2	19.2
Ecuador	0.0	18.1	18.1	18.5	18.5	0.0	18.1	18.1	18.5	18.5
El Salvador	0.9	20.5	20.5	20.5	20.5	0.9	20.5	20.5	20.5	20.5
Guatemala	4.8	4.8	4.8	13.2	13.2	4.8	4.8	4.8	13.2	13.2
Honduras	0.0	0.0	0.0	0.0	0.0	0.0	0.0	0.0	0.0	0.0
Jamaica	16.6	16.6	16.6	16.6	16.6	16.6	16.6	16.6	16.6	16.6
Mexico	16.7	18.8	19.8	20.9	22.4	16.7	18.8	19.8	20.9	22.4
Nicaragua	0.0	0.0	2.0	19.2	19.2	0.0	0.0	2.0	19.2	19.2
Panama	22.9	22.9	22.9	22.9	22.9	22.9	22.9	22.9	22.9	22.9
Paraguay	1.0	1.0	20.9	20.9	20.9	1.0	1.0	20.9	20.9	20.9
Peru	0.0	0.0	0.0	17.5	17.5	0.0	0.0	0.0	17.5	17.5
Trinidad and Tobago	16.1	14.0	13.2	12.8	12.6	16.1	14.0	13.2	12.8	12.6
Uruguay	29.3	30.5	30.5	30.5	30.5	16.7	23.5	25.0	25.9	26.6
Venezuela	17.4	17.4	17.4	17.4	17.4	17.4	17.4	17.4	17.4	17.4
Unweighted average										
LAC[1]	**10.8**	**15.3**	**16.4**	**19.5**	**21.0**	**7.1**	**13.0**	**14.5**	**17.9**	**19.9**

Note: ch denotes children.

1. Represents the average for the group of 20 Latin American and Caribbean countries. Chile and Mexico are also part of the OECD group.

StatLink http://dx.doi.org/10.1787/888933410166

Figure 3.1.b. **Income tax plus employee and employer contributions less cash benefits, 5th income decile, 2013**

As % of labour costs, by family-type

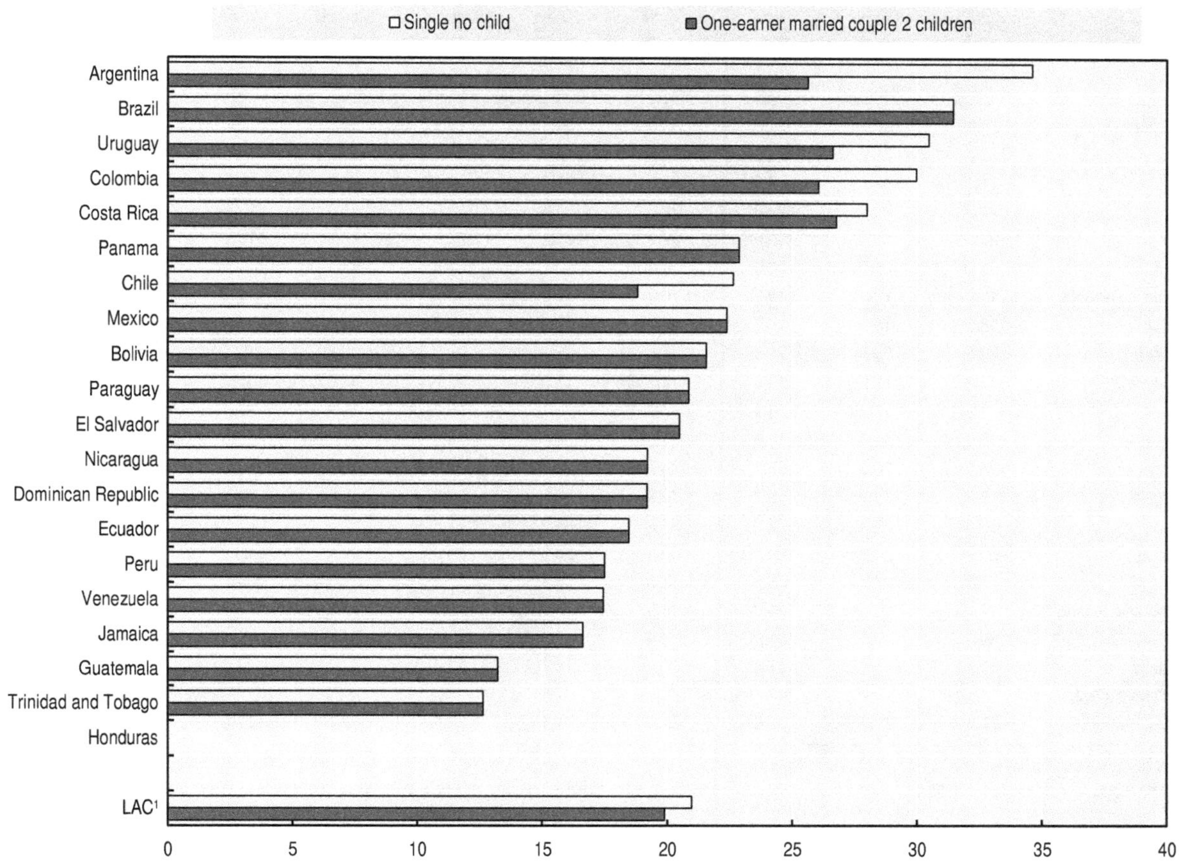

1. Represents the unweighted average for the group of 20 Latin American and Caribbean countries. Chile and Mexico are also part of the OECD group.

StatLink http://dx.doi.org/10.1787/888933407461

Table 3.1.c. **Income tax plus employee and employer contributions less cash benefits, income deciles 6-10, 2013**

As % of labour costs, by family-type and income decile

Country	Single no ch Income decile 6	Single no ch Income decile 7	Single no ch Income decile 8	Single no ch Income decile 9	Single no ch Income decile 10	Married 2 ch Income decile 6	Married 2 ch Income decile 7	Married 2 ch Income decile 8	Married 2 ch Income decile 9	Married 2 ch Income decile 10
Argentina	34.6	34.6	34.6	34.6	34.6	26.9	30.5	32.6	32.9	33.6
Bolivia	21.6	21.6	21.6	21.6	24.0	21.6	21.6	21.6	21.6	24.0
Brazil	31.4	32.2	32.2	34.5	32.1	31.4	32.2	32.2	33.9	32.1
Chile	22.6	22.6	22.6	22.6	24.6	19.3	21.8	22.0	22.6	24.6
Colombia	30.0	30.2	30.2	30.2	31.1	26.6	27.4	27.9	28.6	31.1
Costa Rica	28.0	28.0	28.0	28.0	32.0	27.0	27.1	27.3	27.5	31.7
Dominican Republic	19.2	19.2	19.2	19.2	25.6	19.2	19.2	19.2	19.2	25.6
Ecuador	18.5	18.5	18.5	18.5	20.7	18.5	18.5	18.5	18.5	20.7
El Salvador	20.5	20.5	23.5	24.5	26.3	20.5	20.5	23.5	24.5	26.3
Guatemala	13.2	13.2	13.2	13.3	14.9	13.2	13.2	13.2	13.3	14.9
Honduras	0.0	10.2	8.4	6.7	9.1	0.0	10.2	8.4	6.7	9.1
Jamaica	16.6	16.6	16.6	21.5	30.9	16.6	16.6	16.6	21.5	30.9
Mexico	23.5	26.8	27.8	29.6	33.1	23.5	26.8	27.8	29.6	33.1
Nicaragua	19.2	19.2	19.2	20.8	25.6	19.2	19.2	19.2	20.8	25.6
Panama	22.9	22.9	22.9	24.8	31.0	22.9	22.9	22.9	24.0	30.7
Paraguay	20.9	20.9	20.9	20.9	20.9	20.9	20.9	20.9	20.9	20.9
Peru	17.5	17.5	17.5	17.5	23.9	17.5	17.5	17.5	17.5	23.9
Trinidad and Tobago	12.4	12.0	11.3	15.9	20.7	12.4	12.0	11.3	15.9	20.7
Uruguay	30.5	30.5	31.3	33.4	37.2	29.5	29.8	30.1	32.5	37.0
Venezuela	17.4	17.4	17.4	17.4	18.7	17.4	17.4	17.4	17.4	17.4
Unweighted average										
LAC[1]	**21.0**	**21.7**	**21.8**	**22.8**	**25.9**	**20.2**	**21.3**	**21.5**	**22.5**	**25.7**

Note: ch denotes children.

1. Represents the average for the group of 20 Latin American and Caribbean countries. Chile and Mexico are also part of the OECD group.

StatLink http://dx.doi.org/10.1787/888933410170

Figure 3.1.c. **Income tax plus employee and employer contributions less cash benefits, 10th income decile, 2013**

As % of labour costs, by family-type

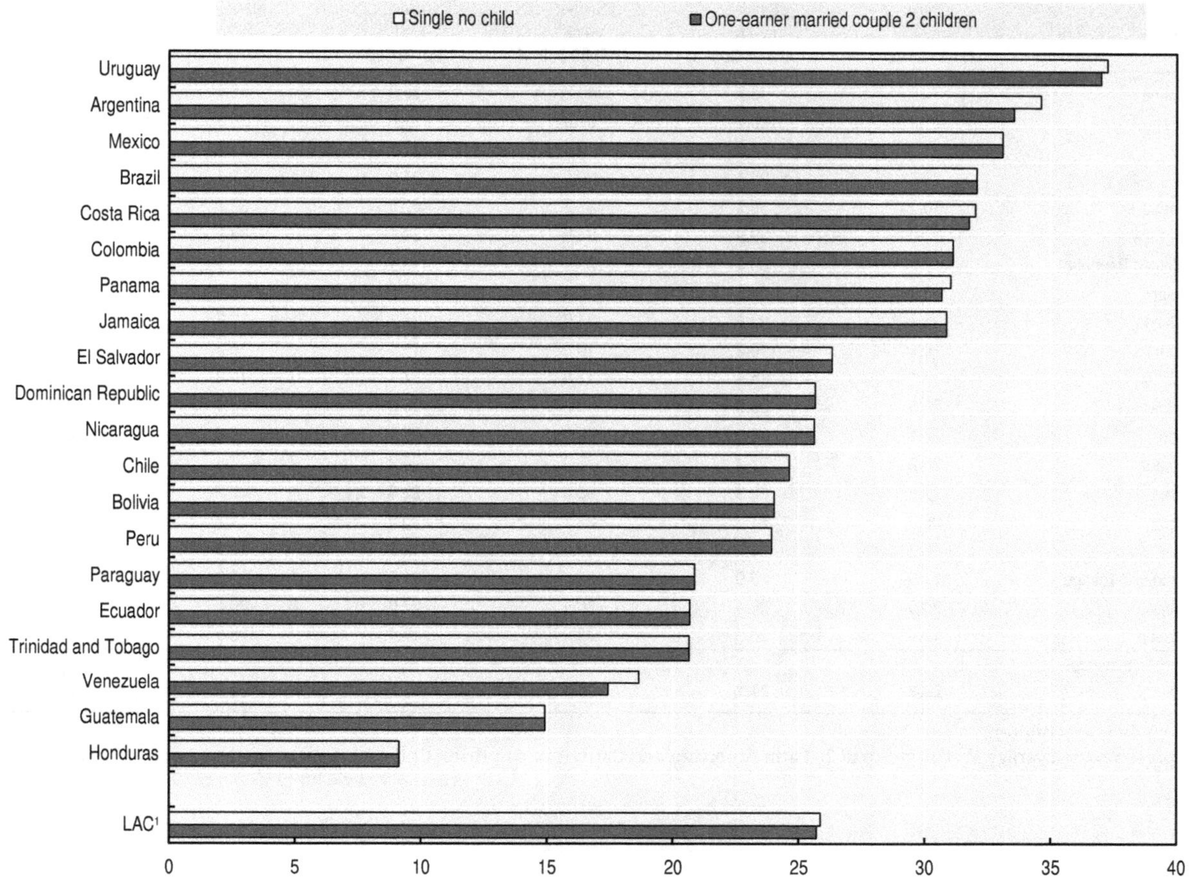

1. Represents the unweighted average for the group of 20 Latin American and Caribbean countries. Chile and Mexico are also part of the OECD group.

StatLink http://dx.doi.org/10.1787/888933407472

Table 3.1.d. Income tax plus employee and employer contributions less cash benefits, USD equivalent earnings, 2013

As % of labour costs, by family-type and annual labour income

Country	Single no ch USD 10 000	Single no ch USD 48 000	Single no ch USD 60 000	Married 2 ch USD 10 000	Married 2 ch USD 48 000	Married 2 ch USD 60 000
Argentina	34.6	43.7	46.2	20.9	39.6	42.8
Bolivia	21.6	28.6	31.8	21.6	28.6	31.8
Brazil	32.2	31.0	30.4	32.2	31.0	30.4
Chile	22.6	22.4	20.5	21.9	22.4	20.5
Colombia	30.2	35.7	37.5	27.9	35.7	37.5
Costa Rica	28.0	33.9	34.9	27.1	33.7	34.7
Dominican Republic	19.4	30.5	29.6	19.4	30.5	29.6
Ecuador	18.5	24.6	25.8	18.5	24.6	25.8
El Salvador	25.1	32.8	34.0	25.1	32.8	34.0
Guatemala	14.1	16.2	16.5	14.1	16.2	16.5
Honduras	7.1	15.9	17.3	7.1	15.9	17.3
Jamaica	26.9	33.9	34.2	26.9	33.9	34.2
Mexico	28.1	36.6	35.5	28.1	36.6	35.5
Nicaragua	26.2	27.4	26.9	26.2	27.4	26.9
Panama	22.9	32.9	35.0	22.9	32.7	34.7
Paraguay	20.9	21.2	22.7	20.9	21.2	22.7
Peru	18.2	28.8	30.4	18.2	28.8	30.4
Trinidad and Tobago	11.5	23.0	23.4	11.5	23.0	23.4
Uruguay	30.5	36.7	36.4	27.0	36.8	36.7
Venezuela	17.4	26.5	33.9	17.4	25.5	33.1
Unweighted average						
LAC[1]	**22.8**	**29.1**	**30.1**	**21.7**	**28.9**	**29.9**

Note: ch denotes children.

1. Represents the average for the group of 20 Latin American and Caribbean countries. Chile and Mexico are also part of the OECD group.

StatLink http://dx.doi.org/10.1787/888933410188

Figure 3.1.d. **Income tax plus employee and employer contributions less cash benefits, USD equivalent earnings, 2013**

As % of labour costs, by family-type for annual labour income of USD 10 000

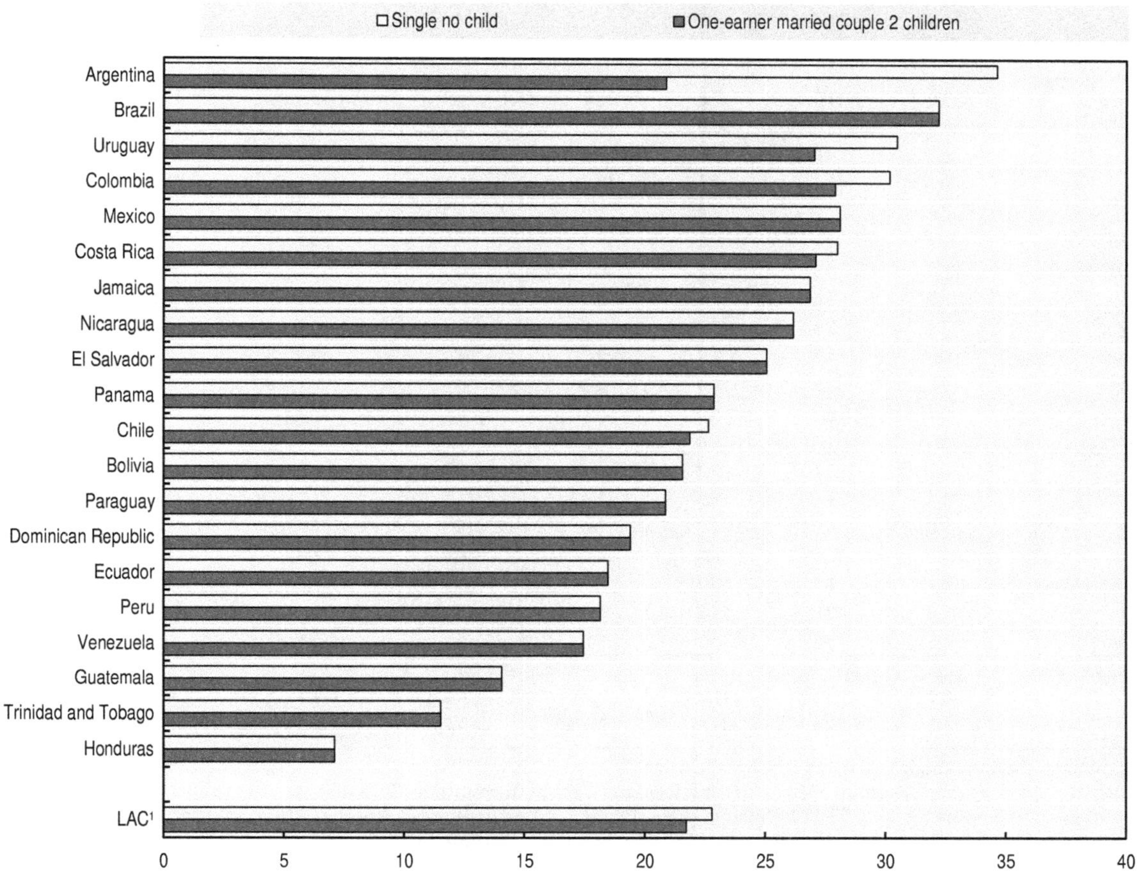

1. Represents the unweighted average for the group of 20 Latin American and Caribbean countries. Chile and Mexico are also part of the OECD group.

StatLink http://dx.doi.org/10.1787/888933407483

Table 3.2.a. **Income tax plus employee social security contributions less cash benefits, family profiles, 2013**

As % of gross wage earnings, by family-type

Country	Single no ch 67 (% AW)	Single no ch 100 (% AW)	Single no ch 167 (% AW)	Single 2 ch 67 (% AW)	Married 2 ch 100 - 0 (% AW)	Married 2 ch 100 -33 (% AW)	Married 2 ch 100 - 67 (% AW)	Married no ch 100 - 33 (% AW)
Argentina	17.0	17.0	17.0	11.5	14.9	15.4	15.8	17.0
Bolivia	10.6	10.6	10.6	10.6	10.6	8.0	10.6	8.0
Brazil	9.0	9.0	12.9	9.0	9.0	6.1	9.0	8.8
Chile	19.1	19.1	19.9	18.2	19.1	16.8	18.7	19.1
Colombia	7.0	7.0	7.0	1.0	3.0	-0.8	2.2	5.3
Costa Rica	9.2	9.2	9.2	8.3	8.2	6.1	8.4	6.6
Dominican Republic	6.0	6.0	6.0	6.0	6.0	4.5	6.0	4.5
Ecuador	9.5	9.5	9.5	9.5	9.5	7.1	9.5	7.1
El Salvador	8.9	8.9	13.9	8.9	8.9	6.7	8.9	6.7
Guatemala	0.8	4.0	4.9	0.8	4.0	3.2	2.8	3.2
Honduras	0.0	3.6	3.0	0.0	3.6	2.7	2.2	2.7
Jamaica	6.7	6.7	9.9	6.7	6.7	6.7	6.7	6.7
Mexico	3.7	11.0	15.6	3.7	11.0	6.4	8.1	6.4
Nicaragua	5.7	5.7	9.2	5.7	5.7	4.3	5.7	4.3
Panama	11.4	11.4	15.7	11.4	11.4	11.4	11.4	11.4
Paraguay	9.0	9.0	9.0	9.0	9.0	6.8	9.0	6.8
Peru	10.9	10.9	12.2	10.9	10.9	8.2	10.9	8.2
Trinidad and Tobago	5.1	4.5	10.3	5.1	4.5	5.0	4.8	5.0
Uruguay	18.0	18.0	22.3	13.0	17.2	17.1	18.1	17.7
Venezuela	5.5	5.5	5.5	5.5	5.5	5.5	5.5	5.5
Unweighted average								
LAC[1]	**8.7**	**9.3**	**11.2**	**7.7**	**8.9**	**7.4**	**8.7**	**8.0**
OECD[2]	**21.2**	**25.4**	**30.8**	**3.8**	**14.2**	**16.7**	**19.9**	**22.1**

Note: ch denotes children and AW denotes the average wage.

1. Represents the average for the group of 20 Latin American and Caribbean countries. Chile and Mexico are also part of the OECD group.
2. The source for OECD averages is OECD (2014) Taxing Wages, Table I.3. It should be noted that the OECD figures are not directly comparable with the other figures in the table as they do not include social security contributions paid to privately managed funds which are not classified as taxes in the OECD methodology.

StatLink http://dx.doi.org/10.1787/888933410199

Figure 3.2.a. **Income tax plus employee social security contributions less cash benefits, 2013**

As % of gross wage earnings, by family-type

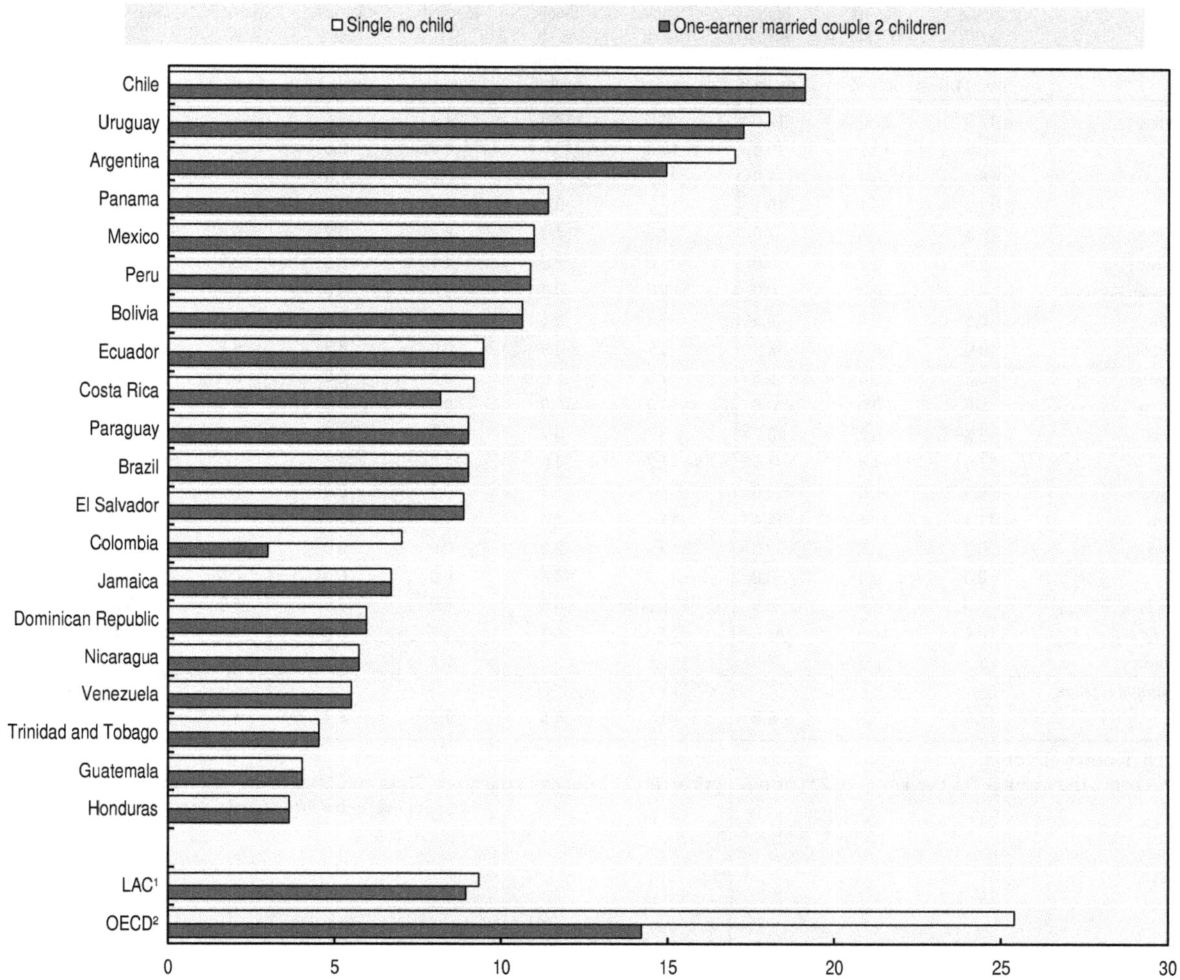

1. Represents the unweighted average for the group of 20 Latin American and Caribbean countries. Chile and Mexico are also part of the OECD group.
2. The source for OECD averages is OECD (2014) Taxing Wages, Table I.3. It should be noted that the OECD figures are not directly comparable with the other figures in the table as they do not include social security contributions paid to privately managed funds which are not classified as taxes in the OECD methodology.

StatLink http://dx.doi.org/10.1787/888933407499

Table 3.2.b. **Income tax plus employee social security contributions less cash benefits, income deciles 1-5, 2013**

As % of gross wage earnings, by family-type and income decile

Country	Single no ch Income decile1	Single no ch Income decile 2	Single no ch Income decile 3	Single no ch Income decile 4	Single no ch Income decile 5	Married 2 ch Income decile1	Married 2 ch Income decile 2	Married 2 ch Income decile 3	Married 2 ch Income decile 4	Married 2 ch Income decile 5
Argentina	17.0	17.0	17.0	17.0	17.0	-24.9	-8.1	-3.3	-0.8	5.6
Bolivia	0.0	10.6	10.6	10.6	10.6	0.0	10.6	10.6	10.6	10.6
Brazil	8.0	8.0	8.0	8.0	8.0	0.8	1.3	2.1	2.8	8.0
Chile	19.1	19.1	19.1	19.1	19.1	7.4	11.2	14.2	14.5	15.1
Colombia	0.0	7.0	7.0	7.0	7.0	-8.2	0.2	0.6	1.1	1.8
Costa Rica	0.0	0.0	0.0	0.0	9.2	-4.1	-2.4	-2.0	-1.8	7.6
Dominican Republic	0.0	0.0	0.0	6.0	6.0	0.0	0.0	0.0	6.0	6.0
Ecuador	0.0	9.5	9.5	9.5	9.5	0.0	9.5	9.5	9.5	9.5
El Salvador	0.0	8.9	8.9	8.9	8.9	0.0	8.9	8.9	8.9	8.9
Guatemala	0.8	0.8	0.8	4.0	4.0	0.8	0.8	0.8	4.0	4.0
Honduras	0.0	0.0	0.0	0.0	0.0	0.0	0.0	0.0	0.0	0.0
Jamaica	6.7	6.7	6.7	6.7	6.7	6.7	6.7	6.7	6.7	6.7
Mexico	-17.0	-4.6	-1.5	1.2	4.0	-17.0	-4.6	-1.5	1.2	4.0
Nicaragua	0.0	0.0	0.0	5.7	5.7	0.0	0.0	0.0	5.7	5.7
Panama	11.4	11.4	11.4	11.4	11.4	11.4	11.4	11.4	11.4	11.4
Paraguay	0.0	0.0	9.0	9.0	9.0	0.0	0.0	9.0	9.0	9.0
Peru	0.0	0.0	0.0	10.9	10.9	0.0	0.0	0.0	10.9	10.9
Trinidad and Tobago	8.9	6.6	5.9	5.6	5.3	8.9	6.6	5.9	5.6	5.3
Uruguay	16.6	18.0	18.0	18.0	18.0	1.7	9.8	11.5	12.7	13.5
Venezuela	5.5	5.5	5.5	5.5	5.5	5.5	5.5	5.5	5.5	5.5
Unweighted average										
LAC[1]	**3.9**	**6.2**	**6.8**	**8.2**	**8.8**	**-0.5**	**3.4**	**4.5**	**6.2**	**7.5**

Note: ch denotes children.

1. Represents the average for the group of 20 Latin American and Caribbean countries. Chile and Mexico are also part of the OECD group.

StatLink http://dx.doi.org/10.1787/888933410205

Figure 3.2.b. **Income tax plus employee social security contributions less cash benefits, 5th Income decile, 2013**

As % of gross wage earnings, by family-type

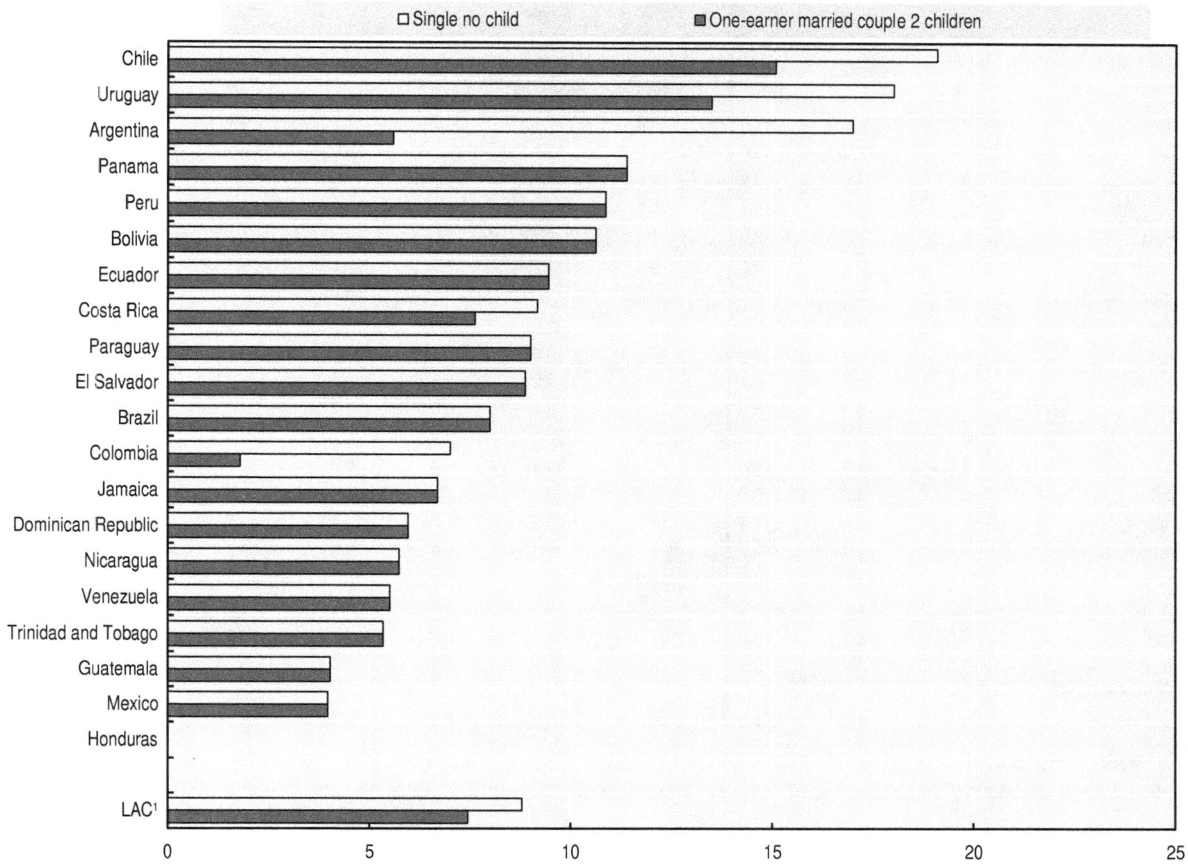

1. Represents the unweighted average for the group of 20 Latin American and Caribbean countries. Chile and Mexico are also part of the OECD group.

StatLink http://dx.doi.org/10.1787/888933407505

Table 3.2.c. **Income tax plus employee social security contributions less cash benefits, income deciles 6-10, 2013**

As % of gross wage earnings, by family-type and income decile

Country	Single no ch Income decile 6	Single no ch Income decile 7	Single no ch Income decile 8	Single no ch Income decile 9	Single no ch Income decile 10	Married 2 ch Income decile 6	Married 2 ch Income decile 7	Married 2 ch Income decile 8	Married 2 ch Income decile 9	Married 2 ch Income decile 10
Argentina	17.0	17.0	17.0	17.0	17.0	7.2	11.7	14.4	14.9	15.6
Bolivia	10.6	10.6	10.6	10.6	13.4	10.6	10.6	10.6	10.6	13.4
Brazil	8.0	9.0	9.0	12.0	16.7	8.0	9.0	9.0	11.2	16.7
Chile	19.1	19.1	19.1	19.1	21.1	15.6	18.2	18.4	19.1	21.1
Colombia	7.0	7.0	7.0	7.0	8.3	2.5	3.3	4.0	4.9	8.3
Costa Rica	9.2	9.2	9.2	9.2	14.2	7.8	8.1	8.3	8.6	13.9
Dominican Republic	6.0	6.0	6.0	6.0	13.5	6.0	6.0	6.0	6.0	13.5
Ecuador	9.5	9.5	9.5	9.5	11.9	9.5	9.5	9.5	9.5	11.9
El Salvador	8.9	8.9	12.3	13.5	18.0	8.9	8.9	12.3	13.5	18.0
Guatemala	4.0	4.0	4.0	4.1	5.9	4.0	4.0	4.0	4.1	5.9
Honduras	0.0	3.7	3.0	2.4	6.7	0.0	3.7	3.0	2.4	6.7
Jamaica	6.7	6.7	6.7	12.1	22.6	6.7	6.7	6.7	12.1	22.6
Mexico	6.0	10.8	12.6	15.4	20.4	6.0	10.8	12.6	15.4	20.4
Nicaragua	5.7	5.7	5.7	7.6	13.2	5.7	5.7	5.7	7.6	13.2
Panama	11.4	11.4	11.4	13.6	20.8	11.4	11.4	11.4	12.7	20.3
Paraguay	9.0	9.0	9.0	9.0	9.0	9.0	9.0	9.0	9.0	9.0
Peru	10.9	10.9	10.9	10.9	17.8	10.9	10.9	10.9	10.9	17.8
Trinidad and Tobago	5.2	4.9	4.5	9.5	16.3	5.2	4.9	4.5	9.5	16.3
Uruguay	18.0	18.0	19.0	21.5	26.0	16.9	17.2	17.6	20.4	25.7
Venezuela	5.5	5.5	5.5	5.5	6.9	5.5	5.5	5.5	5.5	5.5
Unweighted average										
LAC[1]	**8.9**	**9.3**	**9.6**	**10.8**	**15.0**	**7.9**	**8.7**	**9.2**	**10.4**	**14.8**

Note: ch denotes children.

1. Represents the average for the group of 20 Latin American and Caribbean countries. Chile and Mexico are also part of the OECD group.

StatLink http://dx.doi.org/10.1787/888933410217

Figure 3.2.c. **Income tax plus employee social security contributions less cash benefits, 10th income decile, 2013**

As % of gross wage earnings, by family-type

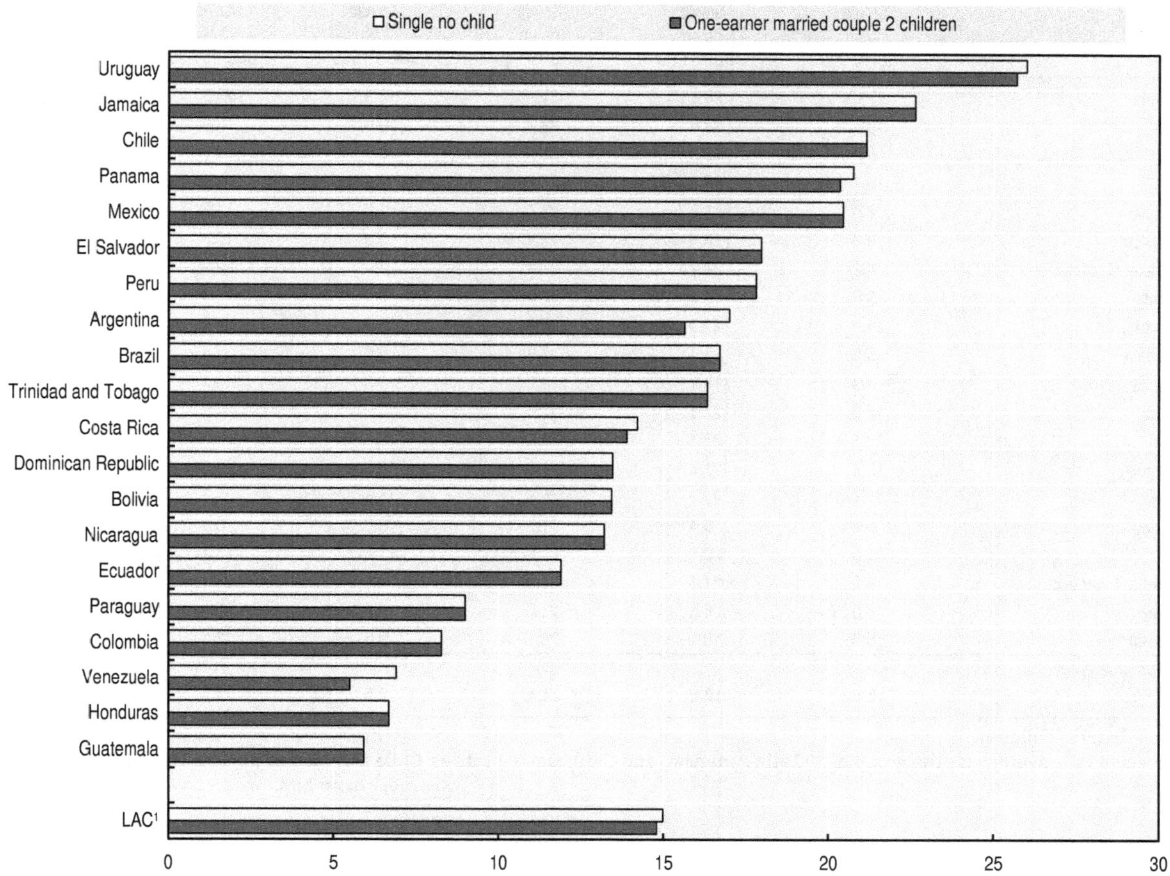

1. Represents the unweighted average for the group of 20 Latin American and Caribbean countries. Chile and Mexico are also part of the OECD group.

StatLink http://dx.doi.org/10.1787/888933407512

Table 3.2.d. **Income tax plus employee social security contributions less cash benefits, USD equivalent earnings, 2013**

As % of gross wage earnings, by family-type and annual labour income

Country	Single no ch USD 10 000	Single no ch USD 48 000	Single no ch USD 60 000	Married 2 ch USD 10 000	Married 2 ch USD 48 000	Married 2 ch USD 60 000
Argentina	17.0	28.5	31.7	-0.5	23.3	27.4
Bolivia	10.6	18.6	22.2	10.6	18.6	22.2
Brazil	9.0	19.6	21.2	9.0	19.6	21.2
Chile	19.1	19.0	17.2	18.3	19.0	17.2
Colombia	7.0	11.2	13.7	4.0	11.2	13.7
Costa Rica	9.2	16.6	17.8	8.0	16.3	17.7
Dominican Republic	6.2	22.2	22.8	6.2	22.2	22.8
Ecuador	9.5	16.3	17.6	9.5	16.3	17.6
El Salvador	14.9	27.0	28.4	14.9	27.0	28.4
Guatemala	5.0	7.4	7.6	5.0	7.4	7.6
Honduras	3.3	15.1	16.7	3.3	15.1	16.7
Jamaica	18.2	27.1	27.6	18.2	27.1	27.6
Mexico	13.1	25.3	26.3	13.1	25.3	26.3
Nicaragua	13.8	21.6	21.8	13.8	21.6	21.8
Panama	11.4	23.0	25.3	11.4	22.7	25.0
Paraguay	9.0	9.4	11.1	9.0	9.4	11.1
Peru	11.6	23.1	24.9	11.6	23.1	24.9
Trinidad & Tobago	4.9	21.1	21.9	4.9	21.1	21.9
Uruguay	18.0	25.3	25.0	14.0	25.4	25.3
Venezuela	5.5	19.1	28.1	5.5	18.1	27.3
Unweighted average						
LAC[1]	**10.8**	**19.8**	**21.4**	**9.5**	**19.5**	**21.2**

Note: ch denotes children.

1. Represents the average for the group of 20 Latin American and Caribbean countries. Chile and Mexico are also part of the OECD group.

StatLink http://dx.doi.org/10.1787/888933410226

Figure 3.2.d. **Income tax plus employee social security contributions less cash benefits, USD equivalent earnings, 2013**

As % of gross wage earnings, by family-type for annual labour income of USD 10 000

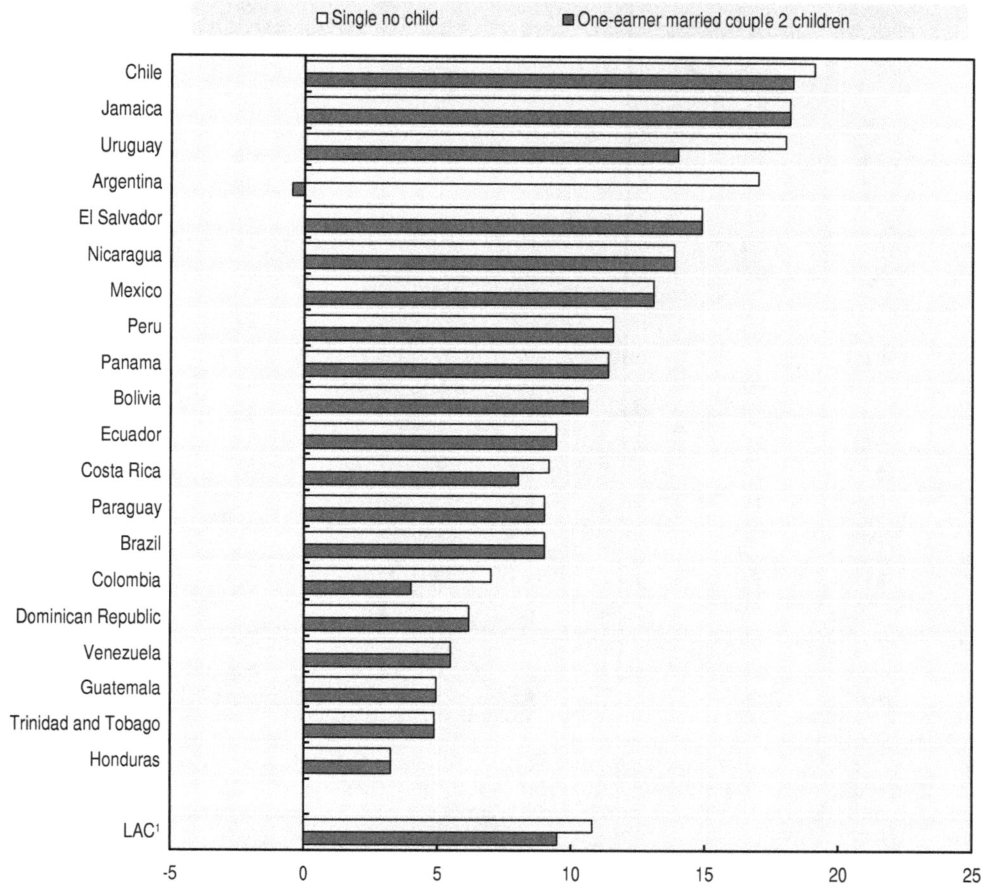

1. Represents the unweighted average for the group of 20 Latin American and Caribbean countries. Chile and Mexico are also part of the OECD group.

StatLink http://dx.doi.org/10.1787/888933407528

Table 3.3.a. **Income tax, family profiles, 2013**

As % of gross wage earnings, by family-type and wage level

Country	Single no ch 67 (% AW)	Single no ch 100 (% AW)	Single no ch 167 (% AW)	Single 2 ch 67 (% AW)	Married 2 ch 100 - 0 (% AW)	Married 2 ch 100 -33 (% AW)	Married 2 ch 100 - 67 (% AW)	Married no ch 100 - 33 (% AW)
Argentina	0.0	0.0	0.0	0.0	0.0	0.0	0.0	0.0
Bolivia	0.0	0.0	0.0	0.0	0.0	0.0	0.0	0.0
Brazil	0.0	0.0	1.9	0.0	0.0	0.0	0.0	0.0
Chile	0.0	0.0	0.8	0.0	0.0	0.0	0.0	0.0
Colombia	0.0	0.0	0.0	0.0	0.0	0.0	0.0	0.0
Costa Rica	0.0	0.0	0.0	-0.9	-1.0	-0.8	-0.6	-0.3
Dominican Republic	0.0	0.0	0.0	0.0	0.0	0.0	0.0	0.0
Ecuador	0.0	0.0	0.0	0.0	0.0	0.0	0.0	0.0
El Salvador	0.0	0.0	5.1	0.0	0.0	0.0	0.0	0.0
Guatemala	0.0	0.0	0.9	0.0	0.0	0.0	0.0	0.0
Honduras	0.0	0.0	0.9	0.0	0.0	0.0	0.0	0.0
Jamaica	0.0	0.0	3.2	0.0	0.0	0.0	0.0	0.0
Mexico	1.4	8.5	13.0	1.4	8.5	4.0	5.6	4.0
Nicaragua	0.0	0.0	3.5	0.0	0.0	0.0	0.0	0.0
Panama	0.0	0.0	4.3	0.0	0.0	0.0	0.0	0.0
Paraguay	0.0	0.0	0.0	0.0	0.0	0.0	0.0	0.0
Peru	0.0	0.0	1.3	0.0	0.0	0.0	0.0	0.0
Trinidad and Tobago	0.0	0.0	5.7	0.0	0.0	0.0	0.0	0.0
Uruguay	0.0	0.0	4.3	0.0	0.0	0.0	0.0	0.0
Venezuela	0.0	0.0	0.0	0.0	0.0	0.0	0.0	0.0
Unweighted average								
LAC[1]	**0.1**	**0.4**	**2.2**	**0.0**	**0.4**	**0.2**	**0.3**	**0.2**
OECD[2]	**11.4**	**15.6**	**21.7**	**6.2**	**10.3**	**10.6**	**12.5**	**12.4**

Note: ch denotes children and AW denotes the average wage.

1. Represents the average for the group of 20 Latin American and Caribbean countries. Chile and Mexico are also part of the OECD group.
2. The source for OECD averages is OECD (2014) Taxing Wages, Table I.4. It should be noted that the OECD figures are not directly comparable with the other figures in the table as they do not include social security contributions paid to privately managed funds which are not classified as taxes in the OECD methodology.

StatLink http://dx.doi.org/10.1787/888933410239

Table 3.3.b. **Income tax, income deciles 1-5, 2013**

As % of gross wage earnings, by family-type and income decile

Country	Single no ch Income decile1	Single no ch Income decile 2	Single no ch Income decile 3	Single no ch Income decile 4	Single no ch Income decile 5	Married 2 ch Income decile1	Married 2 ch Income decile 2	Married 2 ch Income decile 3	Married 2 ch Income decile 4	Married 2 ch Income decile 5
Argentina	0.0	0.0	0.0	0.0	0.0	0.0	0.0	0.0	0.0	0.0
Bolivia	0.0	0.0	0.0	0.0	0.0	0.0	0.0	0.0	0.0	0.0
Brazil	0.0	0.0	0.0	0.0	0.0	0.0	0.0	0.0	0.0	0.0
Chile	0.0	0.0	0.0	0.0	0.0	0.0	0.0	0.0	0.0	0.0
Colombia	0.0	0.0	0.0	0.0	0.0	0.0	0.0	0.0	0.0	0.0
Costa Rica	0.0	0.0	0.0	0.0	0.0	-4.1	-2.4	-2.0	-1.8	-1.5
Dominican Republic	0.0	0.0	0.0	0.0	0.0	0.0	0.0	0.0	0.0	0.0
Ecuador	0.0	0.0	0.0	0.0	0.0	0.0	0.0	0.0	0.0	0.0
El Salvador	0.0	0.0	0.0	0.0	0.0	0.0	0.0	0.0	0.0	0.0
Guatemala	0.0	0.0	0.0	0.0	0.0	0.0	0.0	0.0	0.0	0.0
Honduras	0.0	0.0	0.0	0.0	0.0	0.0	0.0	0.0	0.0	0.0
Jamaica	0.0	0.0	0.0	0.0	0.0	0.0	0.0	0.0	0.0	0.0
Mexico	-19.4	-7.0	-3.9	-1.2	1.6	-19.4	-7.0	-3.9	-1.2	1.6
Nicaragua	0.0	0.0	0.0	0.0	0.0	0.0	0.0	0.0	0.0	0.0
Panama	0.0	0.0	0.0	0.0	0.0	0.0	0.0	0.0	0.0	0.0
Paraguay	0.0	0.0	0.0	0.0	0.0	0.0	0.0	0.0	0.0	0.0
Peru	0.0	0.0	0.0	0.0	0.0	0.0	0.0	0.0	0.0	0.0
Trinidad and Tobago	0.0	0.0	0.0	0.0	0.0	0.0	0.0	0.0	0.0	0.0
Uruguay	0.0	0.0	0.0	0.0	0.0	0.0	0.0	0.0	0.0	0.0
Venezuela	0.0	0.0	0.0	0.0	0.0	0.0	0.0	0.0	0.0	0.0
Unweighted average										
LAC[1]	**-1.0**	**-0.4**	**-0.2**	**-0.1**	**0.1**	**-1.2**	**-0.5**	**-0.3**	**-0.1**	**0.0**

Note: ch denotes children.

1. Represents the unweighted average for the group of 20 Latin American and Caribbean countries. Chile and Mexico are also part of the OECD group.

StatLink http://dx.doi.org/10.1787/888933410245

Table 3.3.c. **Income tax, income deciles 6-10, 2013**

As % of gross wage earnings, by family-type and income decile

Country	Single no ch Income decile 6	Single no ch Income decile 7	Single no ch Income decile 8	Single no ch Income decile 9	Single no ch Income decile 10	Married 2 ch Income decile 6	Married 2 ch Income decile 7	Married 2 ch Income decile 8	Married 2 ch Income decile 9	Married 2 ch Income decile 10
Argentina	0.0	0.0	0.0	0.0	0.0	0.0	0.0	0.0	0.0	0.0
Bolivia	0.0	0.0	0.0	0.0	2.8	0.0	0.0	0.0	0.0	2.8
Brazil	0.0	0.0	0.0	1.0	9.4	0.0	0.0	0.0	0.2	9.4
Chile	0.0	0.0	0.0	0.0	2.1	0.0	0.0	0.0	0.0	2.1
Colombia	0.0	0.0	0.0	0.0	0.4	0.0	0.0	0.0	0.0	0.4
Costa Rica	0.0	0.0	0.0	0.0	5.0	-1.3	-1.1	-0.9	-0.6	4.7
Dominican Republic	0.0	0.0	0.0	0.0	7.5	0.0	0.0	0.0	0.0	7.5
Ecuador	0.0	0.0	0.0	0.0	2.5	0.0	0.0	0.0	0.0	2.5
El Salvador	0.0	0.0	3.4	4.6	10.4	0.0	0.0	3.4	4.6	10.4
Guatemala	0.0	0.0	0.0	0.1	1.9	0.0	0.0	0.0	0.1	1.9
Honduras	0.0	0.0	0.0	0.0	5.3	0.0	0.0	0.0	0.0	5.3
Jamaica	0.0	0.0	0.0	5.5	15.9	0.0	0.0	0.0	5.5	15.9
Mexico	3.6	8.3	10.1	12.8	17.7	3.6	8.3	10.1	12.8	17.7
Nicaragua	0.0	0.0	0.0	1.8	7.5	0.0	0.0	0.0	1.8	7.5
Panama	0.0	0.0	0.0	2.2	9.4	0.0	0.0	0.0	1.3	9.0
Paraguay	0.0	0.0	0.0	0.0	0.0	0.0	0.0	0.0	0.0	0.0
Peru	0.0	0.0	0.0	0.0	6.9	0.0	0.0	0.0	0.0	6.9
Trinidad and Tobago	0.0	0.0	0.0	5.2	13.3	0.0	0.0	0.0	5.2	13.3
Uruguay	0.0	0.0	1.0	3.5	9.4	0.0	0.0	0.0	1.0	7.7
Venezuela	0.0	0.0	0.0	0.0	1.4	0.0	0.0	0.0	0.0	0.0
Unweighted average										
LAC[1]	**0.2**	**0.4**	**0.7**	**1.8**	**6.4**	**0.1**	**0.4**	**0.6**	**1.6**	**6.2**

Note: ch denotes children.

1. Represents the average for the group of 20 Latin American and Caribbean countries. Chile and Mexico are also part of the OECD group.

StatLink http://dx.doi.org/10.1787/888933410252

Figure 3.3. **Income tax, 10th income decile, 2013**

As % of gross wage earnings, by family-type

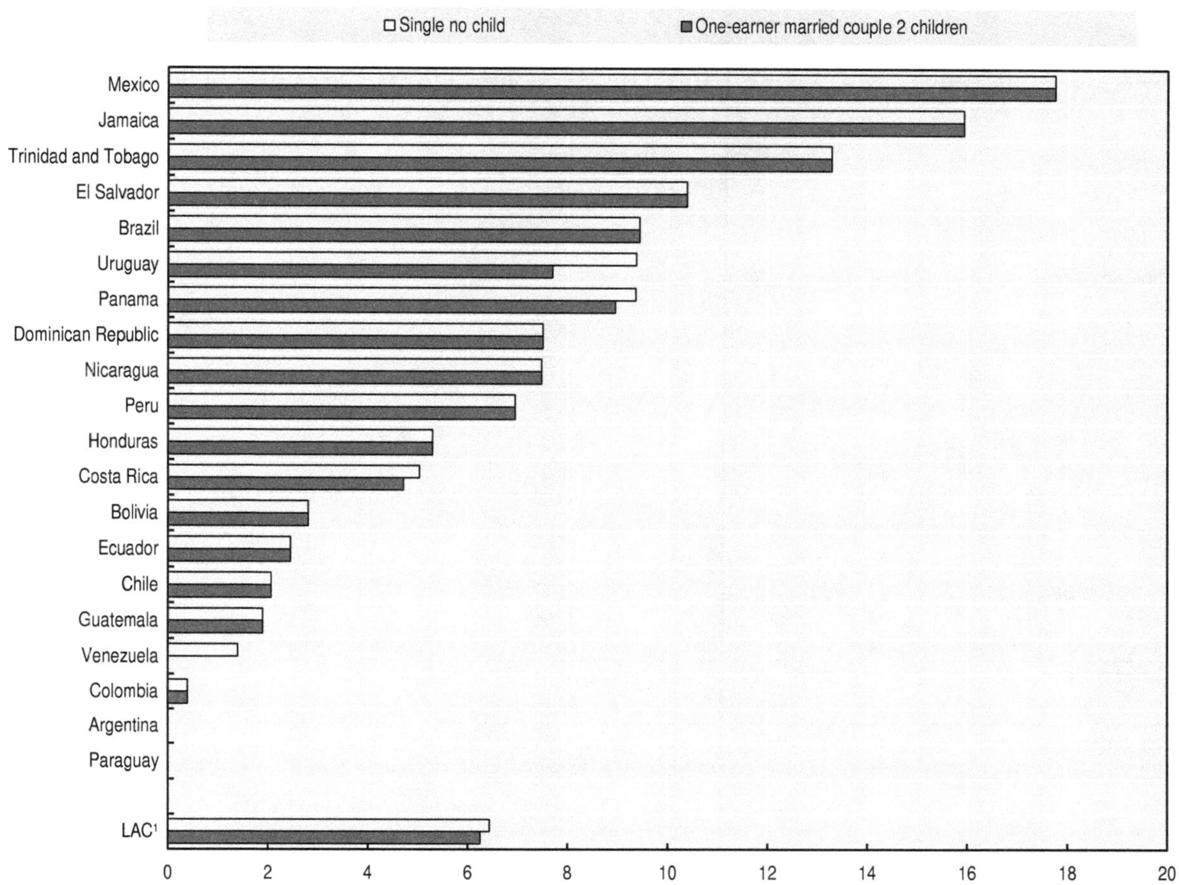

1. Represents the unweighted average for the group of 20 Latin American and Caribbean countries. Chile and Mexico are also part of the OECD group.

StatLink http://dx.doi.org/10.1787/888933407530

Table 3.3.d. **Income tax, USD equivalent earnings, 2013**

As % of gross wage earnings, by family-type and annual labour income

Country	Single no ch USD 10 000	Single no ch USD 48 000	Single no ch USD 60 000	Married 2 ch USD 10 000	Married 2 ch USD 48 000	Married 2 ch USD 60 000
Argentina	0.0	11.5	16.2	0.0	7.2	12.6
Bolivia	0.0	7.1	7.1	0.0	7.1	7.1
Brazil	0.0	14.3	16.9	0.0	14.3	16.9
Chile	0.0	3.2	4.4	0.0	3.2	4.4
Colombia	0.0	3.3	5.8	0.0	3.3	5.8
Costa Rica	0.0	7.4	8.7	-1.1	7.2	8.5
Dominican Republic	0.2	17.7	19.2	0.2	17.7	19.2
Ecuador	0.0	6.8	8.1	0.0	6.8	8.1
El Salvador	6.4	20.5	22.0	6.4	20.5	22.0
Guatemala	0.9	3.3	3.6	0.9	3.3	3.6
Honduras	1.1	14.7	16.3	1.1	14.7	16.3
Jamaica	11.5	22.1	22.7	11.5	22.1	22.7
Mexico	10.5	22.7	24.1	10.5	22.7	24.1
Nicaragua	8.1	19.2	19.9	8.1	19.2	19.9
Panama	0.0	11.6	13.9	0.0	11.3	13.6
Paraguay	0.0	0.4	2.1	0.0	0.4	2.1
Peru	0.7	12.2	14.0	0.7	12.2	14.0
Trinidad and Tobago	0.5	19.8	20.8	0.5	19.8	20.8
Uruguay	0.0	12.2	13.6	0.0	10.9	12.6
Venezuela	0.0	15.3	24.8	0.0	14.3	24.0
Unweighted average						
LAC[1]	**2.0**	**12.3**	**14.2**	**1.9**	**11.9**	**13.9**

Note: ch denotes children.

1. Represents the average for the group of 20 Latin American and Caribbean countries. Chile and Mexico are also part of the OECD group.

StatLink http://dx.doi.org/10.1787/888933410261

Table 3.4.a. **Employee social security contributions, family profiles, 2013**

As % of gross wage earnings, by family-type and wage level

Country	Single no ch 67 (% AW)	Single no ch 100 (% AW)	Single no ch 167 (% AW)	Single 2 ch 67 (% AW)	Married 2 ch 100 - 0 (% AW)	Married 2 ch 100 -33 (% AW)	Married 2 ch 100 - 67 (% AW)	Married no ch 100 - 33 (% AW)
Argentina	17.0	17.0	17.0	17.0	17.0	17.0	17.0	17.0
Bolivia	10.6	10.6	10.6	10.6	10.6	8.0	10.6	8.0
Brazil	9.0	9.0	11.0	9.0	9.0	8.8	9.0	8.8
Chile	19.1	19.1	19.1	19.1	19.1	19.1	19.1	19.1
Colombia	7.0	7.0	7.0	7.0	7.0	5.3	7.0	5.3
Costa Rica	9.2	9.2	9.2	9.2	9.2	6.9	9.0	6.9
Dominican Republic	6.0	6.0	6.0	6.0	6.0	4.5	6.0	4.5
Ecuador	9.5	9.5	9.5	9.5	9.5	7.1	9.5	7.1
El Salvador	8.9	8.9	8.8	8.9	8.9	6.7	8.9	6.7
Guatemala	0.8	4.0	4.0	0.8	4.0	3.2	2.8	3.2
Honduras	0.0	3.6	2.2	0.0	3.6	2.7	2.2	2.7
Jamaica	6.7	6.7	6.7	6.7	6.7	6.7	6.7	6.7
Mexico	2.4	2.5	2.6	2.4	2.5	2.5	2.4	2.5
Nicaragua	5.7	5.7	5.7	5.7	5.7	4.3	5.7	4.3
Panama	11.4	11.4	11.4	11.4	11.4	11.4	11.4	11.4
Paraguay	9.0	9.0	9.0	9.0	9.0	6.8	9.0	6.8
Peru	10.9	10.9	10.9	10.9	10.9	8.2	10.9	8.2
Trinidad and Tobago	5.1	4.5	4.6	5.1	4.5	5.0	4.8	5.0
Uruguay	18.0	18.0	18.0	19.4	19.4	18.7	19.4	17.7
Venezuela	5.5	5.5	5.5	5.5	5.5	5.5	5.5	5.5
Unweighted average								
LAC[1]	**8.6**	**8.9**	**8.9**	**8.7**	**9.0**	**7.9**	**8.8**	**7.9**
OECD[2]	**10.0**	**9.9**	**9.3**	**9.6**	**9.8**	**9.6**	**9.9**	**9.7**

Note: ch denotes children and AW denotes the average wage.

1. Represents the average for the group of 20 Latin American and Caribbean countries. Chile and Mexico are also part of the OECD group.
2. The source for OECD averages is OECD (2014) Taxing Wages, Table I.5. It should be noted that the OECD figures are not directly comparable with the other figures in the table as they do not include social security contributions paid to privately managed funds which are not classified as taxes in the OECD methodology.

StatLink http://dx.doi.org/10.1787/888933410278

Figure 3.4.a. **Employee social security contributions, 2013**

As % of gross wage earnings, by family-type

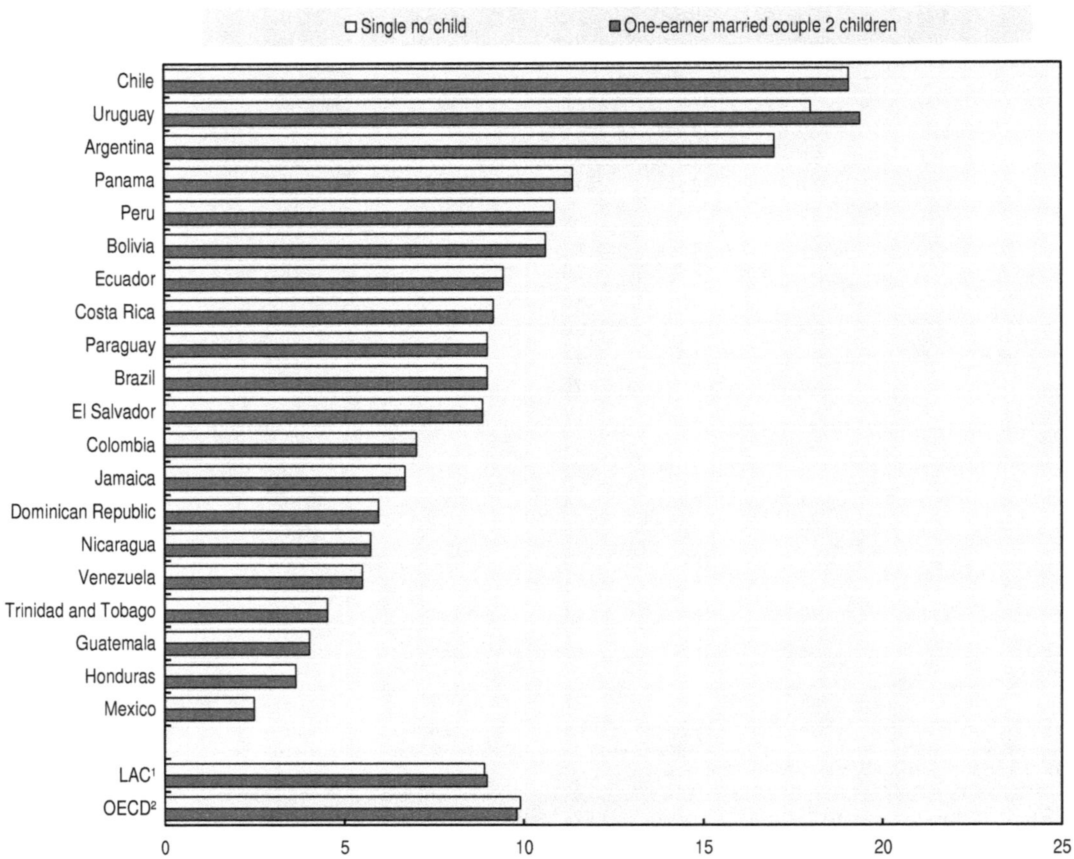

Note: Both the single worker without children and the one-earner married couple with 2 children are assumed to earn the average wage.

1. Represents the unweighted average for the group of 20 Latin American and Caribbean countries. Chile and Mexico are also part of the OECD group.
2. The source for OECD averages is OECD (2014) Taxing Wages, Table I.5. It should be noted that the OECD figures are not directly comparable with the other figures in the table as they do not include social security contributions paid to privately managed funds which are not classified as taxes in the OECD methodology.

StatLink http://dx.doi.org/10.1787/888933407548

Table 3.4.b. **Employee social security contributions, income deciles 1-5, 2013**

As % of gross wage earnings, by family-type and income decile

Country	Single no ch Income decile1	Single no ch Income decile 2	Single no ch Income decile 3	Single no ch Income decile 4	Single no ch Income decile 5	Married 2 ch Income decile1	Married 2 ch Income decile 2	Married 2 ch Income decile 3	Married 2 ch Income decile 4	Married 2 ch Income decile 5
Argentina	17.0	17.0	17.0	17.0	17.0	17.0	17.0	17.0	17.0	17.0
Bolivia	0.0	10.6	10.6	10.6	10.6	0.0	10.6	10.6	10.6	10.6
Brazil	8.0	8.0	8.0	8.0	8.0	8.0	8.0	8.0	8.0	8.0
Chile	19.1	19.1	19.1	19.1	19.1	19.1	19.1	19.1	19.1	19.1
Colombia	0.0	7.0	7.0	7.0	7.0	0.0	7.0	7.0	7.0	7.0
Costa Rica	0.0	0.0	0.0	0.0	9.2	0.0	0.0	0.0	0.0	9.2
Dominican Republic	0.0	0.0	0.0	6.0	6.0	0.0	0.0	0.0	6.0	6.0
Ecuador	0.0	9.5	9.5	9.5	9.5	0.0	9.5	9.5	9.5	9.5
El Salvador	0.0	8.9	8.9	8.9	8.9	0.0	8.9	8.9	8.9	8.9
Guatemala	0.8	0.8	0.8	4.0	4.0	0.8	0.8	0.8	4.0	4.0
Honduras	0.0	0.0	0.0	0.0	0.0	0.0	0.0	0.0	0.0	0.0
Jamaica	6.7	6.7	6.7	6.7	6.7	6.7	6.7	6.7	6.7	6.7
Mexico	2.4	2.4	2.4	2.4	2.4	2.4	2.4	2.4	2.4	2.4
Nicaragua	0.0	0.0	0.0	5.7	5.7	0.0	0.0	0.0	5.7	5.7
Panama	11.4	11.4	11.4	11.4	11.4	11.4	11.4	11.4	11.4	11.4
Paraguay	0.0	0.0	9.0	9.0	9.0	0.0	0.0	9.0	9.0	9.0
Peru	0.0	0.0	0.0	10.9	10.9	0.0	0.0	0.0	10.9	10.9
Trinidad and Tobago	8.9	6.6	5.9	5.6	5.3	8.9	6.6	5.9	5.6	5.3
Uruguay	16.6	18.0	18.0	18.0	18.0	16.6	19.4	19.4	19.4	19.4
Venezuela	5.5	5.5	5.5	5.5	5.5	5.5	5.5	5.5	5.5	5.5
Unweighted average										
LAC[1]	**4.8**	**6.6**	**7.0**	**8.3**	**8.8**	**4.8**	**6.6**	**7.1**	**8.3**	**8.8**

Note: ch denotes children.

1. Represents the average for the group of 20 Latin American and Caribbean countries. Chile and Mexico are also part of the OECD group.

StatLink http://dx.doi.org/10.1787/888933410284

Figure 3.4.b. Employee social security contributions, 5th income decile, 2013

As % of gross wage earnings, by family-type

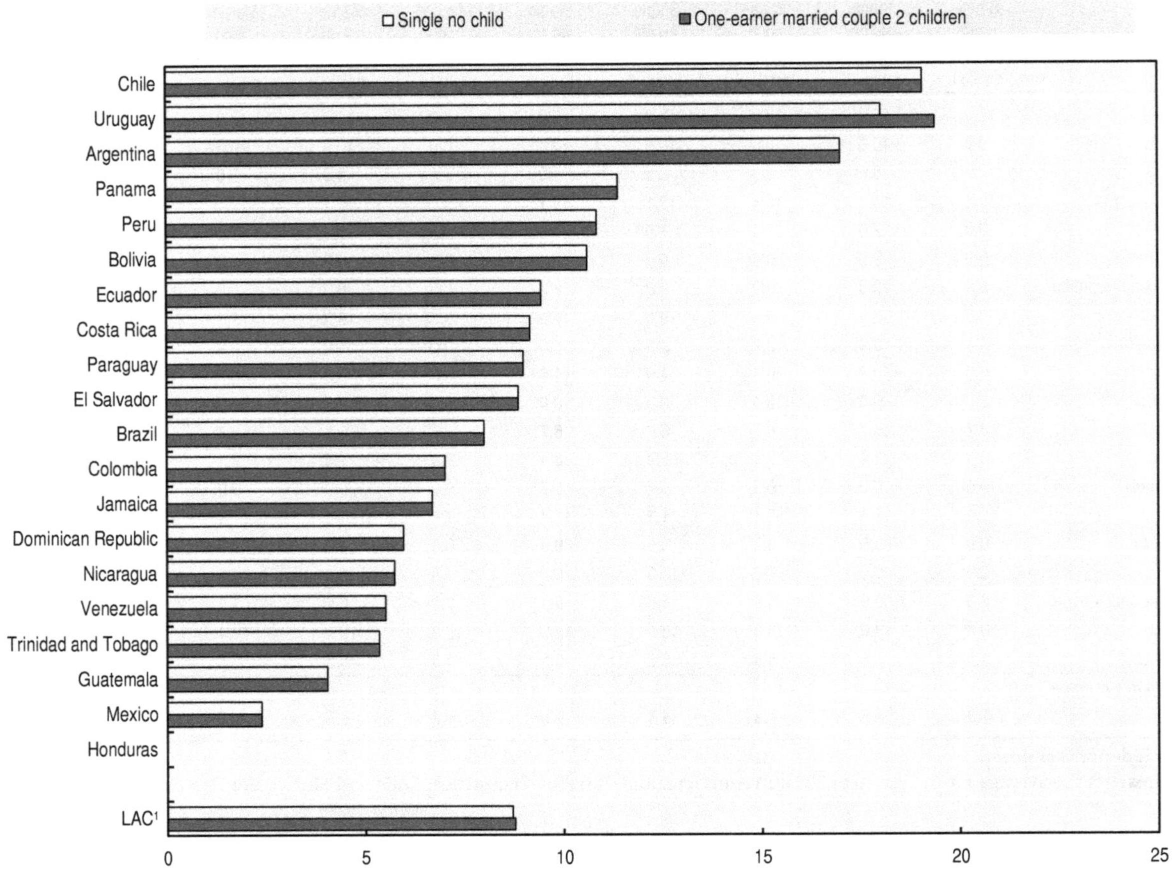

1. Represents the unweighted average for the group of 20 Latin American and Caribbean countries. Chile and Mexico are also part of the OECD group.

StatLink http://dx.doi.org/10.1787/888933407557

Table 3.4.c. **Employee social security contributions, income deciles 6-10, 2013**

As % of gross wage earnings, by family-type and income decile

Country	Single no ch Income decile 6	Single no ch Income decile 7	Single no ch Income decile 8	Single no ch Income decile 9	Single no ch Income decile 10	Married 2 ch Income decile 6	Married 2 ch Income decile 7	Married 2 ch Income decile 8	Married 2 ch Income decile 9	Married 2 ch Income decile 10
Argentina	17.0	17.0	17.0	17.0	17.0	17.0	17.0	17.0	17.0	17.0
Bolivia	10.6	10.6	10.6	10.6	10.6	10.6	10.6	10.6	10.6	10.6
Brazil	8.0	9.0	9.0	11.0	7.3	8.0	9.0	9.0	11.0	7.3
Chile	19.1	19.1	19.1	19.1	19.1	19.1	19.1	19.1	19.1	19.1
Colombia	7.0	7.0	7.0	7.0	7.9	7.0	7.0	7.0	7.0	7.9
Costa Rica	9.2	9.2	9.2	9.2	9.2	9.2	9.2	9.2	9.2	9.2
Dominican Republic	6.0	6.0	6.0	6.0	6.0	6.0	6.0	6.0	6.0	6.0
Ecuador	9.5	9.5	9.5	9.5	9.5	9.5	9.5	9.5	9.5	9.5
El Salvador	8.9	8.9	8.9	8.9	7.6	8.9	8.9	8.9	8.9	7.6
Guatemala	4.0	4.0	4.0	4.0	4.0	4.0	4.0	4.0	4.0	4.0
Honduras	0.0	3.7	3.0	2.4	1.4	0.0	3.7	3.0	2.4	1.4
Jamaica	6.7	6.7	6.7	6.7	6.7	6.7	6.7	6.7	6.7	6.7
Mexico	2.4	2.5	2.5	2.6	2.7	2.4	2.5	2.5	2.6	2.7
Nicaragua	5.7	5.7	5.7	5.7	5.7	5.7	5.7	5.7	5.7	5.7
Panama	11.4	11.4	11.4	11.4	11.4	11.4	11.4	11.4	11.4	11.4
Paraguay	9.0	9.0	9.0	9.0	9.0	9.0	9.0	9.0	9.0	9.0
Peru	10.9	10.9	10.9	10.9	10.9	10.9	10.9	10.9	10.9	10.9
Trinidad and Tobago	5.2	4.9	4.5	4.3	3.0	5.2	4.9	4.5	4.3	3.0
Uruguay	18.0	18.0	18.0	18.0	16.6	19.4	19.4	19.4	19.4	18.0
Venezuela	5.5	5.5	5.5	5.5	5.5	5.5	5.5	5.5	5.5	5.5
Unweighted average										
LAC[1]	**8.7**	**8.8**	**8.9**	**8.9**	**8.5**	**8.8**	**9.0**	**8.9**	**9.0**	**8.6**

Note: ch denotes children.

1. Represents the average for the group of 20 Latin American and Caribbean countries. Chile and Mexico are also part of the OECD group.

StatLink http://dx.doi.org/10.1787/888933410297

Figure 3.4.c. **Employee social security contributions, 10th income decile, 2013**

As % of gross wage earnings, by family-type

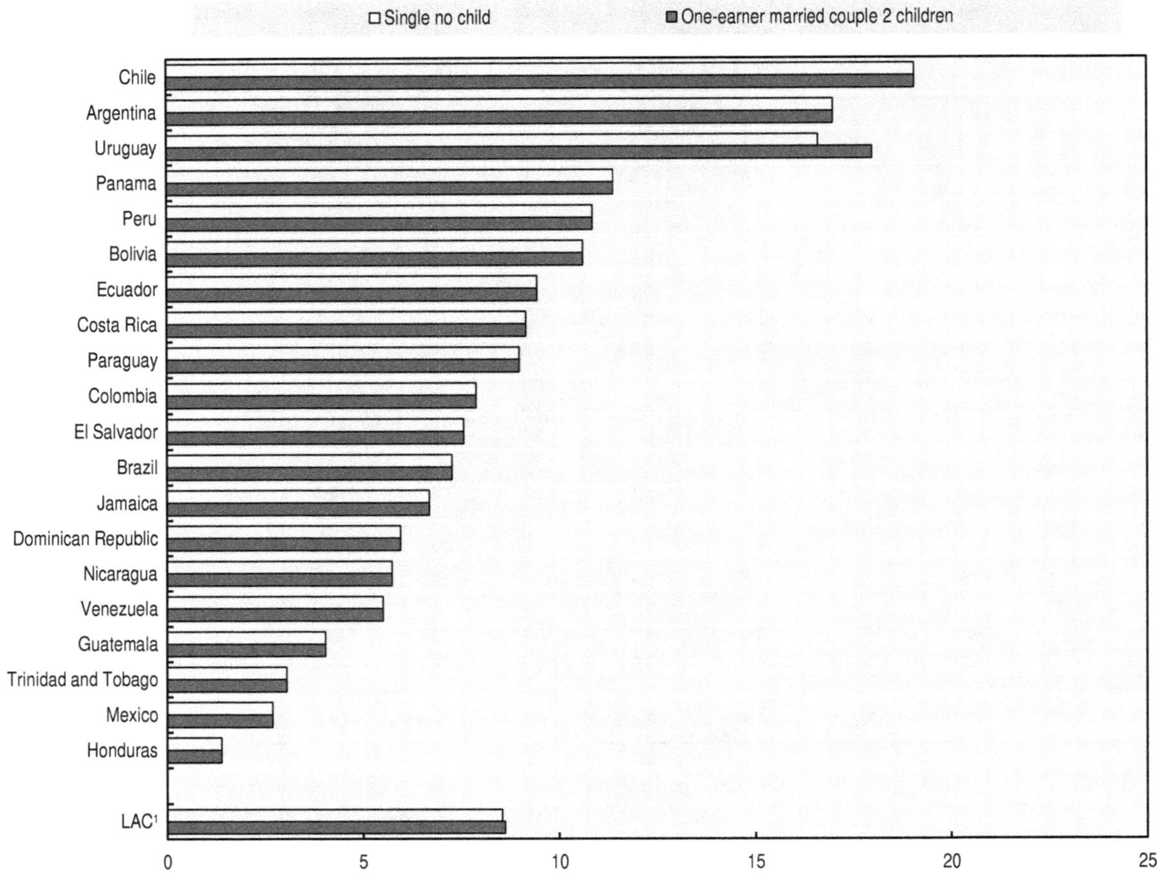

1. Represents the unweighted average for the group of 20 Latin American and Caribbean countries. Chile and Mexico are also part of the OECD group.

StatLink http://dx.doi.org/10.1787/888933407560

Table 3.4.d. **Employee social security contributions, USD equivalent earnings, 2013**

As % of gross wage earnings, by family-type and annual labour income

Country	Single no ch USD 10 000	Single no ch USD 48 000	Single no ch USD 60 000	Married 2 ch USD 10 000	Married 2 ch USD 48 000	Married 2 ch USD 60 000
Argentina	17.0	17.0	15.5	17.0	17.0	15.5
Bolivia	10.6	11.5	15.1	10.6	11.5	15.1
Brazil	9.0	5.3	4.2	9.0	5.3	4.2
Chile	19.1	15.9	12.8	19.1	15.9	12.8
Colombia	7.0	7.9	7.9	7.0	7.9	7.9
Costa Rica	9.2	9.2	9.2	9.2	9.2	9.2
Dominican Republic	6.0	4.5	3.7	6.0	4.5	3.7
Ecuador	9.5	9.5	9.5	9.5	9.5	9.5
El Salvador	8.5	6.5	6.4	8.5	6.5	6.4
Guatemala	4.0	4.0	4.0	4.0	4.0	4.0
Honduras	2.1	0.4	0.4	2.1	0.4	0.4
Jamaica	6.7	5.0	4.9	6.7	5.0	4.9
Mexico	2.6	2.6	2.1	2.6	2.6	2.1
Nicaragua	5.7	2.4	1.9	5.7	2.4	1.9
Panama	11.4	11.4	11.4	11.4	11.4	11.4
Paraguay	9.0	9.0	9.0	9.0	9.0	9.0
Peru	10.9	10.9	10.9	10.9	10.9	10.9
Trinidad and Tobago	4.4	1.4	1.1	4.4	1.4	1.1
Uruguay	18.0	13.1	11.4	19.4	14.5	12.7
Venezuela	5.5	3.8	3.3	5.5	3.8	3.3
Unweighted average						
LAC[1]	**8.8**	**7.6**	**7.2**	**8.9**	**7.6**	**7.3**

Note: ch denotes children.

1. Represents the average for the group of 20 Latin American and Caribbean countries. Chile and Mexico are also part of the OECD group.

StatLink http://dx.doi.org/10.1787/888933410309

Figure 3.4.d. **Employee social security contributions, USD equivalent earnings, 2013**

As % of gross wage earnings, by family-type for annual labour income of USD 10 000

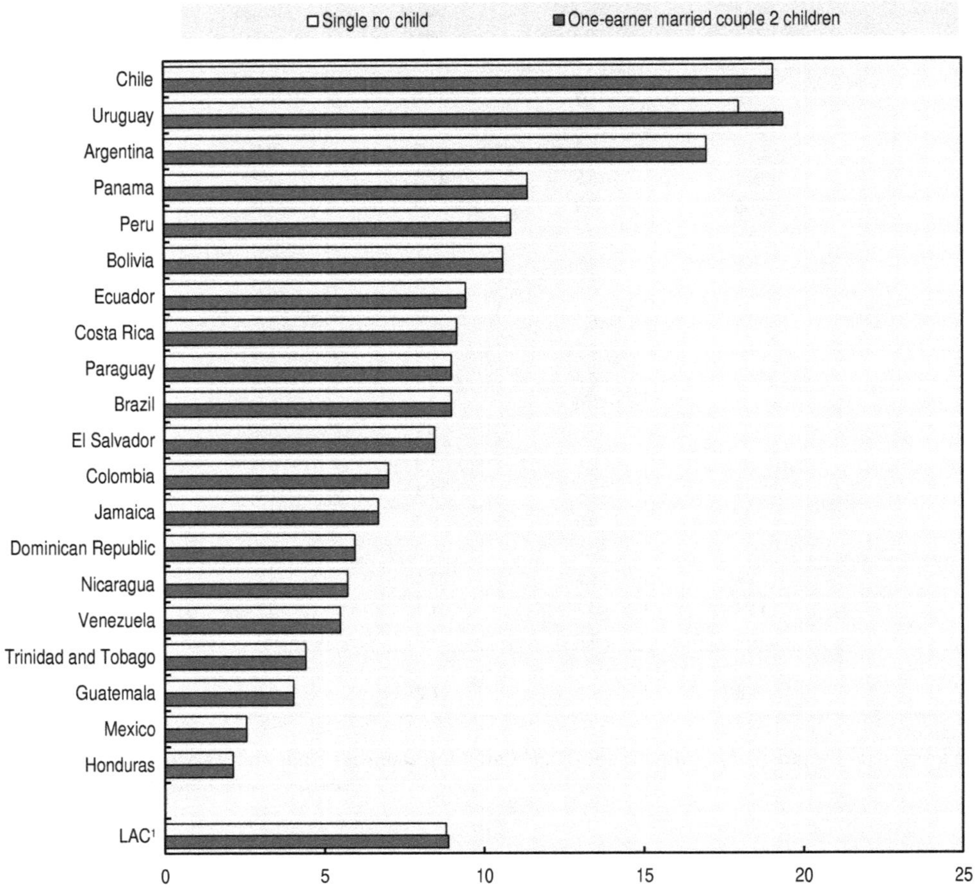

1. Represents the unweighted average for the group of 20 Latin American and Caribbean countries. Chile and Mexico are also part of the OECD group.

StatLink http://dx.doi.org/10.1787/888933407575

Table 3.5.a. **Marginal rate of income tax plus employee and employer contributions less cash benefits, family profiles, 2013**

As % of labour costs, by family-type and wage level

Country	Single no ch 67 (% AW)	Single no ch 100 (% AW)	Single no ch 167 (% AW)	Single 2 ch 67 (% AW)	Married 2 ch 100 - 0 (% AW)	Married 2 ch 100 -33 (% AW)[3]	Married 2 ch 100 - 67 (% AW)[3]	Married no ch 100 - 33 (% AW)[3]
Argentina	34.6	34.6	34.6	34.6	34.6	34.6	34.6	34.6
Bolivia	21.6	21.6	21.6	21.6	21.6	21.6	21.6	21.6
Brazil	32.2	32.2	38.2	32.2	32.2	32.2	32.2	32.2
Chile	22.6	22.6	25.7	22.6	22.6	22.6	22.6	22.6
Colombia	30.0	30.0	30.2	30.0	30.0	30.0	30.0	30.0
Costa Rica	28.0	28.0	35.3	28.0	28.0	28.0	28.0	28.0
Dominican Republic	19.2	19.2	19.2	19.2	19.2	19.2	19.2	19.2
Ecuador	18.5	18.5	18.5	18.5	18.5	18.5	18.5	18.5
El Salvador	20.5	20.5	21.2	20.5	20.5	20.5	20.5	20.5
Guatemala	4.8	13.2	16.8	4.8	13.2	13.2	13.2	13.2
Honduras	0.0	0.0	12.5	0.0	0.0	0.0	0.0	0.0
Jamaica	16.6	16.6	38.4	16.6	16.6	16.6	16.6	16.6
Mexico	25.6	31.0	35.5	25.6	31.0	31.0	31.0	31.0
Nicaragua	19.2	19.2	30.3	19.2	19.2	19.2	19.2	19.2
Panama	22.9	22.9	35.9	22.9	22.9	22.9	22.9	22.9
Paraguay	20.9	20.9	20.9	20.9	20.9	20.9	20.9	20.9
Peru	17.5	17.5	31.4	17.5	17.5	17.5	17.5	17.5
Trinidad and Tobago	0.0	0.0	25.0	0.0	0.0	0.0	0.0	0.0
Uruguay	30.5	30.5	41.7	31.6	31.6	31.6	31.6	30.5
Venezuela	17.4	17.4	17.4	17.4	17.4	17.4	17.4	17.4
Unweighted average								
LAC[1]	**20.1**	**20.8**	**27.5**	**20.2**	**20.9**	**20.9**	**20.9**	**20.8**
OECD[2]	**41.6**	**45.0**	**47.3**	**45.0**	**44.2**	**45.8**	**43.4**	**43.3**

Note: ch denotes children and AW denotes the average wage.

1. Represents the average for the group of 20 Latin American and Caribbean countries. Chile and Mexico are also part of the OECD group.
2. The source for OECD averages is OECD (2014) Taxing Wages, Table I.6. It should be noted that the OECD figures are not directly comparable with the other figures in the table as they do not include social security contributions paid to privately managed funds which are not classified as taxes in the OECD methodology.
3. Assumes a one unit currency rise in labour costs of the principal earner within the household.

StatLink http://dx.doi.org/10.1787/888933410316

Figure 3.5.a. **Marginal rate of income tax plus employee and employer contributions less cash benefits, 2013**

As % of labour costs, by family-type

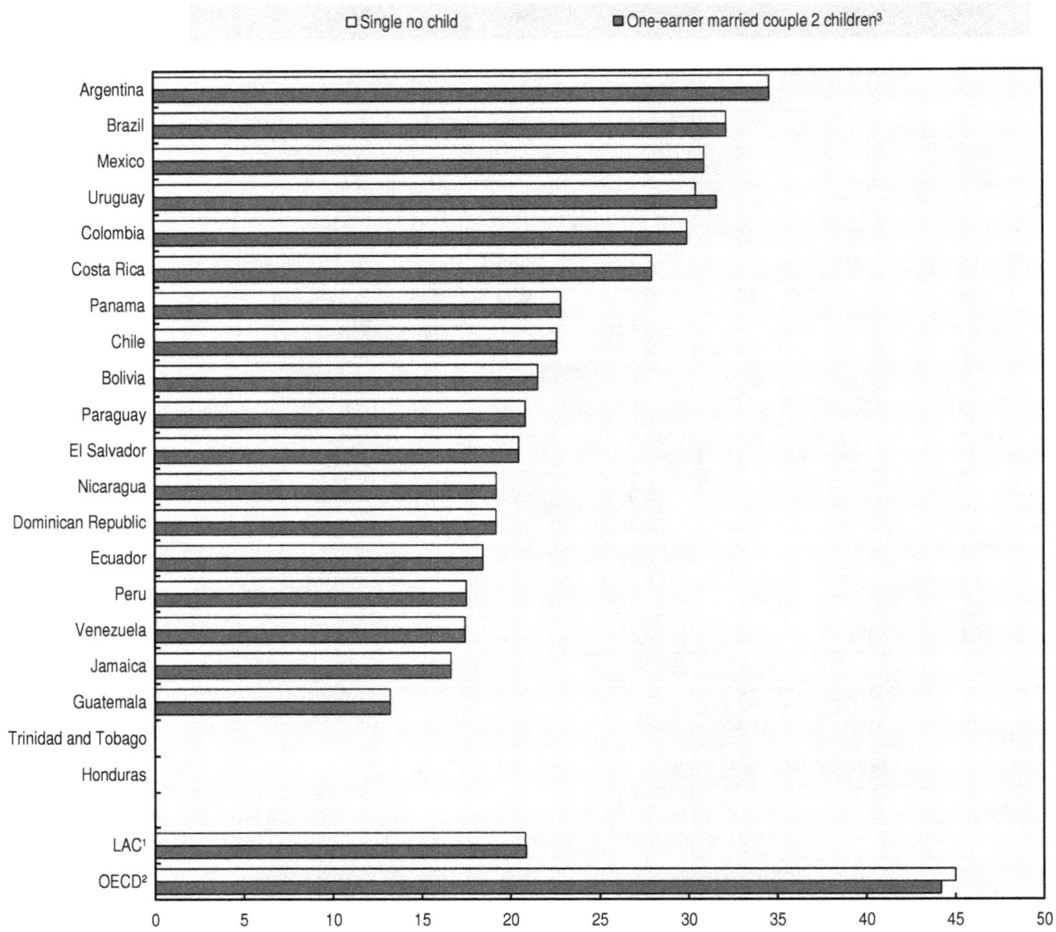

Note: Both the single worker without children and the one-earner married couple with 2 children are assumed to earn the average wage.

1. Represents the unweighted average for the group of 20 Latin American and Caribbean countries. Chile and Mexico are also part of the OECD group.
2. The source for OECD averages is OECD (2014) Taxing Wages, Table I.6. It should be noted that the OECD figures are not directly comparable with the other figures in the table as they do not include social security contributions paid to privately managed funds which are not classified as taxes in the OECD methodology.
3. Assumes a one unit currency rise in labour costs of the principal earner within the household.

StatLink http://dx.doi.org/10.1787/888933407580

Table 3.5.b. Marginal rate of income tax plus employee and employer contributions less cash benefits, income deciles 1-5, 2013

As % of labour costs, by family-type and income decile

Country	Single no ch Income decile1	Single no ch Income decile 2	Single no ch Income decile 3	Single no ch Income decile 4	Single no ch Income decile 5	Married[2] 2 ch Income decile1	Married[2] 2 ch Income decile 2	Married[2] 2 ch Income decile 3	Married[2] 2 ch Income decile 4	Married[2] 2 ch Income decile 5
Argentina	34.6	34.6	34.6	34.6	34.6	34.6	34.6	34.6	34.6	34.6
Bolivia	0.0	21.6	21.6	21.6	21.6	0.0	21.6	21.6	21.6	21.6
Brazil	31.4	31.4	31.4	31.4	31.4	31.4	31.4	31.4	31.4	31.4
Chile	22.6	22.6	22.6	22.6	22.6	22.6	22.6	22.6	22.6	22.6
Colombia	0.0	30.0	30.0	30.0	30.0	0.0	30.0	30.0	30.0	30.0
Costa Rica	0.0	0.0	0.0	0.0	28.0	0.0	0.0	0.0	0.0	28.0
Dominican Republic	1.2	1.2	1.2	19.2	19.2	1.2	1.2	1.2	19.2	19.2
Ecuador	0.0	18.1	18.1	18.5	18.5	0.0	18.1	18.1	18.5	18.5
El Salvador	0.9	20.5	20.5	20.5	20.5	0.9	20.5	20.5	20.5	20.5
Guatemala	4.8	4.8	4.8	13.2	13.2	4.8	4.8	4.8	13.2	13.2
Honduras	0.0	0.0	0.0	0.0	0.0	0.0	0.0	0.0	0.0	0.0
Jamaica	16.6	16.6	16.6	16.6	16.6	16.6	16.6	16.6	16.6	16.6
Mexico	21.5	21.5	21.8	25.6	25.6	21.5	21.5	21.8	25.6	25.6
Nicaragua	0.0	0.0	2.0	19.2	19.2	0.0	0.0	2.0	19.2	19.2
Panama	22.9	22.9	22.9	22.9	22.9	22.9	22.9	22.9	22.9	22.9
Paraguay	1.0	1.0	20.9	20.9	20.9	1.0	1.0	20.9	20.9	20.9
Peru	0.0	0.0	0.0	17.5	17.5	0.0	0.0	0.0	17.5	17.5
Trinidad and Tobago	0.0	0.0	0.0	0.0	0.0	0.0	0.0	0.0	0.0	0.0
Uruguay	29.3	30.5	30.5	30.5	30.5	29.3	31.6	31.6	31.6	31.6
Venezuela	17.4	17.4	17.4	17.4	17.4	17.4	17.4	17.4	17.4	17.4
Unweighted average										
LAC[1]	**10.2**	**14.7**	**15.8**	**19.1**	**20.5**	**10.2**	**14.8**	**15.9**	**19.2**	**20.6**

Note: ch denotes children.

1. Represents the average for the group of 20 Latin American and Caribbean countries. Chile and Mexico are also part of the OECD group.
2. Assumes a one-unit currency rise in labour costs of the principal earner within the household.

StatLink http://dx.doi.org/10.1787/888933410328

Figure 3.5.b. **Marginal rate of income tax plus employee and employer contributions less cash benefits, 5th income decile, 2013**

As % of labour costs, by family-type

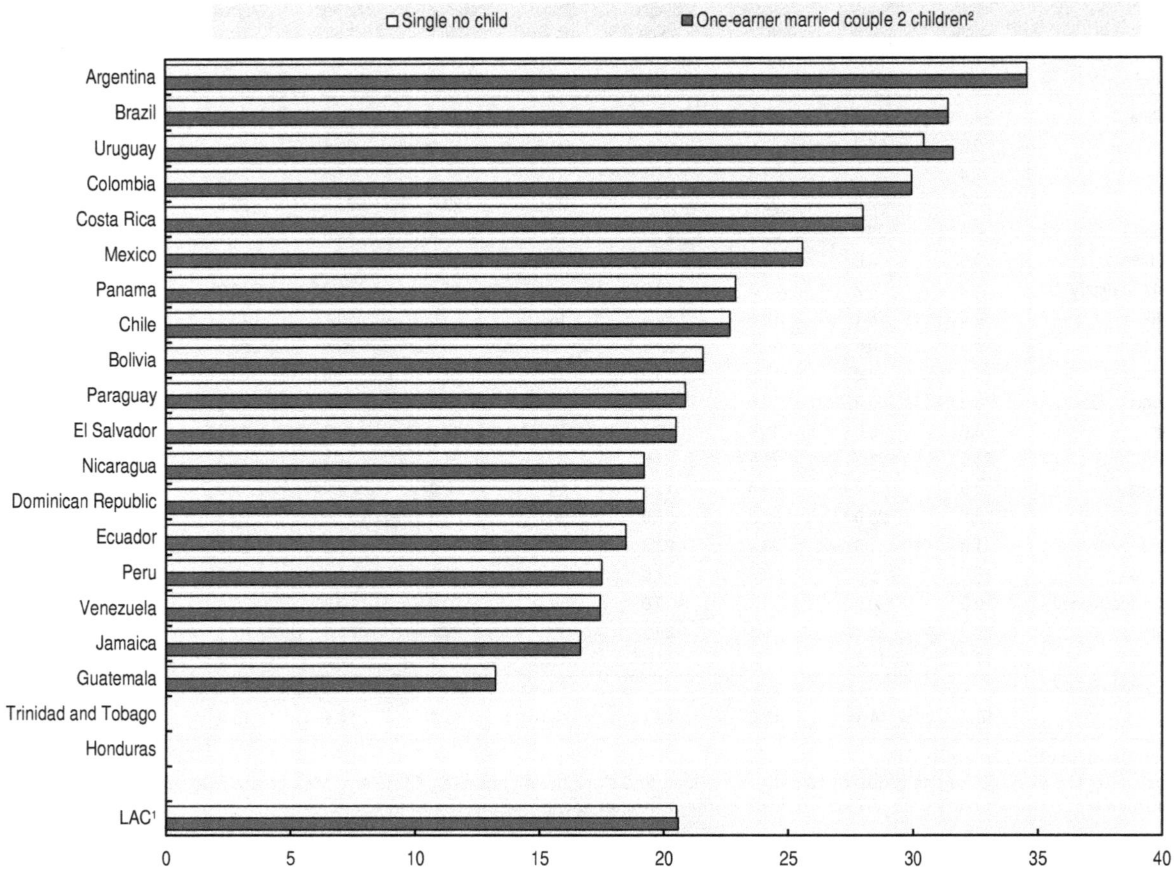

1. Represents the unweighted average for the group of 20 Latin American and Caribbean countries. Chile and Mexico are also part of the OECD group.
2. Assumes a one-unit currency rise in labour costs of the principal earner within the household.

StatLink http://dx.doi.org/10.1787/888933407599

Table 3.5.c. **Marginal rate of income tax plus employee and employer contributions less cash benefits, income deciles 6-10, 2013**

As % of labour costs, by family-type and income decile

Country	Single no ch Income decile 6	Single no ch Income decile 7	Single no ch Income decile 8	Single no ch Income decile 9	Single no ch Income decile 10	Married[2] 2 ch Income decile 6	Married[2] 2 ch Income decile 7	Married[2] 2 ch Income decile 8	Married[2] 2 ch Income decile 9	Married[2] 2 ch Income decile 10
Argentina	34.6	34.6	34.6	34.6	34.6	34.6	34.6	34.6	34.6	34.6
Bolivia	21.6	21.6	21.6	21.6	29.9	21.6	21.6	21.6	21.6	29.9
Brazil	31.4	32.2	32.2	38.2	22.0	31.4	32.2	32.2	38.7	22.0
Chile	22.6	22.6	22.6	22.6	28.8	22.6	22.6	22.6	22.6	28.8
Colombia	30.0	30.2	30.2	30.2	30.8	30.0	30.2	30.2	30.2	30.8
Costa Rica	28.0	28.0	28.0	28.0	38.9	28.0	28.0	28.0	28.0	38.9
Dominican Republic	19.2	19.2	19.2	19.2	35.9	19.2	19.2	19.2	19.2	35.9
Ecuador	18.5	18.5	18.5	18.5	26.5	18.5	18.5	18.5	18.5	26.5
El Salvador	20.5	20.5	28.4	28.4	30.0	20.5	20.5	28.4	28.4	30.0
Guatemala	13.2	13.2	13.2	16.8	16.8	13.2	13.2	13.2	16.8	16.8
Honduras	0.0	0.0	0.0	0.0	16.7	0.0	0.0	0.0	0.0	16.7
Jamaica	16.6	16.6	16.6	38.4	35.4	16.6	16.6	16.6	38.4	35.4
Mexico	26.6	31.0	32.6	35.5	37.4	26.6	31.0	32.6	35.5	37.4
Nicaragua	19.2	19.2	19.2	26.6	30.3	19.2	19.2	19.2	26.6	30.3
Panama	22.9	22.9	22.9	35.9	35.9	22.9	22.9	22.9	35.9	35.9
Paraguay	20.9	20.9	20.9	20.9	20.9	20.9	20.9	20.9	20.9	20.9
Peru	17.5	17.5	17.5	17.5	31.4	17.5	17.5	17.5	17.5	31.4
Trinidad and Tobago	0.0	0.0	0.0	25.0	25.0	0.0	0.0	0.0	25.0	25.0
Uruguay	30.5	30.5	37.4	41.7	35.2	31.6	31.6	31.6	41.9	36.2
Venezuela	17.4	17.4	17.4	17.4	22.7	17.4	17.4	17.4	17.4	17.4
Unweighted average										
LAC[1]	**20.6**	**20.8**	**21.7**	**25.8**	**29.3**	**20.6**	**20.9**	**21.4**	**25.9**	**29.0**

Note: ch denotes children.

1. Represents the average for the group of 20 Latin American and Caribbean countries. Chile and Mexico are also part of the OECD group.
2. Assumes a one-unit currency rise in labour costs of the principal earner within the household.

StatLink http://dx.doi.org/10.1787/888933410334

Figure 3.5.c. **Marginal rate of income tax plus employee and employer contributions less cash benefits, 10th income decile, 2013**

As % of labour costs, by family-type

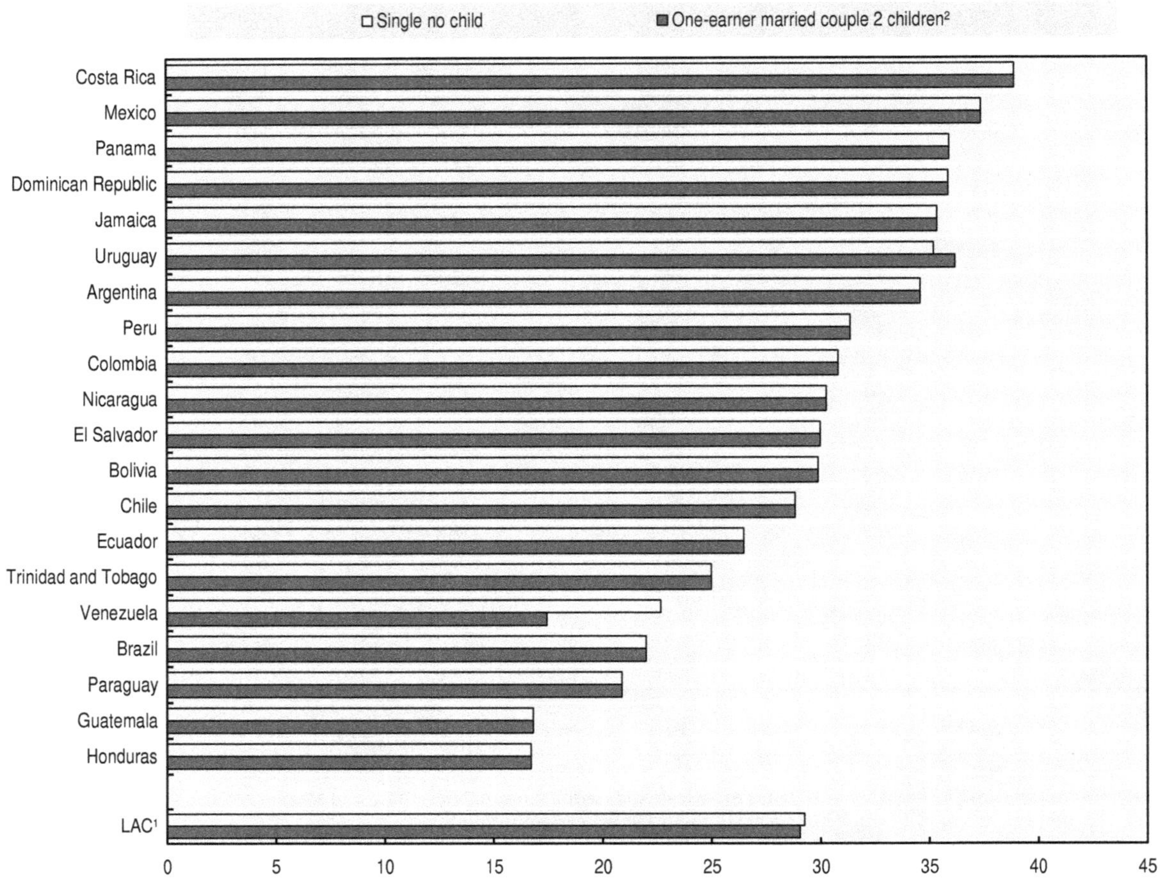

1. Represents the unweighted average for the group of 20 Latin American and Caribbean countries. Chile and Mexico are also part of the OECD group.
2. Assumes a one-unit currency rise in labour costs of the principal earner within the household.

StatLink http://dx.doi.org/10.1787/888933407608

Table 3.5.d. **Marginal rate of income tax plus employee and employer contributions less cash benefits, USD equivalent earnings, 2013**

As % of labour costs, by family-type and annual labour income

Country	Single no ch USD 10 000	Single no ch USD 48 000	Single no ch USD 60 000	Married[2] 2 ch USD 10 000	Married[2] 2 ch USD 48 000	Married[2] 2 ch USD 60 000
Argentina	34.6	57.5	48.8	34.6	52.3	48.8
Bolivia	21.6	30.5	33.1	21.6	30.5	33.1
Brazil	32.2	27.5	27.5	32.2	27.5	27.5
Chile	22.6	11.5	14.3	22.6	11.5	14.3
Colombia	30.2	33.3	33.3	30.2	33.3	33.3
Costa Rica	28.0	38.9	38.9	28.0	38.9	38.9
Dominican Republic	31.7	32.0	25.0	31.7	32.0	25.0
Ecuador	18.5	28.5	31.8	18.5	28.5	31.8
El Salvador	21.2	38.7	38.7	21.2	38.7	38.7
Guatemala	16.8	16.8	18.3	16.8	16.8	18.3
Honduras	12.5	22.9	22.9	12.5	22.9	22.9
Jamaica	38.4	35.4	35.4	38.4	35.4	35.4
Mexico	35.5	31.2	30.0	35.5	31.2	30.0
Nicaragua	34.0	24.5	24.5	34.0	24.5	24.5
Panama	22.9	35.9	44.6	22.9	35.9	44.6
Paraguay	20.9	27.2	28.8	20.9	27.2	28.8
Peru	31.4	36.9	36.9	31.4	36.9	36.9
Trinidad and Tobago	25.0	25.0	25.0	25.0	25.0	25.0
Uruguay	30.5	35.2	35.2	31.6	36.2	36.2
Venezuela	17.4	20.3	24.2	17.4	20.3	24.2
Unweighted average						
LAC[1]	**26.3**	**30.5**	**30.9**	**26.4**	**30.3**	**30.9**

Note: ch denotes children.

1. Represents the average for the group of 20 Latin American and Caribbean countries. Chile and Mexico are also part of the OECD group.
2. Assumes a one-unit currency rise in labour costs of the principal earner within the household.

StatLink http://dx.doi.org/10.1787/888933410347

Figure 3.5.d. **Marginal rate of income tax plus employee and employer contributions less cash benefits, USD equivalent earnings, 2013**

As % of labour costs for USD 10 000 of annual labour income, by family-type

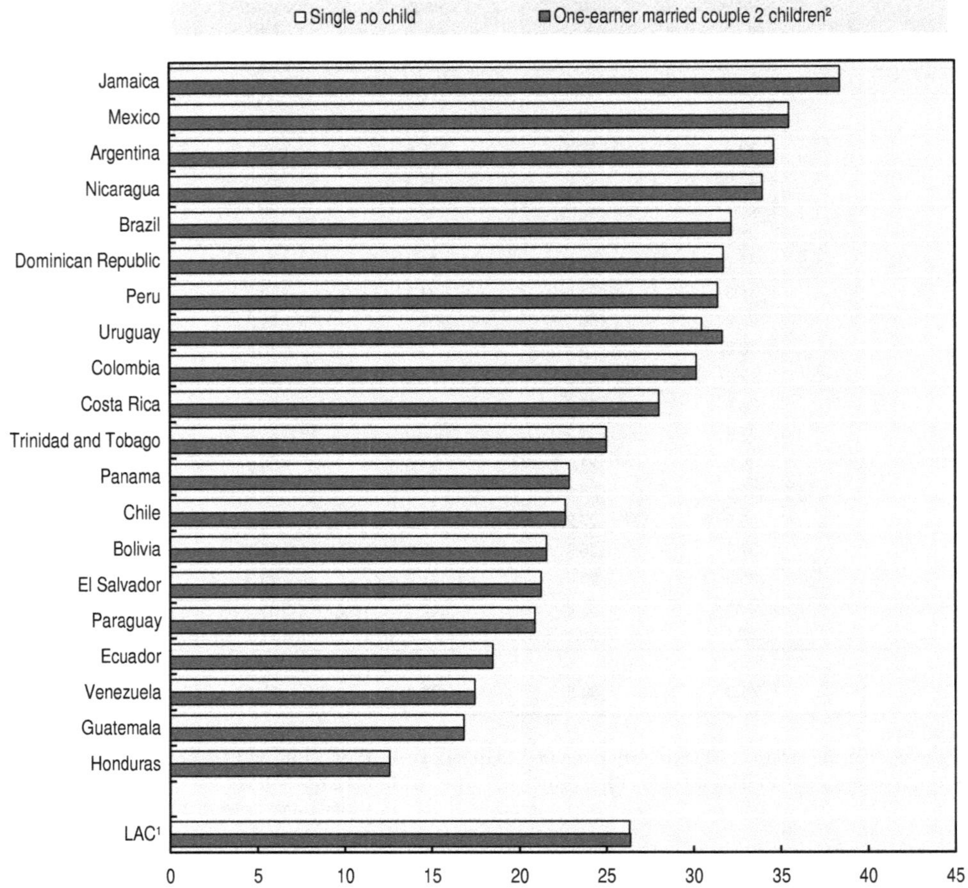

1. Represents the unweighted average for the group of 20 Latin American and Caribbean countries. Chile and Mexico are also part of the OECD group.
2. Assumes a one-unit currency rise in labour costs of the principal earner within the household.

StatLink http://dx.doi.org/10.1787/888933407611

Table 3.6.a. Marginal rate of income tax and employee contributions less cash benefits, family profiles, 2013

As % of gross wage earnings, by family-type

Country	Single no ch 67 (% AW)	Single no ch 100 (% AW)	Single no ch 167 (% AW)	Single 2 ch 67 (% AW)	Married 2 ch 100 - 0 (% AW)	Married [3] 2 ch 100 -33 (% AW)	Married [3] 2 ch 100 - 67 (% AW)	Married [3] no ch 100 - 33 (% AW)
Argentina	17.0	17.0	17.0	17.0	17.0	17.0	17.0	17.0
Bolivia	10.6	10.6	10.6	10.6	10.6	10.6	10.6	10.6
Brazil	9.0	9.0	17.0	9.0	9.0	9.0	9.0	9.0
Chile	19.1	19.1	22.3	19.1	19.1	19.1	19.1	19.1
Colombia	7.0	7.0	7.0	7.0	7.0	7.0	7.0	7.0
Costa Rica	9.2	9.2	18.3	9.2	9.2	9.2	9.2	9.2
Dominican Republic	6.0	6.0	6.0	6.0	6.0	6.0	6.0	6.0
Ecuador	9.5	9.5	9.5	9.5	9.5	9.4	9.5	9.4
El Salvador	8.9	8.9	15.4	8.9	8.9	8.9	8.9	8.9
Guatemala	0.8	4.0	8.0	0.8	4.0	4.0	4.0	4.0
Honduras	0.0	0.0	12.5	0.0	0.0	0.0	0.0	0.0
Jamaica	6.7	6.7	31.1	6.7	6.7	6.7	6.7	6.7
Mexico	13.2	18.7	24.0	13.2	18.7	18.7	18.7	18.7
Nicaragua	5.7	5.7	18.6	5.7	5.7	5.7	5.7	5.7
Panama	11.4	11.4	26.4	11.4	11.4	11.4	11.4	11.4
Paraguay	9.0	9.0	9.0	9.0	9.0	9.0	9.0	9.0
Peru	10.9	10.9	25.9	10.9	10.9	10.9	10.9	10.9
Trinidad and Tobago	0.0	0.0	25.0	0.0	0.0	0.0	0.0	0.0
Uruguay	18.0	18.0	31.2	19.4	19.4	19.4	19.4	18.0
Venezuela	5.5	5.5	5.5	5.5	5.5	5.5	5.5	5.5
Unweighted average								
LAC[1]	**8.9**	**9.3**	**17.0**	**8.9**	**9.4**	**9.4**	**9.4**	**9.3**
OECD[2]	**31.8**	**36.1**	**40.4**	**35.5**	**34.9**	**36.8**	**34.3**	**34.2**

Note: ch denotes children and AW denotes the average wage.

1. Represents the average for the group of 20 Latin American and Caribbean countries. Chile and Mexico are also part of the OECD group.
2. The source for OECD averages is OECD (2014) Taxing Wages, Table I.7. It should be noted that the OECD figures are not directly comparable with the other figures in the table as they do not include social security contributions paid to privately managed funds which are not classified as taxes in the OECD methodology.
3. Assumes a one unit currency rise in gross wage earnings of the principal earner within the household.

StatLink http://dx.doi.org/10.1787/888933410357

Figure 3.6.a. **Marginal rate of income tax and employee contributions less cash benefits, 2013**

As % of gross wage earnings, by family-type

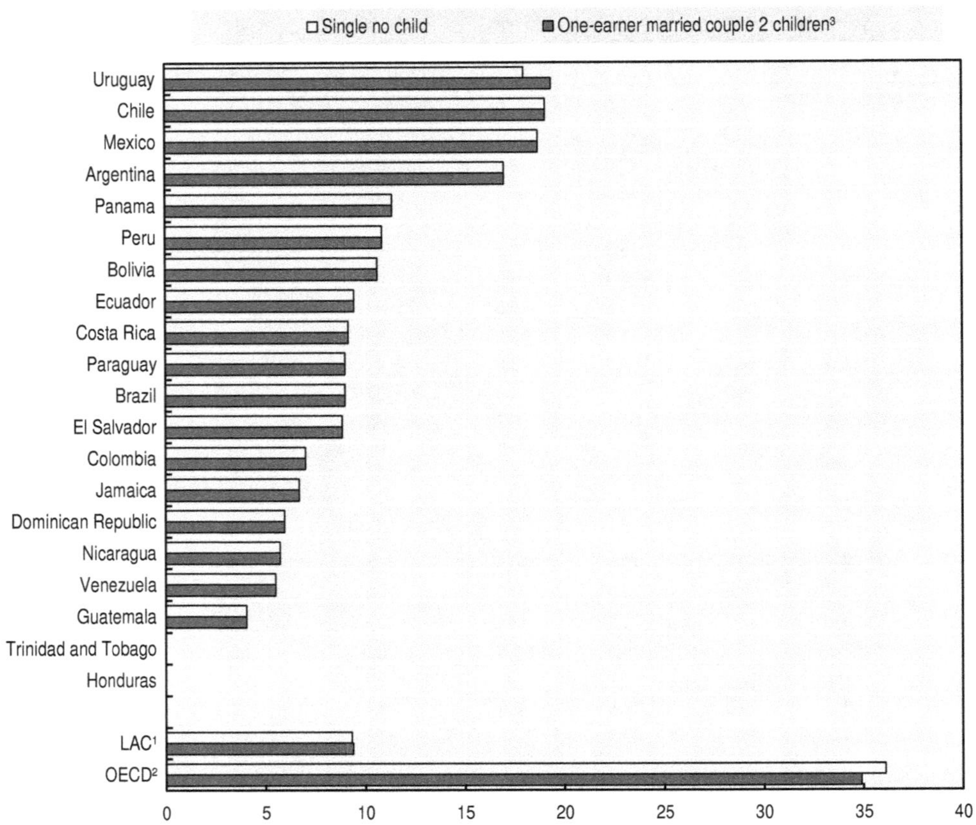

Note: Both the single worker without children and the one-earner married couple with 2 children are assumed to earn the average wage.

1. Represents the unweighted average for the group of 20 Latin American and Caribbean countries. Chile and Mexico are also part of the OECD group.
2. The source for OECD averages is OECD (2014) Taxing Wages, Table I.7. It should be noted that the OECD figures are not directly comparable with the other figures in the table as they do not include social security contributions paid to privately managed funds which are not classified as taxes in the OECD methodology.
3. Assumes a one unit currency rise in labour costs of the principal earner within the household.

StatLink http://dx.doi.org/10.1787/888933407621

Table 3.6.b. **Marginal rate of income tax and employee contributions less cash benefits, income deciles 1-5, 2013**

As % of gross wage earnings, by family-type and income decile

Country	Single no ch Income decile1	Single no ch Income decile 2	Single no ch Income decile 3	Single no ch Income decile 4	Single no ch Income decile 5	Married[2] 2 ch Income decile1	Married[2] 2 ch Income decile 2	Married[2] 2 ch Income decile 3	Married[2] 2 ch Income decile 4	Married[2] 2 ch Income decile 5
Argentina	17.0	17.0	17.0	17.0	17.0	17.0	17.0	17.0	17.0	17.0
Bolivia	0.0	10.6	10.6	10.6	10.6	0.0	10.6	10.6	10.6	10.6
Brazil	8.0	8.0	8.0	8.0	8.0	8.0	8.0	8.0	8.0	8.0
Chile	19.1	19.1	19.1	19.1	19.1	19.1	19.1	19.1	19.1	19.1
Colombia	0.0	7.0	7.0	7.0	7.0	0.0	7.0	7.0	7.0	7.0
Costa Rica	0.0	0.0	0.0	0.0	9.2	0.0	0.0	0.0	0.0	9.2
Dominican Republic	0.0	0.0	0.0	6.0	6.0	0.0	0.0	0.0	6.0	6.0
Ecuador	0.0	9.4	9.4	9.4	9.4	0.0	9.4	9.4	9.4	9.4
El Salvador	0.0	8.9	8.9	8.9	8.9	0.0	8.9	8.9	8.9	8.9
Guatemala	0.8	0.8	0.8	4.0	4.0	0.8	0.8	0.8	4.0	4.0
Honduras	0.0	0.0	0.0	0.0	0.0	0.0	0.0	0.0	0.0	0.0
Jamaica	6.7	6.7	6.7	6.7	6.7	6.7	6.7	6.7	6.7	6.7
Mexico	8.5	8.5	8.7	13.2	13.2	8.5	8.5	8.7	13.2	13.2
Nicaragua	0.0	0.0	0.0	5.7	5.7	0.0	0.0	0.0	5.7	5.7
Panama	11.4	11.4	11.4	11.4	11.4	11.4	11.4	11.4	11.4	11.4
Paraguay	0.0	0.0	9.0	9.0	9.0	0.0	0.0	9.0	9.0	9.0
Peru	0.0	0.0	0.0	10.9	10.9	0.0	0.0	0.0	10.9	10.9
Trinidad and Tobago	0.0	0.0	0.0	0.0	0.0	0.0	0.0	0.0	0.0	0.0
Uruguay	16.6	18.0	18.0	18.0	18.0	16.6	19.4	19.4	19.4	19.4
Venezuela	5.5	5.5	5.5	5.5	5.5	5.5	5.5	5.5	5.5	5.5
Unweighted average										
LAC[1]	**4.7**	**6.5**	**7.0**	**8.5**	**9.0**	**4.7**	**6.6**	**7.1**	**8.6**	**9.0**

Note: ch denotes children.

1. Represents the average for the group of 20 Latin American and Caribbean countries. Chile and Mexico are also part of the OECD group.
2. Assumes a one-unit currency rise in gross wage earnings of the principal earner within the household.

StatLink http://dx.doi.org/10.1787/888933410362

Figure 3.6.b. **Marginal rate of income tax and employee contributions less cash benefits, 5th income decile, 2013**

As % of gross wage earnings, by family-type

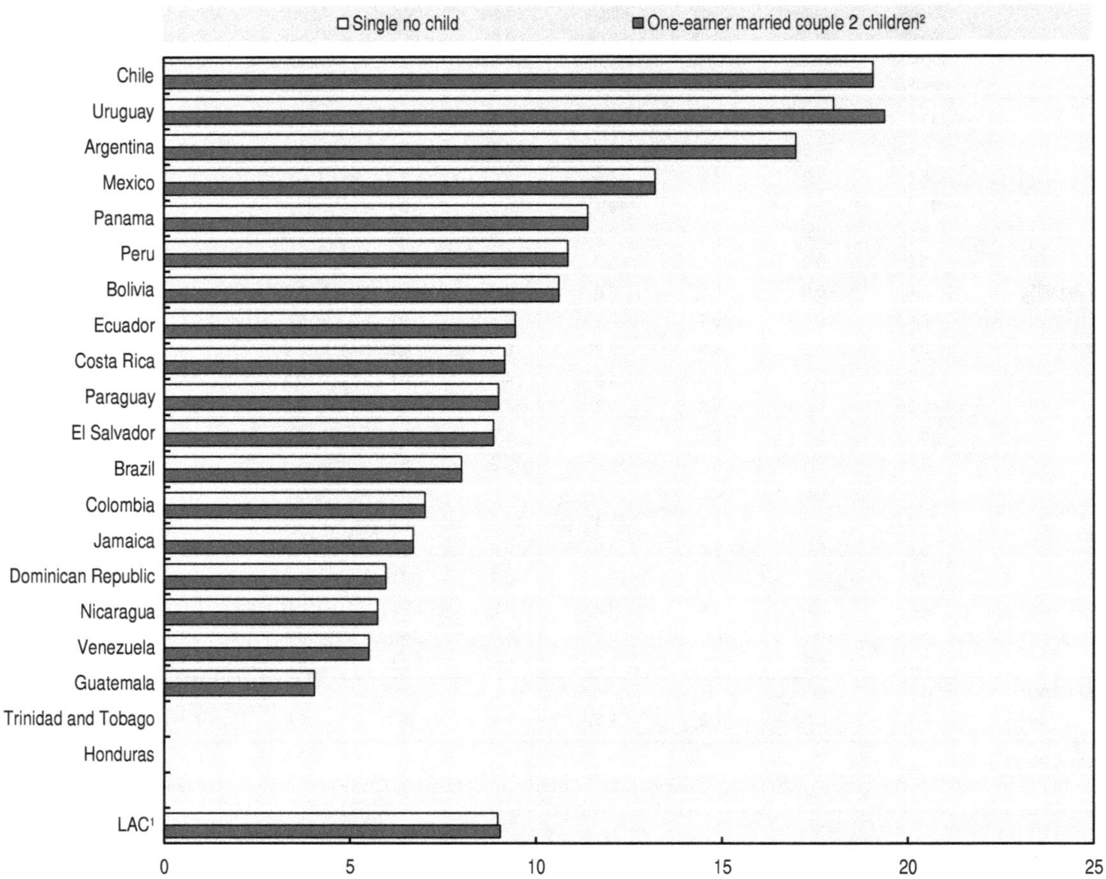

1. Represents the unweighted average for the group of 20 Latin American and Caribbean countries. Chile and Mexico are also part of the OECD group.
2. Assumes a one-unit currency rise in gross wage earnings of the principal earner within the household.

StatLink http://dx.doi.org/10.1787/888933407631

Table 3.6.c. Marginal rate of income tax and employee contributions less cash benefits, income deciles 6-10, 2013

As % of gross wage earnings, by family-type and income decile

Country	Single no ch Income decile 6	Single no ch Income decile 7	Single no ch Income decile 8	Single no ch Income decile 9	Single no ch Income decile 10	Married[2] 2 ch Income decile 6	Married[2] 2 ch Income decile 7	Married[2] 2 ch Income decile 8	Married[2] 2 ch Income decile 9	Married[2] 2 ch Income decile 10
Argentina	17.0	17.0	17.0	17.0	17.0	17.0	17.0	17.0	17.0	17.0
Bolivia	10.6	10.6	10.6	10.6	20.1	10.6	10.6	10.6	10.6	20.1
Brazil	8.0	9.0	9.0	17.0	22.0	8.0	9.0	9.0	17.7	22.0
Chile	19.1	19.1	19.1	19.1	25.6	19.1	19.1	19.1	19.1	25.6
Colombia	7.0	7.0	7.0	7.0	7.9	7.0	7.0	7.0	7.0	7.9
Costa Rica	9.2	9.2	9.2	9.2	22.9	9.2	9.2	9.2	9.2	22.9
Dominican Republic	6.0	6.0	6.0	6.0	25.4	6.0	6.0	6.0	6.0	25.4
Ecuador	9.4	9.4	9.5	9.4	18.3	9.4	9.4	9.5	9.4	18.3
El Salvador	8.9	8.9	18.0	18.0	24.8	8.9	8.9	18.0	18.0	24.8
Guatemala	4.0	4.0	4.0	8.0	8.0	4.0	4.0	4.0	8.0	8.0
Honduras	0.0	0.0	0.0	0.0	16.7	0.0	0.0	0.0	0.0	16.7
Jamaica	6.7	6.7	6.7	31.1	29.2	6.7	6.7	6.7	31.1	29.2
Mexico	13.6	18.7	20.6	24.0	26.3	13.6	18.7	20.6	24.0	26.3
Nicaragua	5.7	5.7	5.7	14.3	18.6	5.7	5.7	5.7	14.3	18.6
Panama	11.4	11.4	11.4	26.4	26.4	11.4	11.4	11.4	26.4	26.4
Paraguay	9.0	9.0	9.0	9.0	9.0	9.0	9.0	9.0	9.0	9.0
Peru	10.9	10.9	10.9	10.9	25.9	10.9	10.9	10.9	10.9	25.9
Trinidad and Tobago	0.0	0.0	0.0	25.0	25.0	0.0	0.0	0.0	25.0	25.0
Uruguay	18.0	18.0	26.2	31.2	23.6	19.4	19.4	19.4	31.5	24.8
Venezuela	5.5	5.5	5.5	5.5	11.5	5.5	5.5	5.5	5.5	5.5
Unweighted average										
LAC[1]	**9.0**	**9.3**	**10.3**	**14.9**	**20.2**	**9.1**	**9.4**	**9.9**	**15.0**	**20.0**

Note: ch denotes children.

1. Represents the average for the group of 20 Latin American and Caribbean countries. Chile and Mexico are also part of the OECD group.
2. Assumes a one-unit currency rise in gross wage earnings of the principal earner within the household.

StatLink http://dx.doi.org/10.1787/888933410374

Figure 3.6.c. **Marginal rate of income tax and employee contributions less cash benefits, 10th income decile, 2013**

As % of gross wage earnings, by family-type

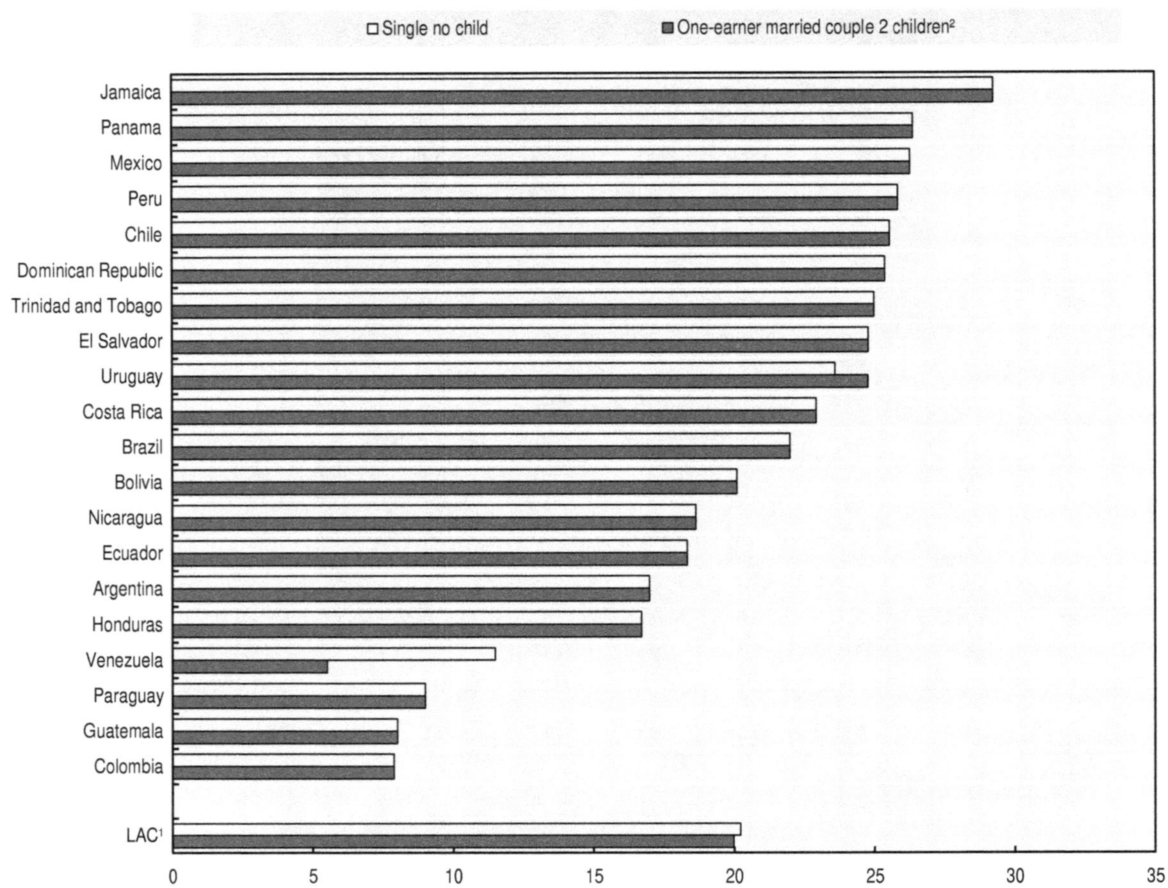

1. Represents the unweighted average for the group of 20 Latin American and Caribbean countries. Chile and Mexico are also part of the OECD group.
2. Assumes a one-unit currency rise in gross wage earnings of the principal earner within the household.

StatLink http://dx.doi.org/10.1787/888933407646

Table 3.6.d. **Marginal rate of income tax and employee contributions less cash benefits, USD equivalent earnings, 2013**

As % of gross wage earnings, by family-type and annual labour income

Country	Single no ch USD 10 000	Single no ch USD 48 000	Single no ch USD 60 000	Married[2] 2 ch USD 10 000	Married[2] 2 ch USD 48 000	Married[2] 2 ch USD 60 000
Argentina	17.0	46.1	35.0	17.0	39.4	35.0
Bolivia	10.6	20.8	23.7	10.6	20.8	23.7
Brazil	9.0	27.5	27.5	9.0	27.5	27.5
Chile	19.1	8.6	13.5	19.1	8.6	13.5
Colombia	7.0	7.9	7.9	7.0	7.9	7.9
Costa Rica	9.2	22.9	22.9	9.2	22.9	22.9
Dominican Republic	20.5	27.2	25.0	20.5	27.2	25.0
Ecuador	9.5	20.6	24.3	9.5	20.6	24.3
El Salvador	15.4	34.2	34.2	15.4	34.2	34.2
Guatemala	8.0	8.0	9.6	8.0	8.0	9.6
Honduras	12.5	22.9	22.9	12.5	22.9	22.9
Jamaica	31.1	29.3	29.2	31.1	29.3	29.2
Mexico	24.0	30.4	30.0	24.0	30.4	30.0
Nicaragua	22.9	22.9	22.9	22.9	22.9	22.9
Panama	11.4	26.4	36.4	11.4	26.4	36.4
Paraguay	9.0	16.3	18.1	9.0	16.3	18.1
Peru	25.9	31.9	31.9	25.9	31.9	31.9
Trinidad and Tobago	25.0	25.0	25.0	25.0	25.0	25.0
Uruguay	18.0	23.6	23.6	19.4	24.8	24.8
Venezuela	5.5	17.4	21.4	5.5	17.4	21.4
Unweighted average						
LAC[1]	**15.5**	**23.5**	**24.3**	**15.6**	**23.2**	**24.3**

Note: ch denotes children.

1. Represents the average for the group of 20 Latin American and Caribbean countries. Chile and Mexico are also part of the OECD group.
2. Assumes a one-unit currency rise in gross wage earnings of the principal earner within the household.

StatLink http://dx.doi.org/10.1787/888933410387

Figure 3.6.d. **Marginal rate of income tax and employee contributions less cash benefits, USD equivalent earnings, 2013**

As % of gross wage earnings and for annual labour income of USD 10 000, by family-type

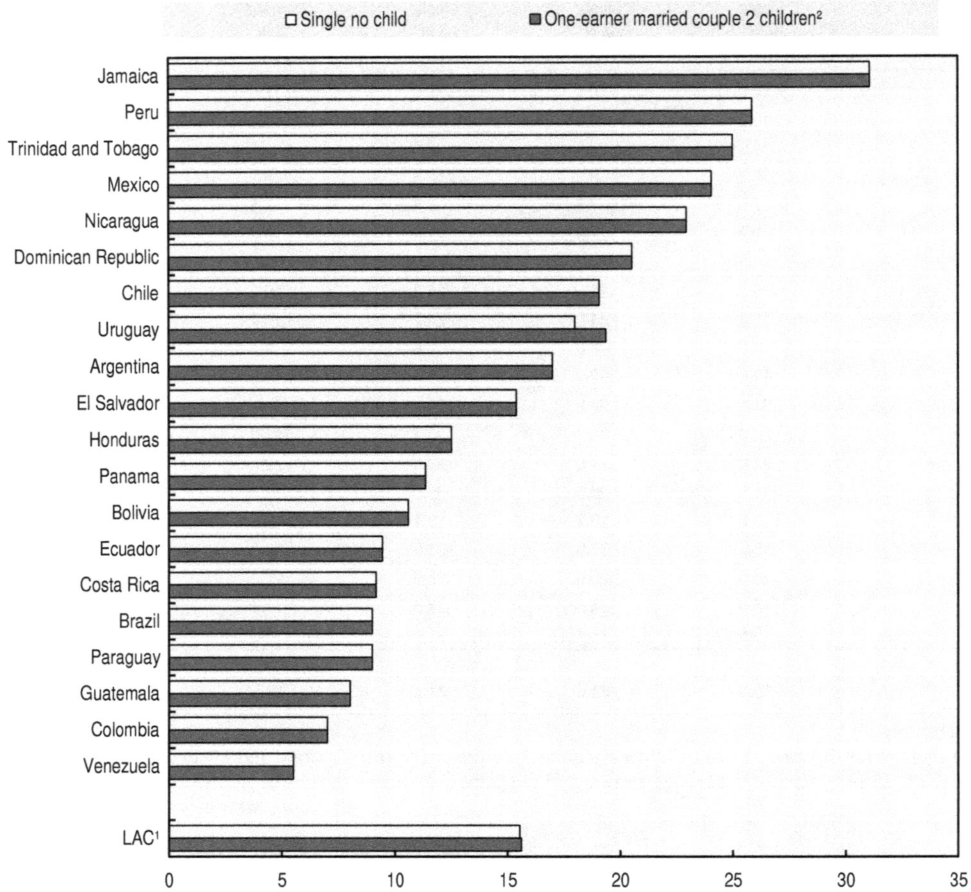

1. Represents the unweighted average for the group of 20 Latin American and Caribbean countries. Chile and Mexico are also part of the OECD group.
2. Assumes a one-unit currency rise in gross wage earnings of the principal earner within the household.

StatLink http://dx.doi.org/10.1787/888933407658

Table 3.7.a. Increase in net income after an increase of 1 currency unit in gross wage earnings, family profiles, 2013[1]

By family-type and wage level

Country	Single no ch 67 (% AW)	Single no ch 100 (% AW)	Single no ch 167 (% AW)	Single 2 ch 67 (% AW)	Married 2 ch 100 - 0 (% AW)	Married 2 ch 100 -33 (% AW)[4]	Married 2 ch 100 - 67 (% AW)[4]	Married no ch 100 - 33 (% AW)[4]
Argentina	1.00	1.00	1.00	0.94	0.98	0.98	0.99	1.00
Bolivia	1.00	1.00	1.00	1.00	1.00	0.97	1.00	0.97
Brazil	1.00	1.00	0.95	1.00	1.00	0.97	1.00	1.00
Chile	1.00	1.00	0.97	0.99	1.00	0.97	1.00	1.00
Colombia	1.00	1.00	1.00	0.94	0.96	0.92	0.95	0.98
Costa Rica	1.00	1.00	0.90	0.99	0.99	0.97	0.99	0.97
Dominican Republic	1.00	1.00	1.00	1.00	1.00	0.98	1.00	0.98
Ecuador	1.00	1.00	1.00	1.00	1.00	0.97	1.00	0.97
El Salvador	1.00	1.00	0.98	1.00	1.00	0.98	1.00	0.98
Guatemala	1.00	1.00	0.97	1.00	1.00	0.99	0.99	0.99
Honduras	1.00	1.04	0.90	1.00	1.04	1.03	1.02	1.03
Jamaica	1.00	1.00	0.77	1.00	1.00	1.00	1.00	1.00
Mexico	0.90	0.91	0.90	0.90	0.91	0.87	0.88	0.87
Nicaragua	1.00	1.00	0.90	1.00	1.00	0.99	1.00	0.99
Panama	1.00	1.00	0.87	1.00	1.00	1.00	1.00	1.00
Paraguay	1.00	1.00	1.00	1.00	1.00	0.98	1.00	0.98
Peru	1.00	1.00	0.84	1.00	1.00	0.97	1.00	0.97
Trinidad and Tobago	1.05	1.05	0.84	1.05	1.05	1.05	1.05	1.05
Uruguay	1.00	1.00	0.89	0.93	0.97	0.97	0.98	1.00
Venezuela	1.00	1.00	1.00	1.00	1.00	1.00	1.00	1.00
Unweighted average								
LAC[2]	**1.00**	**1.00**	**0.93**	**0.99**	**0.99**	**0.98**	**0.99**	**0.99**
OECD[3]	**0.87**	**0.85**	**0.86**	**0.69**	**0.73**	**0.74**	**0.79**	**0.83**

Note: ch denotes children and AW denotes average wage.

1. The reported elasticities are calculated as (100 – METR)/(100 – AETR), where METR is the marginal rate of income tax plus employee social security contributions less cash benefits reported in Table 3.6a and AETR is the average rate of income tax plus employee social security contributions less cash benefits reported in Table 3.2a.
2. Represents the average for the group of 20 Latin American and Caribbean countries. Chile and Mexico are also part of the OECD group.
3. The source for OECD averages is OECD (2014) Taxing Wages, Table I.8. It should be noted that the OECD figures are not directly comparable with the other figures in the table as they do not include social security contributions paid to privately managed funds which are not classified as taxes in the OECD methodology.
4. Assumes a one-unit currency rise in gross wage earnings of the principal earner within the household.

StatLink http://dx.doi.org/10.1787/888933410396

Table 3.7.b. Increase in net income after an increase of 1 currency unit in gross wage earnings, income deciles 1-5, 2013[1]

By family-type and income decile

Country	Single no ch Income decile1	Single no ch Income decile 2	Single no ch Income decile 3	Single no ch Income decile 4	Single no ch Income decile 5	Married[3] 2 ch Income decile1	Married[3] 2 ch Income decile 2	Married[3] 2 ch Income decile 3	Married[3] 2 ch Income decile 4	Married[3] 2 ch Income decile 5
Argentina	1.00	1.00	1.00	1.00	1.00	0.66	0.77	0.80	0.82	0.88
Bolivia	1.00	1.00	1.00	1.00	1.00	1.00	1.00	1.00	1.00	1.00
Brazil	1.00	1.00	1.00	1.00	1.00	0.93	0.93	0.94	0.95	1.00
Chile	1.00	1.00	1.00	1.00	1.00	0.87	0.91	0.94	0.95	0.95
Colombia	1.00	1.00	1.00	1.00	1.00	0.92	0.93	0.94	0.94	0.95
Costa Rica	1.00	1.00	1.00	1.00	1.00	0.96	0.98	0.98	0.98	0.98
Dominican Republic	1.00	1.00	1.00	1.00	1.00	1.00	1.00	1.00	1.00	1.00
Ecuador	1.00	1.00	1.00	1.00	1.00	1.00	1.00	1.00	1.00	1.00
El Salvador	1.00	1.00	1.00	1.00	1.00	1.00	1.00	1.00	1.00	1.00
Guatemala	1.00	1.00	1.00	1.00	1.00	1.00	1.00	1.00	1.00	1.00
Honduras	1.00	1.00	1.00	1.00	1.00	1.00	1.00	1.00	1.00	1.00
Jamaica	1.00	1.00	1.00	1.00	1.00	1.00	1.00	1.00	1.00	1.00
Mexico	0.78	0.87	0.90	0.88	0.90	0.78	0.87	0.90	0.88	0.90
Nicaragua	1.00	1.00	1.00	1.00	1.00	1.00	1.00	1.00	1.00	1.00
Panama	1.00	1.00	1.00	1.00	1.00	1.00	1.00	1.00	1.00	1.00
Paraguay	1.00	1.00	1.00	1.00	1.00	1.00	1.00	1.00	1.00	1.00
Peru	1.00	1.00	1.00	1.00	1.00	1.00	1.00	1.00	1.00	1.00
Trinidad and Tobago	1.10	1.07	1.06	1.06	1.06	1.10	1.07	1.06	1.06	1.06
Uruguay	1.00	1.00	1.00	1.00	1.00	0.85	0.89	0.91	0.92	0.93
Venezuela	1.00	1.00	1.00	1.00	1.00	1.00	1.00	1.00	1.00	1.00
Unweighted average										
LAC[2]	**0.99**	**1.00**	**1.00**	**1.00**	**1.00**	**0.95**	**0.97**	**0.97**	**0.97**	**0.98**

Note: ch denotes children.

1. The reported elasticities are calculated as (100 – METR)/(100 – AETR), where METR is the marginal rate of income tax plus employee social security contributions less cash benefits reported in Table 3.6.b and AETR is the average rate of income tax plus employee social security contributions less cash benefits reported in Table 3.2.b.
2. Represents the average for the group of 20 Latin American and Caribbean countries. Chile and Mexico are also part of the OECD group.
3. Assumes a one-unit currency rise in gross wage earnings of the principal earner within the household.

StatLink http://dx.doi.org/10.1787/888933410405

Table 3.7.c. Increase in net income after an increase of 1 currency unit in gross wage earnings, income deciles 6-10, 2013[1]

By family-type and income decile

Country	Single no ch decile 6	Single no ch decile 7	Single no ch decile 8	Single no ch decile 9	Single no ch decile 10	Married[3] 2 ch decile 6	Married[3] 2 ch decile 7	Married[3] 2 ch decile 8	Married[3] 2 ch decile 9	Married[3] 2 ch decile 10
Argentina	1.00	1.00	1.00	1.00	1.00	0.89	0.94	0.97	0.98	0.98
Bolivia	1.00	1.00	1.00	1.00	0.92	1.00	1.00	1.00	1.00	0.92
Brazil	1.00	1.00	1.00	0.94	0.94	1.00	1.00	1.00	0.93	0.94
Chile	1.00	1.00	1.00	1.00	0.94	0.96	0.99	0.99	1.00	0.94
Colombia	1.00	1.00	1.00	1.00	1.00	0.95	0.96	0.97	0.98	1.00
Costa Rica	1.00	1.00	1.00	1.00	0.90	0.99	0.99	0.99	0.99	0.89
Dominican Republic	1.00	1.00	1.00	1.00	0.86	1.00	1.00	1.00	1.00	0.86
Ecuador	1.00	1.00	1.00	1.00	0.93	1.00	1.00	1.00	1.00	0.93
El Salvador	1.00	1.00	0.94	0.95	0.92	1.00	1.00	0.94	0.95	0.92
Guatemala	1.00	1.00	1.00	0.96	0.98	1.00	1.00	1.00	0.96	0.98
Honduras	1.00	1.04	1.03	1.02	0.89	1.00	1.04	1.03	1.02	0.89
Jamaica	1.00	1.00	1.00	0.78	0.91	1.00	1.00	1.00	0.78	0.91
Mexico	0.92	0.91	0.91	0.90	0.93	0.92	0.91	0.91	0.90	0.93
Nicaragua	1.00	1.00	1.00	0.93	0.94	1.00	1.00	1.00	0.93	0.94
Panama	1.00	1.00	1.00	0.85	0.93	1.00	1.00	1.00	0.84	0.92
Paraguay	1.00	1.00	1.00	1.00	1.00	1.00	1.00	1.00	1.00	1.00
Peru	1.00	1.00	1.00	1.00	0.90	1.00	1.00	1.00	1.00	0.90
Trinidad and Tobago	1.05	1.05	1.05	0.83	0.90	1.05	1.05	1.05	0.83	0.90
Uruguay	1.00	1.00	0.91	0.88	1.03	0.97	0.97	0.98	0.86	1.01
Venezuela	1.00	1.00	1.00	1.00	0.95	1.00	1.00	1.00	1.00	1.00
Unweighted average										
LAC[2]	**1.00**	**1.00**	**0.99**	**0.95**	**0.94**	**0.99**	**0.99**	**0.99**	**0.95**	**0.94**

Note: ch denotes children.

1. The reported elasticities are calculated as (100 – METR)/(100 – AETR), where METR is the marginal rate of income tax plus employee social security contributions less cash benefits reported in Table 3.6.c and AETR is the average rate of income tax plus employee social security contributions less cash benefits reported in Table 3.2.c.
2. Represents the average for the group of 20 Latin American and Caribbean countries. Chile and Mexico are also part of the OECD group.
3. Assumes a one-unit currency rise in gross wage earnings of the principal earner within the household.

StatLink http://dx.doi.org/10.1787/888933410419

Table 3.7.d. Increase in net income after an increase of 1 currency unit in gross wage earnings, USD equivalent earnings, 2013

By family-type and annual labour income

Country	Single no ch USD 10 000	Single no ch USD 48 000	Single no ch USD 60 000	Married[3] 2 ch USD 10 000	Married[3] 2 ch USD 48 000	Married[3] 2 ch USD 60 000
Argentina	1.00	0.75	0.95	0.83	0.79	0.90
Bolivia	1.00	0.97	0.98	1.00	0.97	0.98
Brazil	1.00	0.90	0.92	1.00	0.90	0.92
Chile	1.00	1.13	1.04	0.99	1.13	1.04
Colombia	1.00	1.04	1.07	0.97	1.04	1.07
Costa Rica	1.00	0.92	0.94	0.99	0.92	0.94
Dominican Republic	0.85	0.94	0.97	0.85	0.94	0.97
Ecuador	1.00	0.95	0.92	1.00	0.95	0.92
El Salvador	0.99	0.90	0.92	0.99	0.90	0.92
Guatemala	0.97	0.99	0.98	0.97	0.99	0.98
Honduras	0.90	0.91	0.92	0.90	0.91	0.92
Jamaica	0.84	0.97	0.98	0.84	0.97	0.98
Mexico	0.87	0.93	0.95	0.87	0.93	0.95
Nicaragua	0.89	0.98	0.99	0.89	0.98	0.99
Panama	1.00	0.96	0.85	1.00	0.95	0.85
Paraguay	1.00	0.92	0.92	1.00	0.92	0.92
Peru	0.84	0.89	0.91	0.84	0.89	0.91
Trinidad and Tobago	0.79	0.95	0.96	0.79	0.95	0.96
Uruguay	1.00	1.02	1.02	0.94	1.01	1.01
Venezuela	1.00	1.02	1.09	1.00	1.01	1.08
Unweighted average						
LAC[2]	**0.95**	**0.95**	**0.96**	**0.93**	**0.95**	**0.96**

Note: ch denotes children.

1. The reported elasticities are calculated as (100 – METR)/(100 – AETR), where METR is the marginal rate of income tax plus employee social security contributions less cash benefits reported in Table 3.6.d and AETR is the average rate of income tax plus employee social security contributions less cash benefits reported in Table 3.2.d.
2. Represents the average for the group of 20 Latin American and Caribbean countries. Chile and Mexico are also part of the OECD group.
3. Assumes a one-unit currency rise in gross wage earnings of the principal earner within the household.

StatLink http://dx.doi.org/10.1787/888933410425

Figure 3.7. **LAC average: Increase in net income after an increase of 1 currency unit in gross wage earnings, 2013**[1]

by family-type and income decile

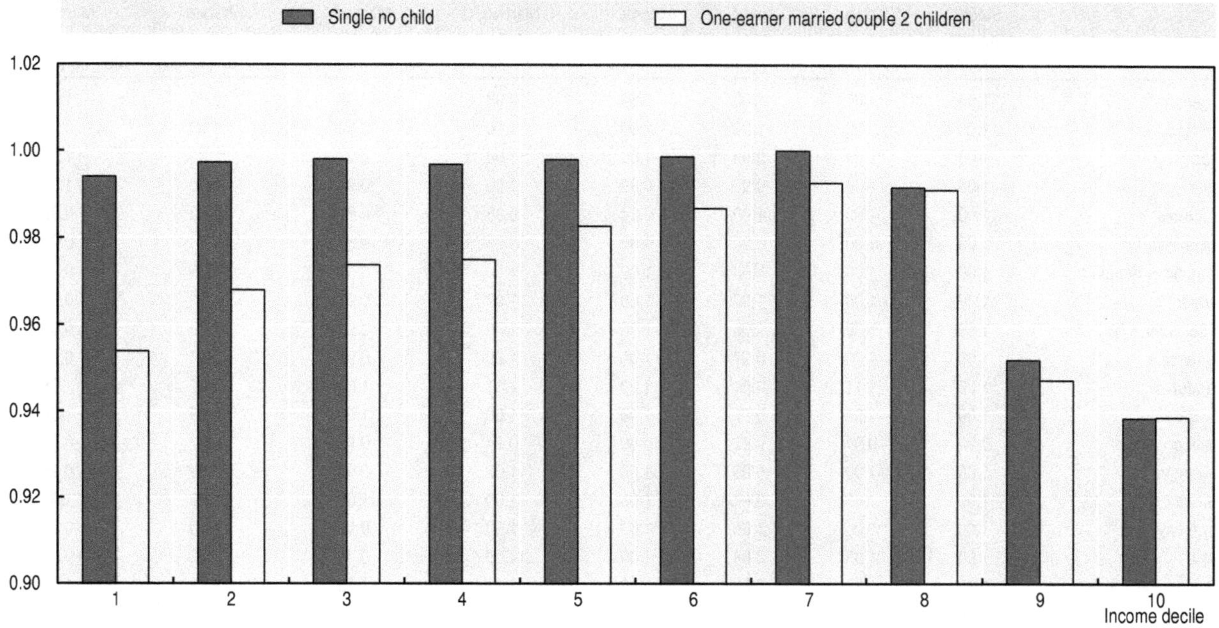

1. The reported elasticities are calculated as (100 – METR)/(100 – AETR), where METR is the marginal rate of income tax plus employee social security contributions less cash benefits reported in Table 3.6b and 3.6b and AETR is the average rate of income tax plus employee social security contributions less cash benefits reported in Table 3.2b and Table 3.2c.

StatLink http://dx.doi.org/10.1787/888933407665

Figure 3.8. **LAC average: Increase in net income after an increase of 1 currency unit in labour costs, 2013**[1]

by family-type and income decile

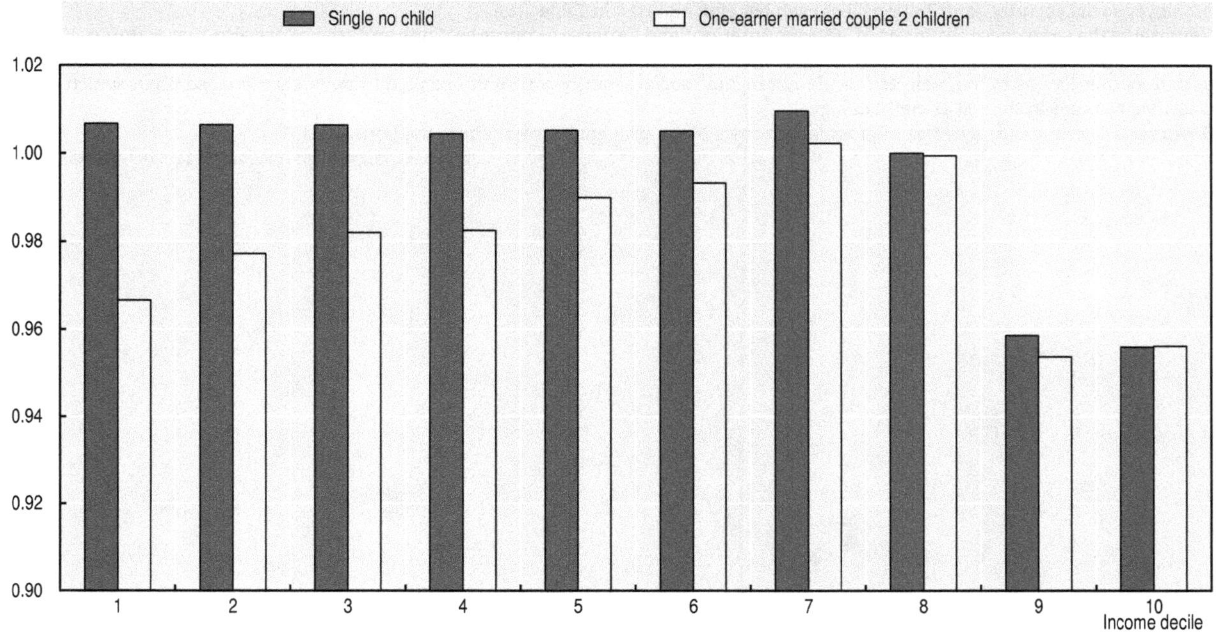

1. The reported elasticities are calculated as (100 – METR)/(100 – AETR), where METR is the marginal rate of income tax plus employee and employer social security contributions less cash benefits reported in Tables 3.5.b and 3.5.c and AETR is the average rate of income tax plus employee and employer social security contributions less cash benefits reported in Tables 3.1.b and 3.1.c.

StatLink http://dx.doi.org/10.1787/888933407677

Table 3.8.a. **Increase in net income after an increase of 1 currency unit in gross labour costs, family profiles, 2013**[1]

By family-type and wage level

Country	Single no ch 67 (% AW)	Single no ch 100 (% AW)	Single no ch 167 (% AW)	Single 2 ch 67 (% AW)	Married 2 ch 100 - 0 (% AW)	Married 2 ch 100 -33 (% AW)[4]	Married 2 ch 100 - 67 (% AW)[4]	Married no ch 100 - 33 (% AW)[4]
Argentina	1.00	1.00	1.00	0.94	0.98	0.98	0.99	1.00
Bolivia	1.00	1.00	1.00	1.00	1.00	0.94	1.00	0.94
Brazil	1.00	1.00	0.95	1.00	1.00	0.97	1.00	1.00
Chile	1.00	1.00	0.97	0.99	1.00	0.97	1.00	1.00
Colombia	1.00	1.00	1.00	0.94	0.96	0.87	0.95	0.92
Costa Rica	1.00	1.00	0.90	0.99	0.99	0.92	0.99	0.92
Dominican Republic	1.00	1.00	1.00	1.00	1.00	0.95	1.00	0.95
Ecuador	1.00	1.00	1.00	1.00	1.00	0.95	1.00	0.95
El Salvador	1.00	1.00	1.05	1.00	1.00	0.95	1.00	0.95
Guatemala	1.00	1.00	0.97	1.00	1.00	0.98	0.96	0.98
Honduras	1.00	1.11	0.94	1.00	1.11	1.08	1.07	1.08
Jamaica	1.00	1.00	0.77	1.00	1.00	1.00	1.00	1.00
Mexico	0.96	0.94	0.92	0.96	0.94	0.92	0.92	0.92
Nicaragua	1.00	1.00	0.90	1.00	1.00	0.95	1.00	0.95
Panama	1.00	1.00	0.87	1.00	1.00	1.00	1.00	1.00
Paraguay	1.00	1.00	1.00	1.00	1.00	0.95	1.00	0.95
Peru	1.00	1.00	0.84	1.00	1.00	0.95	1.00	0.95
Trinidad and Tobago	1.13	1.12	0.90	1.13	1.12	1.13	1.13	1.13
Uruguay	1.00	1.00	0.89	0.93	0.97	0.97	0.98	1.00
Venezuela	1.00	1.00	1.00	1.00	1.00	1.00	1.00	1.00
Unweighted averages								
LAC[2]	**1.00**	**1.01**	**0.94**	**0.99**	**1.00**	**0.97**	**1.00**	**0.98**
OECD[3]	**0.87**	**0.85**	**0.86**	**0.69**	**0.73**	**0.74**	**0.79**	**0.83**

Note: ch denotes children and AW denotes the average wage.

1. The reported elasticities are calculated as (100 – METR)/(100 – AETR), where METR is the marginal rate of income tax plus employee and employer social security contributions less cash benefits reported in Table 3.5.a and AETR is the average rate plus employee and employer social security contributions less cash benefits reported in Table 3.1.a.
2. Represents the average for the group of 20 Latin American and Caribbean countries. Chile and Mexico are also part of the OECD group.
3. The source for OECD averages is OECD (2014) Taxing Wages, Table I.9. It should be noted that the OECD figures are not directly comparable with the other figures in the table as they do not include social security contributions paid to privately managed funds which are not classified as taxes in the OECD methodology.
4. Assumes a one-unit currency rise in gross labour costs of the principal earner within the household.

StatLink http://dx.doi.org/10.1787/888933410436

Table 3.8.b. Increase in net income after an increase of 1 currency unit in gross labour costs, income deciles 1-5, 2013[1]

By family-type and income decile

Country	Single no ch Income decile1	Single no ch Income decile 2	Single no ch Income decile 3	Single no ch Income decile 4	Single no ch Income decile 5	Married[3] 2 ch Income decile1	Married[3] 2 ch Income decile 2	Married[3] 2 ch Income decile 3	Married[3] 2 ch Income decile 4	Married[3] 2 ch Income decile 5
Argentina	1.00	1.00	1.00	1.00	1.00	0.66	0.77	0.80	0.82	0.88
Bolivia	1.00	1.00	1.00	1.00	1.00	1.00	1.00	1.00	1.00	1.00
Brazil	1.00	1.00	1.00	1.00	1.00	0.93	0.93	0.94	0.95	1.00
Chile	1.00	1.00	1.00	1.00	1.00	0.87	0.91	0.94	0.95	0.95
Colombia	1.00	1.00	1.00	1.00	1.00	0.92	0.93	0.94	0.94	0.95
Costa Rica	1.00	1.00	1.00	1.00	1.00	0.96	0.98	0.98	0.98	0.98
Dominican Republic	1.00	1.00	1.00	1.00	1.00	1.00	1.00	1.00	1.00	1.00
Ecuador	1.00	1.00	1.00	1.00	1.00	1.00	1.00	1.00	1.00	1.00
El Salvador	1.00	1.00	1.00	1.00	1.00	1.00	1.00	1.00	1.00	1.00
Guatemala	1.00	1.00	1.00	1.00	1.00	1.00	1.00	1.00	1.00	1.00
Honduras	1.00	1.00	1.00	1.00	1.00	1.00	1.00	1.00	1.00	1.00
Jamaica	1.00	1.00	1.00	1.00	1.00	1.00	1.00	1.00	1.00	1.00
Mexico	0.94	0.97	0.98	0.94	0.96	0.94	0.97	0.98	0.94	0.96
Nicaragua	1.00	1.00	1.00	1.00	1.00	1.00	1.00	1.00	1.00	1.00
Panama	1.00	1.00	1.00	1.00	1.00	1.00	1.00	1.00	1.00	1.00
Paraguay	1.00	1.00	1.00	1.00	1.00	1.00	1.00	1.00	1.00	1.00
Peru	1.00	1.00	1.00	1.00	1.00	1.00	1.00	1.00	1.00	1.00
Trinidad and Tobago	1.19	1.16	1.15	1.15	1.14	1.19	1.16	1.15	1.15	1.14
Uruguay	1.00	1.00	1.00	1.00	1.00	0.85	0.89	0.91	0.92	0.93
Venezuela	1.00	1.00	1.00	1.00	1.00	1.00	1.00	1.00	1.00	1.00
Unweighted average										
LAC[2]	**1.01**	**1.01**	**1.01**	**1.00**	**1.01**	**0.97**	**0.98**	**0.98**	**0.98**	**0.99**

Note: ch denotes children.

1. The reported elasticities are calculated as (100 – METR)/(100 – AETR), where METR is the marginal rate of income tax plus employee and employer social security contributions less cash benefits reported in Tables 3.5.b and AETR is the average rate plus employee and employer social security contributions less cash benefits reported in Table 3.1.b.
2. Represents the average for the group of 20 Latin American and Caribbean countries. Chile and Mexico are also part of the OECD group.
3. Assumes a one-unit currency rise in gross labour costs of the principal earner within the household.

StatLink http://dx.doi.org/10.1787/888933410445

Table 3.8.c. **Increase in net income after an increase of 1 currency unit in gross labour costs, income deciles 6-10, 2013[1]**

By family-type and income decile

Country	Single no ch Income decile 6	Single no ch Income decile 7	Single no ch Income decile 8	Single no ch Income decile 9	Single no ch Income decile 10	Married[3] 2 ch Income decile 6	Married[3] 2 ch Income decile 7	Married[3] 2 ch Income decile 8	Married[3] 2 ch Income decile 9	Married[3] 2 ch Income decile 10
Argentina	1.00	1.00	1.00	1.00	1.00	0.86	0.94	0.97	0.98	0.98
Bolivia	1.00	1.00	1.00	1.00	0.92	1.00	1.00	1.00	1.00	0.92
Brazil	1.00	1.00	1.00	0.94	1.15	1.00	1.00	1.00	0.93	1.15
Chile	1.00	1.00	1.00	1.00	0.94	0.96	0.99	0.99	1.00	0.94
Colombia	1.00	1.00	1.00	1.00	1.00	0.95	0.96	0.97	0.98	1.00
Costa Rica	1.00	1.00	1.00	1.00	0.90	0.99	0.99	0.99	0.99	0.89
Dominican Republic	1.00	1.00	1.00	1.00	0.86	1.00	1.00	1.00	1.00	0.86
Ecuador	1.00	1.00	1.00	1.00	0.93	1.00	1.00	1.00	1.00	0.93
El Salvador	1.00	1.00	0.94	0.95	0.95	1.00	1.00	0.94	0.95	0.95
Guatemala	1.00	1.00	1.00	0.96	0.98	1.00	1.00	1.00	0.96	0.98
Honduras	1.00	1.11	1.09	1.07	0.92	1.00	1.11	1.09	1.07	0.92
Jamaica	1.00	1.00	1.00	0.78	0.93	1.00	1.00	1.00	0.78	0.93
Mexico	0.96	0.94	0.93	0.92	0.94	0.96	0.94	0.93	0.92	0.94
Nicaragua	1.00	1.00	1.00	0.93	0.94	1.00	1.00	1.00	0.93	0.94
Panama	1.00	1.00	1.00	0.85	0.93	1.00	1.00	1.00	0.84	0.92
Paraguay	1.00	1.00	1.00	1.00	1.00	1.00	1.00	1.00	1.00	1.00
Peru	1.00	1.00	1.00	1.00	0.90	1.00	1.00	1.00	1.00	0.90
Trinidad and Tobago	1.14	1.14	1.13	0.89	0.95	1.14	1.14	1.13	0.89	0.95
Uruguay	1.00	1.00	0.91	0.88	1.03	0.97	0.97	0.98	0.86	1.01
Venezuela	1.00	1.00	1.00	1.00	0.95	1.00	1.00	1.00	1.00	1.00
Unweighted average										
LAC[2]	**1.01**	**1.01**	**1.00**	**0.96**	**0.96**	**0.99**	**1.00**	**1.00**	**0.95**	**0.96**

Note: ch denotes children.

1. The reported elasticities are calculated as (100 – METR)/(100 – AETR), where METR is the marginal rate of income tax plus employee and employer social security contributions less cash benefits reported in Tables 3.5.c and AETR is the average rate plus employee and employer social security contributions less cash benefits reported in Table 3.1.c.
2. Represents the average for the group of 20 Latin American and Caribbean countries. Chile and Mexico are also part of the OECD group.
3. Assumes a one-unit currency rise in gross labour costs of the principal earner within the household.

StatLink http://dx.doi.org/10.1787/888933410450

Table 3.8.d. **Increase in net income after an increase of 1 currency unit in gross labour costs, USD equivalent earnings, 2013**

By family-type and annual labour income

Country	Single no ch USD 10 000	Single no ch USD 48 000	Single no ch USD 60 000	Married[3] 2 ch USD 10 000	Married[3] 2 ch USD 48 000	Married[3] 2 ch USD 60 000
Argentina	1.00	0.75	0.95	0.83	0.79	0.90
Bolivia	1.00	0.97	0.98	1.00	0.97	0.98
Brazil	1.00	1.05	1.04	1.00	1.05	1.04
Chile	1.00	1.14	1.08	0.99	1.14	1.08
Colombia	1.00	1.04	1.07	0.97	1.04	1.07
Costa Rica	1.00	0.92	0.94	0.99	0.92	0.94
Dominican Republic	0.85	0.98	1.07	0.85	0.98	1.07
Ecuador	1.00	0.95	0.92	1.00	0.95	0.92
El Salvador	1.05	0.91	0.93	1.05	0.91	0.93
Guatemala	0.97	0.99	0.98	0.97	0.99	0.98
Honduras	0.94	0.92	0.93	0.94	0.92	0.93
Jamaica	0.84	0.98	0.98	0.84	0.98	0.98
Mexico	0.90	1.09	1.09	0.90	1.09	1.09
Nicaragua	0.89	1.04	1.03	0.89	1.04	1.03
Panama	1.00	0.96	0.85	1.00	0.95	0.85
Paraguay	1.00	0.92	0.92	1.00	0.92	0.92
Peru	0.84	0.89	0.91	0.84	0.89	0.91
Trinidad and Tobago	0.85	0.97	0.98	0.85	0.97	0.98
Uruguay	1.00	1.02	1.02	0.94	1.01	1.01
Venezuela	1.00	1.08	1.15	1.00	1.07	1.13
Unweighted average						
LAC[2]	**0.96**	**0.98**	**0.99**	**0.94**	**0.98**	**0.99**

Note: ch denotes children.

1. The reported elasticities are calculated as (100 – METR)/(100 – AETR), where METR is the marginal rate of income tax plus employee and employer social security contributions less cash benefits reported in Tables 3.5.c and AETR is the average rate plus employee and employer social security contributions less cash benefits reported in Table 3.1.c.
2. Represents the average for the group of 20 Latin American and Caribbean countries. Chile and Mexico are also part of the OECD group.
3. Assumes a one-unit currency rise in gross labour costs of the principal earner within the household.

StatLink http://dx.doi.org/10.1787/888933410461

Table 3.9.a. **Annual gross wage and net income, single person, 2013**

In US dollars using PPP, by family-type and wage level

Country	Single no ch 67 (% AW)		Single no ch 100 (% AW)		Single no ch 167 (% AW)		Single 2 ch 67 (% AW)	
	Total gross earnings before taxes	Net income after taxes	Total gross earnings before taxes	Net income after taxes	Total gross earnings before taxes	Net income after taxes	Total gross earnings before taxes	Net income after taxes
Argentina	21 331	17 688	31 808	26 400	53 119	44 089	21 311	18 869
Bolivia	8 382	7 492	12 510	11 182	20 892	18 673	8 382	7 492
Brazil	9 482	8 629	14 152	12 879	23 634	20 577	9 482	8 629
Chile	12 815	10 370	19 127	15 478	31 943	25579	12 815	10 486
Colombia	7 958	7 400	11 878	11 045	19 836	18 444	7 958	7 878
Costa Rica	10 338	9 390	15 430	14 015	25 768	23 397	10 338	9 478
Dominican Republic	7 512	7 064	11 212	10 543	18 724	17 608	7 512	7 064
Ecuador	9 755	8 833	14 559	13 183	24 313	22 016	9 755	8 833
El Salvador	7 213	6 574	10 766	9 811	17 980	15 480	7 213	6 574
Guatemala	8 337	8 267	12 443	11 941	20 780	19 757	8 337	8 267
Honduras	7 692	7 692	11 480	11 062	19 171	18 588	7 692	7 692
Jamaica	3 974	3 708	5 932	5 535	9 906	8 924	3 974	3 708
Mexico	8 512	8 193	12 705	11 312	21 218	17 913	8 512	8 193
Nicaragua	5 520	5 203	8239	7 766	13 759	12 493	5 520	5 203
Panama	10 855	9 619	16 202	14 356	27 057	22 821	10 855	9 619
Paraguay	10 454	9 513	15602	14 198	26 056	23 711	10 454	9 513
Peru	7 494	6 680	11 185	9 970	18 678	16 398	7 494	6 680
Trinidad and Tobago	7 977	7 570	11 906	11367	19884	17 840	7 977	7 570
Uruguay	9 766	8 007	14 576	11 950	24 342	18 908	9 766	8 498
Venezuela	9 180	8674	13 701	12 947	22 881	21 621	9 180	8 674
Unweighted averages								
LAC[1]	**9 226**	**8 328**	**13 771**	**12 347**	**22 997**	**20 242**	**9 226**	**8 446**
OECD[2]	**26 862**	**20 890**	**40 292**	**29 592**	**67 154**	**45 428**	**26 924**	**25 816**

Note: ch denotes children and AW denotes average wage.

1. Represents the average for the group of 20 Latin American and Caribbean countries. Chile and Mexico are also part of the OECD group.
2. The source for OECD averages is OECD (2014) Taxing Wages, Table I.10a. It should be noted that the OECD figures are not directly comparable with the other figures in the table as they do not include social security contributions paid to privately managed funds which are not classified as taxes in the OECD methodology.

StatLink http://dx.doi.org/10.1787/888933410477

Table 3.9.b. **Annual gross wage and net income, married couple, 2013**

In USD using PPP, by family-type and wage level

Country	Married 2 ch Income decile 100 - 0 (% AW)		Married 2 ch Income decile 100 - 33 (% AW)		Married 2 ch Income decile 100 - 67 (% AW)		Married no ch Income decile 100 - 33 (% AW)	
	Total gross earnings before taxes	Net income after taxes	Total gross earnings before taxes	Net income after taxes	Total gross earnings before taxes	Net income after taxes	Total gross earnings before taxes	Net income after taxes
Argentina	31 808	27 056	42 304	35 768	53 119	44 745	42 304	35 112
Bolivia	12 510	11 182	16 639	15 310	20 892	18 673	16 639	15 310
Brazil	14 152	12 879	18 822	17 672	23 634	21 507	18 822	17 175
Chile	19 127	15 478	25 439	21 155	31 943	25 964	25 439	20 586
Colombia	11 878	11 522	15 797	15 920	19 836	19 400	15 797	14 964
Costa Rica	15 430	14 169	20 521	19 261	25 768	23 606	20 521	19 173
Dominican Republic	11 212	10 543	14 912	14 243	18 724	17 608	14 912	14 243
Ecuador	14 559	13 183	19 363	17 988	24 313	22 016	19 363	17 988
El Salvador	10 766	9 811	14 319	13 364	17 980	16 385	14 319	13 364
Guatemala	12 443	11 941	16 550	16 013	20 780	20 208	16 550	16 013
Honduras	11 480	11 062	15 268	14 851	19 171	18 754	15 268	14 851
Jamaica	5 932	5 535	7 889	7 361	9 906	9 243	7 889	7 361
Mexico	12 705	11 312	16 898	15 810	21 218	19 506	16 898	15 810
Nicaragua	8 239	7 766	10 957	10 485	13 759	12 969	10 957	10 485
Panama	16 202	14 356	21 548	19 094	27 057	23 975	21 548	19 094
Paraguay	15 602	14 198	20 751	19 347	26 056	23 711	20 751	19 347
Peru	11 185	9 970	14 875	13 661	18 678	16 649	14 875	13 661
Trinidad and Tobago	11 906	11 367	15 836	15 051	19 884	18 937	15 836	15 051
Uruguay	14 576	12 062	19 386	16 072	24 342	19 934	19 386	15 960
Venezuela	13 701	12 947	18 223	17 219	22 881	21 621	18 223	17 219
Unweighted average								
LAC[1]	**13 771**	**12 417**	**18 315**	**16 782**	**22 997**	**20 771**	**18 315**	**16 638**
OECD[2]	40 480	34 366	53 973	44 504	67 467	53 422	53 848	41 462

Note: ch denotes children and AW denotes average wage.

1. Represents the average for the group of 20 Latin American and Caribbean countries. Chile and Mexico are also part of the OECD group.
2. The source for OECD averages is OECD (2014) Taxing Wages, Table I.10a. It should be noted that the OECD figures are not directly comparable with the other figures in the table as they do not include social security contributions paid to privately managed funds which are not classified as taxes in the OECD methodology.

StatLink http://dx.doi.org/10.1787/888933410482

Table 3.9.c. Annual gross wage and net income, single person without children, income deciles 1-5, 2013

In USD using PPP, by family-type and income decile

Country	Single no ch Income decile 1		Single no ch Income decile 2		Single no ch Income decile 3		Single no ch Income decile 4		Single no ch Income decile 5	
	Total gross earnings before taxes	Net income after taxes	Total gross earnings before taxes	Net income after taxes	Total gross earnings before taxes	Net income after taxes	Total gross earnings before taxes	Net income after taxes	Total gross earnings before taxes	Net income after taxes
Argentina	6 256	5 193	10 440	8 665	12 909	10 714	14 749	12 242	16 391	13 604
Bolivia	4 267	4 267	6 056	5 413	7 350	6 570	8 446	7 549	9 713	8 682
Brazil	4 841	4 453	5 233	4 815	5 898	5 426	6 726	6 188	7 710	7 093
Chile	4 882	3 950	7 252	5 869	7 422	6 006	7 954	6 436	9 134	7 391
Colombia	5 847	5 847	7 047	6 553	7 470	6 946	8 114	7 545	9 150	8 509
Costa Rica	3 750	3 750	6 499	6 499	7 799	7 799	8 818	8 818	9 991	9 075
Dominican Republic	2 941	2 941	4 146	4 146	5 088	5 088	6 148	5 782	7 289	6 854
Ecuador	6 110	6 110	7 341	6 647	7 714	6 985	8 651	7 833	10 034	9 086
El Salvador	4 321	4 321	5 124	4 669	5 683	5 179	6 164	5 617	7 080	6 452
Guatemala	5 510	5 464	7 626	7 563	8 464	8 394	9 184	8 813	9 944	9 542
Honduras	4 674	4 674	6 810	6 810	7 651	7 651	8 320	8 320	8 760	8 760
Jamaica	973	908	1 016	948	1279	193	3 198	2 984	3 409	3 181
Mexico	2 595	3 037	5 034	5 268	6 229	6 323	7 469	7 380	8 722	8 375
Nicaragua	3 253	3 253	4 193	4 193	4 875	4 875	5 395	5 085	6 091	5 741
Panama	6 262	5 549	8 420	7 461	9 274	8 217	10 393	9 209	11 335	10 044
Paraguay	6 341	6 341	8 312	8 312	8 927	8 124	10 076	9 169	11 145	10 142
Peru	4 187	4 187	5 591	5 591	6 376	6 376	7 160	6 382	8 210	7 318
Trinidad and Tobago	2 266	2 065	4 442	4 148	5 930	5 579	7 332	6 924	8 809	8 338
Uruguay	4 203	3 504	6 537	5 359	7 956	6 523	9 303	7 627	10 614	8 702
Venezuela	7 365	6 959	8 819	8 334	9 630	9 100	10 534	9 954	11 401	10 773
Unweighted average										
LAC[1]	**4 542**	**4 339**	**6 297**	**5 863**	**7 196**	**6 653**	**8 207**	**7 493**	**9 247**	**8 383**

Note: ch denotes children.

1. Represents the average for the group of 20 Latin American and Caribbean countries. Chile and Mexico are also part of the OECD group.

StatLink http://dx.doi.org/10.1787/888933410496

Table 3.9.d. **Annual gross wage and net income, single person without children, income deciles 6-10, 2013**

In USD using PPP, by family-type and income decile

Country	Single no ch Income decile 6		Single no ch Income decile 7		Single no ch Income decile 8		Single no ch Income decile 9		Single no ch Income decile 10	
	Total gross earnings before taxes	Net income after taxes	Total gross earnings before taxes	Net income after taxes	Total gross earnings before taxes	Net income after taxes	Total gross earnings before taxes	Net income after taxes	Total gross earnings before taxes	Net income after taxes
Argentina	19 039	15 803	22 341	18 543	25 722	21 349	30 924	25 667	48 254	40 051
Bolivia	11 141	9 958	12 821	11 459	15 233	13 615	19 226	17 184	34 727	30 064
Brazil	9 188	8 453	10 855	9 878	13 846	12 600	19 403	17 065	47 118	39 246
Chile	10 529	8 520	12 886	10 428	16 645	13 469	23 271	18 831	55 960	44 126
Colombia	10 530	9 791	12 766	11 871	15 989	14 868	22 339	20 773	50 404	46 231
Costa Rica	11 586	10 523	13 916	12 640	17 812	16 179	25 296	22 977	47 277	40 559
Dominican Republic	8 554	8 044	9 992	9 396	12 936	12 165	18 669	17 556	37 444	32 403
Ecuador	11 612	10 515	13 711	12 415	17 080	15 466	21 823	19 761	41 857	36 872
El Salvador	8 605	7 842	10 743	9 790	12 671	11 111	15 978	13 824	31 759	26 057
Guatemala	11 012	10 568	12 035	11 550	13 738	13 184	16 583	15 896	30 749	28 926
Honduras	9 485	9 485	11 244	10 826	13 783	13 366	17 640	17 223	30 048	28 039
Jamaica	4 399	4 105	6 374	5 947	6 767	6 314	11 074	9 729	24 795	19 188
Mexico	10 285	9 664	12 422	11 082	15 515	13 559	20 753	17 560	43 095	34 286
Nicaragua	6 856	6 462	7 627	7 190	8 865	8 356	11 530	10 657	23 930	20 769
Panama	12 574	11 142	14 623	12 958	17 607	15 602	22 747	19 649	51 547	40 848
Paraguay	13 050	11 875	15 192	13 825	17 938	16 324	23 139	21 056	42 426	38 607
Peru	9 339	8 325	10 655	9 498	12 873	11 475	16 576	14 776	31 668	26 028
Trinidad and Tobago	10 465	9 925	12 451	11 843	15 082	14 401	19 288	17 456	32 999	27 610
Uruguay	12 337	10 114	14 345	11 762	17 461	14 147	22 280	17 489	39 902	29 531
Venezuela	12 236	11 562	13 512	12 768	15 051	14 222	18 430	17 415	32 982	30 706
Unweighted average										
LAC[1]	**10 641**	**9 634**	**12 526**	**11 283**	**15 131**	**13 589**	**19 849**	**17 627**	**38 947**	**33 007**

Note: ch denotes children.

1. Represents the average for the group of 20 Latin American and Caribbean countries. Chile and Mexico are also part of the OECD group.

StatLink http://dx.doi.org/10.1787/888933410506

Table 3.9.e. Annual gross wage and net income, one-earner married couple with two children, income deciles 1-5, 2013

In USD using PPP, by family-type and income decile

Country	Married 2 ch Income decile 1		Married 2 ch Income decile 2		Married 2 ch Income decile 3		Married 2 ch Income decile 4		Married 2 ch Income decile 5	
	Total gross earnings before taxes	Net income after taxes	Total gross earnings before taxes	Net income after taxes	Total gross earnings before taxes	Net income after taxes	Total gross earnings before taxes	Net income after taxes	Total gross earnings before taxes	Net income after taxes
Argentina	6 256	7 817	10 440	11 290	12 909	13 339	14 749	14 866	16 391	15 474
Bolivia	4 267	4 267	6 056	5 413	7 350	6 570	8 446	7 549	9 713	8 682
Brazil	4 841	4 803	5 233	5 164	5 898	5 776	6 726	6 538	7 710	7 093
Chile	4 882	4 519	7 252	6 438	7 422	6 372	7 954	6 802	9 134	7 757
Colombia	5 847	6 324	7 047	7 030	7 470	7 424	8 114	8 023	9 150	8 986
Costa Rica	3 750	3 905	6 499	6 653	7 799	7 953	8 818	8 972	9 991	9 230
Dominican Republic	2 941	2 941	4 146	4 146	5 088	5 088	6 148	5 782	7 289	6 854
Ecuador	6 110	6 110	7 341	6 647	7 714	6 985	8 651	7 833	10 034	9 086
El Salvador	4 321	4 321	5 124	4 669	5 683	5 179	6 164	5 617	7 080	6 452
Guatemala	5 510	5 464	7 626	7 563	8 464	8 394	9 184	8 813	9 944	9 542
Honduras	4 674	4 674	6 810	6 810	7 651	7 651	8 320	8 320	8 760	8 760
Jamaica	973	908	1 016	948	1 279	1 193	3 198	2 984	3 409	3 181
Mexico	2 595	3 037	5 034	5 268	6 229	6 323	7 469	7 380	8 722	8 375
Nicaragua	3 253	3 253	4 193	4 193	4 875	4 875	5 395	5 085	6 091	5 741
Panama	6 262	5 549	8 420	7 461	9 274	8 217	10 393	9 209	11 335	10 044
Paraguay	6 341	6 341	8 312	8 312	8 927	8 124	10 076	9 169	11 145	10 142
Peru	4 187	4 187	5 591	5 591	6 376	6 376	7 160	6 382	8 210	7 318
Trinidad and Tobago	2 266	2 065	4 442	4 148	5 930	5 579	7 332	6 924	8 809	8 338
Uruguay	4 203	4 130	6 537	5 895	7 956	7 039	9 303	8 125	10 614	9 182
Venezuela	7 365	6 959	8 819	8 334	9 630	9 100	10 534	9 954	11 401	10 773
Unweighted average										
LAC[1]	**4 542**	**4 579**	**6 297**	**6 099**	**7 196**	**6 878**	**8 207**	**7 716**	**9 247**	**8 551**

Note: ch denotes children.

1. Represents the average for the group of 20 Latin American and Caribbean countries. Chile and Mexico are also part of the OECD group.

StatLink http://dx.doi.org/10.1787/888933410518

Table 3.9.f. **Annual gross wage and net income, one-earner married couple with two children, income deciles 6-10, 2013**

In USD using PPP, by family-type and income decile

Country	Married 2 ch Income decile 6		Married 2 ch Income decile 7		Married 2 ch Income decile 8		Married 2 ch Income decile 9		Married 2 ch Income decile 10	
	Total gross earnings before taxes	Net income after taxes	Total gross earnings before taxes	Net income after taxes	Total gross earnings before taxes	Net income after taxes	Total gross earnings before taxes	Net income after taxes	Total gross earnings before taxes	Net income after taxes
Argentina	19 039	17 672	22 341	19 724	25 722	22 005	30 924	26 323	48 254	40 707
Bolivia	11 141	9 958	12 821	11 459	15 233	13 615	19 226	17 184	34 727	30 064
Brazil	9 188	8 453	10 855	9 878	13 846	12 600	19 403	17 224	47 118	39 246
Chile	10 529	8 885	12 886	10 543	16 645	13 585	23 271	18 831	55 960	44 126
Colombia	10 530	10 269	12 766	12 348	15 989	15 346	22 339	21 250	50 404	46 231
Costa Rica	11 586	10 678	13 916	12 795	17 812	16 333	25 296	23 131	47 277	40 714
Dominican Republic	8 554	8 044	9 992	9 396	12 936	12 165	18 669	17 556	37 444	32 403
Ecuador	11 612	10 515	13 711	12 415	17 080	15 466	21 823	19 761	41 857	36 872
El Salvador	8 605	7 842	10 743	9 790	12 671	11 111	15 978	13 824	31 759	26 057
Guatemala	11 012	10 568	12 035	11 550	13 738	13 184	16 583	15 896	30 749	28 926
Honduras	9 485	9 485	11 244	10 826	13 783	13 366	17 640	17 223	30 048	28 039
Jamaica	4 399	4 105	6 374	5 947	6 767	6 314	11 074	9 729	24 795	19 188
Mexico	10 285	9 664	12 422	11 082	15 515	13 559	20 753	17 560	43 095	34 286
Nicaragua	6 856	6 462	7 627	7 190	8 865	8 356	11 530	10 657	23 930	20 769
Panama	12 574	11 142	14 623	12 958	17 607	15 602	22 747	19 860	51 547	41 059
Paraguay	13 050	11 875	15 192	13 825	17 938	16 324	23 139	21 056	42 426	38 607
Peru	9 339	8 325	10 655	9 498	12 873	11 475	16 576	14 776	31 668	26 028
Trinidad and Tobago	10 465	9 925	12 451	11 843	15 082	14 401	19 288	17 456	32 999	27 610
Uruguay	12 337	10 257	14 345	11 876	17 461	14 388	22 280	17 745	39 902	29 650
Venezuela	12 236	11 562	13 512	12 768	15 051	14 222	18 430	17 415	32 982	31 166
Unweighted average										
LAC[1]	**10 641**	**9 784**	**12 526**	**11 386**	**15 131**	**13 671**	**19 849**	**17 723**	**38 947**	**33 087**

Note: ch denotes children.

1. Represents the average for the group of 20 Latin American and Caribbean countries. Chile and Mexico are also part of the OECD group.

StatLink http://dx.doi.org/10.1787/888933410520

Table 3.10.a. **Annual labour costs and net income, single person, 2013**

In USD using PPP, by family-type and wage level

Country	Single no ch 67 (% AW)		Single no ch 100 (% AW)		Single no ch 167 (% AW)		Single 2 ch 67 (% AW)	
	Total gross labour costs before taxes	Net income after taxes	Total gross labour costs before taxes	Net income after taxes	Total gross labour costs before taxes	Net income after taxes	Total gross labour costs before taxes	Net income after taxes
Argentina	27 055	17 688	40 380	26 400	67 435	44 089	27 055	18 869
Bolivia	9 552	7 492	14 257	11 182	23 809	18 673	9 552	7 492
Brazil	12 725	8 629	18 992	12 879	31 717	20 577	12 725	8 629
Chile	13 406	10 370	20 009	15 478	33 415	25 579	13 406	10 486
Colombia	10 568	7 400	15 774	11 045	26 411	18 444	10 568	7 878
Costa Rica	13 043	9 390	19 468	14 015	32 511	23 397	13 043	9 478
Dominican Republic	8 743	7 064	13 049	10 543	21 792	17 608	8 743	7 064
Ecuador	10 833	8 833	16 169	13 183	27 002	22 016	10 833	8 833
El Salvador	8 268	6 574	12 341	9 811	20 567	15 480	8 268	6 574
Guatemala	8 685	8 267	13 761	11 941	22 980	19 757	8 685	8 267
Honduras	7 692	7 692	12 290	11 062	19 982	18 588	7 692	7 692
Jamaica	4 448	3 708	6 639	5 535	11 087	8 924	4 448	3 708
Mexico	10 547	8 193	15 477	11 312	25 499	17 913	10 547	8 193
Nicaragua	6 441	5 203	9 613	7 766	16 054	12 493	6 441	5 203
Panama	12 472	9 619	18 615	14 356	31 087	22 821	12 472	9 619
Paraguay	12 022	9 513	17 943	14 198	29 964	23 711	12 022	9 513
Peru	8 097	6 680	12 085	9 970	20 181	16 398	8 097	6 680
Trinidad and Tobago	8 585	7 570	12 778	11 367	21 510	17 840	8 585	7 570
Uruguay	11 516	8 007	17 188	11 950	28 704	18 908	11 516	8 498
Venezuela	10 507	8 674	15 682	12 947	26 189	21 621	10 507	8 674
Unweighted averages								
LAC[1]	**10 760**	**8 328**	**16 125**	**12 347**	**26 895**	**20 242**	**10 760**	**8 446**
OECD[2]	**31 317**	**20 890**	**47 082**	**29 592**	**78 162**	**45 428**	**31 397**	**25 816**

Note: ch denotes children and AW denotes average wage.

1. Represents the average for the group of 20 Latin American and Caribbean countries. Chile and Mexico are also part of the OECD group.
2. The source for OECD averages is OECD (2014) Taxing Wages, Table I.11.a. It should be noted that the OECD figures are not directly comparable with the other figures in the table as they do not include social security contributions paid to privately managed funds which are not classified as taxes in the OECD methodology.

StatLink http://dx.doi.org/10.1787/888933410536

Table 3.10.b. **Annual labour costs and net income, married couple, 2013**

In USD using PPP, by family-type and wage level

Country	Married 2 ch 100 - 0 (% AW)		Married 2 ch 100 - 33 (% AW)		Married 2 ch 100 - 67 (% AW)		Married no ch 100 - 33 (% AW)	
	Total gross labour costs before taxes	Net income after taxes	Total gross labour costs before taxes	Net income after taxes	Total gross labour costs before taxes	Net income after taxes	Total gross labour costs before taxes	Net income after taxes
Argentina	40 380	27 056	53 706	35 768	67 435	44 745	53 706	35 112
Bolivia	14 257	11 182	18 385	15 310	23 809	18 673	18 385	15 310
Brazil	18 992	12 879	25 260	17 672	31 717	21 507	25 260	17 175
Chile	20 009	15 478	26 612	21 155	33 415	25 964	26 612	20 586
Colombia	15 774	11 522	19 693	15 920	26 342	19 400	19 693	14 964
Costa Rica	19 468	14 169	24 559	19 261	32 511	23 606	24 559	19 173
Dominican Republic	13 049	10 543	16 794	14 243	21 792	17 608	16 794	14 243
Ecuador	16 169	13 183	20 974	17 988	27 002	22 016	20 974	17 988
El Salvador	12 341	9 811	15 927	13 364	20 609	16 385	15 927	13 364
Guatemala	13 761	11 941	18 039	16 013	22 446	20 208	18 039	16 013
Honduras	12 290	11 062	16 078	14 851	19 982	18 754	16 078	14 851
Jamaica	6 639	5 535	8 830	7 361	11 087	9 243	8 830	7 361
Mexico	15 477	11 312	20 986	15 810	26 024	19 506	20 986	15 810
Nicaragua	9 613	7 766	12 332	10 485	16 054	12 969	12 332	10 485
Panama	18 615	14 356	24 758	19 094	31 087	23 975	24 758	19 094
Paraguay	17 943	14 198	23 143	19 347	29 964	23 711	23 143	19 347
Peru	12 085	9 970	15 776	13 661	20 181	16 649	15 776	13 661
Trinidad and Tobago	12 778	11 367	16 991	15 051	21 363	18 937	16 991	15 051
Uruguay	17 188	12 062	22 860	16 072	28 704	19 934	22 860	15 960
Venezuela	15 682	12 947	20 857	17 219	26 189	21 621	20 857	17 219
Unweighted averages								
LAC[1]	**16 125**	**12 417**	**21 128**	**16 782**	**26 886**	**20 771**	**21 128**	**16 638**
OECD[2]	**47 322**	**34 366**	**62 853**	**44 504**	**78 798**	**53 422**	**62 694**	**41 462**

Note: ch denotes children and AW denotes average wage.

1. Represents the average for the group of 20 Latin American and Caribbean countries. Chile and Mexico are also part of the OECD group.
2. The source for OECD averages is OECD (2014) Taxing Wages, Table I.11.b. It should be noted that the OECD figures are not directly comparable with the other figures in the table as they do not include social security contributions paid to privately managed funds which are not classified as taxes in the OECD methodology.

StatLink http://dx.doi.org/10.1787/888933410545

Table 3.10.c. **Annual labour costs and net income, single person without children, income deciles 1-5, 2013**

In USD using PPP, by family-type and income decile

Country	Single no ch Income decile 1		Single no ch Income decile 2		Single no ch Income decile 3		Single 2 ch Income decile 4		Single 2 ch Income decile 5	
	Total gross labour costs before taxes	Net income after taxes	Total gross labour costs before taxes	Net income after taxes	Total gross labour costs before taxes	Net income after taxes	Total gross labour costs before taxes	Net income after taxes	Total gross labour costs before taxes	Net income after taxes
Argentina	7 943	5 193	13 254	8 665	16 388	10 714	18 725	12 242	20 808	13 604
Bolivia	4 267	4 267	6 902	5 413	8 377	6 570	9 625	7 549	11 069	8 682
Brazil	6 496	4 453	7 023	4 815	7 915	5 426	9 027	6 188	10 347	7 093
Chile	5 107	3 950	7 587	5 869	7 765	6 006	8 320	6 436	9 555	7 391
Colombia	5 847	5 847	9 358	6 553	9 920	6 946	10 775	7 545	12 152	8 509
Costa Rica	3 750	3 750	6 499	6 499	7 799	7 799	8 818	8 818	12 606	9 075
Dominican Republic	2 977	2 941	4 195	4 146	5 149	5 088	7 156	5 782	8 483	6 854
Ecuador	6 110	6 110	8 119	6 647	8 531	6 985	9 607	7 833	11 144	9 086
El Salvador	4 363	4 321	5 873	4 669	6 514	5 179	7 065	5 617	8 116	6 452
Guatemala	5 740	5 464	7 945	7 563	8 818	8 394	10 156	8 813	10 996	9 542
Honduras	4 674	4 674	6 810	6 810	7 651	7 651	8 320	8 320	8 760	8 760
Jamaica	1 089	908	1 137	948	1 431	1 193	3 580	2 984	3 816	3 181
Mexico	3 646	3 037	6 490	5 268	7 884	6 323	9 331	7 380	10 791	8 375
Nicaragua	3 253	3 253	4 193	4 193	4 973	4 875	6 295	5 085	7 107	5 741
Panama	7 195	5 549	9 674	7 461	10 655	8 217	11 941	9 209	13 023	10 044
Paraguay	6 404	6 341	8 395	8 312	10 267	8 124	11 587	9 169	12 817	10 142
Peru	4 187	4 187	5 591	5 591	6 376	6 376	7 736	6 382	8 870	7 318
Trinidad and Tobago	2 462	2 065	4 824	4 148	6 425	5 579	7 939	6 924	9 543	8 338
Uruguay	4 956	3 504	7 708	5 359	9 381	6 523	10 970	7 627	12 516	8 702
Venezuela	8 429	6 959	10 095	8 334	11 023	9 100	12 057	9 954	13 049	10 773
Unweighted average										
LAC[1]	**4 945**	**4 339**	**7 084**	**5 863**	**8 162**	**6 653**	**9 451**	**7 493**	**10 778**	**8 383**

Note: ch denotes children and AW denotes average wage.

1. Represents the average for the group of 20 Latin American and Caribbean countries. Chile and Mexico are also part of the OECD group.

StatLink http://dx.doi.org/10.1787/888933410551

Table 3.10.d. **Annual labour costs and net income, single person without children, income deciles 6-10, 2013**

In USD using PPP, by family-type and income decile

Country	Single no ch Income decile 6		Single no ch Income decile 7		Single no ch Income decile 8		Single 2 ch Income decile 9		Single 2 ch Income decile 10	
	Total gross labour costs before taxes	Net income after taxes	Total gross labour costs before taxes	Net income after taxes	Total gross labour costs before taxes	Net income after taxes	Total gross labour costs before taxes	Net income after taxes	Total gross labour costs before taxes	Net income after taxes
Argentina	24 171	15 803	28 363	18 543	32 654	21 349	39 259	25 667	61 260	40 051
Bolivia	12 696	9 958	14 611	11 459	17 360	13 615	21 910	17 184	39 576	30 064
Brazil	12 330	8 453	14 568	9 878	18 582	12 600	26 039	17 065	57 766	39 246
Chile	11 014	8 520	13 480	10 428	17 413	13 469	24 343	18 831	58 540	44 126
Colombia	13 983	9 791	16 998	11 871	21 289	14 868	29 745	20 773	67 113	46 231
Costa Rica	14 618	10 523	17 558	12 640	22 473	16 179	31 916	22 977	59 650	40 559
Dominican Republic	9 956	8 044	11 629	9 396	15 056	12 165	21 729	17 556	43 581	32 403
Ecuador	12 897	10 515	15 227	12 415	18 969	15 466	24 237	19 761	46 486	36 872
El Salvador	9 864	7 842	12 314	9 790	14 524	11 111	18 315	13 824	35 371	26 057
Guatemala	12 178	10 568	13 310	11 550	15 193	13 184	18 339	15 896	34 004	28 926
Honduras	9 485	9 485	12 054	10 826	14 594	13 366	18 451	17 223	30 858	28 039
Jamaica	4 924	4 105	7 134	5 947	7 574	6 314	12 394	9 729	27 752	19 188
Mexico	12 628	9 664	15 144	11 082	18 785	13 559	24 952	17 560	51 255	34 286
Nicaragua	7 999	6 462	8 900	7 190	10 344	8 356	13 454	10 657	27 923	20 769
Panama	14 447	11 142	16 802	12 958	20 230	15 602	26 135	19 649	59 225	40 848
Paraguay	15 007	11 875	17 471	13 825	20 629	16 324	26 610	21 056	48 789	38 607
Peru	10 091	8 325	11 513	9 498	13 909	11 475	17 910	14 776	34 216	26 028
Trinidad and Tobago	11 336	9 925	13 460	11 843	16 238	14 401	20 747	17 456	34 801	27 610
Uruguay	14 547	10 114	16 916	11 762	20 590	14 147	26 272	17 489	47 053	29 531
Venezuela	14 005	11 562	15 466	12 768	17 227	14 222	21 094	17 415	37 751	30 706
Unweighted average										
LAC[1]	**12 409**	**9 634**	**14 646**	**11 283**	**17 682**	**13 589**	**23 193**	**17 627**	**45 149**	**33 007**

Note: ch denotes children and AW denotes average wage.

1. Represents the average for the group of 20 Latin American and Caribbean countries. Chile and Mexico are also part of the OECD group.

StatLink http://dx.doi.org/10.1787/888933410567

Table 3.10.e. **Annual labour costs and net income, one-earner married couple with two children, income deciles 1-5, 2013**

In USD using PPP, by family-type and income decile

Country	Married 2 ch Income decile 1		Married 2 ch Income decile 2		Married 2 ch Income decile 3		Married 2 ch Income decile 4		Married 2 ch Income decile 5	
	Total gross labour costs before taxes	Net income after taxes	Total gross labour costs before taxes	Net income after taxes	Total gross labour costs before taxes	Net income after taxes	Total gross labour costs before taxes	Net income after taxes	Total gross labour costs before taxes	Net income after taxes
Argentina	7 943	7 817	13 254	11 290	16 388	13 339	18 725	14 866	20 808	15 474
Bolivia	4 267	4 267	6 902	5 413	8 377	6 570	9 625	7 549	11 069	8 682
Brazil	6 496	4 803	7 023	5 164	7 915	5 776	9 027	6 538	10 347	7 093
Chile	5 107	4 519	7 587	6 438	7 765	6 372	8 320	6 802	9 555	7 757
Colombia	5 847	6 324	9 358	7 030	9 920	7 424	10 775	8 023	12 152	8 986
Costa Rica	3 750	3 905	6 499	6 653	7 799	7 953	8 818	8 972	12 606	9 230
Dominican Republic	2 977	2 941	4 195	4 146	5 149	5 088	7 156	5 782	8 483	6 854
Ecuador	6 110	6 110	8 119	6 647	8 531	6 985	9 607	7 833	11 144	9 086
El Salvador	4 363	4 321	5 873	4 669	6 514	5 179	7 065	5 617	8 116	6 452
Guatemala	5 740	5 464	7 945	7 563	8 818	8 394	10 156	8 813	10 996	9 542
Honduras	4 674	4 674	6 810	6 810	7 651	7 651	8 320	8 320	8 760	8 760
Jamaica	1 089	908	1 137	948	1 431	1 193	3 580	2 984	3 816	3 181
Mexico	3 646	3 037	6 490	5 268	7 884	6 323	9 331	7 380	10 791	8 375
Nicaragua	3 253	3 253	4 193	4 193	4 973	4 875	6 295	5 085	7 107	5 741
Panama	7 195	5 549	9 674	7 461	10 655	8 217	11 941	9 209	13 023	10 044
Paraguay	6 404	6 341	8 395	8 312	10 267	8 124	11 587	9 169	12 817	10 142
Peru	4 187	4 187	5 591	5 591	6 376	6 376	7 736	6 382	8 870	7 318
Trinidad and Tobago	2 462	2 065	4 824	4 148	6 425	5 579	7 939	6 924	9 543	8 338
Uruguay	4 956	4 130	7 708	5 895	9 381	7 039	10 970	8 125	12 516	9 182
Venezuela	8 429	6 959	10 095	8 334	11 023	9 100	12 057	9 954	13 049	10 773
Unweighted average										
LAC[1]	**4 945**	**4 579**	**7 084**	**6 099**	**8 162**	**6 878**	**9 451**	**7 716**	**10 778**	**8 551**

Note: ch denotes children and AW denotes average wage.

1. Represents the average for the group of 20 Latin American and Caribbean countries. Chile and Mexico are also part of the OECD group.

StatLink http://dx.doi.org/10.1787/888933410574

Table 3.10.f. **Annual labour costs and net income, one-earner married couple with two children, income deciles 6-10, 2013**

In USD using PPP, by family-type and income decile

Country	Married 2 ch Income decile 6		Married 2 ch Income decile 7		Married 2 ch Income decile 8		Married 2 ch Income decile 9		Married 2 ch Income decile 10	
	Total gross labour costs before taxes	Net income after taxes	Total gross labour costs before taxes	Net income after taxes	Total gross labour costs before taxes	Net income after taxes	Total gross labour costs before taxes	Net income after taxes	Total gross labour costs before taxes	Net income after taxes
Argentina	24 171	17 672	28 363	19 724	32 654	22 005	39 259	26 323	61 260	40 707
Bolivia	12 696	9 958	14 611	11 459	17 360	13 615	21 910	17 184	39 576	30 064
Brazil	12 330	8 453	14 568	9 878	18 582	12 600	26 039	17 224	57 766	39 246
Chile	11 014	8 885	13 480	10 543	17 413	13 585	24 343	18 831	58 540	44 126
Colombia	13 983	10 269	16 998	12 348	21 289	15 346	29 745	21 250	67 113	46 231
Costa Rica	14 618	10 678	17 558	12 795	22 473	16 333	31 916	23 131	59 650	40 714
Dominican Republic	9 956	8 044	11 629	9 396	15 056	12 165	21 729	17 556	43 581	32 403
Ecuador	12 897	10 515	15 227	12 415	18 969	15 466	24 237	19 761	46 486	36 872
El Salvador	9 864	7 842	12 314	9 790	14 524	11 111	18 315	13 824	35 371	26 057
Guatemala	12 178	10 568	13 310	11 550	15 193	13 184	18 339	15 896	34 004	28 926
Honduras	9 485	9 485	12 054	10 826	14 594	13 366	18 451	17 223	30 858	28 039
Jamaica	4 924	4 105	7 134	5 947	7 574	6 314	12 394	9 729	27 752	19 188
Mexico	12 628	9 664	15 144	11 082	18 785	13 559	24 952	17 560	51 255	34 286
Nicaragua	7 999	6 462	8 900	7 190	10 344	8 356	13 454	10 657	27 923	20 769
Panama	14 447	11 142	16 802	12 958	20 230	15 602	26 135	19 860	59 225	41 059
Paraguay	15 007	11 875	17 471	13 825	20 629	16 324	26 610	21 056	48 789	38 607
Peru	10 091	8 325	11 513	9 498	13 909	11 475	17 910	14 776	34 216	26 028
Trinidad and Tobago	11 336	9 925	13 460	11 843	16 238	14 401	20 747	17 456	34 801	27 610
Uruguay	14 547	10 257	16 916	11 876	20 590	14 388	26 272	17 745	47 053	29 650
Venezuela	14 005	11 562	15 466	12 768	17 227	14 222	21 094	17 415	37 751	31 166
Unweighted average										
LAC[1]	**12 409**	**9 784**	**14 646**	**11 386**	**17 682**	**13 671**	**23 193**	**17 723**	**45 149**	**33 087**

Note: ch denotes children and AW denotes average wage.

1. Represents the average for the group of 20 Latin American and Caribbean countries. Chile and Mexico are also part of the OECD group.

StatLink http://dx.doi.org/10.1787/888933410588

PART I

Chapter 4

Graphical exposition of the 2013 tax burden

This chapter presents a graphical exposition of the tax burdens on labour income in 2013 by income decile. These are illustrated in separate graphs for each of two family types in each Latin American and Caribbean country. The family types are single taxpayers without children and one-earner married couples with two children.

The graphs are divided into two sets showing the average and the marginal tax wedge components as percentage of total labour costs (income taxes; employee and employer social security contributions and family benefits). The graphs also show the net personal average and marginal tax rates.

The graphs in this section show the estimated tax burden on labour income in 2013 for gross wage earnings over the whole of the distribution of labour income for formal workers ordered by deciles. For each of the Latin America and Caribbean countries, there are separate graphs for two family types: a single person without children and a one-earner married couple with two children. The net personal average tax rate and the net personal marginal tax rate (defined as the change in personal income taxes and employee social security contributions net of cash benefits as a result of an increase in gross wage earnings) are included in the graphs.[1] The graphs also show respectively the composition of the average and marginal tax wedge.

The graphs for the average tax wedges illustrate the relative importance of the different components of the tax wedges; personal income taxes, employee social security contributions, employer social security contributions (including payroll taxes where applicable) and family benefits as a percentage of total labour costs. Those for the marginal tax wedge are the same except they present the change in value of each tax/benefit component as a percentage of the change in labour costs. For each earnings point on the charts, the earnings level represents the average earnings within the decile. It should be noted that a decreasing share in total labour costs does not necessarily imply that the corresponding taxes or cash benefits are decreasing in cash terms. A decreasing share of the tax wedge only implies that the total value of the taxes and social security contributions less benefits is not increasing as rapidly as total labour costs.

Families, especially at the lower levels of the labour income distribution, are treated favourably by tax-benefit schemes in 7 of the 20 countries in the region. When taking into account cash benefits paid to the family together with income taxes and employee social security contributions, one-earner married couples with two children have a negative net personal average tax rate in some parts of the income distribution in 4 countries. In Argentina the net personal average rate of the family becomes positive at earnings levels contained in the fifth income decile. Mexico provides a formal employment subsidy credit to workers resulting in a negative personal average tax rate up to an earnings level contained in the fourth income decile. This applies to all workers with and without children. In Costa Rica, where there are reimbursable tax credits to families, the negative personal average tax rate exists at earnings levels up to the fourth income decile.

Cash benefits are provided to families in 5 countries in the region; Argentina, Brazil, Chile, Colombia and Uruguay. In the case of Brazil, these benefits cease for the one-earner married couple at an earnings level in the fifth income decile. In the other 4 countries, this position is not reached until the ninth or tenth income decile.

For both family types, in the cases of Brazil, El Salvador, Honduras, Jamaica, Trinidad and Tobago and Uruguay, the average payments burden attributed to employee social security contributions declines in the last decile of income. The same applies to employer social security contributions. However, at these income levels, individuals have also started to pay income tax, which contributes to increases in the tax wedge and the net personal average rate as earnings rise. In most countries, workers start to pay income tax at earnings levels in the eighth, ninth and tenth income deciles. The exceptions are El Salvador and Mexico where payments of income tax start in the seventh and fifth income deciles respectively.

The marginal tax wedge is relatively flat throughout the labour income distribution for most countries for two reasons. These are the existence of proportional social security systems and also because income tax payments only commence at the upper deciles of the labour income distribution. The cases of Honduras and Trinidad and Tobago are special since the marginal tax wedge is zero before becoming positive at the higher levels of income; the tenth and ninth deciles respectively. This is because, at the specific earnings levels focussed in the chart, there is no change in the payment of employee social security contributions for a one unit increase in labour income The marginal tax wedge is therefore only shown as positive when the income tax comes into play at very high levels of income.

For most countries, the marginal tax wedge becomes positive in the first or second income deciles. Costa Rica, Honduras, Nicaragua, Peru and Trinidad and Tobago are the exceptions starting at the fifth, seventh, third, fourth and eighth levels of decile income respectively.

In Paraguay and Venezuela, the marginal tax wedge appears to be constant throughout the income distribution for the one-earner married couple. In Paraguay, the same is true for the single worker. This is because the income tax payments commence at earnings levels higher than the average earnings in the tenth income decile.

Note:

1. Some of the graphs have bars where the average tax wedge is shown but not the net personal average tax rate. In these cases the two measures are the same. The same point applies to the figures showing the marginal tax wedge and the net personal marginal tax rate.

Argentina 2013: Average tax wedge decomposition

By level of gross earnings expressed in income deciles

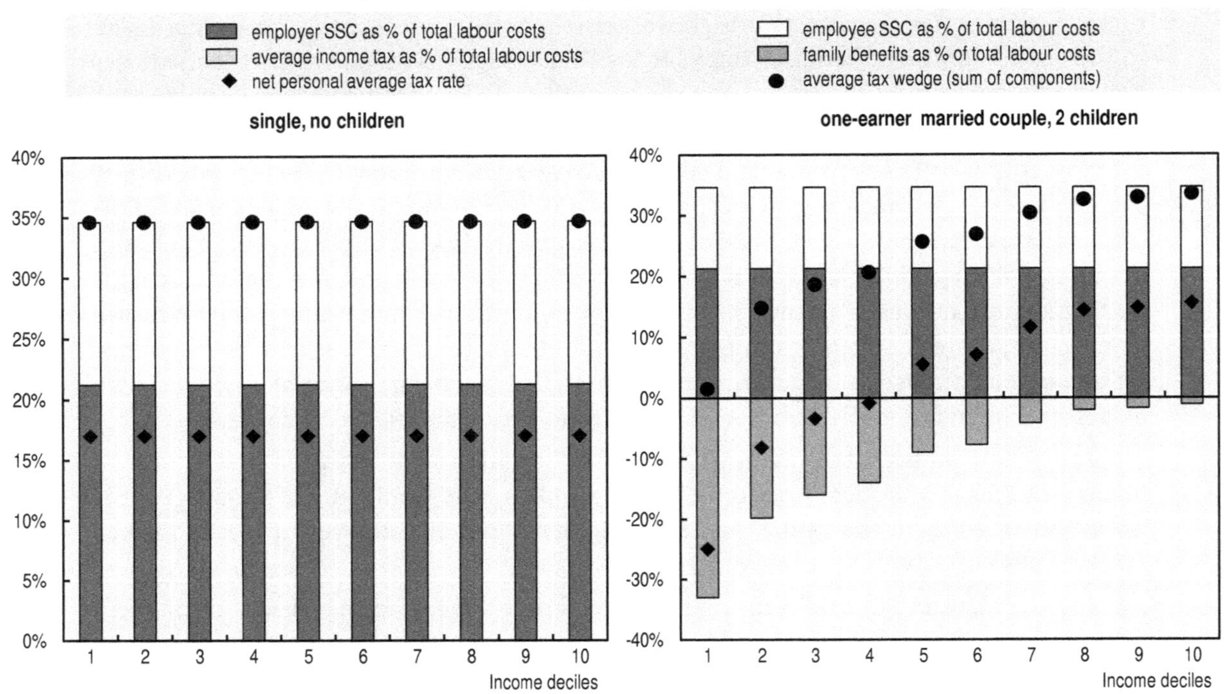

StatLink http://dx.doi.org/10.1787/888933407689

Argentina 2013: Marginal tax wedge decomposition

By level of gross earnings expressed in income deciles

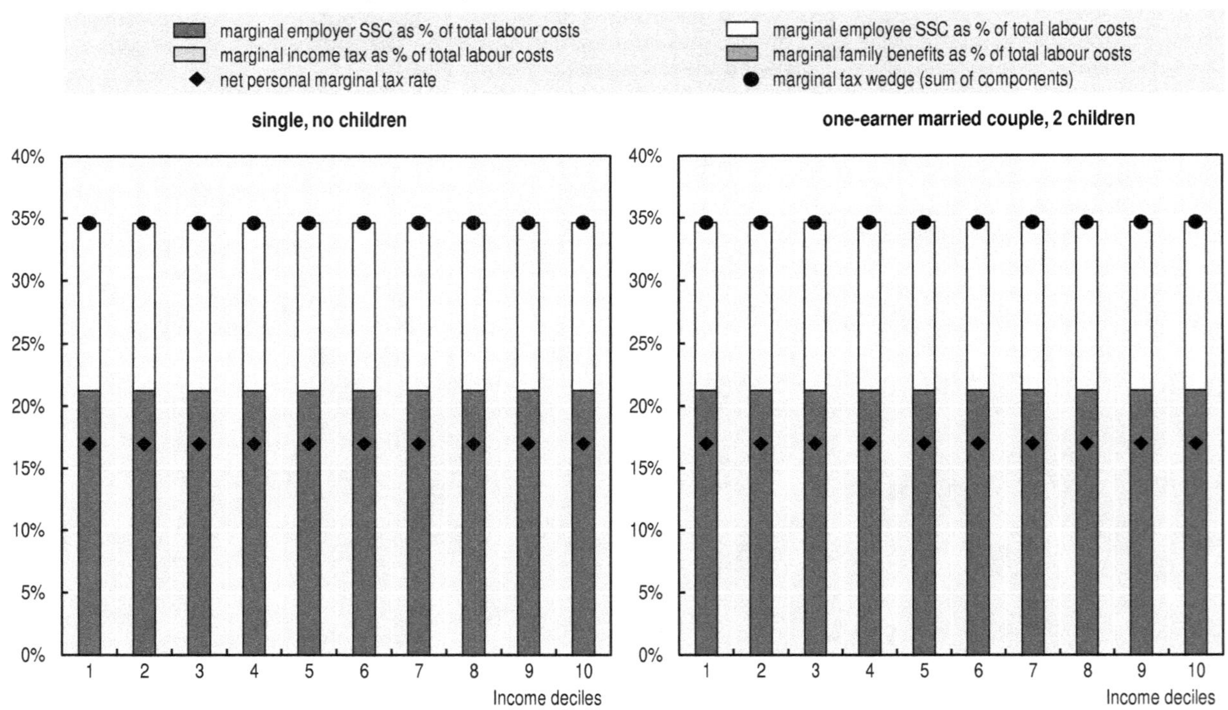

StatLink http://dx.doi.org/10.1787/888933407694

Bolivia 2013: Average tax wedge decomposition

By level of gross earnings expressed in income deciles

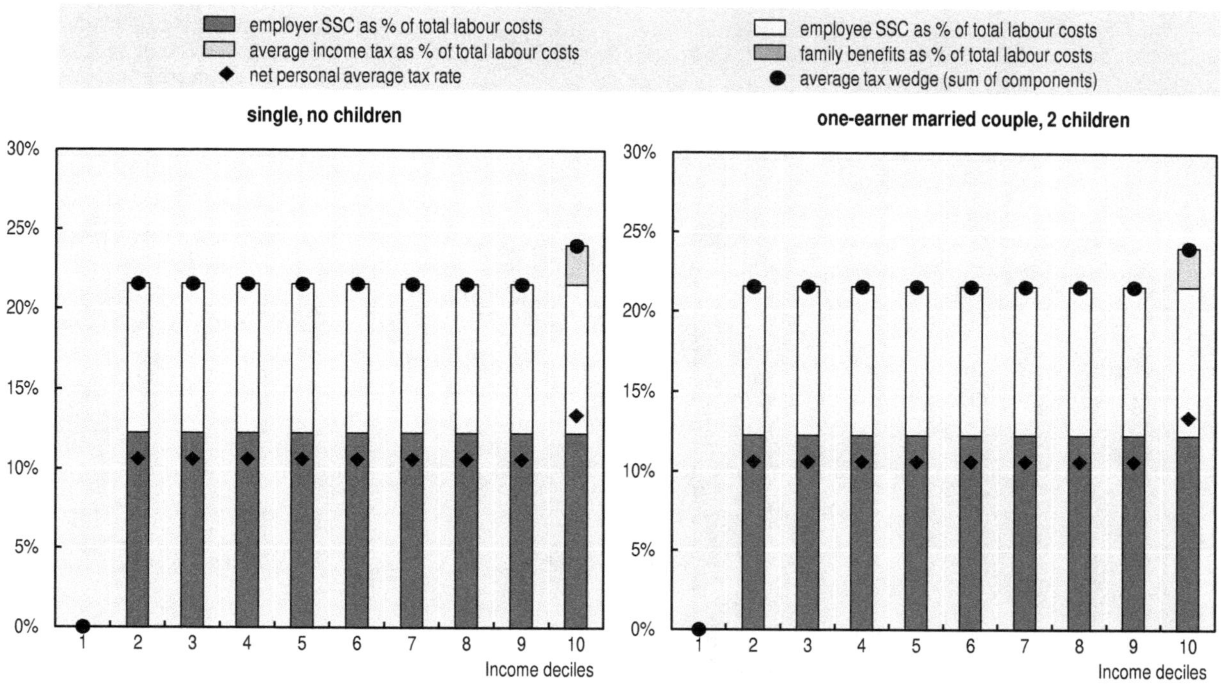

StatLink http://dx.doi.org/10.1787/888933407708

Bolivia 2013: Marginal tax wedge decomposition

By level of gross earnings expressed in income deciles

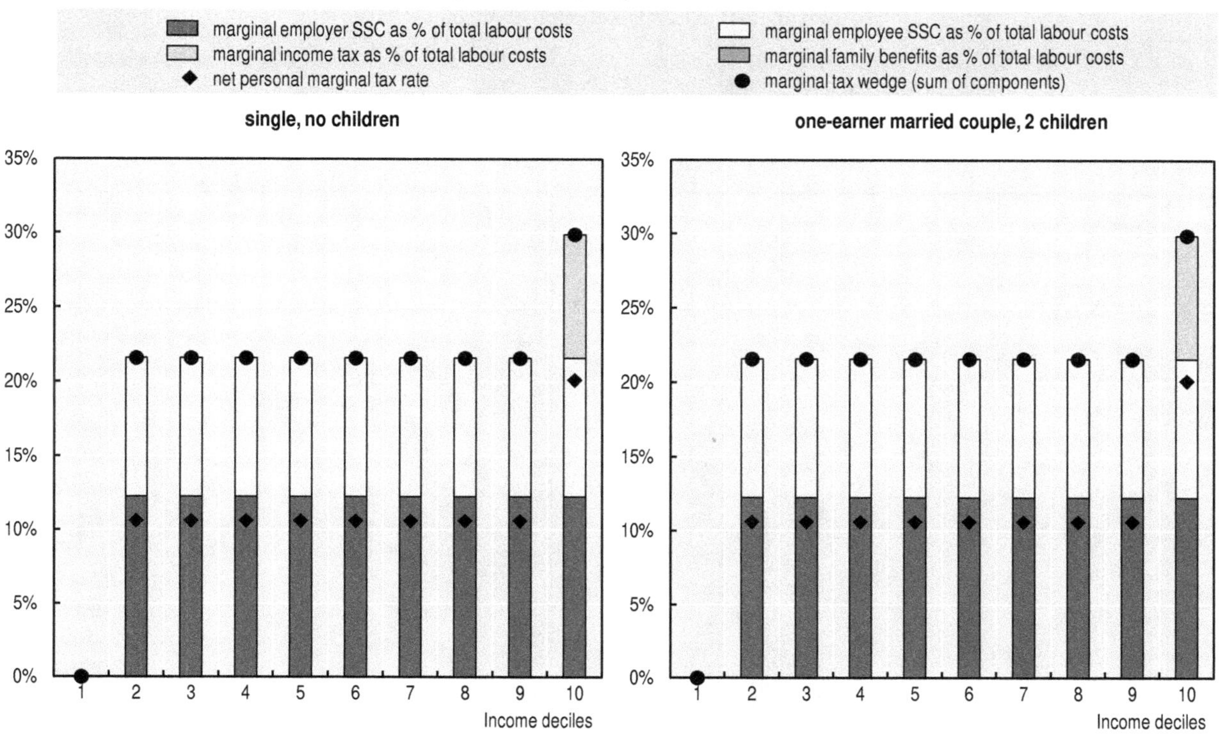

StatLink http://dx.doi.org/10.1787/888933407717

Brazil 2013: Average tax wedge decomposition

By level of gross earnings expressed in income deciles

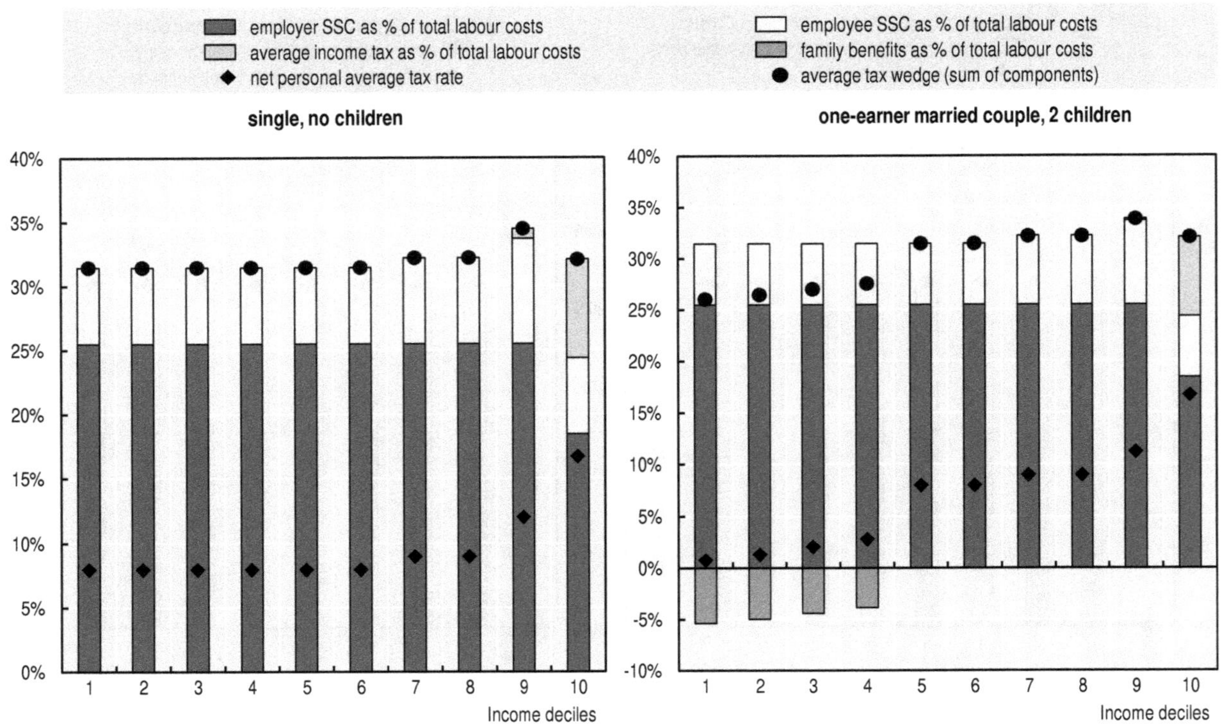

StatLink http://dx.doi.org/10.1787/888933407729

Brazil 2013: Marginal tax wedge decomposition

By level of gross earnings expressed in income deciles

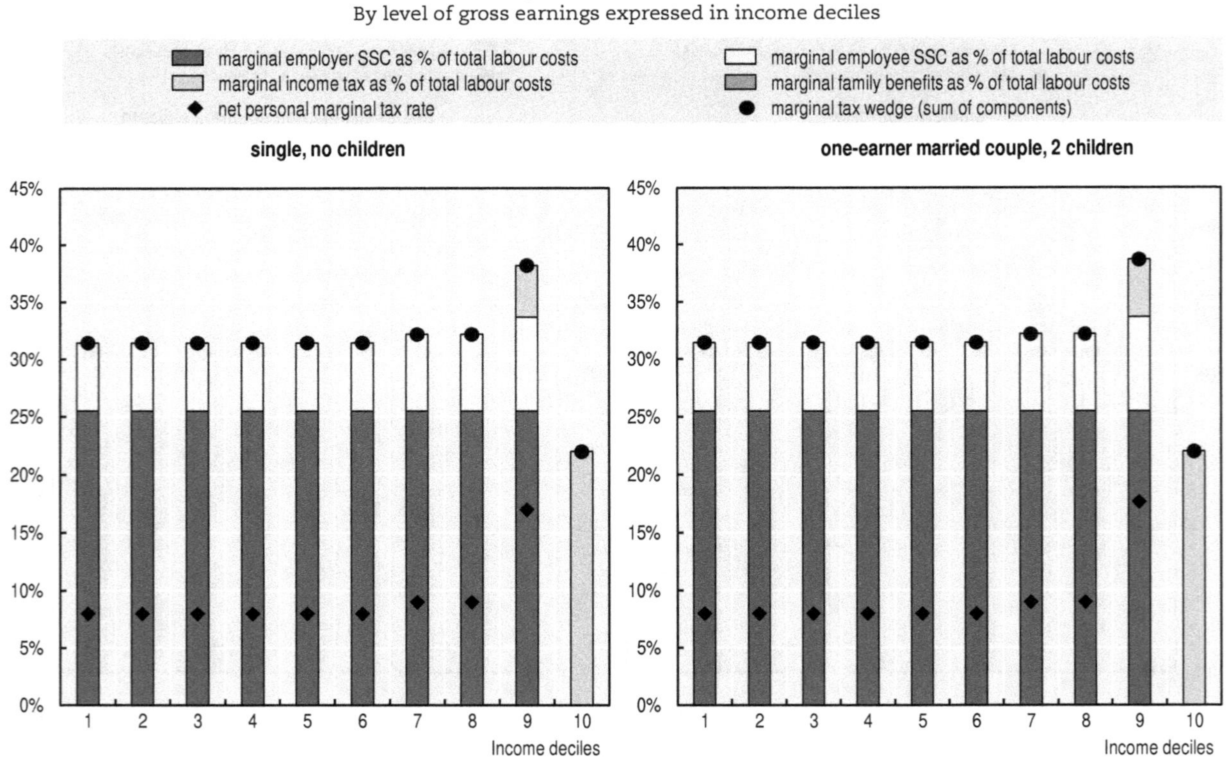

StatLink http://dx.doi.org/10.1787/888933407732

Chile 2013: Average tax wedge decomposition

By level of gross earnings expressed in income deciles

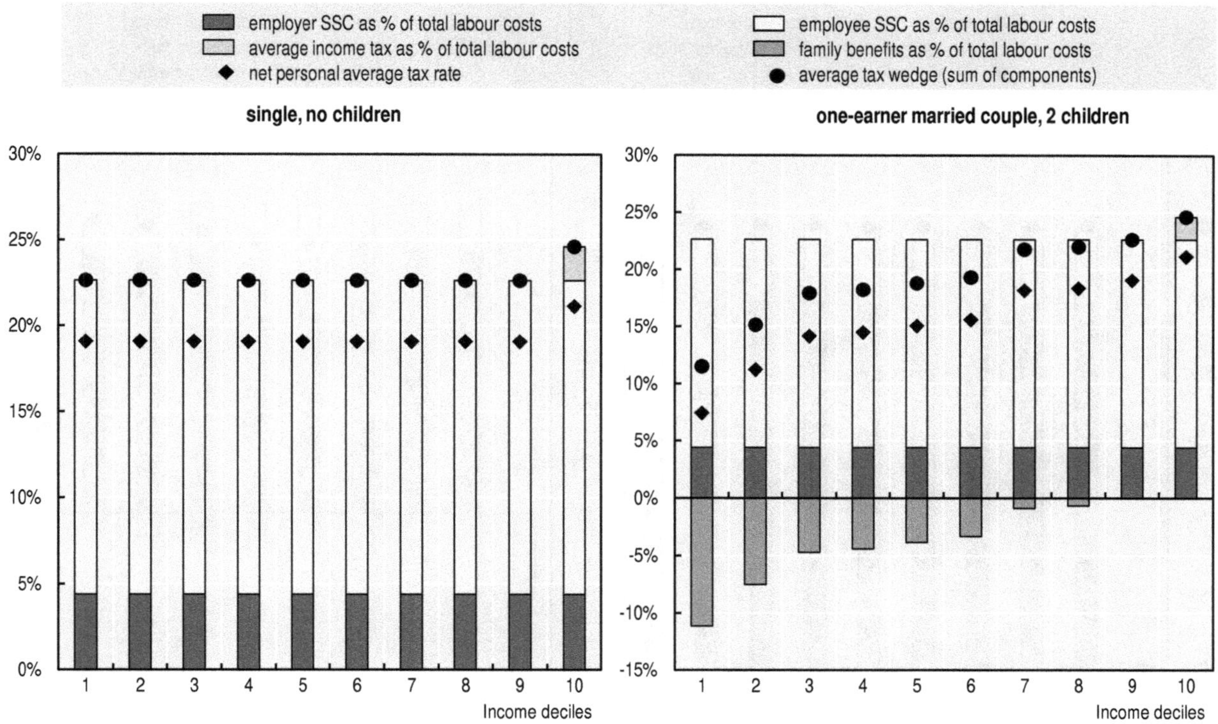

StatLink http://dx.doi.org/10.1787/888933407748

Chile 2013: Marginal tax wedge decomposition

By level of gross earnings expressed in income deciles

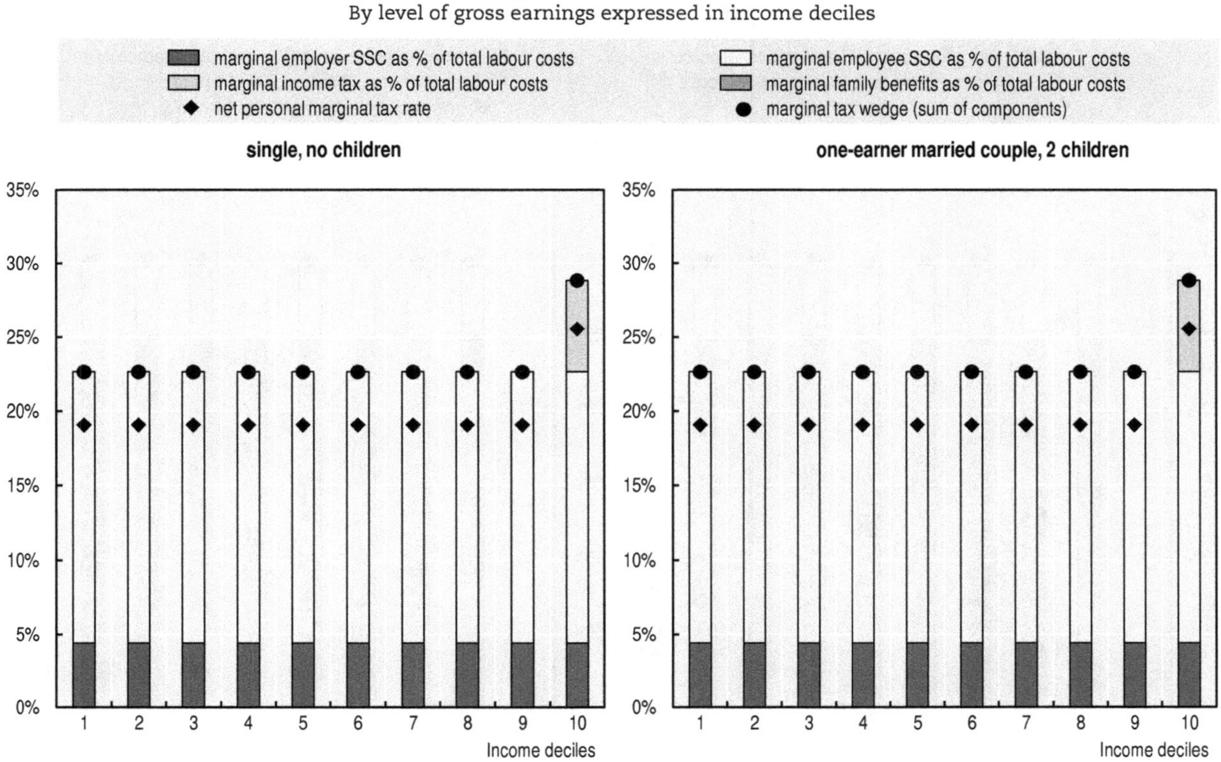

StatLink http://dx.doi.org/10.1787/888933407758

Colombia 2013: Average tax wedge decomposition

By level of gross earnings expressed in income deciles

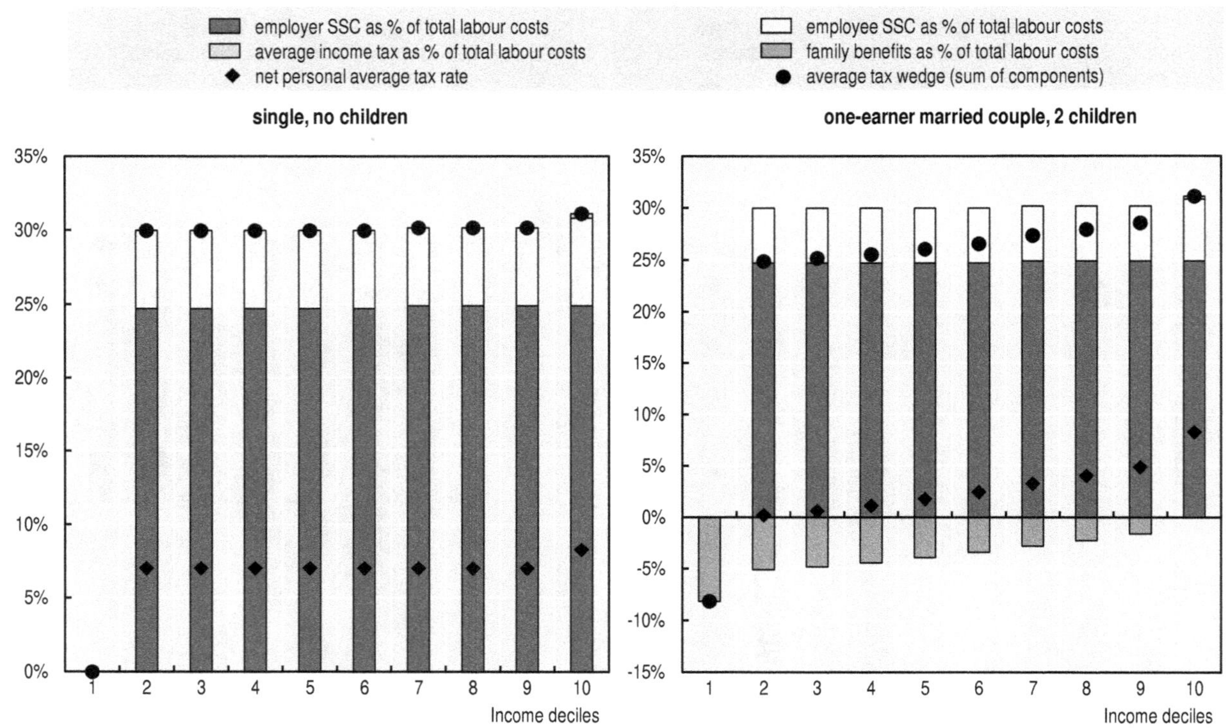

StatLink http://dx.doi.org/10.1787/888933407765

Colombia 2013: Marginal tax wedge decomposition

By level of gross earnings expressed in income deciles

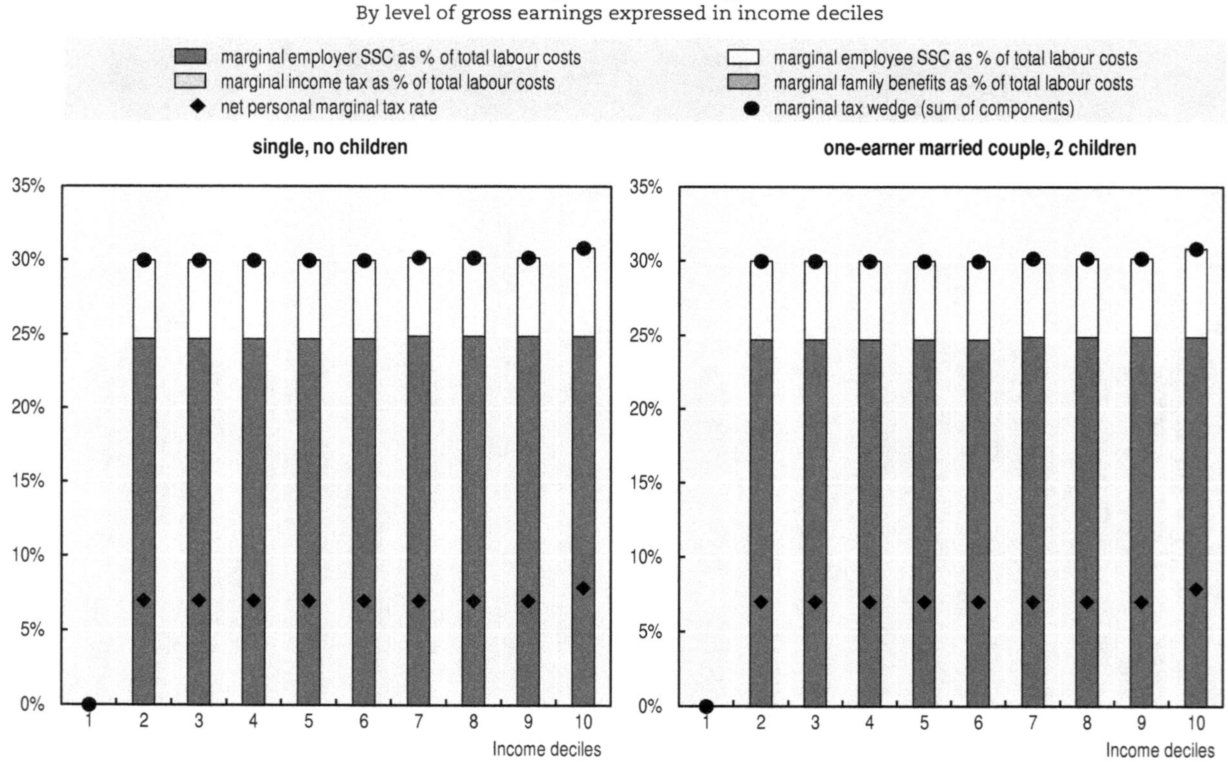

StatLink http://dx.doi.org/10.1787/888933407778

Costa Rica 2013: Average tax wedge decomposition

By level of gross earnings expressed in income deciles

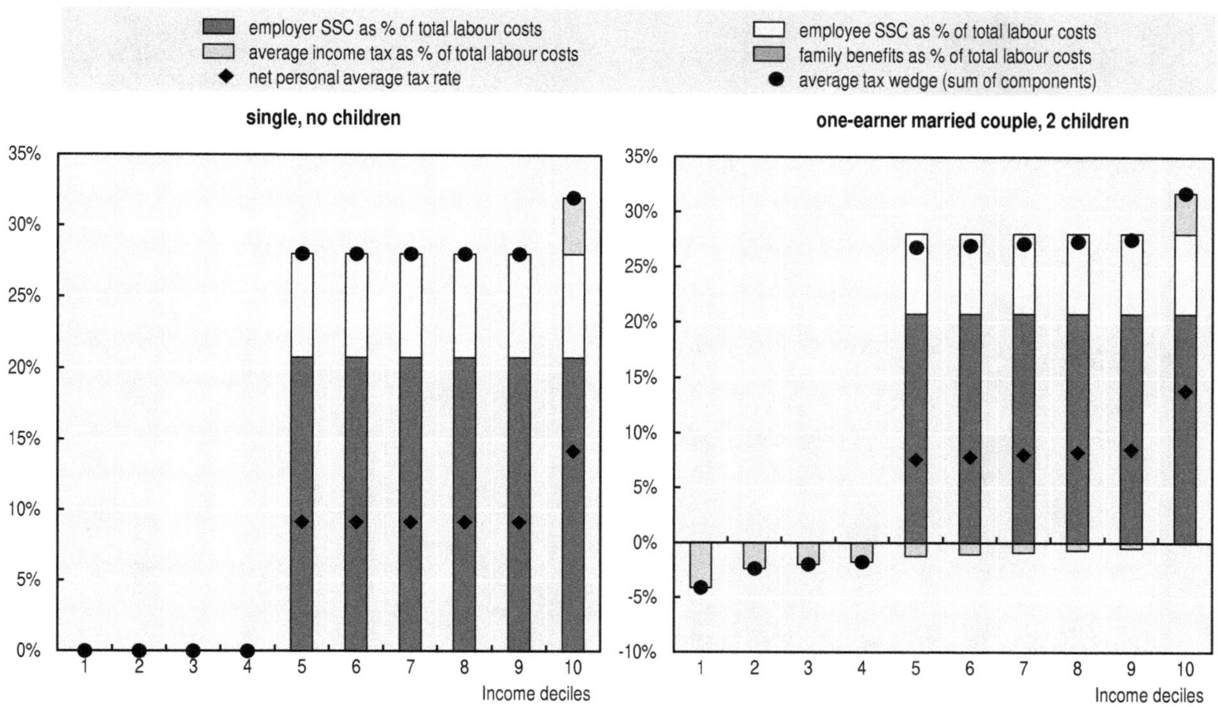

StatLink http://dx.doi.org/10.1787/888933407784

Costa Rica 2013: Marginal tax wedge decomposition

By level of gross earnings expressed in income deciles

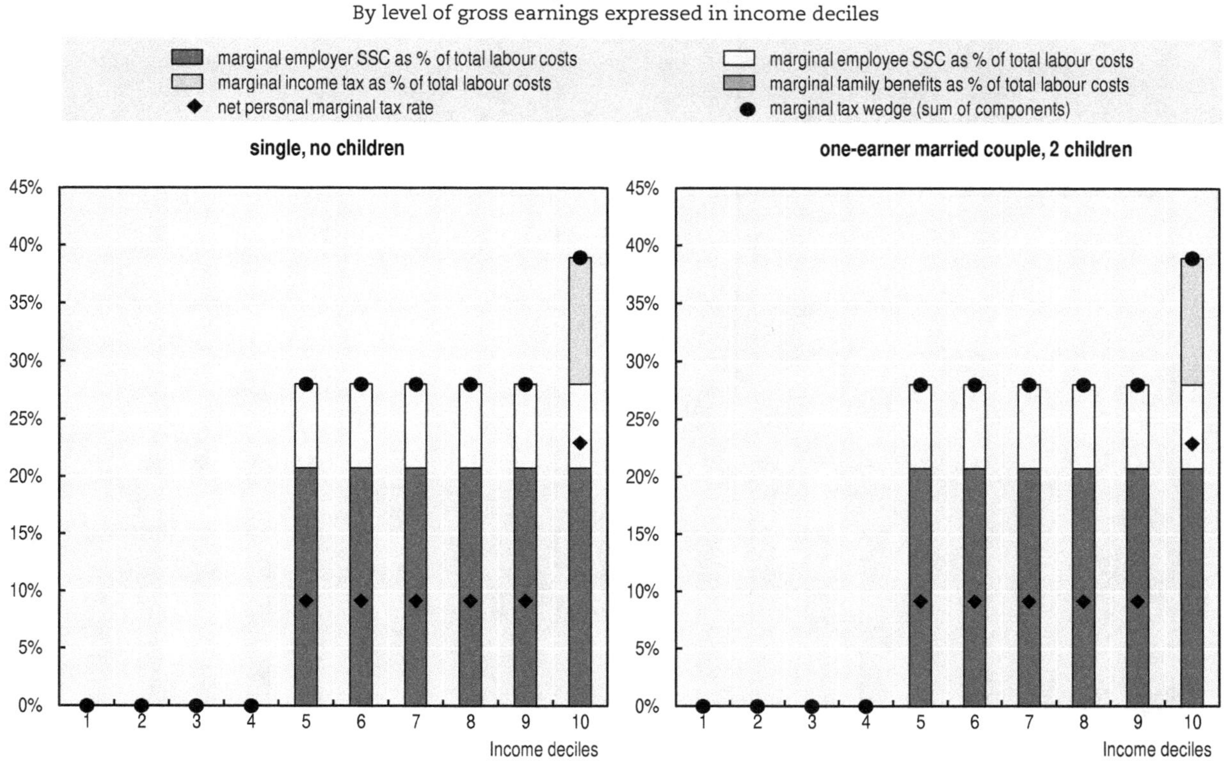

StatLink http://dx.doi.org/10.1787/888933407797

Dominican Republic 2013: Average tax wedge decomposition

By level of gross earnings expressed in income deciles

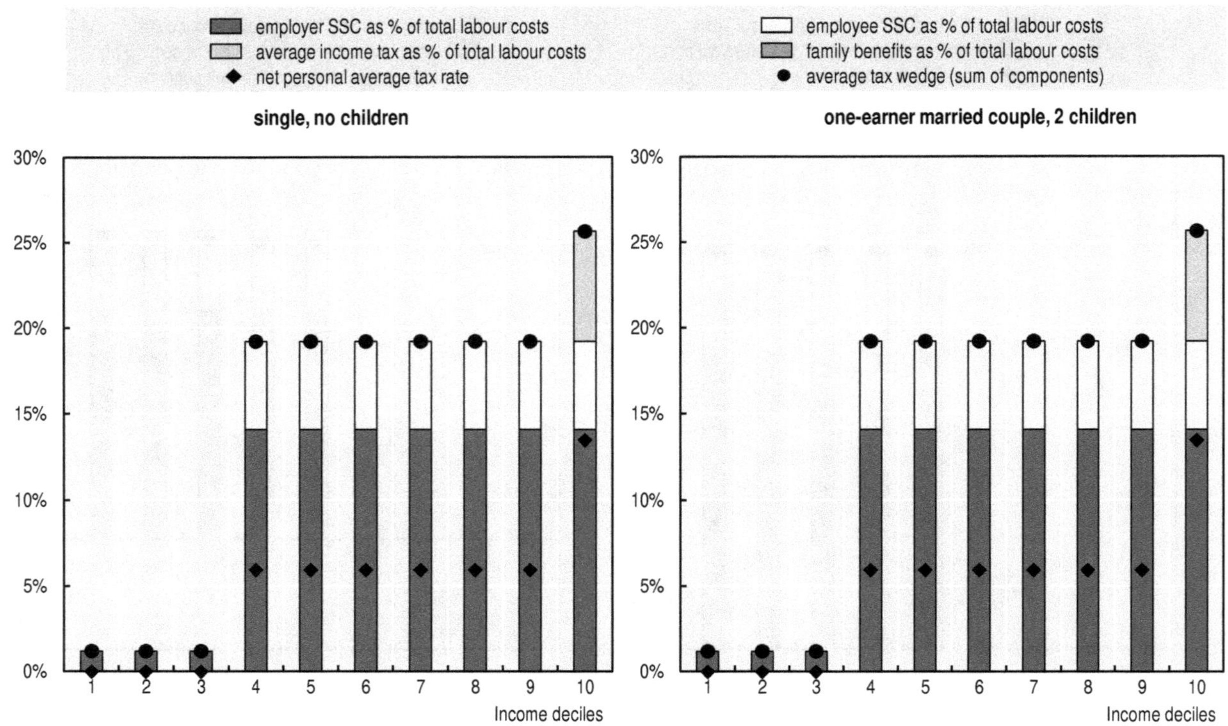

StatLink http://dx.doi.org/10.1787/888933407802

Dominican Republic 2013: Marginal tax wedge decomposition

By level of gross earnings expressed in income deciles

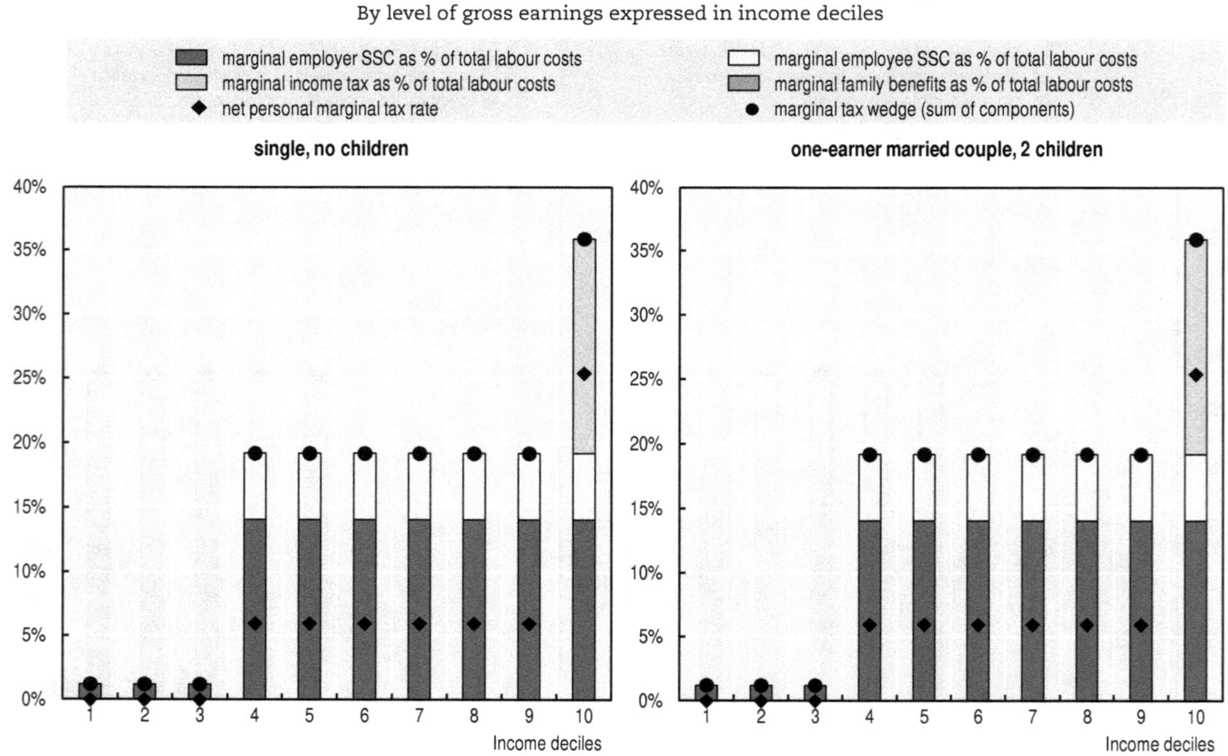

StatLink http://dx.doi.org/10.1787/888933407816

Ecuador 2013: Average tax wedge decomposition

By level of gross earnings expressed in income deciles

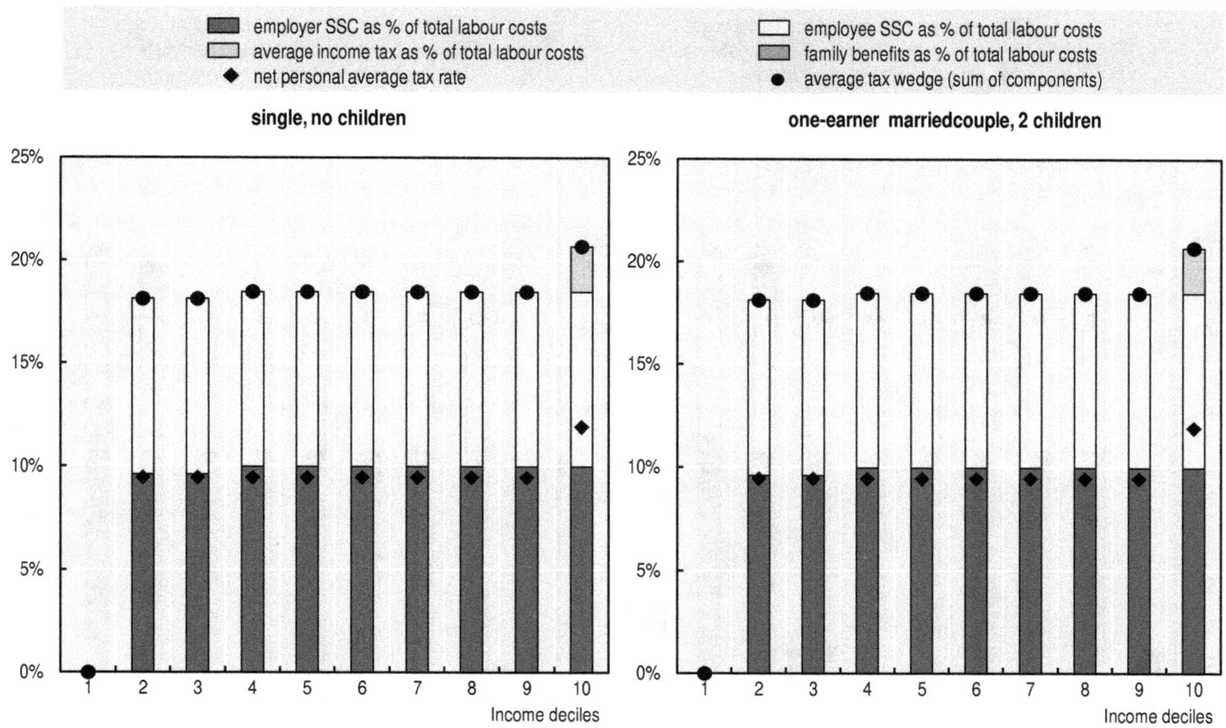

StatLink http://dx.doi.org/10.1787/888933407823

Ecuador 2013: Marginal tax wedge decomposition

By level of gross earnings expressed in income deciles

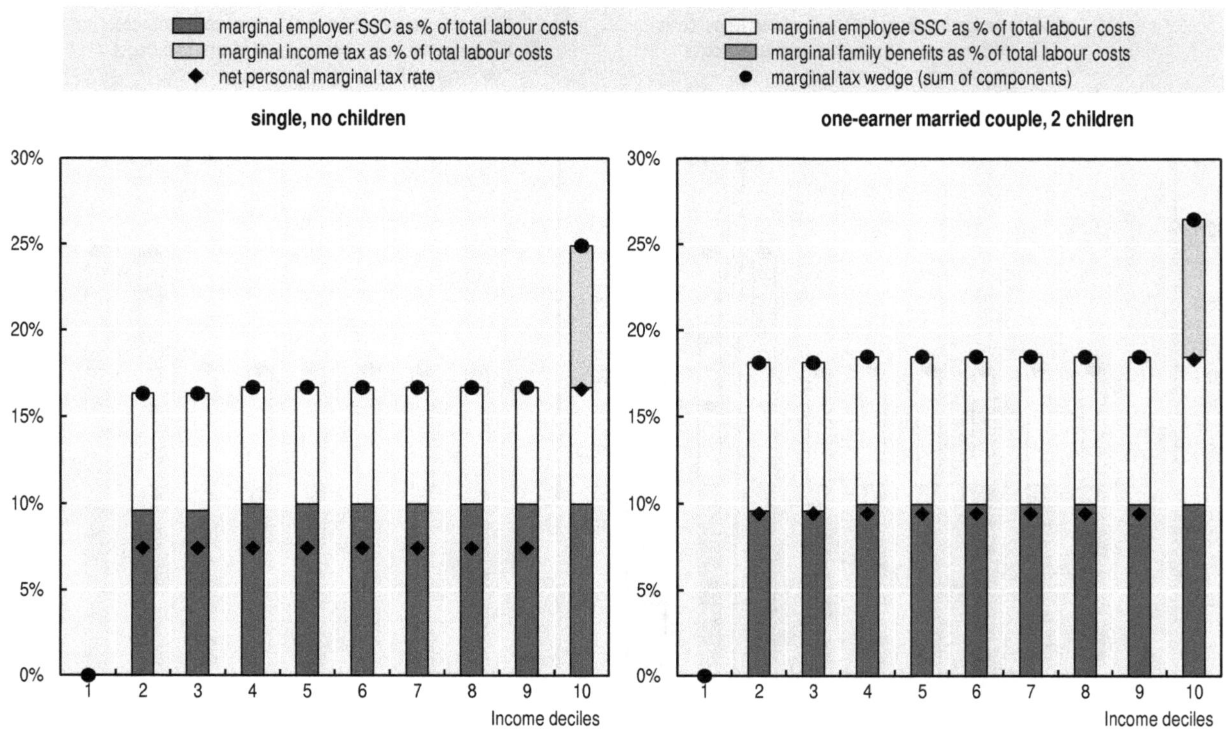

StatLink http://dx.doi.org/10.1787/888933407835

El Salvador 2013: Average tax wedge decomposition

By level of gross earnings expressed in income deciles

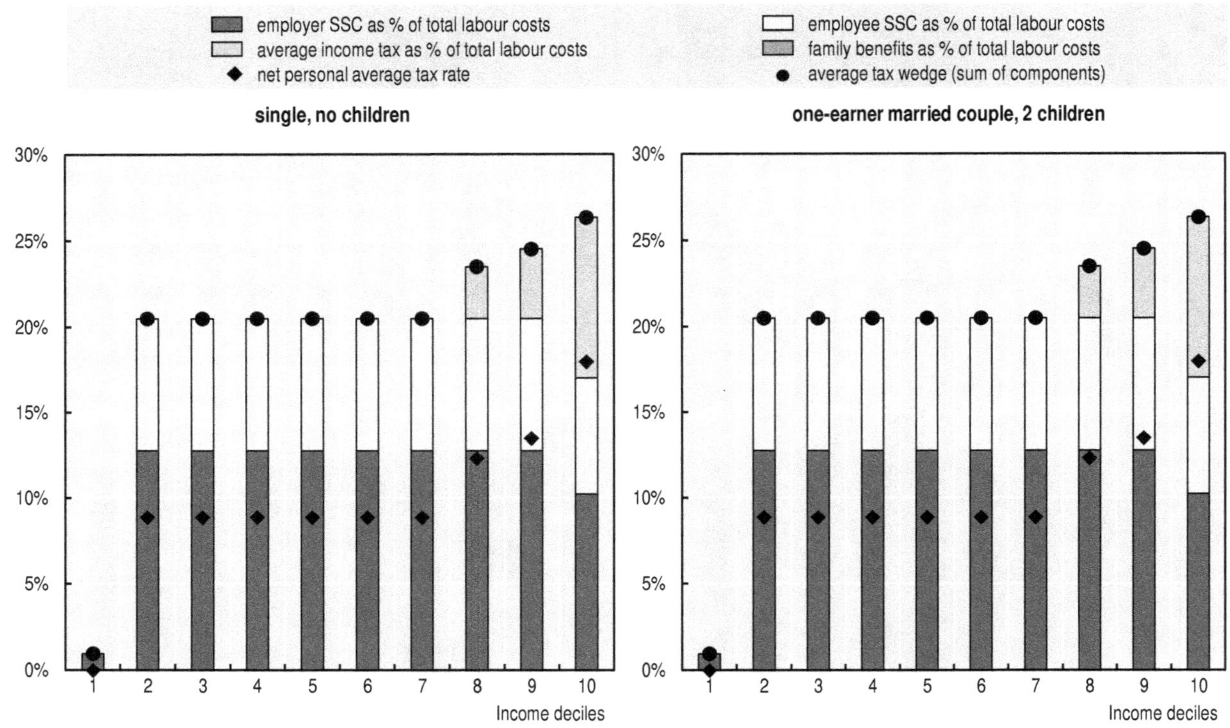

StatLink http://dx.doi.org/10.1787/888933407848

El Salvador 2013: Marginal tax wedge decomposition

By level of gross earnings expressed in income deciles

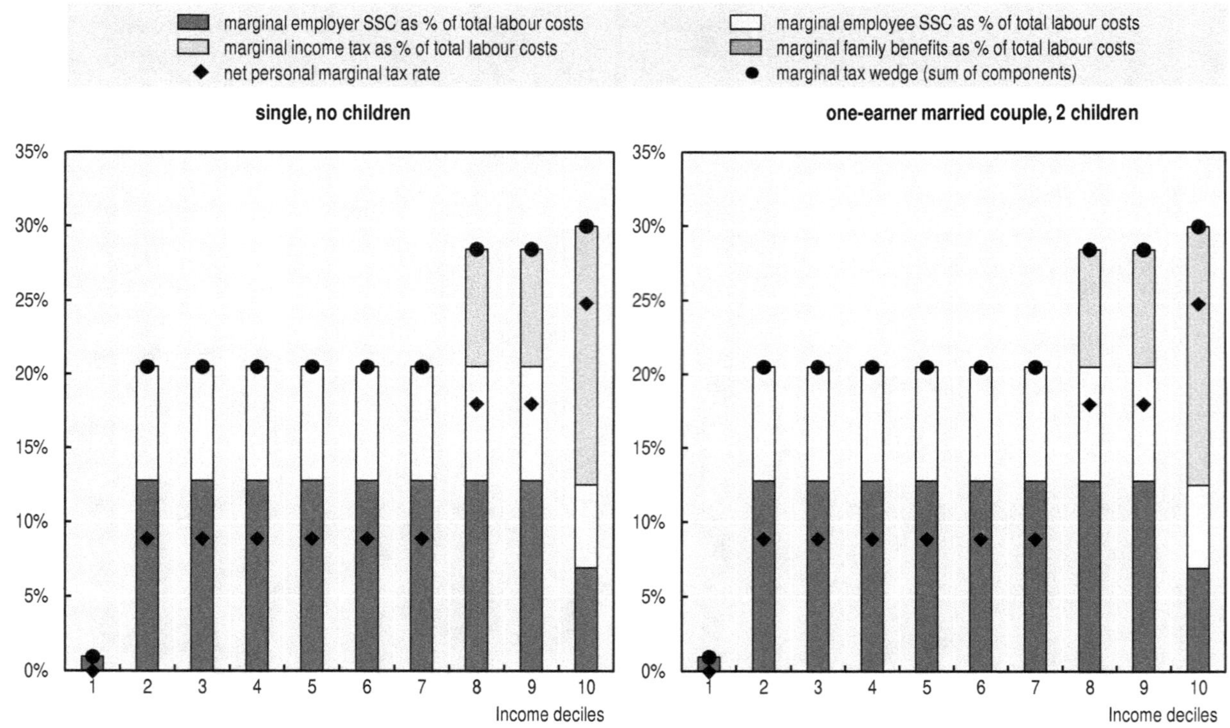

StatLink http://dx.doi.org/10.1787/888933407859

Guatemala 2013: Average tax wedge decomposition

By level of gross earnings expressed in income deciles

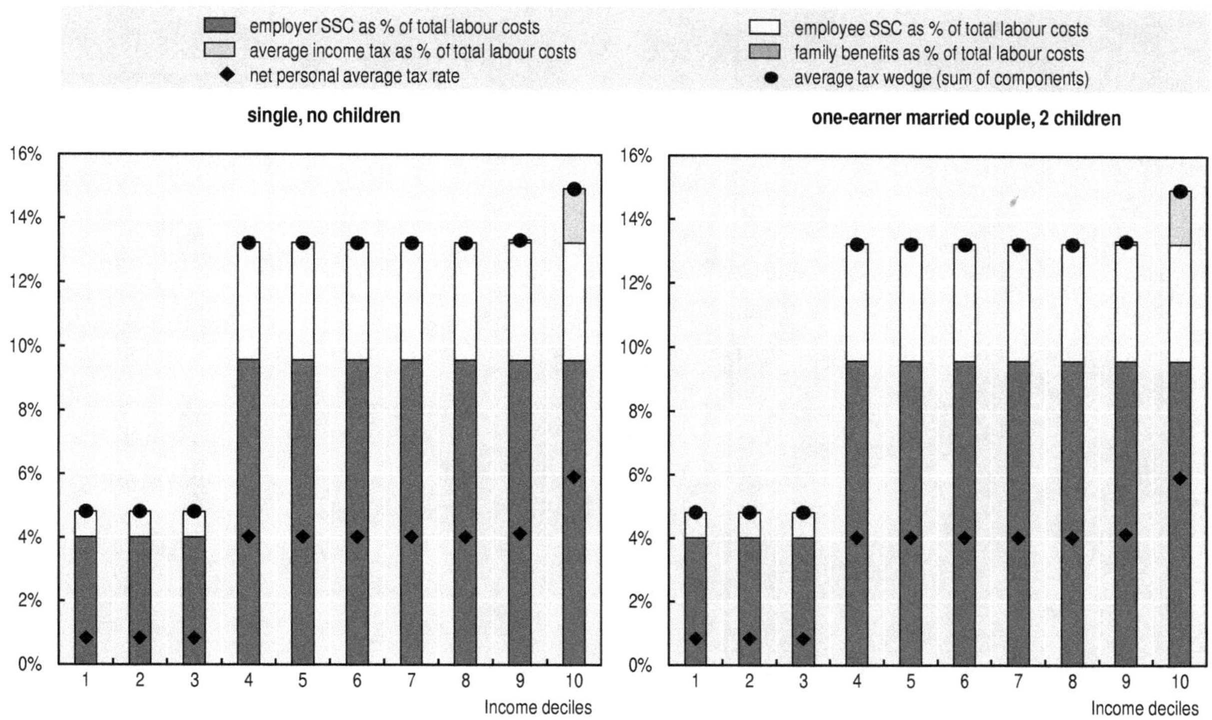

StatLink http://dx.doi.org/10.1787/888933407861

Guatemala 2013: Marginal tax wedge decomposition

By level of gross earnings expressed in income deciles

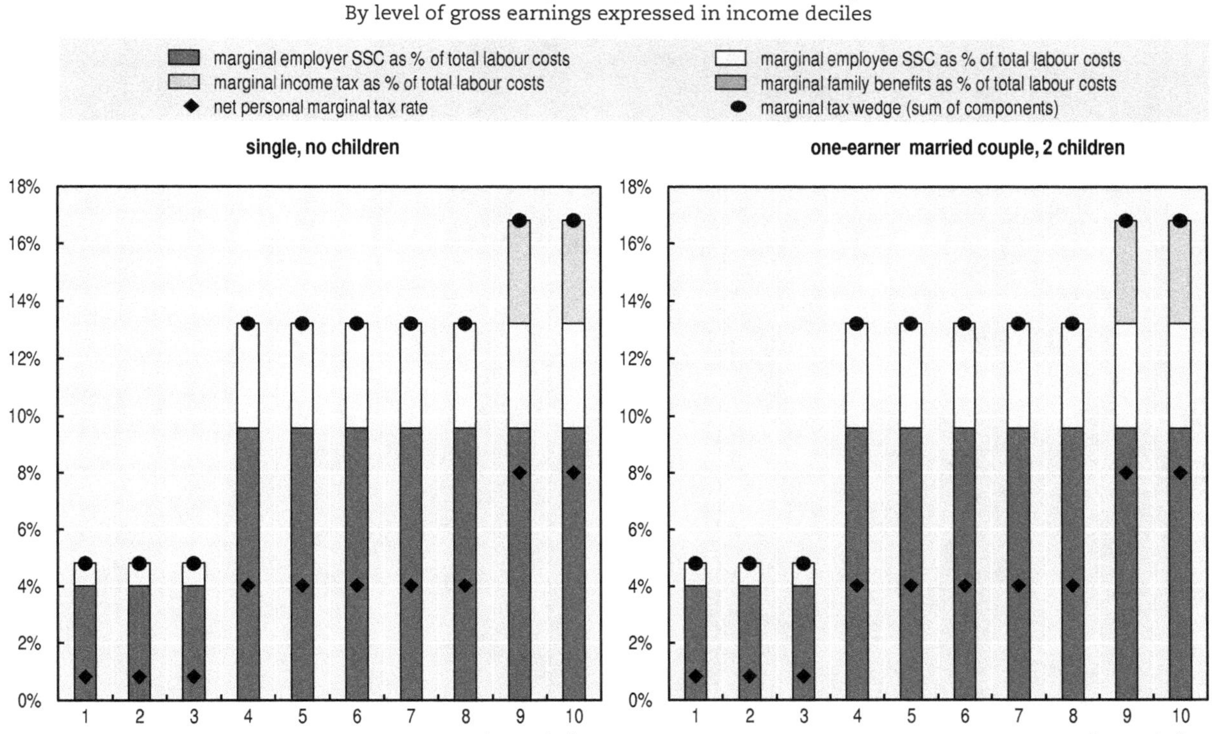

StatLink http://dx.doi.org/10.1787/888933407872

Honduras 2013: Average tax wedge decomposition

By level of gross earnings expressed in income deciles

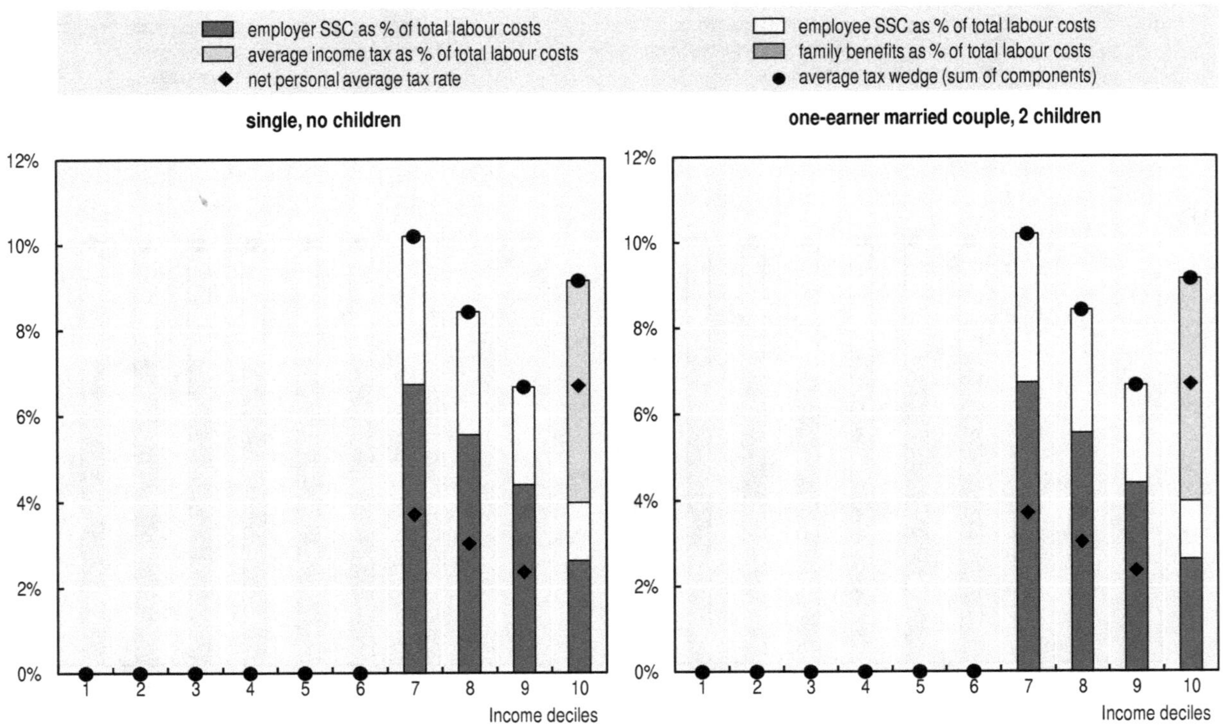

StatLink http://dx.doi.org/10.1787/888933407880

Honduras 2013: Marginal tax wedge decomposition

By level of gross earnings expressed in income deciles

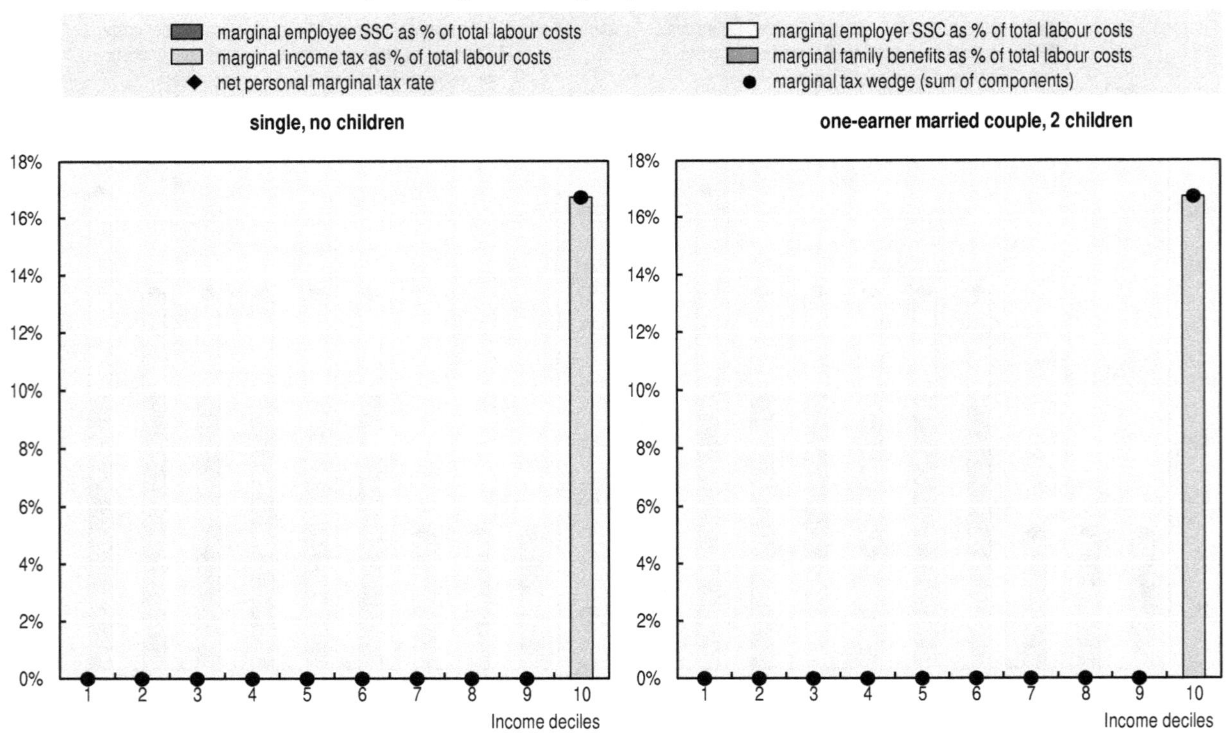

StatLink http://dx.doi.org/10.1787/888933407891

Jamaica 2013: Average tax wedge decomposition

By level of gross earnings expressed in income deciles

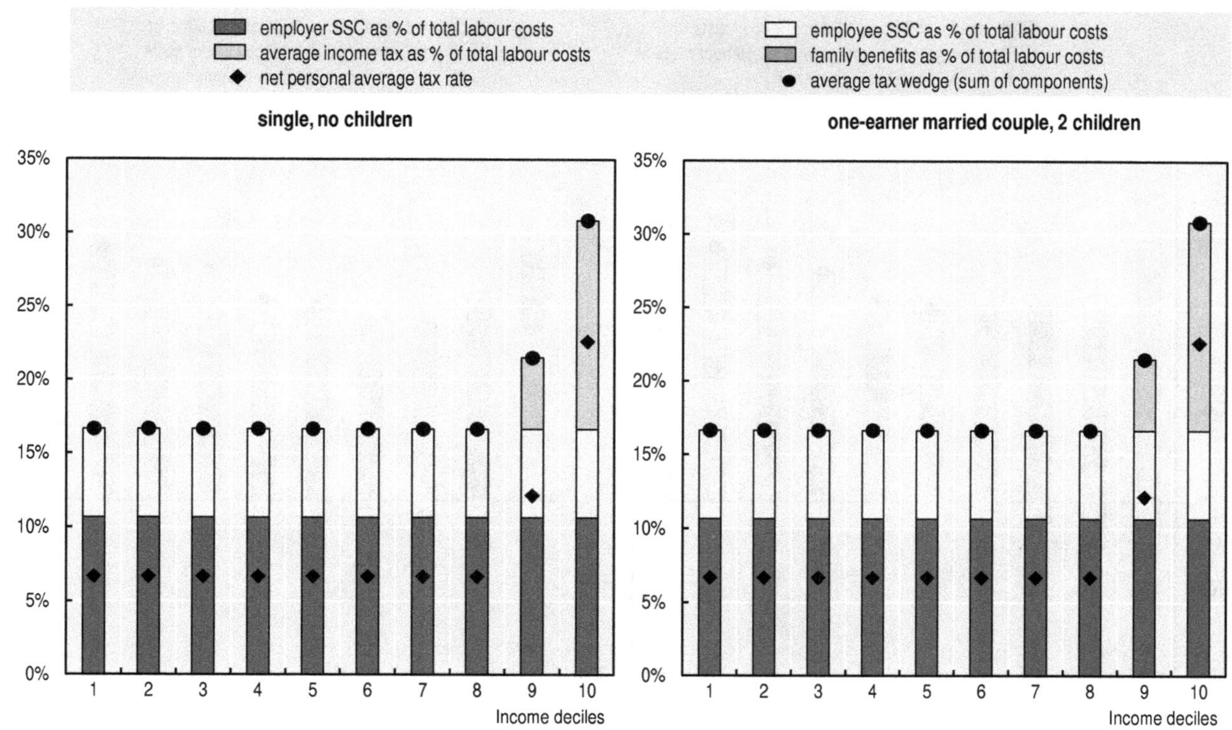

StatLink http://dx.doi.org/10.1787/888933407904

Jamaica 2013: Marginal tax wedge decomposition

By level of gross earnings expressed in income deciles

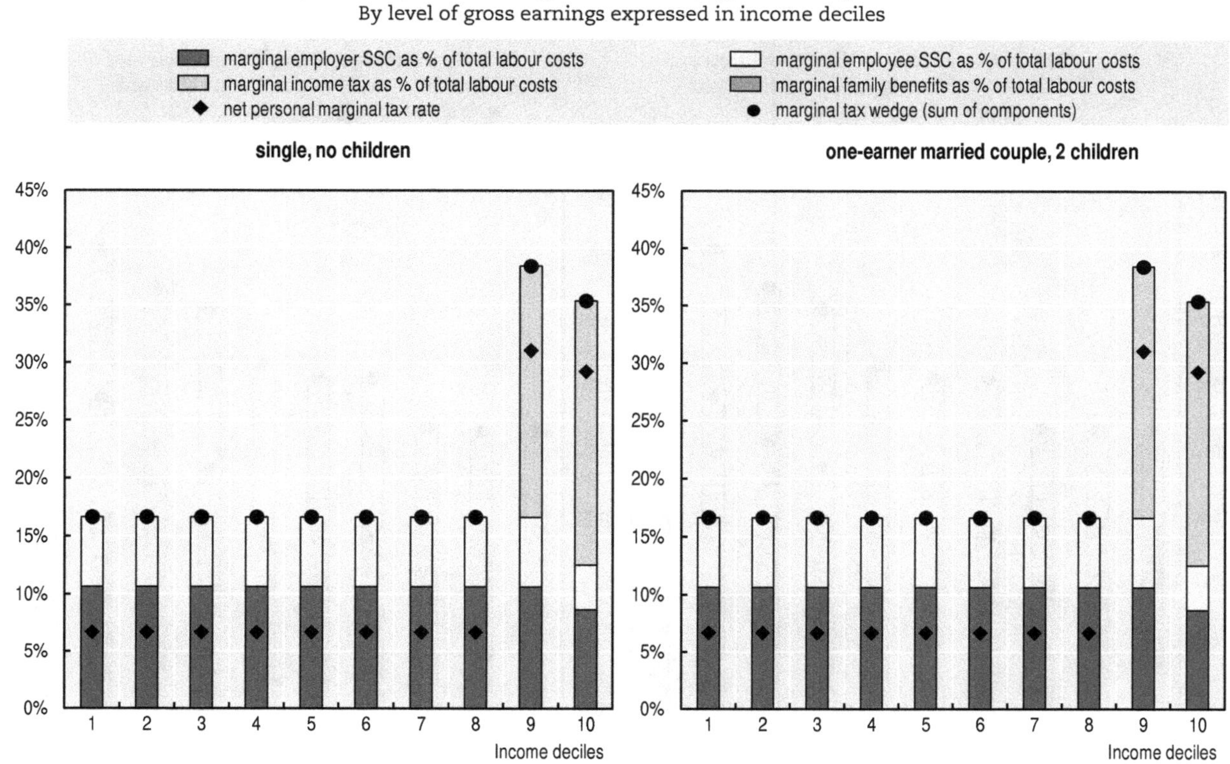

StatLink http://dx.doi.org/10.1787/888933407913

Mexico 2013: Average tax wedge decomposition

By level of gross earnings expressed in income deciles

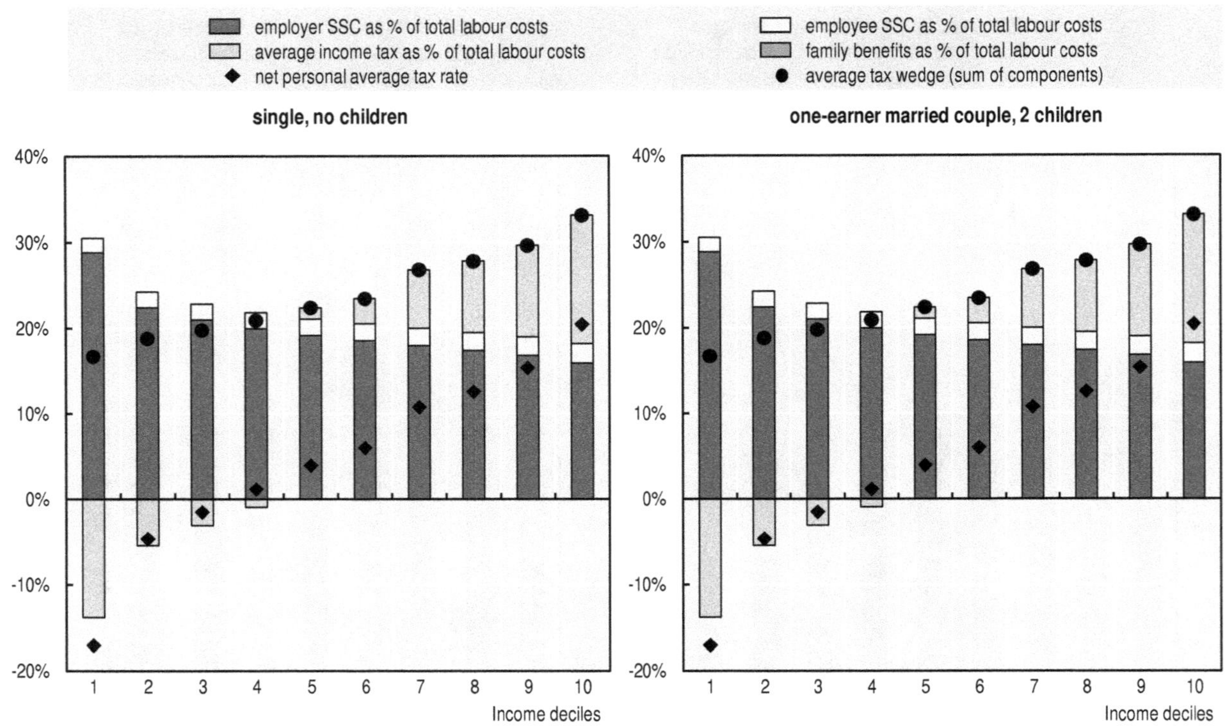

StatLink http://dx.doi.org/10.1787/888933407922

Mexico 2013: Marginal tax wedge decomposition

By level of gross earnings expressed in income deciles

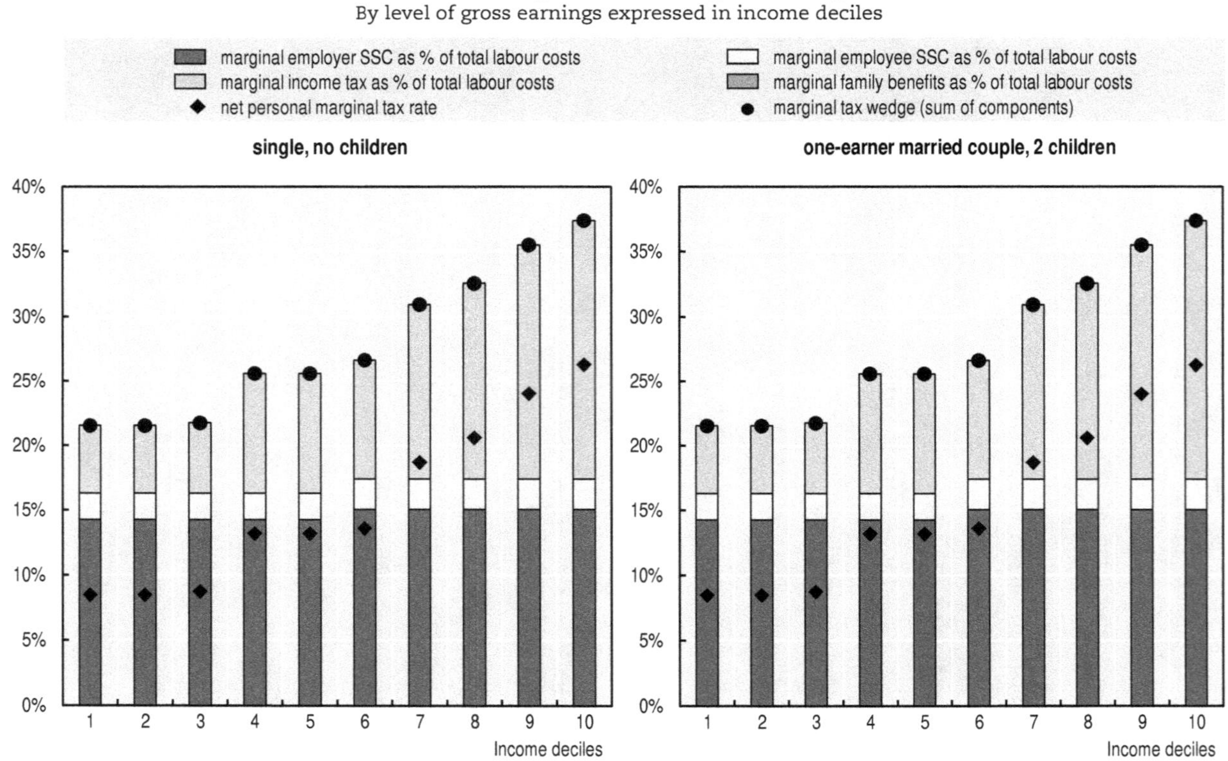

StatLink http://dx.doi.org/10.1787/888933407933

Nicaragua 2013: Average tax wedge decomposition

By level of gross earnings expressed in income deciles

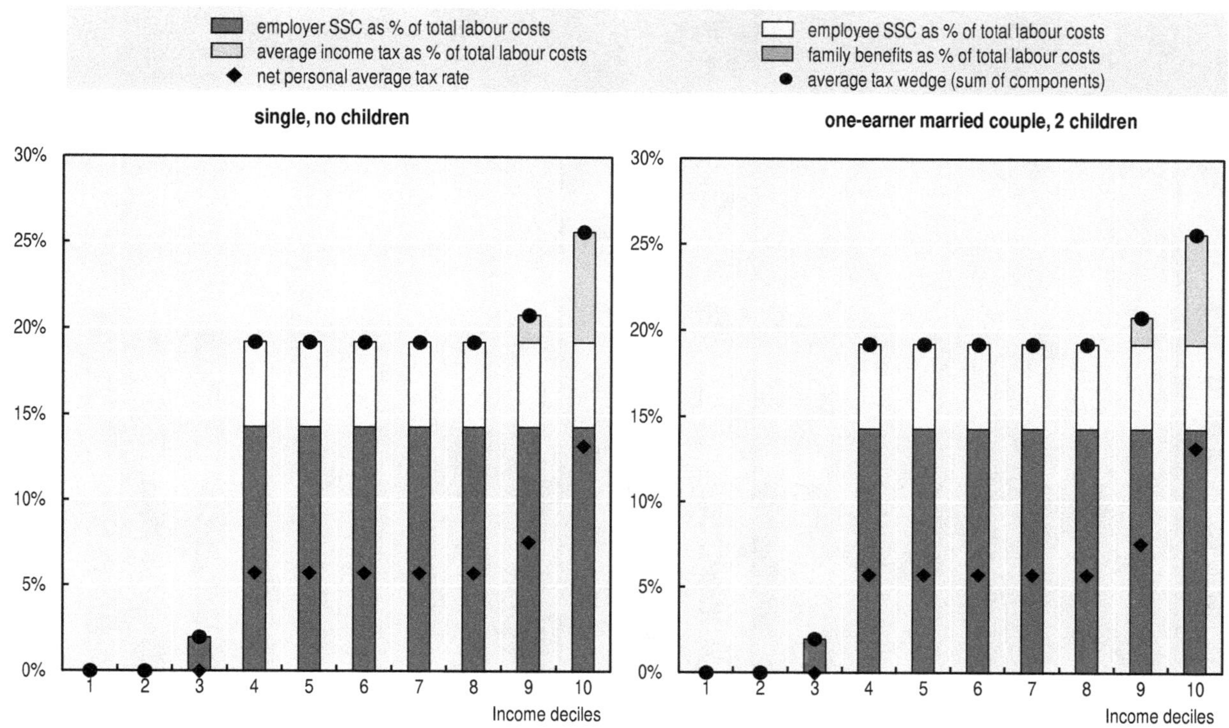

StatLink http://dx.doi.org/10.1787/888933407942

Nicaragua 2013: Marginal tax wedge decomposition

By level of gross earnings expressed in income deciles

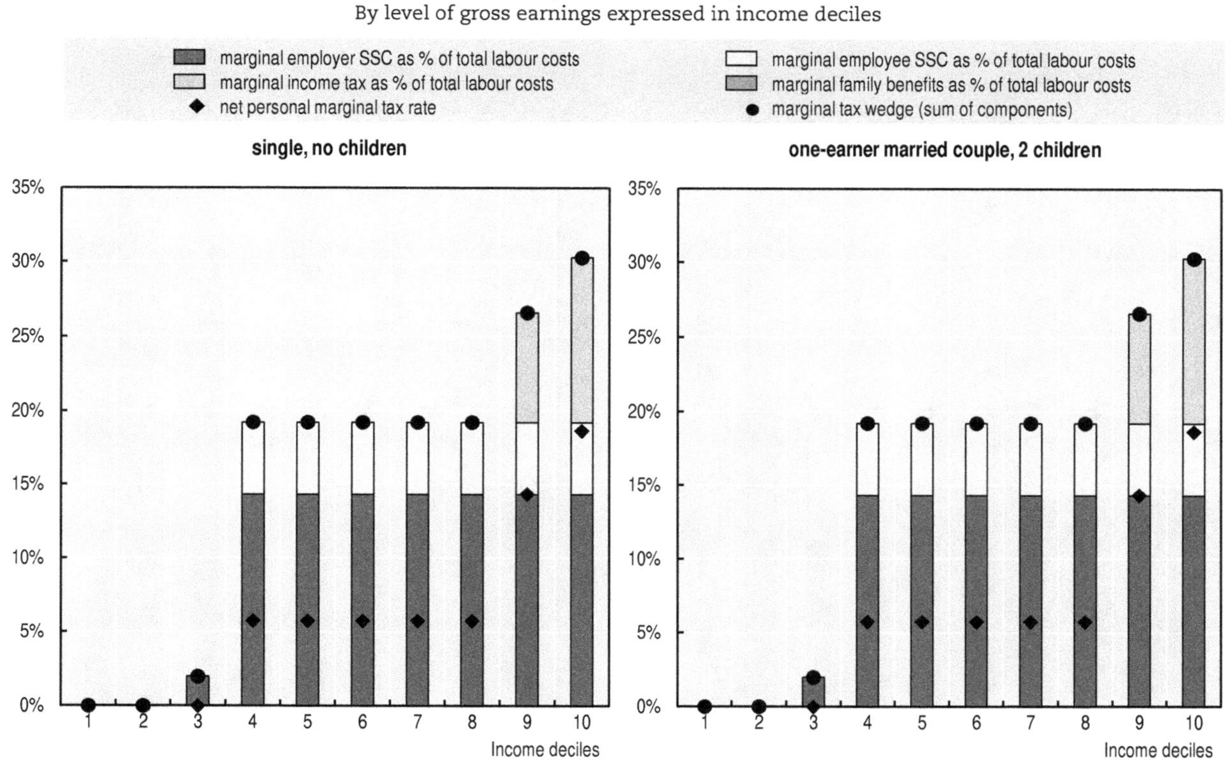

StatLink http://dx.doi.org/10.1787/888933407955

Panama 2013: Average tax wedge decomposition

By level of gross earnings expressed in income deciles

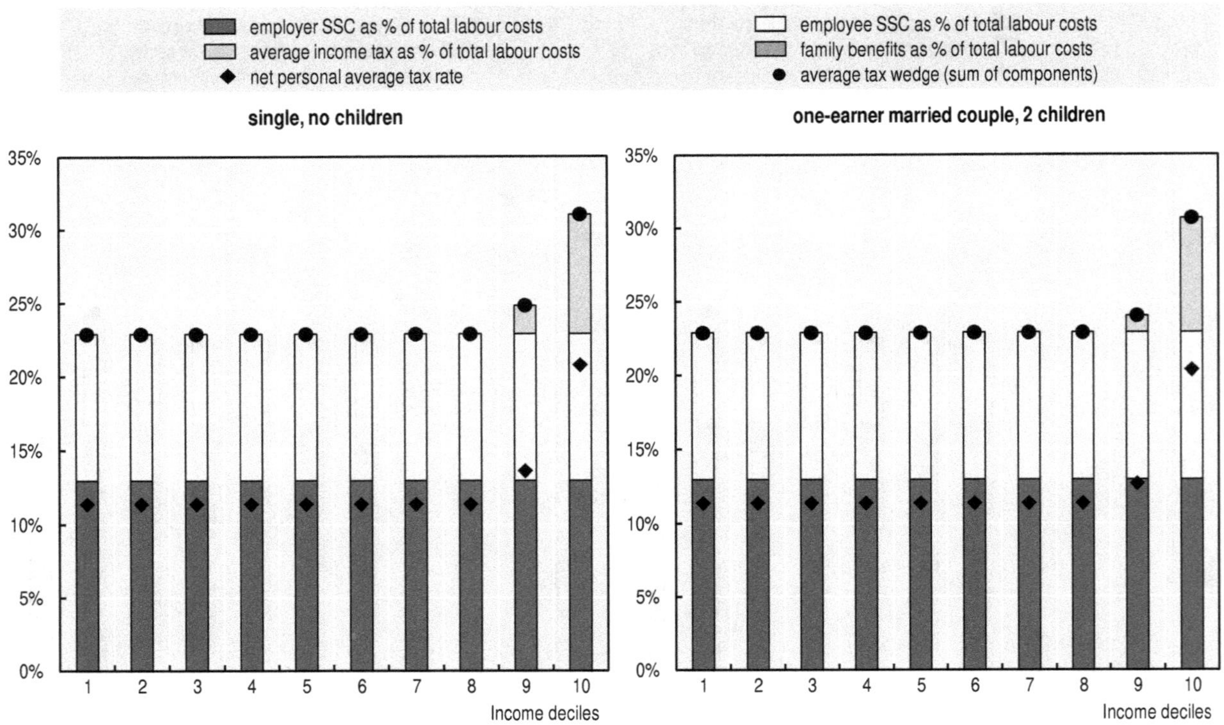

StatLink http://dx.doi.org/10.1787/888933407968

Panama 2013: Marginal tax wedge decomposition

By level of gross earnings expressed in income deciles

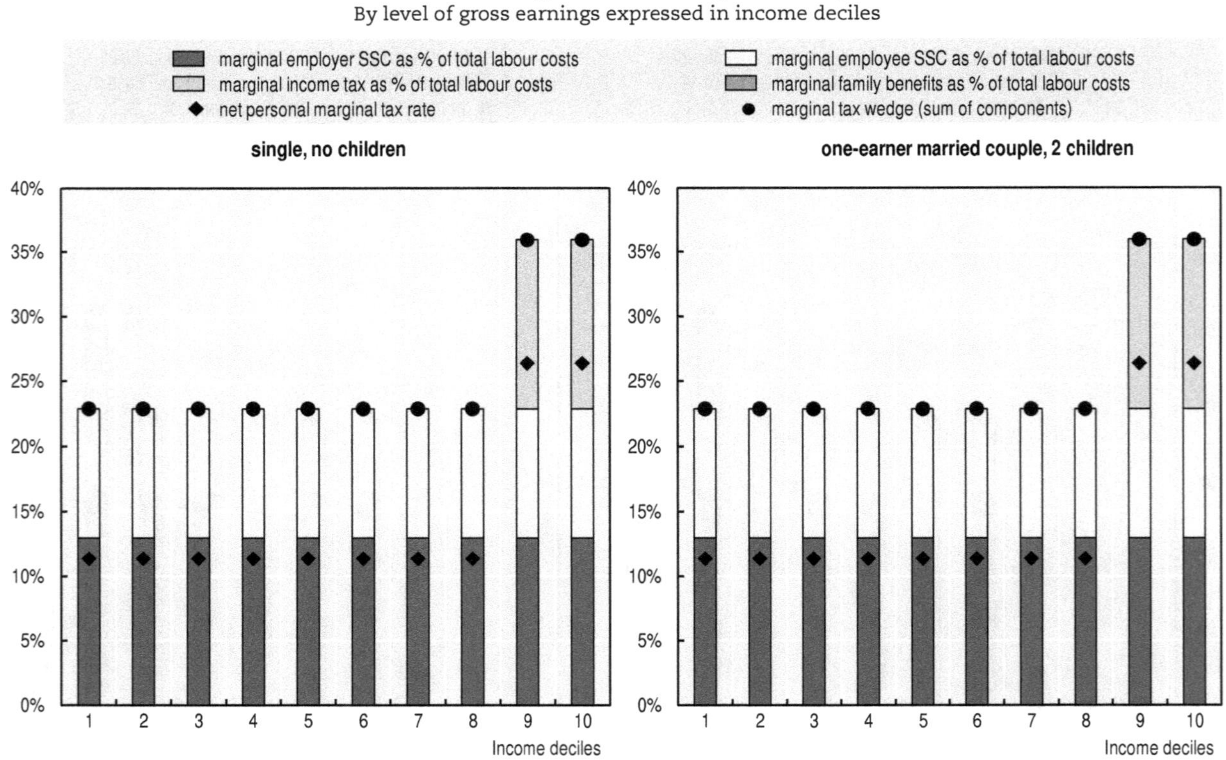

StatLink http://dx.doi.org/10.1787/888933407976

Paraguay 2013: Average tax wedge decomposition

By level of gross earnings expressed in income deciles

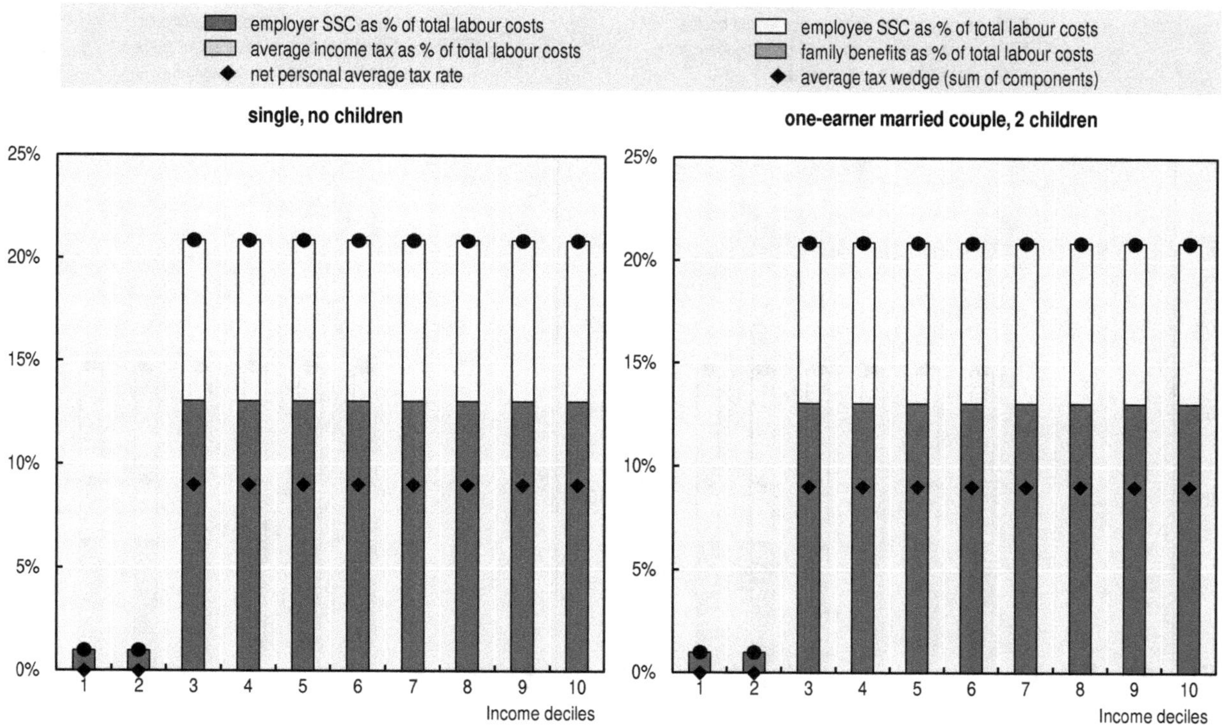

StatLink http://dx.doi.org/10.1787/888933407984

Paraguay 2013: Marginal tax wedge decomposition

By level of gross earnings expressed in income deciles

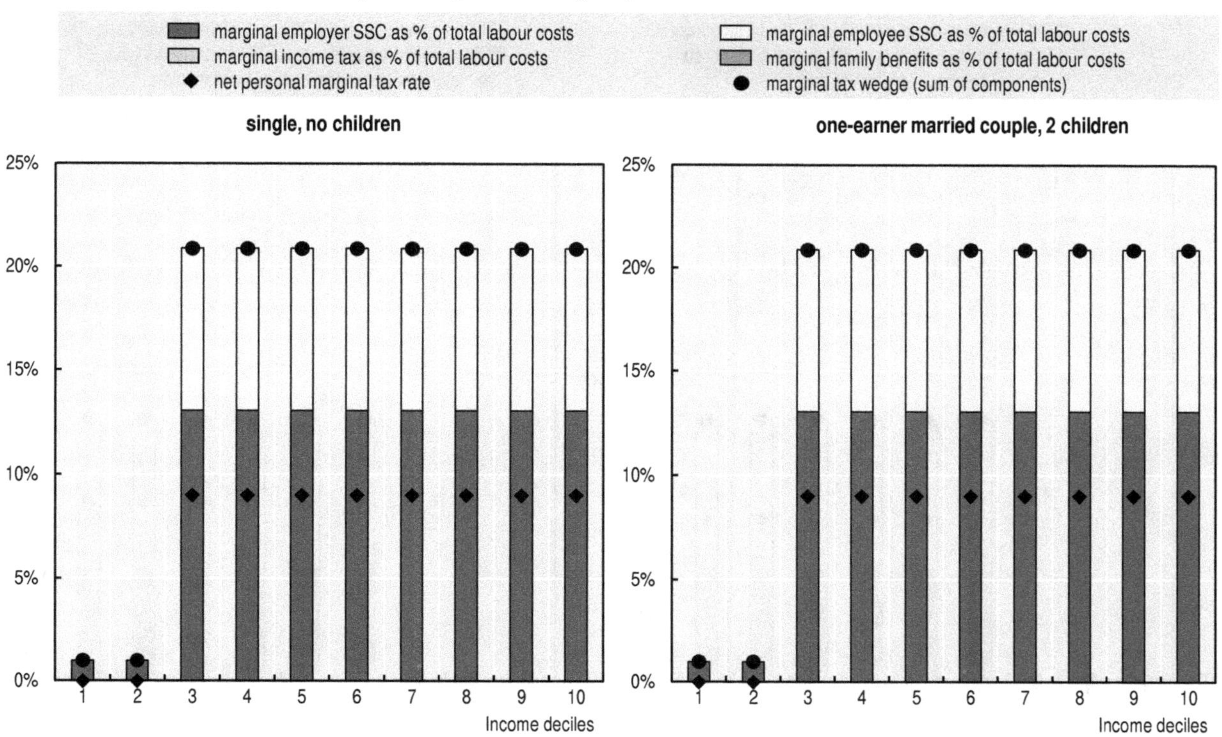

StatLink http://dx.doi.org/10.1787/888933407991

Peru 2013: Average tax wedge decomposition

By level of gross earnings expressed in income deciles

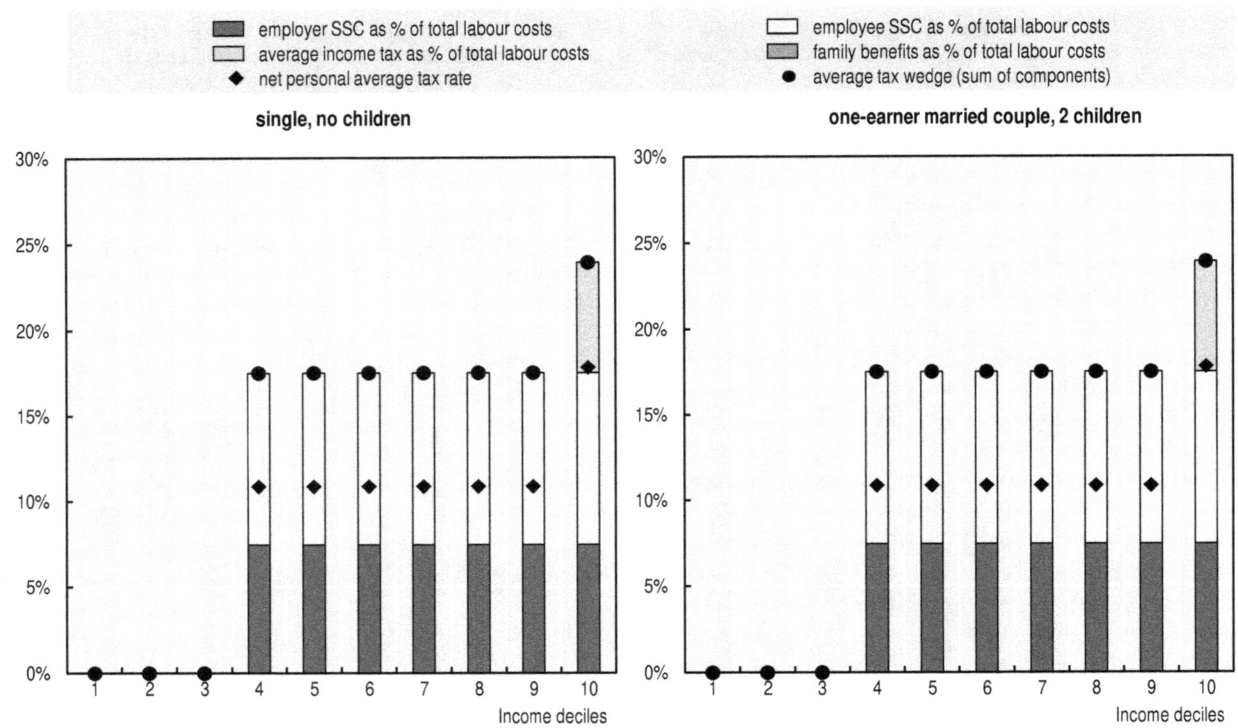

StatLink http://dx.doi.org/10.1787/888933408006

Peru 2013: Marginal tax wedge decomposition

By level of gross earnings expressed in income deciles

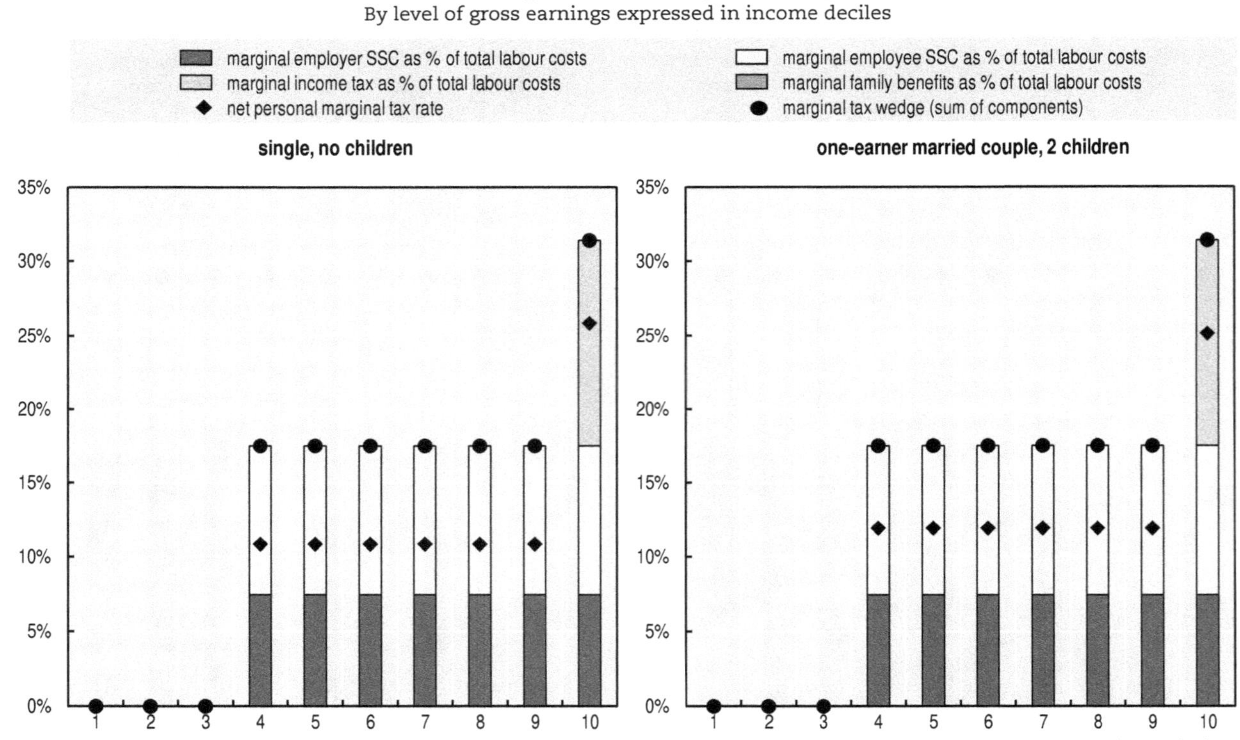

StatLink http://dx.doi.org/10.1787/888933408013

Trinidad and Tobago 2013: Average tax wedge decomposition

By level of gross earnings expressed in income deciles

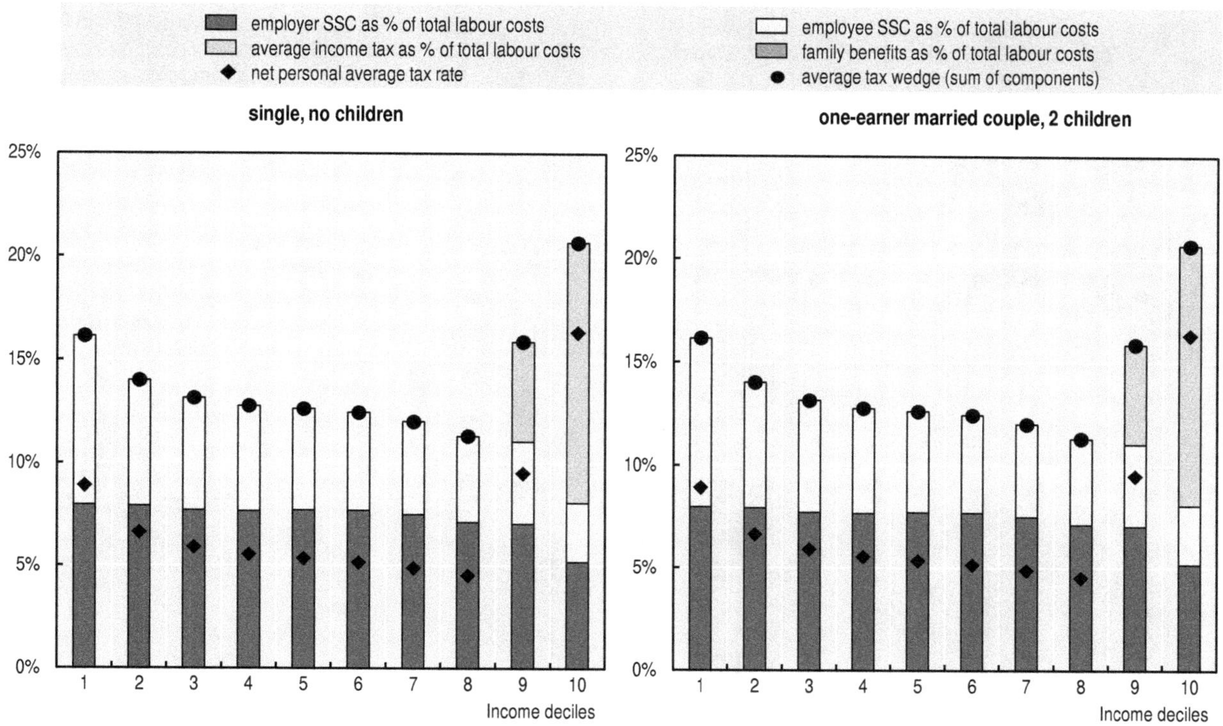

StatLink http://dx.doi.org/10.1787/888933408024

Trinidad and Tobago 2013: Marginal tax wedge decomposition

By level of gross earnings expressed in income deciles

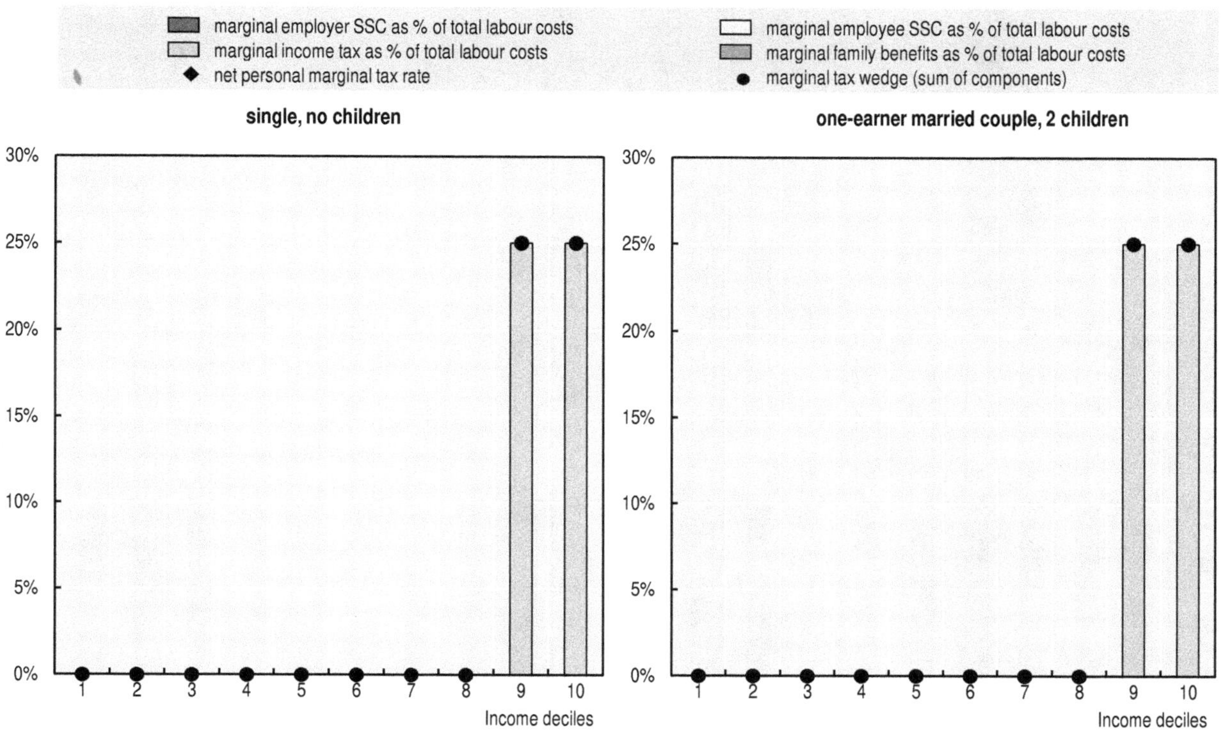

StatLink http://dx.doi.org/10.1787/888933408032

Uruguay 2013: Average tax wedge decomposition

By level of gross earnings expressed in income deciles

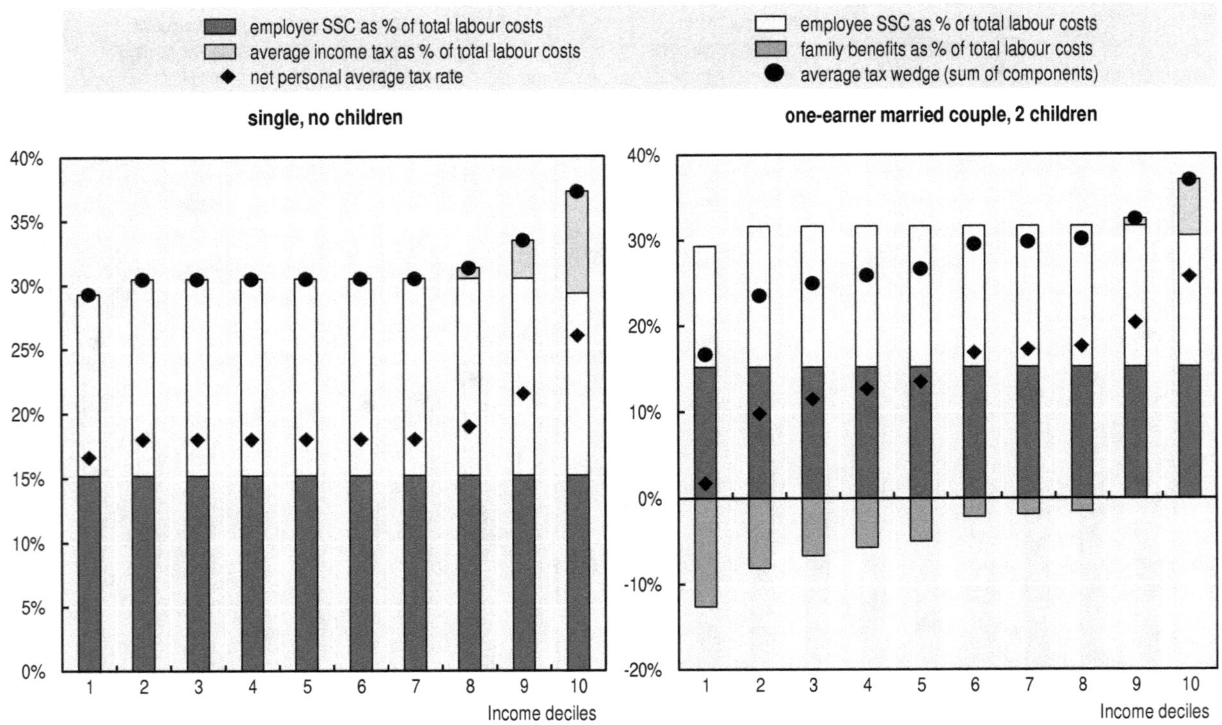

StatLink http://dx.doi.org/10.1787/888933408046

Uruguay 2013: Marginal tax wedge decomposition

By level of gross earnings expressed in income deciles

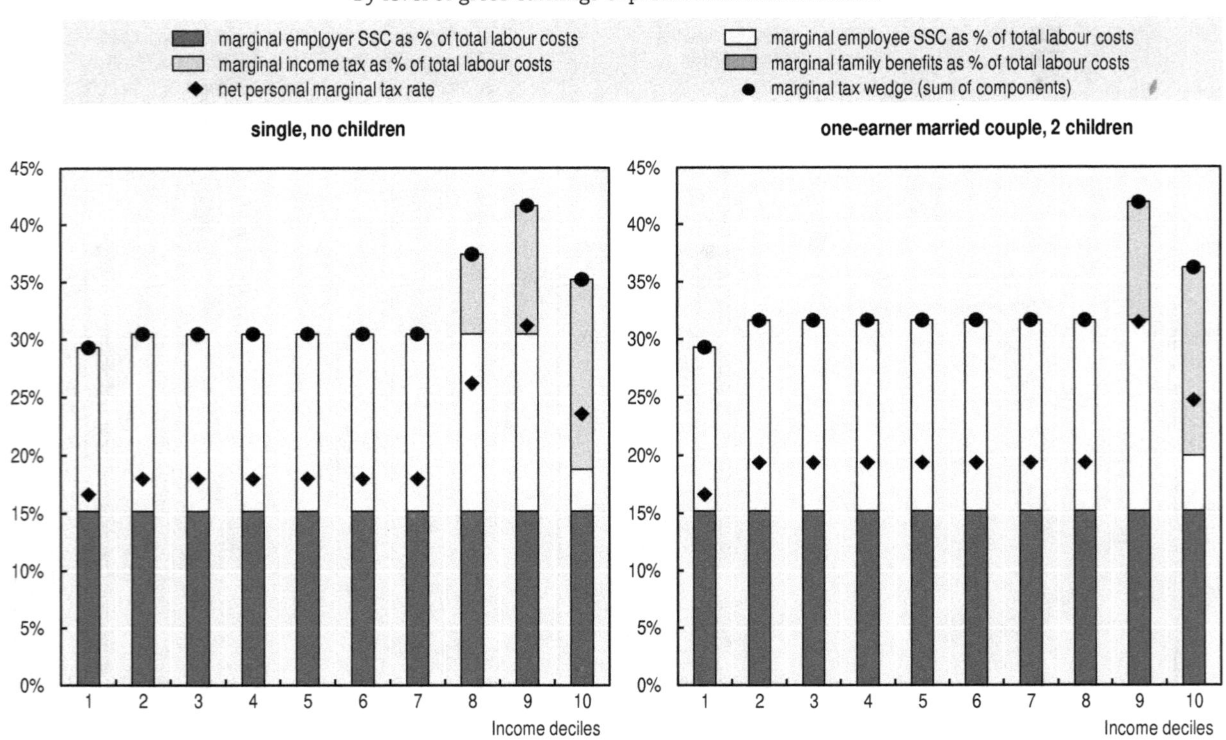

StatLink http://dx.doi.org/10.1787/888933408057

Venezuela 2013: Average tax wedge decomposition

By level of gross earnings expressed in income deciles

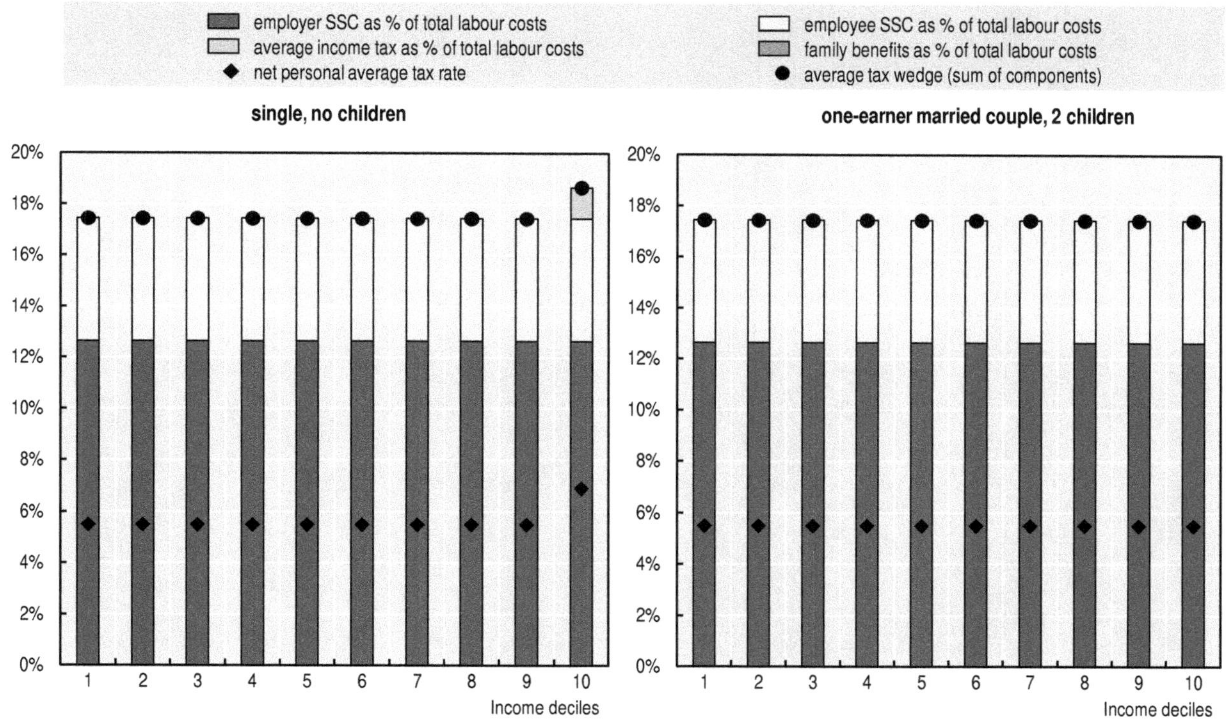

StatLink http://dx.doi.org/10.1787/888933408065

Venezuela 2013: Marginal tax wedge decomposition

By level of gross earnings expressed in income deciles

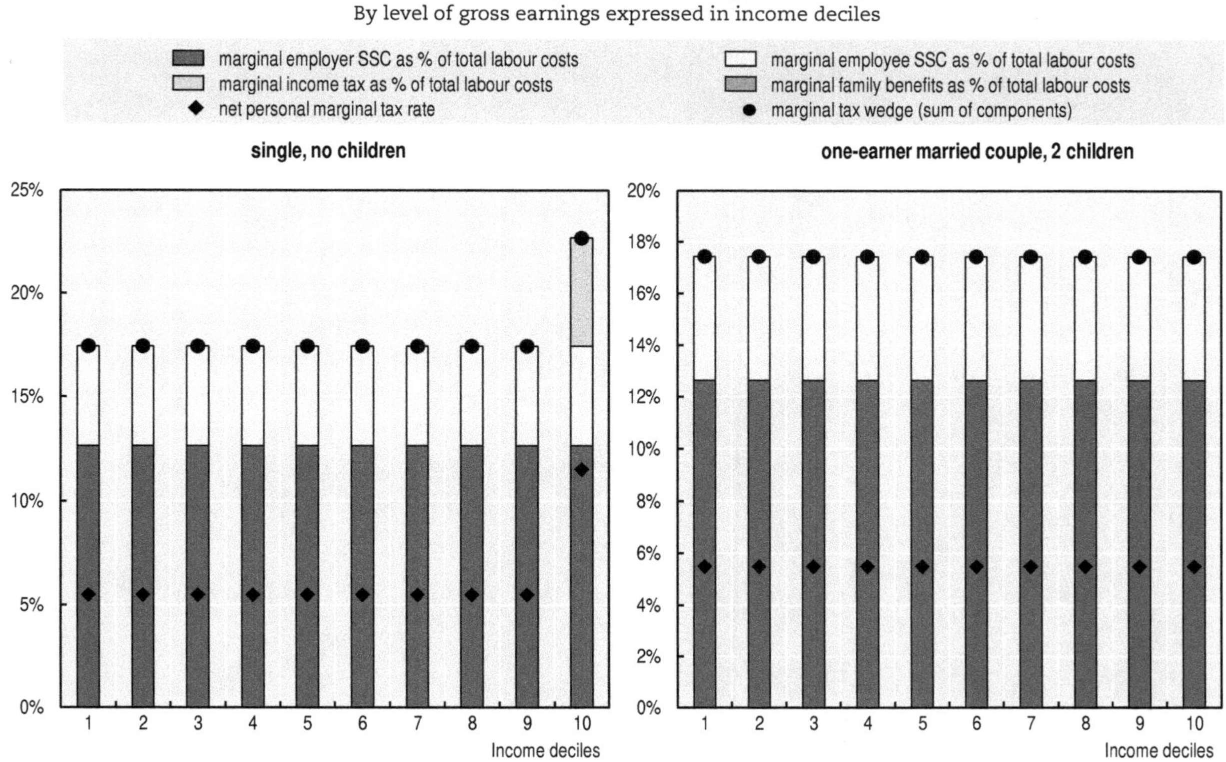

StatLink http://dx.doi.org/10.1787/888933408076

PART II

Country details

This part of the publication provides the individual country details for 2013 that lie behind the comparative analysis of the previous chapters. For each country, a table of detailed country results is followed by a description of the tax/benefit system.

There is a standardized summary for each country for single persons and married couples, each in four different scenarios, which differ by the number of earners in a couple, the level of income and the presence of children in the household (0/2).

All tables begin with the gross wage earnings (line 1) and derive the taxable income for the personal income tax levied by the central government (line 4) taking into account standard deductions (line 2) and taxable cash transfers (line 3). Taxable income leads to a calculation of central government income tax paid (line 7); including reductions in the form of tax credits (line 6). Total payments to the general government (line 10) also include state and local income taxes (line 8) and compulsory employee social security contributions (line 9). Take-home pay (line 12) is calculated as gross wage earnings less all payments to the general government, plus universal cash transfers, usually in respect of children, received from the government.

Line 13 reports social security contributions (including payroll taxes) paid by employers.

The average tax rates (line 14) are then shown as:

- *income tax as a share of gross wage earnings.*
- *employee social security contributions as a share of gross wage earnings;*
- *the share of income tax and employees' social security contributions minus benefits in gross wage earnings; and*
- *the share of income tax and all social security contributions (paid by the employee and the employer) minus benefits in gross labour costs.*

Marginal tax rates (line 15) are presented as:

- *the increase in income tax and employee contributions minus benefits as a share of the related increase in gross wage earnings (both for the principal earner and the spouse); and*
- *the increase in tax and all social security contributions (paid by the employee and the employer) minus cash benefits as a share of the related increase in gross labour costs (both for the principal earner and the spouse).*

Argentina

The country profile includes data on the income taxes paid by workers, their social security contributions, the family benefits they receive in the form of cash transfers as well as the social security contributions and payroll taxes paid by the employers. Results reported include the average and marginal tax burdens for eight different family types.

It also describes the personal income tax systems, all compulsory social security contribution schemes and universal cash transfers as well as recent changes in the tax/benefit system.

Argentina 2013

Tax / benefit of single persons

	Wage level (% of average wage)	67	100	167	67
	Number of children	0	0	0	2
1.	**Gross wage earnings**	77 956	116 352	194 308	77 956
2.	**Standard tax allowances**	106 962	116 352	194 308	124 914
	Basic allowance	16 157	16 157	16 157	16 157
	Married or head of family	0	0	0	0
	Dependent children	0	0	0	17 952
	Deduction for social security contributions and income taxes	13 253	19 780	33 032	13 253
	Work-related expenses	0	0	0	0
	Other	77 553	80 416	145 119	77 553
3.	**Tax credits or cash transfers included in taxable income**	0	0	0	0
4.	**Central government taxable income (1-2+3)**	0	0	0	0
5.	**Central government income tax liability (exclusive of tax credits)**	0	0	0	0
6.	**Tax credits**	0	0	0	0
	Basic credit	0	0	0	0
	Married or head of family	0	0	0	0
	Children	0	0	0	0
	Other	0	0	0	0
7.	**Central government income tax finally paid (5-6)**	0	0	0	0
8.	**State and local taxes**	0	0	0	0
9.	**Employees' compulsory social security contributions**				
	Gross earnings	13 253	19 780	33 032	13 253
10.	**Total payments to general government (7+8+9)**	13 253	19 780	33 032	13 253
11.	**Cash transfers from general government**	0	0	0	4 320
	For head of family	0	0	0	0
	For two children	0	0	0	4 320
12.	**Take-home pay (1-10+11)**	64 703	96 572	161 276	69 023
13.	**Employer's compulsory social security contributions**	21 011	31 360	52 371	21 011
14.	**Average rates**				
	Income tax (7 / 1)	0.0%	0.0%	0.0%	0.0%
	Employees' social security contributions (9 / 1)	17.0%	17.0%	17.0%	17.0%
	Total payments less cash transfers [(10-11) / 1]	17.0%	17.0%	17.0%	17.0%
	Total tax wedge including employer's social security contributions [(10+13-11) / (1+13)]	34.6%	34.6%	34.6%	34.6%
15.	**Marginal rates**				
	Total payments less cash transfers: principal earner	17.0%	17.0%	17.0%	17.0%
	Total payments less cash transfers: spouse	N.A.	N.A.	N.A.	N.A.
	Total tax wedge: principal earner	34.6%	34.6%	34.6%	34.6%
	Total tax wedge: spouse	N.A.	N.A.	N.A.	N.A.

Argentina 2013

Tax / benefit of married couples

		100-0	100-33	100-67	100-33
	Wage level (% of average wage)	100-0	100-33	100-67	100-33
	Number of children	2	2	2	0
1.	**Gross wage earnings**	116 352	154 748	194 308	154 748
2.	**Standard tax allowances**	149 393	249 630	256 355	216 589
	Basic allowance	16 157	32 314	32 314	32 314
	Married or head of family	17 952	0	0	0
	Dependent children	17 952	35 904	35 904	0
	Deduction for social security contributions and income taxes	19 780	26 307	33 032	26 307
	Work-related expenses	0	0	0	0
	Other	77 553	155 105	155 105	157 968
3.	**Tax credits or cash transfers included in taxable income**	0	0	0	0
4.	**Central government taxable income (1-2+3)**	0	0	0	0
5.	**Central government income tax liability (exclusive of tax credits)**	0	0	0	0
6.	**Tax credits**	0	0	0	0
	Basic credit	0	0	0	0
	Married or head of family	0	0	0	0
	Children	0	0	0	0
	Other	0	0	0	0
7.	**Central government income tax finally paid (5-6)**	0	0	0	0
8.	**State and local taxes**	0	0	0	0
9.	**Employees' compulsory social security contributions**				
	Gross earnings	19 780	26 307	33 032	26 307
10.	**Total payments to general government (7+8+9)**	19 780	26 307	33 032	26 307
11.	**Cash transfers from general government**	2 400	2 400	2 400	0
	For head of family	0	0	0	0
	For two children	2 400	2 400	2 400	0
12.	**Take-home pay (1-10+11)**	98 972	130 841	163 676	128 441
13.	**Employer's compulsory social security contributions**	31 360	41 708	52 371	41 708
14.	**Average rates**				
	Income tax (7 / 1)	0.0%	0.0%	0.0%	0.0%
	Employees' social security contributions (9 / 1)	17.0%	17.0%	17.0%	17.0%
	Total payments less cash transfers [(10-11) / 1]	14.9%	15.4%	15.8%	17.0%
	Total tax wedge including employer's social security contributions [(10+13-11) / (1+13)]	33.0%	33.4%	33.6%	34.6%
15.	**Marginal rates**				
	Total payments less cash transfers: principal earner	17.0%	17.0%	17.0%	17.0%
	Total payments less cash transfers: spouse	17.0%	17.0%	17.0%	17.0%
	Total tax wedge: principal earner	34.6%	34.6%	34.6%	34.6%
	Total tax wedge: spouse	34.6%	34.6%	34.6%	34.6%

The national currency is the Argentinian Peso (ARS). In 2013, the average exchange rate was ARS 5.50 to USD 1. In that year, the average worker earned ARS 116 352.

The Report includes estimates of the tax wedge over the whole of the income distribution ordered by deciles of total labour income of formal wage earners derived from the household surveys.

	Deciles of Incomes									
	1	2	3	4	5	6	7	8	9	10
Local currency (ARS)	22 886	38 190	47 220	53 953	59 957	69 645	81 725	94090	113 120	176 514
USD[1]	4 161	6 944	8 586	9 810	10 901	12 663	14 859	17 107	20 567	32093
Dollars in PPP[2]	6 256	10 440	12 909	14 749	16 391	19039	22 341	25 722	30 924	48 254
Ratio to the minimum wage[3]	0.6	1.1	1.3	1.5	1.7	2.0	2.3	2.7	3.2	5.0

1. Average official exchange rates published by the central bank.
2. Calculated using the implied conversion rate (national currency per current international dollar in purchasing power parity) published by the IMF in the World Economic Outlook dataset.
3. Ratio of the income decile to the official minimum wage of the country.

1. Personal income tax system

The fiscal year is the calendar year.

1.1. *Central government income tax*

The income tax law in Argentina recognises several types of income. The first category taxes income and gains obtained from estates and land; the second category applies to investment income and other capital gains; the third category encompasses profits from enterprises and certain trade activities; the fourth category taxes wages from personal work. The latter encompasses all wages, income or compensation from employment; pensions or compensation from previous employment; and any other form of compensation received in exchange for professional services.

Exempt income:

The most noteworthy types of exempt income include:

- Interest paid on deposits by financial institutions subject to the legal financial scheme including savings, special savings accounts, fixed term savings and other forms of deposits as determined by the Central Bank of Argentina.
- Severance payments or payments made with respect to accidents or illness.

1.1.1. *Tax unit*

Members of the family are taxed separately.

The personal income tax applies to all residents levied on their worldwide income. Non-residents are taxed on Argentine-source income only. A legal resident for tax purposes includes persons who are natives of Argentina, those who have become naturalised citizens and foreigners who have either been granted a residence permit or who remain in the country with authorisation to work for a period of 12 years or more.

1.1.2. *Tax allowances and tax credits*

1.1.2.1. Standard tax allowances and tax credits

The decree 1234/2013, that institutes counter-cyclical measures aimed at strengthening the purchasing power of workers and their families, established standard allowances that varied according to three levels of monthly earnings.

- For workers earning up to ARS 15 000 per month, the special deduction for employment was increased by the amount of the difference between the taxable income and the sum of the basic allowance and the deductions for spouse and children. This meant that the taxable income is always exhausted and the tax liability zero.
- For taxpayers earning up to ARS 25 000 per month, allowances are as follows:
  - ARS 16 157 in respect of a basic allowance.
  - ARS 17 952 in respect of the spouse.
  - ARS 8 976 for each child or stepchild aged less than 24 or unable to work.
  - ARS 77 553 for the taxpayer when income relates to employment (fourth category).
  - Social security contributions paid.
- For taxpayers earning above ARS 25 000 per month, allowances are as follows:
  - ARS 15 120 in respect of a basic allowance.
  - ARS 16 800 in respect of the spouse.
  - ARS 8 400 for each child or stepchild aged less than 24 or unable to work.
  - ARS 72 576 for the taxpayer when income relates to employment (fourth category).
  - Social security contributions paid.

1.1.2.2. Main non-standard tax allowances and tax credits

- Life assurance premiums.

1.1.3. *Tax schedule*

The annual income tax liability is calculated on the taxable income according to the following schedule in 2013:

Income (ARS) up to	Marginal rate (%)
10 000	9.0
20 000	14.0
30 000	19.0
60 000	23.0
90 000	27.0
12 000	31.0
above	35.0

1.2. *State and local taxes*

No state or local taxes are levied on wages.

2. Compulsory social security contribution to schemes operated within the government sector

2.1. *Employee contributions*

Program	Marginal rate (%)
Old age, disability and death program	11.0
Integral Medical Attention Program (PAMI)	3.0
Social work (Obra social)	3.0

The employee contributions are levied on gross wages. The lower threshold of earnings was ARS 9 272.00 per year (ARS 772.67 per month) with a ceiling of ARS 301 343.00 per year (ARS 25 111.92 per month) in 2013.

2.1. *Employer contributions*

Employers are required to pay either 17% or 21% of the payroll in social security contributions (depending on the company activities), excluding the component of the Social Work (Obra social). The 17% rate is adopted in this Report as more than 60% of employers pay at this rate. Within this frame, employers are required to contribute to the public programs as follows:

Program	Marginal rate (%)
Old age, disability and death program	10.2
Integral Medical Attention Program (PAMI)	1.5
Unemployment insurance	0.9
Family allowances	4.4
Social work (Obra social)	6.0
Work injury insurance	4.0

The lower threshold for the employer social security contributions is ARS 9 272 per year (ARS 772.67 per month) in 2013. There is no upper threshold.

3. Universal cash transfer

3.1. *Amount for spouse and for dependent children*

Income (ARS) up to	Amount per child (ARS)
2 400	2 400
48 000	3 420
62 400	2 160
82 800	1 200
264 000	0
above	0

4. Main changes in tax/benefits since 2013

The monthly ceiling for social security contributions paid by employees was increased to ARG 56 057 since March 2016.

5. Memorandum items

5.1. *Identification of an AW*

The data refer to the earnings of workers within the formal sector. The average worker's wage was calculated using microdata from the national household surveys.

Bolivia

The country profile includes data on the income taxes paid by workers, their social security contributions, the family benefits they receive in the form of cash transfers as well as the social security contributions and payroll taxes paid by the employers. Results reported include the average and marginal tax burdens for eight different family types.

It also describes the personal income tax systems, all compulsory social security contribution schemes and universal cash transfers as well as recent changes in the tax/benefit system.

Bolivia 2013

Tax / benefit of single persons

	Wage level (% of average wage)	67	100	167	67
	Number of children	0	0	0	2
1.	**Gross wage earnings**	27 082	40 420	67 502	27 082
2.	**Standard tax allowances**	36 128	39 737	47 065	36 128
	Basic allowance	28 800	28 800	28 800	28 800
	Married or head of family	0	0	0	0
	Dependent children	0	0	0	0
	Deduction for social security contributions and income taxes	2 876	4 293	7 169	2 876
	Work-related expenses	0	0	0	0
	Other	4 452	6 644	11096	4 452
3.	**Tax credits or cash transfers included in taxable income**	0	0	0	0
4.	**Central government taxable income (1-2+3)**	0	683	20 437	0
5.	**Central government income tax liability (exclusive of tax credits)**	0	89	2 657	0
6.	**Tax credits**	0	89	2 657	0
	Basic credit	0	89	2 657	0
	Married or head of family	0	0	0	0
	Children	0	0	0	0
	Other	0	0	0	0
7.	**Central government income tax finally paid (5-6)**	0	0	0	0
8.	**State and local taxes**	0	0	0	0
9.	**Employees' compulsory social security contributions**				
	Gross earnings	2 876	4 293	7 169	2 876
10.	**Total payments to general government (7+8+9)**	2 876	4 293	7 169	2 876
11.	**Cash transfers from general government**	0	0	0	0
	For head of family	0	0	0	0
	For two children	0	0	0	0
12.	**Take-home pay (1-10+11)**	24 205	36 127	60 333	24 205
13.	**Employer's compulsory social security contributions**	3 781	5 644	9 425	3 781
14.	**Average rates**				
	Income tax (7 / 1)	0.0%	0.0%	0.0%	0.0%
	Employees' social security contributions (9 / 1)	10.6%	10.6%	10.6%	10.6%
	Total payments less cash transfers [(10-11) / 1]	10.6%	10.6%	10.6%	10.6%
	Total tax wedge including employer's social security contributions [(10+13-11) / (1+ 13)]	21.6%	21.6%	21.6%	21.6%
15.	**Marginal rates**				
	Total payments less cash transfers: principal earner	10.6%	10.6%	10.6%	10.6%
	Total payments less cash transfers: spouse	N.A.	N.A.	N.A.	N.A.
	Total tax wedge: principal earner	21.6%	21.6%	21.6%	21.6%
	Total tax wedge: spouse	N.A.	N.A.	N.A.	N.A.

Bolivia 2013

Tax / benefit of married couples

		Wage level (% of average wage)	100-0	100-33	100-67	100-33
		Number of children	2	2	2	0
1.	**Gross wage earnings**		40 420	53 759	67 502	53 759
2.	**Standard tax allowances**		39 737	70 730	72 989	70 730
	Basic allowance		28 800	57 600	57 600	57 600
	Married or head of family		0	0	0	0
	Dependent children		0	0	0	0
	Deduction for social security contributions and income taxes		4 293	4 293	4 293	4 293
	Work-related expenses		0	0	0	0
	Other		6 644	8 837	11 096	8 837
3.	**Tax credits or cash transfers included in taxable income**		0	0	0	0
4.	**Central government taxable income (1-2+3)**		683	683	683	683
5.	**Central government income tax liability (exclusive of tax credits)**		89	89	89	89
6.	**Tax credits**		89	89	89	89
	Basic credit		89	89	89	89
	Married or head of family		0	0	0	0
	Children		0	0	0	0
	Other		0	0	0	0
7.	**Central government income tax finally paid (5-6)**		0	0	0	0
8.	**State and local taxes**		0	0	0	0
9.	**Employees' compulsory social security contributions**					
	Gross earnings		4 293	4 293	7 169	4 293
10.	**Total payments to general government (7+8+9)**		4 293	4 293	7 169	4 293
11.	**Cash transfers from general government**		0	0	0	0
	For head of family		0	0	0	0
	For two children		0	0	0	0
12.	**Take-home pay (1-10+11)**		36 127	49 466	60 333	49 466
13.	**Employer's compulsory social security contributions**		5 644	5 644	9 425	5 644
14.	**Average rates**					
	Income tax (7 / 1)		0.0%	0.0%	0.0%	0.0%
	Employees' social security contributions (9 / 1)		10.6%	8.0%	10.6%	8.0%
	Total payments less cash transfers [(10-11) / 1]		10.6%	8.0%	10.6%	8.0%
	Total tax wedge including employer's social security contributions [(10+13-11) / (1+13)]		21.6%	16.7%	21.6%	16.7%
15.	**Marginal rates**					
	Total payments less cash transfers: principal earner		10.6%	10.6%	10.6%	10.6%
	Total payments less cash transfers: spouse		0.0%	0.0%	10.6%	0.0%
	Total tax wedge: principal earner		21.6%	21.6%	21.6%	21.6%
	Total tax wedge: spouse		0.0%	0.0%	21.6%	0.0%

The national currency is the Boliviano (BOB). In 2013, the average exchange rate was BOB 6.98 to USD 1. In that year, the average worker earned BOB 40 420.36.

The Report includes estimates of the tax wedge over the whole of the income distribution ordered by deciles of total labour income of formal wage earners derived from the household surveys.

	Deciles of Incomes									
	1	2	3	4	5	6	7	8	9	10
Local currency (BOB)	13 786	19 567	23 749	27 290	31 383	35 996	41 424	49 217	62 119	112 204
USD[1]	1 975	2 803	3 402	3 910	4 496	5 157	5 935	7051	8 900	16075
Dollars in PPP[2]	4 267	6056	7 350	8 446	9 713	11 141	12 821	15 233	19 226	34 727
Ratio to the minimum wage[3]	1.0	1.4	1.6	1.9	2.2	2.5	2.9	3.4	4.3	7.8

1. Average official exchange rates published by the central bank.
2. Calculated using the implied conversion rate (National currency per current international dollar in purchasing power parity) published by the IMF in the World Economic Outlook dataset.
3. Ratio of the income decile to the official minimum wage of the country.

1. Personal income tax system

The tax is paid on a monthly basis and the fiscal year is the calendar year.

1.1. *Central government income tax*

The complementary scheme to the Value Added Tax (RC-IVA according to its initials in Spanish) taxes personal income, inheritances and gains from both capital and labour. Personal income covers wages, salaries, bonuses, and compensations in money received for the provision of services.

Bolivian-source income is derived from any economic activity using assets located in the country. For tax purposes, the nationality, domicile or residence of the recipient is not deemed to be relevant.

Exempt provisions include:

- The Christmas bonus
- Social benefits
- Birth, lactation, pre-family, wedding, family and burial allowances paid to the individuals according to the social security laws.
- Retirement income, pension income, allowances paid due to illness and work injury allowances.

1.1.1. *Tax unit*

Members of the family are taxed separately.

Personal income tax applies to both residents and non-residents who derive income in the country.

1.1.2. *Tax allowances and tax credits*

1.1.2.1. Standard tax allowances and tax credits

- BOB 2 400 (i.e. twice the minimum monthly national wage).
- Employee social security contributions.
- 13% of twice the national minimum wage.

1.1.2.2. Main non-standard tax allowances and tax credits

- A value-added credit can be offset against the tax if the proper documentation is presented.

1.1.3. *Tax schedule*

The tax rate for the complementary scheme to the VAT was 13%:

1.2. *State and local taxes*

No state or local taxes are levied on wages.

2. Compulsory social security contribution to schemes operated within the government sector

2.1. *Employee contributions*

Program	Marginal rate (%)
Old age, disability and death program (SIP)	12.21
Solidarity Fund*	0.50

*These contributions are mandatory and paid to privately managed funds.

Employee contributions are levied on gross wages. The lower earnings threshold was BOB 14 400. The ceiling was BOB 864 000. Mid- and end-year bonuses are exempt from social security contributions.

For employees with earnings higher than BOB 156 000, an additional variable contribution was paid to the Solidarity Fund. In 2013, the schedule was as follows:

Income (BOB) up to	Marginal rate (%)
156 000	0
300 000	1
420 000	5
above	10

2.2. *Employer contributions*

The schedule for employer social security contributions was as follows.

Program	Marginal rate (%)
Healthcare programs	10.0
Work Injury	1.71
Solidarity Fund	3.0
Housing Fund (Provivienda)	2.0

These employer contributions are levied on the payroll. The lower and upper earnings thresholds are the same as for the employee social security contributions. Bonuses paid to employees are exempt from social security contributions.

3. Universal cash transfer

3.1. *Amount for spouse and for dependent children*

None.

4. Main changes in tax/benefit since 2013

The minimum wage increased to BOB 1 656 per month for 2015 and consequently the standard income tax allowances and the lower threshold for employee social security contributions were increased.

5. Memorandum items

5.1. *Identification of an AW*

The data refer to the earnings of workers within the formal sector. The average worker's wage was calculated using microdata from the national household surveys.

Brazil

The country profile includes data on the income taxes paid by workers, their social security contributions, the family benefits they receive in the form of cash transfers as well as the social security contributions and payroll taxes paid by the employers. Results reported include the average and marginal tax burdens for eight different family types.

It also describes the personal income tax systems, all compulsory social security contribution schemes and universal cash transfers as well as recent changes in the tax/benefit system.

Brazil 2013

Tax / benefit of single persons

	Wage level (% of average wage)	67	100	167	67
	Number of children	0	0	0	2
1.	**Gross wage earnings**	15 200	22 686	37 886	15 200
2.	**Standard tax allowances**	3 040	4 537	7 577	5 495
	Basic allowance	0	0	0	0
	Married or head of family	0	0	0	0
	Dependent children	0	0	0	4 127
	Deduction for social security contributions and income taxes	1 368	2042	4 167	1 368
	Work-related expenses	0	0	0	0
	Other	0	0	0	0
3.	**Tax credits or cash transfers included in taxable income**	0	0	0	0
4.	**Central government taxable income (1-2+3)**	12 160	18 149	30 308	9 704
5.	**Central government income tax liability (exclusive of tax credits)**	0	0	733	0
6.	**Tax credits**	0	0	0	0
	Basic credit	0	0	0	0
	Married or head of family	0	0	0	0
	Children	0	0	0	0
	Other	0	0	0	0
7.	**Central government income tax finally paid (5-6)**	0	0	733	0
8.	**State and local taxes**	0	0	0	0
9.	**Employees' compulsory social security contributions**				
	Gross earnings	1 368	2 042	4 167	1 368
10.	**Total payments to general government (7+8+9)**	1 368	2 042	4 901	1 368
11.	**Cash transfers from general government**	0	0	0	0
	For head of family	0	0	0	0
	For two children	0	0	0	0
12.	**Take-home pay (1-10+11)**	13 832	20 644	32 985	13 832
13.	**Employer's compulsory social security contributions**	5 198	7 759	12 957	5 198
14.	**Average rates**				
	Income tax (7 / 1)	0.0%	0.0%	1.9%	0.0%
	Employees' social security contributions (9 / 1)	9.0%	9.0%	11.0%	9.0%
	Total payments less cash transfers [(10-11) / 1]	9.0%	9.0%	12.9%	9.0%
	Total tax wedge including employer's social security contributions [(10+13-11) / (1+13)]	32.2%	32.2%	35.1%	32.2%
15.	**Marginal rates**				
	Total payments less cash transfers: principal earner	9.0%	9.0%	17.0%	9.0%
	Total payments less cash transfers: spouse	N.A.	N.A.	N.A.	N.A.
	Total tax wedge: principal earner	32.2%	32.2%	38.2%	32.2%
	Total tax wedge: spouse	N.A.	N.A.	N.A.	N.A.

Brazil 2013

Tax / benefit of married couples

	Wage level (% of average wage)	100-0	100-33	100-67	100-33
	Number of children	2	2	2	0
1.	**Gross wage earnings**	22 686	30 172	37 886	30 172
2.	**Standard tax allowances**	8 233	12 338	12 338	6 579
	Basic allowance	0	0	0	0
	Married or head of family	2 064	0	0	0
	Dependent children	4 127	4 127	4 127	0
	Deduction for social security contributions and income taxes	2 042	2 641	3 410	2 641
	Work-related expenses	0	0	0	0
	Other	0	0	0	0
3.	**Tax credits or cash transfers included in taxable income**	0	0	0	0
4.	**Central government taxable income (1-2+3)**	14 453	17 834	25 548	23 593
5.	**Central government income tax liability (exclusive of tax credits)**	0	0	0	0
6.	**Tax credits**	0	0	0	0
	Basic credit	0	0	0	0
	Married or head of family	0	0	0	0
	Children	0	0	0	0
	Other	0	0	0	0
7.	**Central government income tax finally paid (5-6)**	0	0	0	0
8.	**State and local taxes**	0	0	0	0
9.	**Employees' compulsory social security contributions**				
	Gross earnings	2 042	2 641	3 410	2 641
10.	**Total payments to general government (7+8+9)**	2 042	2 641	3 410	2 641
11.	**Cash transfers from general government**	0	796	0	0
	For head of family	0	0	0	0
	For two children	0	796	0	0
12.	**Take-home pay (1-10+11)**	20 644	28 328	34 476	27 532
13.	**Employer's compulsory social security contributions**	7 759	10 319	12 957	10 319
14.	**Average rates**				
	Income tax (7 / 1)	0.0%	0.0%	0.0%	0.0%
	Employees' social security contributions (9 / 1)	9.0%	8.8%	9.0%	8.8%
	Total payments less cash transfers [(10-11) / 1]	9.0%	6.1%	9.0%	8.8%
	Total tax wedge including employer's social security contributions [(10+13-11) / (1+ 13)]	32.2%	30.0%	32.2%	32.0%
15.	**Marginal rates**				
	Total payments less cash transfers: principal earner	9.0%	9.0%	9.0%	9.0%
	Total payments less cash transfers: spouse	-2.6%	8.0%	9.0%	8.0%
	Total tax wedge: principal earner	32.2%	32.2%	32.2%	32.2%
	Total tax wedge: spouse	23.5%	31.4%	32.2%	31.4%

The national currency is the Real (BRL). In 2013, the average exchange rate was BRL 2.16 to USD 1. In that year, the average worker earned BRL 22 686.

The Report includes estimates of the tax wedge over the whole of the income distribution ordered by deciles of total labour income of formal wage earners derived from the household surveys.

	Deciles of Incomes									
	1	2	3	4	5	6	7	8	9	10
Local currency (BRL)	7 760	8 389	9 454	10 782	12 359	14 728	17 401	22 196	31 104	75 530
USD[1]	3 600	3 892	4 386	5002	5 734	6 833	8073	10 298	14 431	35 042
Dollars in PPP[2]	4 841	5 233	5 898	6 726	7 710	9 188	10 855	13 846	19 403	47 118
Ratio to the minimum wage[3]	1.0	1.0	1.2	1.3	1.5	1.8	2.1	2.7	3.8	9.3

1. Average official exchange rates published by the central bank.
2. Calculated using the implied conversion rate (national currency per current international dollar in purchasing power parity) published by the IMF in the World Economic Outlook dataset.
3. Ratio of the income decile to official minimum wage of the country.

1. Personal income tax system

The fiscal year is the calendar year.

1.1. Central government income tax

The personal income tax is levied on wages, capital gains, pension income and all types of profits.

In the context of employment, the income tax is applied on wages, salaries, subsidies and vacation remuneration or any other benefits received in exchange for labour services. It is also applied to the profits made by a worker in exchange for services or self-employment.

1.1.1. Tax unit

In this report, it is assumed that members of the family are taxed separately. In practice, spouses may opt to file a joint tax return for the household.

The personal income tax applies to all residents and non-residents receiving an income in the country.

1.1.2. Tax allowances and tax credits

1.1.2.1. Standard tax allowances and tax credits

The Brazilian tax code establishes two alternative mechanisms to establish deductions. The first one is a percentage of the taxable income up to a ceiling and the second involves the summation of individual amounts. The taxpayer is entitled to deduct whichever of these two is the highest.

- Individuals are entitled to a simplified deduction of 20% of the taxable income up to BRL 15 197.

- Alternatively, individuals are entitled to deduct the sum of:
  - BRL 2 063.64 for the spouse.
  - BRL 2 063.64 for each child aged 24 years or less.
  - Employee social security contributions paid to the general government.

1.1.2.2. *Main non-standard tax allowances and tax credits*

- Medical expenses incurred by the taxpayer or his/ her dependents that are not reimbursed through a healthcare insurance program.
- Amounts paid in alimony.
- Contributions to privately managed Brazilian based pension funds.
- Contributions to the Individual Retirement Program (FAPI) up to 12% of the taxable base.
- Annual education expenses up to BRL 3 091.35.
- Social security contributions paid on behalf of a maid who works at the taxpayer's household.
- Contributions to the cultural, sports and children's fund up to 6% of the income tax due.

1.1.3. *Tax schedule*

The annual income tax liability was calculated on the taxable income according to the following schedule in 2013:

Income (BRL) up to	Marginal rate (%)
20 529.36	0.0
30 766.92	7.5
41 023.08	15.0
51 259.08	22.5
above	27.5

1.1.4. *State and local taxes*

No state or local taxes are levied on wages.

2. Compulsory social security contribution to schemes operated within the government sector

2.1. *Employee contributions*

Program	Marginal rate (%)
Old age, disability and death program	8 – 11

Employee social security contributions were levied on the gross income of the individual according to the following schedule in 2013:

Income (BRL) up to	Marginal rate (%)
14 972.40	8
24 954.00	9
49 908.00	11

The lower threshold for contributions was set at BRL 14 972 and the ceiling at BRL 49 908.

2.1. *Employer contributions*

Employers were required to make contributions to the following public programs.

Program	Marginal rate (%)
Old age, disability and healthcare programs	20.0
Work Injury	1.0
Education wage	2.5
FGTS	8.0
National Learning Service	1.0
Social Service	1.5
National Institute for Colonisation and Reform (INCRA)	0.2

The employer contribution rates are applied to the payroll. The ceiling for the contributions was BRL 49 908.

3. Universal cash transfer

3.1. *Amount for spouse and for dependent children*

Income (BRL) up to	Amount per child
7 758.60	397.92
11 661.36	280.32
Above	0

4. Main changes in tax/benefit since 2013

The annual tax schedule was updated as follows for 2015:

Income (BRL) up to	Marginal rate (%)
22 449.13	0
33 477.72	7.5
44 476.74	15.0
55 373.55	22.5
above	27.5

5. Memorandum items

5.1. *Identification of an AW*

The data refer to the earnings of workers within the formal sector. The average worker's wage was calculated using microdata from the national household surveys.

Chile

The country profile includes data on the income taxes paid by workers, their social security contributions, the family benefits they receive in the form of cash transfers as well as the social security contributions and payroll taxes paid by the employers. Results reported include the average and marginal tax burdens for eight different family types.

It also describes the personal income tax systems, all compulsory social security contribution schemes and universal cash transfers as well as recent changes in the tax/benefit system.

Chile 2013

Tax / benefit of single persons

	Wage level (% of average wage)	67	100	167	67
	Number of children	0	0	0	2
1.	**Gross wage earnings**	4 424 961	6 604 419	11 029 380	4 424 961
2.	**Standard tax allowances**	844 283	1 260 123	2 104 406	844 283
	Basic allowance	0	0	0	0
	Married or head of family	0	0	0	0
	Dependent children	0	0	0	0
	Deduction for social security contributions and income taxes	844 283	1 260 123	2 104 406	844 283
	Work-related expenses	0	0	0	0
	Other	0	0	0	0
3.	**Tax credits or cash transfers included in taxable income**	0	0	0	0
4.	**Central government taxable income (1-2+3)**	3 580 678	5 344 296	8 924 974	3 580 678
5.	**Central government income tax liability (exclusive of tax credits)**	0	0	92 796	0
6.	**Tax credits**	0	0	0	205 124
	Basic credit	0	0	0	0
	Married or head of family	0	0	0	0
	Children	0	0	0	205 124
	Other	0	0	0	0
7.	**Central government income tax finally paid (5-6)**	0	0	92 796	0
8.	**State and local taxes**	0	0	0	0
9.	**Employees' compulsory social security contributions**				
	Gross earnings	844 283	1 260 123	2 104 406	844 283
10.	**Total payments to general government (7+8+9)**	844 283	1 260 123	2 197 202	844 283
11.	**Cash transfers from general government**	0	0	0	39 876
	For head of family	0	0	0	0
	For two children	0	0	0	39 876
12.	**Take-home pay (1-10+11)**	3 580 678	5 344 296	8 832 178	3 620 554
13.	**Employer's compulsory social security contributions**	203 991	304 464	508 454	203 991
14.	**Average rates**				
	Income tax (7 / 1)	0.0%	0.0%	0.0%	0.0%
	Employees' social security contributions (9 / 1)	19.1%	19.1%	19.1%	19.1%
	Total payments less cash transfers [(10-11) / 1]	19.1%	19.1%	19.9%	18.2%
	Total tax wedge including employer's social security contributions [(10+13-11) / (1+ 13)]	22.6%	22.6%	23.5%	21.8%
15.	**Marginal rates**				
	Total payments less cash transfers: principal earner	19.1%	19.1%	22.3%	19.1%
	Total payments less cash transfers: spouse	N.A.	N.A.	N.A.	N.A.
	Total tax wedge: principal earner	22.6%	22.6%	25.7%	22.6%
	Total tax wedge: spouse	N.A.	N.A.	N.A.	N.A.

Chile 2013

Tax / benefit of married couples

		Wage level (% of average wage)	100-0	100-33	100-67	100-33
		Number of children	2	2	2	0
1.	**Gross wage earnings**		6 604 419	8 783 877	11 029 380	8 783 877
2.	**Standard tax allowances**		1 260 123	1 675 964	2 104 406	1 675 964
	Basic allowance		0	0	0	0
	Married or head of family		0	0	0	0
	Dependent children		0	0	0	0
	Deduction for social security contributions and income taxes		1 260 123	1 675 964	2 104 406	1 675 964
	Work-related expenses		0	0	0	0
	Other		0	0	0	0
3.	**Tax credits or cash transfers included in taxable income**		0	0	0	0
4.	**Central government taxable income (1-2+3)**		5 344 296	7 107 914	8 924 974	7 107 914
5.	**Central government income tax liability (exclusive of tax credits)**		0	0	0	0
6.	**Tax credits**		102 562	102 562	102 562	0
	Basic credit		0	0	0	0
	Married or head of family		0	0	0	0
	Children		102 562	205 124	205 124	0
	Other		0	0	0	0
7.	**Central government income tax finally paid (5-6)**		0	0	0	0
8.	**State and local taxes**		0	0	0	0
9.	**Employees' compulsory social security contributions**					
	Gross earnings		1 260 123	1 675 964	2 104 406	1 675 964
10.	**Total payments to general government (7+8+9)**		1 260 123	1 675 964	2 104 406	1 675 964
11.	**Cash transfers from general government**		0	196 440	39 876	0
	For head of family		0	0	0	0
	For two children		0	196 440	39 876	0
12.	**Take-home pay (1-10+11)**		5 344 296	7 304 354	8 964 850	7 107 914
13.	**Employer's compulsory social security contributions**		304 464	404 937	508 454	404 937
14.	**Average rates**					
	Income tax (7 / 1)		0.0%	0.0%	0.0%	0.0%
	Employees' social security contributions (9 / 1)		19.1%	19.1%	19.1%	19.1%
	Total payments less cash transfers [(10-11) / 1]		19.1%	16.8%	18.7%	19.1%
	Total tax wedge including employer's social security contributions [(10+13-11) / (1+13)]		22.6%	20.5%	22.3%	22.6%
15.	**Marginal rates**					
	Total payments less cash transfers: principal earner		19.1%	19.1%	19.1%	19.1%
	Total payments less cash transfers: spouse		10.1%	19.1%	19.1%	19.1%
	Total tax wedge: principal earner		22.6%	22.6%	22.6%	22.6%
	Total tax wedge: spouse		14.0%	22.6%	22.6%	22.6%

The national currency is the Chilean Peso (CLP). In 2013, the average exchange rate was CLP 491.31 to USD 1. In that year, the average worker in Chile earned CLP 6 604 419.00.

The Report includes estimates of the tax wedge over the whole of the income distribution ordered by deciles of total labour income of formal wage earners derived from the household surveys.

	Deciles of Incomes									
	1	2	3	4	5	6	7	8	9	10
Local currency (thousands of CLP)	1 685	2 504	2 562	2 746	3 153	3 635	4 449	5 747	8 034	19 322
USD[1]	3 403	5 056	5 174	5 545	6 367	7 340	8 983	11 604	16 222	39 010
Dollars in PPP[2]	4 882	7 252	7 422	7 954	9 134	10 529	12 886	16 645	23 271	55 960
Ratio to the minimum wage[3]	0.7	1.1	1.1	1.2	1.3	1.5	1.9	2.4	3.4	8.1

1. Average official exchange rates published by the central bank.
2. Calculated using the implied conversion rate (national currency per current international dollar in purchasing power parity) published by the IMF in the World Economic Outlook dataset.
3. Ratio of the income decile to the official minimum wage of the country.

Tax allowances and tax thresholds for the personal income tax system and upper earning ceilings for social security contributions are determined by using the Annual Tax Unit (Unidad Tributaria Anual – UTA) and the Foment Unit (Unidad de Fomento – UF). These are expressed in Consumer Price Index (CPI) units. The latter are subject to daily adjustments in line with CPI variations.

Revenue items	Unit	CLP	USD
Social security contributions	Unidad de Fomento (UF)	23 000.56	46.44
Monthly tax thresholds	Unidad Tributaria Mensual (UTM)	40 772.00	82.32
Annual tax thresholds	Unidad Tributaria Anual (UTA)	489 264.00	987.79

1. Personal income tax system

The fiscal year for the income tax is the calendar year.

1.1. *Central government income tax*

The income tax is separately applied in respect of the different categories of income. The first category pertains to capital gains and profits from commercial, industrial, mining and other companies. Labour income is taxed under the second category of income tax. It encompasses salaries, bonuses, allowances, shares and any compensation paid for personal services. The resulting tax liability is credited to the global complementary tax which is calculated and paid on an annual basis.

1.1.1. *Tax unit*

Each family member declares and pays taxes separately.

1.1.2. *Tax allowances and tax credits*

1.1.2.1. Standard tax reliefs

- Employee social security contributions regardless of whether they are paid to government or privately managed insurers.
- A tax credit on education of 4.4 UFs for each child aged 24 years or less possessing an enrollment certificate from an accredited education institution. This credit is paid to households whose combined income does not exceed 792 UFs (CLP 18 461 171.52).

1.1.2.2. Main non-standard tax allowances and tax credits

- Voluntary contributions to pension funds and retirement savings funds with an upper limit of 600 UFs (CPL 13 985 736).
- Taxpayers whose annual income falls below 90 UTAs (44 033 760) are entitled to a 100% deduction of mortgage interest paid. The percentage of the deduction is reduced as the taxpayer's income increases.

1.1.3. *Tax schedule*

The annual income tax liability was calculated on the taxable income according to the following schedule in 2013:

Income (UTA) up to	Income (CLP) up to	Marginal rate (%)
13.5	6 605 064	0.0
30	14 677 920	4.0
50	24 463 200	8.0
70	34 248 480	13.5
90	44 033 760	23.0
120	58 711 680	30.4
150	73 389 600	35.5
above	above	40.0

1.2. *State and local taxes*

No state or local taxes are levied on wages.

2. Compulsory social security contribution to schemes operated within the government sector

2.1. *Employee contributions*

Program	Marginal rate (%)
Old age, disability and survivors programs*	10.0
Healthcare (FONASA)	7.0
Unemployment Insurance*	0.6
AFP Fee*	2.25

*These contributions are mandatory and paid to privately managed insurance funds. Workers can choose whether to pay the healthcare contributions to the government scheme (FONASA) or to a private managed fund.

Employee social security contributions are levied on gross earnings. The upper earnings ceiling for contributions to the old age, disability and survivors program and AFP fees was 70.3 UFs (CLP 19 403 272). The corresponding ceilings for the healthcare program and the unemployment insurance were 70 UFs (CLP 19 320 470) and 105.4 UFs (CLP 29 091 108) respectively.

2.2. Employer contributions

Employers are required to contribute to the following public programs.

Program	Marginal rate (%)
Work injury*	0.95
Unemployment insurance*	2.40
Disability insurance*	1.26
High Risk Occupation Insurance*	0 – 6.8

*Mandatory contributions paid to privately managed funds.

Employer social security contributions are levied on the payroll. The upper earnings ceilings were the same as those applying to the employee contributions.

3. Universal cash transfer

3.1. Amount for spouse and for dependent children

Family allowances are paid to workers with dependent children on a monthly basis. They encompass: a) adopted children; b) children up to the age of 18 or 24 provided they are students in an elementary, secondary, technical or specialised school or higher education in families whose income is less than or equal to half the minimum wage. The amount a household receives is contingent on the number of children and the household's income. The modelling assumes that the benefit is assessed on the spouse with the lower earning level in the cases where both spouses are working.

Schedule of transfers per dependant	
Income (CLP) up to	Annual payment (CLP)
2 537 232.00	98 220.00
3 835 560.00	63 090.00
5 982 162.00	19 938.00
above	0

4. Main changes in tax/benefit since 2013

- The tax schedules and upper earnings ceilings for social security contributions were subject to the CPI variations.

5. Memorandum items

5.1. Identification of an AW

The source of information is a survey conducted by the National Statistics Institute (INE) to determine the Salary and Labour Cost Index. This nationwide survey is carried out on a monthly sample and gathers information on salaries and labour costs. It applies to companies with at least 5-worker payrolls grouped in accordance with UN ISIC Rev. 3 international economic activity standard, covering workers in industry sectors C-O.*

The average gross earnings was obtained by multiplying the average hourly wage by the average number of hours worked. It covers both full and part-time workers.

The average deciles of income were constructed using the national household survey of 2011. The income deciles were adjusted using the Central Bank's real wage index.

Taxing Wages in Latin America and the Caribbean

Colombia

The country profile includes data on the income taxes paid by workers, their social security contributions, the family benefits they receive in the form of cash transfers as well as the social security contributions and payroll taxes paid by the employers. Results reported include the average and marginal tax burdens for eight different family types.

It also describes the personal income tax systems, all compulsory social security contribution schemes and universal cash transfers as well as recent changes in the tax/benefit system.

Colombia 2013

Tax / benefit of single persons

	Wage level (% of average wage)	67	100	167	67
	Number of children	0	0	0	2
1.	**Gross wage earnings**	9 349 326	13 954 218	23 303 544	9 349 326
2.	**Standard tax allowances**	2 829 132	4 222 585	7 051 716	3 764 064
	Basic allowance	0	0	0	0
	Married or head of family	0	0	0	0
	Dependent children	0	0	0	934 933
	Deduction for social security contributions and income taxes	655 734	978 707	1 634 440	655 734
	Work-related expenses	0	0	0	0
	Other	2 173 398	3 243 878	5 417 276	2 173 398
3.	**Tax credits or cash transfers included in taxable income**	0	0	0	0
4.	**Central government taxable income (1-2+3)**	6 520 194	9 731 633	16 251 828	5 585 262
5.	**Central government income tax liability (exclusive of tax credits)**	0	0	0	0
6.	**Tax credits**	0	0	0	0
	Basic credit	0	0	0	0
	Married or head of family	0	0	0	0
	Children	0	0	0	0
	Other	0	0	0	0
7.	**Central government income tax finally paid (5-6)**	0	0	0	0
8.	**State and local taxes**	0	0	0	0
9.	**Employees' compulsory social security contributions**				
	Gross earnings	655 734	978 707	1 634 440	655 734
10.	**Total payments to general government (7+8+9)**	655 734	978 707	1 634 440	655 734
11.	**Cash transfers from general government**	0	0	0	561 332
	For head of family	0	0	0	0
	For two children	0	0	0	561 332
12.	**Take-home pay (1-10+11)**	8 693 593	12 975 511	21 669 104	9 254 925
13.	**Employer's compulsory social security contributions**	3 066 579	4 576 984	7 724 659	3 066 579
14.	**Average rates**				
	Income tax (7 / 1)	0.0%	0.0%	0.0%	0.0%
	Employees' social security contributions (9 / 1)	7.0%	7.0%	7.0%	7.0%
	Total payments less cash transfers [(10-11) / 1]	7.0%	7.0%	7.0%	1.0%
	Total tax wedge including employer's social security contributions [(10+13-11) / (1+13)]	30.0%	30.0%	30.2%	25.5%
15.	**Marginal rates**				
	Total payments less cash transfers: principal earner	7.0%	7.0%	7.0%	7.0%
	Total payments less cash transfers: spouse	N.A.	N.A.	N.A.	N.A.
	Total tax wedge: principal earner	30.0%	30.0%	30.2%	30.0%
	Total tax wedge: spouse	N.A.	N.A.	N.A.	N.A.

Colombia 2013

Tax / benefit of married couples

	Wage level (% of average wage)	100-0	100-33	100-67	100-33
	Number of children	2	2	2	0
1.	**Gross wage earnings**	13 954 218	18 559 110	23 303 544	18 559 110
2.	**Standard tax allowances**	5 618 006	6 769 229	8 447 138	5 373 808
	Basic allowance	0	0	0	0
	Married or head of family	0	0	0	0
	Dependent children	1 395 422	1 395 422	1 395 422	0
	Deduction for social security contributions and income taxes	978 707	978 707	1 634 440	978 707
	Work-related expenses	0	0	0	0
	Other	3 243 878	4 395 101	5 417 276	4 395 101
3.	**Tax credits or cash transfers included in taxable income**	0	0	0	0
4.	**Central government taxable income (1-2+3)**	8 336 212	11 789 881	14 856 406	13 185 302
5.	**Central government income tax liability (exclusive of tax credits)**	0	0	0	0
6.	**Tax credits**	0	0	0	0
	Basic credit	0	0	0	0
	Married or head of family	0	0	0	0
	Children	0	0	0	0
	Other	0	0	0	0
7.	**Central government income tax finally paid (5-6)**	0	0	0	0
8.	**State and local taxes**	0	0	0	0
9.	**Employees' compulsory social security contributions**				
	Gross earnings	978 707	978 707	1 634 440	978 707
10.	**Total payments to general government (7+8+9)**	978 707	978 707	1 634 440	978 707
11.	**Cash transfers from general government**	561 332	1 122 664	1 122 664	0
	For head of family	0	0	0	0
	For two children	561 332	1 122 664	1 122 664	0
12.	**Take-home pay (1-10+11)**	13 536 843	18 703 067	22 791 768	17 580 403
13.	**Employer's compulsory social security contributions**	4 576 984	4 576 984	7 643 562	4 576 984
14.	**Average rates**				
	Income tax (7 / 1)	0.0%	0.0%	0.0%	0.0%
	Employees' social security contributions (9 / 1)	7.0%	5.3%	7.0%	5.3%
	Total payments less cash transfers [(10-11) / 1]	3.0%	-0.8%	2.2%	5.3%
	Total tax wedge including employer's social security contributions [(10+13-11) / (1+13)]	27.0%	19.2%	26.4%	24.0%
15.	**Marginal rates**				
	Total payments less cash transfers: principal earner	7.0%	7.0%	7.0%	7.0%
	Total payments less cash transfers: spouse	-12.2%	0.0%	7.0%	0.0%
	Total tax wedge: principal earner	30.0%	30.0%	30.0%	30.0%
	Total tax wedge: spouse	-12.2%	0.0%	30.0%	0.0%

The national currency is the Colombian Peso (COP). In 2013, the average exchange rate for the year was COP 1 869.10 to USD 1. In that year, the average worker earned COP 13 954 218. There is a Unit of Tax Value (Unidad de Valor Tributario – UVT) which varies over time. The 2012 UVT is applicable to the estimation of the tax liability on income earned in 2013. In that year, the UVT was COP 26 841.

The Report includes estimates of the tax wedge over the whole of the income distribution ordered by deciles of total labour income of formal wage earners derived from the household surveys

	Deciles of Incomes									
	1	2	3	4	5	6	7	8	9	10
Local currency (thousands of COP)	6 868	8 278	8 775	9 532	10 750	12 370	14 997	18 784	26 245	59 216
USD[1]	3 675	4 429	4 695	5 100	5 751	6 618	8 024	10 050	14 042	31 682
Dollars in PPP[2]	5 847	7 047	7 470	8 114	9 150	10 530	12 766	15 989	22 339	50 404
Ratio to the minimum wage[3]	1.0	1.2	1.2	1.3	1.5	1.7	2.1	2.7	3.7	8.4

1. Average official exchange rates published by the central bank.
2. Calculated using the implied conversion rate (National currency per current international dollar in purchasing parity power) published by the IMF in the World Economic Outlook dataset.
3. Ratio of the income decile to the official minimum wage of the country.

1. Personal income tax system

The fiscal year is the calendar year.

1.1. Central government income tax

Colombian tax legislation provides for two alternative systems in addition to the basic model for determining the personal income tax liability. Under the basic model, individual taxpayers are mandated to self-assess their income tax on labour earnings, capital gains on sales of property, occasional profits, as well as profits from companies and foreign entities. The first alternative is the Minimum Alternative Simple Tax (Impuesto Mínimo Alternativo Simple – IMAS) which is an optional system aimed at low wage-earning individuals. The second is the National Minimum Alternative Tax (Impuesto Mínimo Alternativo Nacional – IMAN). This is a presumptive and mandatory system for the determination of the tax base and income tax rate on income and complementary income.

The alternative systems have different allowances and exemptions compared with the ordinary income and complementary tax system.

The determination of the income tax liability takes several steps. An individual must first self-assess the tax liabilities using the IMAN and the basic income tax system and choose the higher of the resulting tax liabilities. If the taxpayer is entitled to use the optional IMAS system, then he/she may elect to pay the lower of the IMAS tax liability and the higher of the IMAN and the basic system.

Exempt income under the basic income tax:

- Work injury or sickness compensation.
- Compensations paid due to maternity leave.
- Funeral expenses
- Old age, disability and work injury compensation that exceed 1 000 UVTs per month.
- Other exemptions applying to public servants such as police officers and members of the military.
- Interest paid on deposits held by financial institutions subject to the financial institutions' legal scheme.
- Severance payments or payments made due to accidents or illness, regardless of whether the payments are made under civil laws, social security or insurance contracts.

1.1.1. *Tax unit*

Each family member declares and pays taxes separately.

1.1.2. *Tax allowances and tax credits*

1.1.2.1. Standard tax allowances and tax credits applying to the basic income tax model

- 25% of wages up to 240 UVTs per month.
- Compulsory employee social security contributions (also applicable to the alternative tax systems – IMAS and IMAN).
- 10% of dependents' gross earnings, regardless of the number of dependents, up to 32 UVTs per month. In the case of married couples, this deduction has been applied to the principal earner in the modelling.

1.1.2.2. Main non-standard tax allowances and tax credits

- Voluntary and mandatory contributions to pension plans limited to either 30% of the annual employment income or 3 800 UVTs in 2013, whichever is lowest.
- Mortgage interest payments made by an employee up to 16 UVTs per month.
- Dividends and interest.
- Health insurance premiums paid in respect of the taxpayer, the spouse and any dependents.
- Charitable donations.

1.1.3. *Tax schedule*

The annual income tax liabilities were calculated on the taxable income according to the following alternative schedules in 2013:

Basic income tax system (2013)		
Income (UVT) up to	Income (COP) up to	Marginal rate (%)
1 090	29 257 000	0
1 700	45 630 000	19
4 100	110 048 000	28
above	above	33

IMAN Tax Schedule (2013)

Income up to (UVT)	Income up to (COP)	Tax liability (UVT)	Tax liability (COP)
1 548	41 549 868	0	0
1 588	42 623 508	1.05	28 183
1 629	43 723 989	1.08	28 988
1 670	44 824 470	1.11	29 794
1 710	45 898 110	1.14	30 599
1 751	46 998 591	1.16	31 136
1 792	48 099 072	2.38	63 882
1 833	49 199 553	2.43	65 224
1 873	50 273 193	2.49	66 834
1 914	51 373 674	4.76	127 763
1 955	52 474 155	4.86	130 447
1 996	53 574 636	4.96	133 131
2 036	54 648 276	8.43	226 270
2 118	56 849 238	8.71	233 785
2 199	59 023 359	13.74	368 795
2 281	61 224 321	14.26	382 753
2 362	63 398 442	19.81	531 720
2 443	65 572 563	25.70	689 814
2 525	67 773 525	26.57	713 165
2 606	69 947 646	35.56	954 466
2 688	72 148 608	45.05	1 209 187
2 769	74 322 729	46.43	1 246 228
2 851	76 523 691	55.58	1 491 823
2 932	78 697 812	60.70	1 629 249
3 014	80 898 774	66.02	1 772 043
3 095	83 072 895	71.54	1 920 205
3 177	85 273 857	77.24	2 073 199
3 258	87 447 978	83.14	2 231 561
3 339	89 622 099	89.23	2 395 022
3 421	91 823 061	95.51	2 563 584
3 502	93 997 182	101.98	2 737 245
3 584	96 198 144	108.64	2 916 006
3 665	98 372 265	115.49	3 099 867
3 747	100 573 227	122.54	3 289 096
3 828	102 747 348	129.76	3 482 888
3 910	104 948 310	137.18	3 682 048
3 991	107 122 431	144.78	3 886 040
4 072	109 296 552	152.58	4 095 400
4 276	114 772 116	168.71	4 528 345
4 480	120 247 680	189.92	5 097 643
4 683	125 696 403	212.27	5 697 539
4 887	131 171 967	235.75	6 327 766
5 091	136 647 531	260.34	6 987 786
5 294	142 096 254	286.03	7 677 331
5 498	147 571 818	312.81	8 396 133
5 701	153 020 541	340.66	9 143 655
5 905	158 496 105	369.57	9 919 628
6 109	163 971 669	399.52	10 723 516
6 312	169 420 392	430.49	11 554 782
6 516	174 895 956	462.46	12 412 889
6 720	180 371 520	495.43	13 297 837
6 923	185 820 243	529.36	14 208 552
7 127	191 295 807	564.23	15 144 497
7 330	196 744 530	600.04	16 105 674
7 534	202 220 094	636.75	17 091 007
7 738	207 695 658	674.35	18 100 228

IMAN Tax Schedule (2013)

Income up to (UVT)	Income up to (COP)	Tax liability (UVT)	Tax liability (COP)
7 941	213 144 381	712.80	19 132 265
8 145	218 619 945	752.10	20 187 116
8 349	224 095 509	792.22	21 263 977
8 552	229 544 232	833.12	22 361 774
8 756	235 019 796	874.79	23 480 238
8 959	240 468 519	917.21	24 618 834
9 163	245 944 083	960.34	25 776 486
9 367	251 419 647	1 004.16	26 952 659
9 570	256 868 370	1 048.64	28 146 546
9 774	262 343 934	1 093.75	29 357 344
9 978	267 819 498	1 139.48	30 584 783
10 181	273 268 221	1 185.78	31 827 521
10 385	278 743 785	1 232.62	33 084 753
10 588	284 192 508	1 279.99	34 356 212
10 792	289 668 072	1 327.85	35 640 822
10 996	295 143 636	1 376.16	36 937 511
11 199	300 592 359	1 424.90	38 245 741
11 403	306 067 923	1 474.04	39 564 708
11 607	311 543 487	1 523.54	40 893 337
11 810	316 992 210	1 573.37	42 230 824
12 014	322 467 774	1 623.49	43 576 095
12 217	327 916 497	1 673.89	44 928 881
12 421	333 392 061	1 724.51	46 287 573
12 625	338 867 625	1 775.33	47 651 633
12 828	344 316 348	1 826.31	49 019 987
13 032	349 791 912	1 877.42	50 391 830
13 236	355 267 476	1 928.63	51 766 358
13 439	360 716 199	1 979.89	53 142 227
13 643	366 191 763	2 031.18	54 518 902
above	above	= (27% of taxable income) – 1 622	= (27% of taxable income) – 43 506 102

IMAS Tax Schedule (2013)

Income up to (UVT)	Income up to (COP)	Tax liability (UVT)	Tax liability (COP)
1 548	41 549 868	0.00	0
1 588	42 623 508	1.08	28 988
1 629	43 723 989	1.10	29 525
1 670	44 824 470	1.13	30 330
1 710	45 898 110	1.16	31 136
1 751	46 998 591	1.19	31 941
1 792	48 099 072	2.43	65 224
1 833	49 199 553	2.48	66 566
1 873	50 273 193	2.54	68 176
1 914	51 373 674	4.85	130 179
1 955	52 474 155	4.96	133 131
1 996	53 574 636	5.06	135 815
2 036	54 648 276	8.60	230 833
2 118	56 849 238	8.89	238 616
2 199	59 023 359	14.02	376 311
2 281	61 224 321	20.92	561 514
2 362	63 398 442	29.98	804 693
2 443	65 572 563	39.03	1 047 604
2 525	67 773 525	48.08	1 290 515
2 606	69 947 646	57.14	1 533 695

IMAS Tax Schedule (2013)			
Income up to (UVT)	Income up to (COP)	Tax liability (UVT)	Tax liability (COP)
2 688	72 148 608	66.19	1 776 606
2 769	74 322 729	75.24	2 019 517
2 851	76 523 691	84.30	2 262 696
2 932	78 697 812	93.35	2 505 607
3 014	80 898 774	102.40	2 748 518
3 095	83 072 895	111.46	2 991 698
3 177	85 273 857	122.79	3 295 806
3 258	87 447 978	136.13	3 653 865
3 339	89 622 099	149.47	4 011 924
3 421	91 823 061	162.82	4 370 252
3 502	93 997 182	176.16	4 728 311
3 584	96 198 144	189.50	5 086 370
3 665	98 372 265	202.84	5 444 428
3 747	100 573 227	216.18	5 802 487
3 828	102 747 348	229.52	6 160 546
3 910	104 948 310	242.86	6 518 605
3 991	107 122 431	256.21	6 876 933
4 072	109 296 552	269.55	7 234 992
4 276	114 772 116	282.89	7 593 050
4 480	120 247 680	316.24	8 488 198
4 683	125 696 403	349.60	9 383 614
4 700	126 152 700	382.95	10 278 761

1.2. State and local taxes

No state or local taxes are levied on wages.

2. Compulsory social security contribution to schemes operated within the government sector

2.1. Employee contributions

Employee social security contributions are levied on gross earnings. Income in respect of vacations and other monetary bonuses received by workers are exempt.

- There is a rate of 4% for the old age, disability and survivors programs. The lower earnings threshold is the minimum wage (the annual minimum wage was COP 7 704 000 in 2013). The upper ceiling is 25 times the minimum wage (COP 176 850 000 per year in 2013).
- The contribution rate and earnings thresholds for the healthcare contributions are the same as for the old age program.

In addition, contributions to the Solidarity Fund for Pensions are levied on taxable income above 4 times the minimum wage according to the following monthly schedule:

Income up to (Number of times the minimum wage)	Income up to (COP)	Marginal rate (%)
4	28 296 000	0
16	113 184 000	1.0
17	120 258 000	1.2
18	127 332 000	1.4
19	134 406 000	1.6
20	141 480 000	1.8
above	above	2.0

2.2. Employer contributions

Program	Marginal rate (%)	Lower threshold (COP)	Upper threshold (COP)
Old age pensions	12.0	7 074 000	176 850 000
Healthcare	8.5	7 074 000	176 850 000
Work injury	0.348	14 148 000	176 850 000
Unemployment insurance	8.3	7 074 000	176 850 000
Instituto Colombiano de Bienestar Familiar	3.0	70 740 000	176 850 000
Servicio Nacional de Aprendizaje	2.0	70 740 000	176 850 000
Cajas de Compensación Familiar	4.0	7 074 000	176 850 000

The employer social security contributions are levied on the payroll. The lower earnings thresholds and the upper ceilings constitute various multiples of the minimum wage (COP 7 074 000 in 2013).

3. Universal cash transfer

3.1. Amount for spouse and for dependent children

The "Family Subsidy" is paid on a monthly basis, in respect of all dependents in the household, to a single earner working 96 hours or more per month with a monthly wage not exceeding COP 2 358 000 (4 times the minimum wages). For employed couples, the requirement to receive this subsidy is that the sum of their gross wages does not exceed COP 3 537 000 (6 times the minimum wage).

Eligible individuals, economically dependent on the worker, include children, stepchildren, orphans, and parents aged over 60.

The amount of the monthly transfer which is constant throughout the year varies between geographical regions. The annual average allowance in 2013 was COP 280 666 per dependent.

4. Main changes in tax/benefit since 2013

The amount of the UVT is adjusted each year impacting on each of the three personal income tax schedules. The UVT for 2016 is 29 753.

5. Memorandum items

5.1. Identification of an AW

The source of information is the Integrated Household Survey conducted by the National Administrative Department of Statistics (DANE). The average gross earnings are obtained by multiplying the average hourly wage by the average number of hours worked, according to the quarterly reports and expressed on a monthly basis. The figures cover full time workers (taking into account people working 40 hours or more per week in their main jobs). The data on the income deciles distribution refers to the earnings of workers within the formal sector.

Costa Rica

The country profile includes data on the income taxes paid by workers, their social security contributions, the family benefits they receive in the form of cash transfers as well as the social security contributions and payroll taxes paid by the employers. Results reported include the average and marginal tax burdens for eight different family types.

It also describes the personal income tax systems, all compulsory social security contribution schemes and universal cash transfers as well as recent changes in the tax/benefit system.

Costa Rica 2013

Tax / benefit of single persons

		67	100	167	67
	Wage level (% of average wage)	67	100	167	67
	Number of children	0	0	0	2
1.	**Gross wage earnings**	3 756 893	5 607 303	9 364 195	3 756 893
2.	**Standard tax allowances**	308 786	460 874	769 660	308 786
	Basic allowance	0	0	0	0
	Married or head of family	0	0	0	0
	Dependent children	0	0	0	0
	Deduction for social security contributions and income taxes	0	0	0	0
	Work-related expenses	0	0	0	0
	Other	308 786	460 874	769 660	308 786
3.	**Tax credits or cash transfers included in taxable income**	0	0	0	0
4.	**Central government taxable income (1-2+3)**	3 448 107	5 146 428	8 594 535	3 448 107
5.	**Central government income tax liability (exclusive of tax credits)**	0	0	2 654	0
6.	**Tax credits**	0	0	0	32 160
	Basic credit	0	0	0	0
	Married or head of family	0	0	0	0
	Children	0	0	0	32 160
	Other	0	0	0	0
7.	**Central government income tax finally paid (5-6)**	0	0	2 654	-32 160
8.	**State and local taxes**	0	0	0	0
9.	**Employees' compulsory social security contributions**				
	Gross earnings	344 507	514 190	858 697	344 507
10.	**Total payments to general government (7+8+9)**	344 507	514 190	861 350	312 347
11.	**Cash transfers from general government**	0	0	0	0
	For head of family	0	0	0	0
	For two children	0	0	0	0
12.	**Take-home pay (1-10+11)**	3 412 386	5 093 113	8 502 845	3 444 546
13.	**Employer's compulsory social security contributions**	983 179	1 467 431	2 450 610	983 179
14.	**Average rates**				
	Income tax (7 / 1)	0.0%	0.0%	0.0%	-0.9%
	Employees' social security contributions (9 / 1)	9.2%	9.2%	9.2%	9.2%
	Total payments less cash transfers [(10-11) / 1]	9.2%	9.2%	9.2%	8.3%
	Total tax wedge including employer's social security contributions [(10+13-11) / (1+13)]	28.0%	28.0%	28.0%	27.3%
15.	**Marginal rates**				
	Total payments less cash transfers: principal earner	9.2%	9.2%	18.3%	9.2%
	Total payments less cash transfers: spouse	N.A.	N.A.	N.A.	N.A.
	Total tax wedge: principal earner	28.0%	28.0%	35.3%	28.0%
	Total tax wedge: spouse	N.A.	N.A.	N.A.	N.A.

Costa Rica

Tax / benefit of married couples

		100-0	100-33	100-67	100-33
	Wage level (% of average wage)	100-0	100-33	100-67	100-33
	Number of children	2	2	2	0
1.	**Gross wage earnings**	5 607 303	7 457 712	9 364 195	7 457 712
2.	**Standard tax allowances**	460 874	612 963	769 660	612 963
	Basic allowance	0	0	0	0
	Married or head of family	0	0	0	0
	Dependent children	0	0	0	0
	Deduction for social security contributions and income taxes	0	0	0	0
	Work-related expenses	0	0	0	0
	Other	460 874	612 963	769 660	612 963
3.	**Tax credits or cash transfers included in taxable income**	0	0	0	0
4.	**Central government taxable income (1-2+3)**	5 146 428	6 844 750	8 594 535	6 844 750
5.	**Central government income tax liability (exclusive of tax credits)**	0	0	0	0
6.	**Tax credits**	56 160	56 160	56 160	24 000
	Basic credit	0	0	0	0
	Married or head of family	24 000	24 000	24 000	24 000
	Children	32 160	32 160	32 160	0
	Other	0	0	0	0
7.	**Central government income tax finally paid (5-6)**	-56 160	-56 160	-56 160	-24 000
8.	**State and local taxes**	0	0	0	0
9.	**Employees' compulsory social security contributions**				
	Gross earnings	514 190	514 190	841 714	514 190
10.	**Total payments to general government (7+8+9)**	458 030	458 030	785 554	490 190
11.	**Cash transfers from general government**	0	0	0	0
	For head of family	0	0	0	0
	For two children	0	0	0	0
12.	**Take-home pay (1-10+11)**	5 149 273	6 999 683	8 578 642	6 967 523
13.	**Employer's compulsory social security contributions**	1 467 431	1 467 431	2 450 610	1 467 431
14.	**Average rates**				
	Income tax (7 / 1)	-1.0%	-0.8%	-0.6%	-0.3%
	Employees' social security contributions (9 / 1)	9.2%	6.9%	9.0%	6.9%
	Total payments less cash transfers [(10-11) / 1]	8.2%	6.1%	8.4%	6.6%
	Total tax wedge including employer's social security contributions [(10+13-11) / (1+13)]	27.2%	21.6%	27.4%	21.9%
15.	**Marginal rates**				
	Total payments less cash transfers: principal earner	9.2%	9.2%	9.2%	9.2%
	Total payments less cash transfers: spouse	0.0%	0.0%	8.7%	0.0%
	Total tax wedge: principal earner	28.0%	28.0%	28.0%	28.0%
	Total tax wedge: spouse	0.0%	0.0%	27.7%	0.0%

The national currency is the Costa Rican colon (CRC). In 2013, the average exchange rate was CRC 490.67 to USD 1. In that year, the average worker earned CRC 5 607 302.63.

The Report includes estimates of the tax wedge over the whole of the income distribution ordered by deciles of total labour income of formal wage earners derived from the household surveys.

	Deciles of Incomes									
	1	2	3	4	5	6	7	8	9	10
Local currency (thousands of CRC)	1 362	2 361	2 834	3 204	3 630	4 210	5057	6 473	9 192	17 181
USD[1]	2 777	4 813	5 776	6 531	7 400	8 581	10 307	13 192	18 736	35016
Dollars in PPP[2]	3 750	6 499	7 799	8 818	9 991	11 586	13 916	17 812	25 296	47 277
Ratio to the minimum wage[3]	0.4	0.7	0.8	0.9	1.1	1.2	1.5	1.9	2.7	5.0

1. Average official exchange rates published by the central bank.
2. Calculated using the implied conversion rate (National currency per current international dollar in purchasing power parity) published by the IMF in the World Economic Outlook dataset.
3. Ratio of the income decile to the official minimum wage of the country.

1. Personal income tax system

The fiscal year runs from October to September.

1.1. *Central government income tax*

The Costa Rican income tax is applied to the income in cash or in kind, both continuous or occasional, from any Costa Rican source obtained or accrued by individuals or legal entities domiciled in the country;

Costa Rica's labour legislation provides for a payment of an additional salary or «bonus» paid in December of each year. The amount is determined by the worker's monthly average wage from all sources. It is exempt from the income tax.

1.1.1. *Tax unit*

In this report, it is assumed that members of the family are taxed separately. In practice, spouses may opt to file a joint tax return for the household.

The personal income tax applies to Costa Rican nationals receiving income from a Costa Rican source, regardless of whether or not they have resided in the country during the relevant fiscal period.

1.1.2. *Tax allowances and tax credits*

1.1.2.1. Standard tax credits

- CRC 16 080 for each child in the household.
- CRC 24 000 for the spouse, which can only be claimed by one of the spouses.

1.1.2.2. Main non-standard tax allowances and tax credits

None

1.1.3. *Tax schedule*

The annual income tax liability was calculated on the taxable income according to the following schedule in 2013:

Income (CRC) up to	Marginal rate (%)
8 568 000	0
12 852 000	10
above	15

1.2. *State and local taxes*

No state or local taxes are levied on wages.

2. Compulsory social security contribution to schemes operated within the government sector

2.1. *Employee contributions*

Program	Marginal rate (%)
Old age, disability and death program (IVM)	2.67
Healthcare and Maternity Insurance (SEM)	5.50
Popular Bank Fee	1.0

The employee contributions are levied on the gross wage. The lower earnings threshold is the minimum national wage, which was equal to CRC 3 106 464 in 2013.

2.2. *Employer contributions*

Employers are required to contribute to the following public programs.

Program	Marginal rate (%)
Old age, disability and death program (IVM)	4.92
Healthcare and Maternity Insurance (SEM)	9.25
Popular Bank Fee	0.50
Unemployment insurance	3.00
Family allowances	5.00
Complementary pensions	1.50
Learning National Institute (INA)	1.50
Joint Institute for Social Aid (IMAS)	0.50

The employer contributions are levied on the gross payroll.

3. Universal cash transfer

3.1. *Amount for spouse and for dependent children*

None.

4. Main changes in tax/benefit since 2013

The tax schedule for the 2015 fiscal year was as follows:

Income (CRC) up to	Marginal rate (%)
9 516 000	0
14 280 000	10
above	15

The contribution rate for the employee social security contributions to the old age, disability and death program were increased in 2015.

Program	Marginal rate (%)
Old age, disability and death program (IVM)	2.84

The employer social security contribution rate for the same program was also increased.

Program	Marginal rate (%)
Old age, disability and death program (IVM)	5.08

5. Memorandum items

5.1. *Identification of an AW*

The data refer to the earnings of workers within the formal sector. The average worker's wage was calculated using microdata from the national household surveys.

Dominican Republic

The country profile includes data on the income taxes paid by workers, their social security contributions, the family benefits they receive in the form of cash transfers as well as the social security contributions and payroll taxes paid by the employers. Results reported include the average and marginal tax burdens for eight different family types.

It also describes the personal income tax systems, all compulsory social security contribution schemes and universal cash transfers as well as recent changes in the tax/benefit system.

Dominican Republic 2013

Tax / benefit of single persons

	Wage level (% of average wage)	67	100	167	67
	Number of children	0	0	0	2
1.	**Gross wage earnings**	151 394	225 961	377 355	151 394
2.	**Standard tax allowances**	4 345	6 485	10 830	4 345
	Basic allowance	0	0	0	0
	Married or head of family	0	0	0	0
	Dependent children	0	0	0	0
	Deduction for social security contributions and income taxes	4 345	6 485	10 830	4 345
	Work-related expenses	0	0	0	0
	Other	0	0	0	0
3.	**Tax credits or cash transfers included in taxable income**	0	0	0	0
4.	**Central government taxable income (1-2+3)**	147 049	219 476	366 525	147 049
5.	**Central government income tax liability (exclusive of tax credits)**	0	0	0	0
6.	**Tax credits**	0	0	0	0
	Basic credit	0	0	0	0
	Married or head of family	0	0	0	0
	Children	0	0	0	0
	Other	0	0	0	0
7.	**Central government income tax finally paid (5-6)**	0	0	0	0
8.	**State and local taxes**	0	0	0	0
9.	**Employees' compulsory social security contributions**				
	Gross earnings	9 023	13 467	22 490	9 023
10.	**Total payments to general government (7+8+9)**	9 023	13 467	22 490	9 023
11.	**Cash transfers from general government**	0	0	0	0
	For head of family	0	0	0	0
	For two children	0	0	0	0
12.	**Take-home pay (1-10+11)**	142 371	212 494	354 864	142 371
13.	**Employer's compulsory social security contributions**	24 813	37 035	61 848	24 813
14.	**Average rates**				
	Income tax (7 / 1)	0.0%	0.0%	0.0%	0.0%
	Employees' social security contributions (9 / 1)	6.0%	6.0%	6.0%	6.0%
	Total payments less cash transfers [(10-11) / 1]	6.0%	6.0%	6.0%	6.0%
	Total tax wedge including employer's social security contributions [(10+13-11) / (1+13)]	19.2%	19.2%	19.2%	19.2%
15.	**Marginal rates**				
	Total payments less cash transfers: principal earner	6.0%	6.0%	6.0%	6.0%
	Total payments less cash transfers: spouse	N.A.	N.A.	N.A.	N.A.
	Total tax wedge: principal earner	19.2%	19.2%	19.2%	19.2%
	Total tax wedge: spouse	N.A.	N.A.	N.A.	N.A.

Dominican Republic 2013

Tax / benefit of married couples

	Wage level (% of average wage)	100-0	100-33	100-67	100-33
	Number of children	2	2	2	0
1.	**Gross wage earnings**	225 961	300 528	377 355	300 528
2.	**Standard tax allowances**	6 485	6 485	10 830	6 485
	Basic allowance	0	0	0	0
	Married or head of family	0	0	0	0
	Dependent children	0	0	0	0
	Deduction for social security contributions and income taxes	6 485	6 485	10 830	6 485
	Work-related expenses	0	0	0	0
	Other	0	0	0	0
3.	**Tax credits or cash transfers included in taxable income**	0	0	0	0
4.	**Central government taxable income (1-2+3)**	219 476	294 043	366 525	294 043
5.	**Central government income tax liability (exclusive of tax credits)**	0	0	0	0
6.	**Tax credits**	0	0	0	0
	Basic credit	0	0	0	0
	Married or head of family	0	0	0	0
	Children	0	0	0	0
	Other	0	0	0	0
7.	**Central government income tax finally paid (5-6)**	0	0	0	0
8.	**State and local taxes**	0	0	0	0
9.	**Employees' compulsory social security contributions**				
	Gross earnings	13 467	13 467	22 490	13 467
10.	**Total payments to general government (7+8+9)**	13 467	13 467	22 490	13 467
11.	**Cash transfers from general government**	0	0	0	0
	For head of family	0	0	0	0
	For two children	0	0	0	0
12.	**Take-home pay (1-10+11)**	212 494	287 061	354 864	287 061
13.	**Employer's compulsory social security contributions**	37 035	37 930	61 848	37 930
14.	**Average rates**				
	Income tax (7 / 1)	0.0%	0.0%	0.0%	0.0%
	Employees' social security contributions (9 / 1)	6.0%	4.5%	6.0%	4.5%
	Total payments less cash transfers [(10-11) / 1]	6.0%	4.5%	6.0%	4.5%
	Total tax wedge including employer's social security contributions [(10+13-11) / (1+13)]	19.2%	15.2%	19.2%	15.2%
15.	**Marginal rates**				
	Total payments less cash transfers: principal earner	6.0%	6.0%	6.0%	6.0%
	Total payments less cash transfers: spouse	0.0%	0.0%	6.0%	0.0%
	Total tax wedge: principal earner	19.2%	19.2%	19.2%	19.2%
	Total tax wedge: spouse	1.2%	1.2%	19.2%	1.2%

The national currency is the Dominican Peso (DOP). In 2013, the average exchange rate was DOP 41.81 to USD 1. In that year, the average worker earned DOP 225 960.84.

The Report includes estimates of the tax wedge over the whole of the income distribution ordered by deciles of total labour income of formal wage earners derived from the household surveys.

	Deciles of Incomes									
	1	2	3	4	5	6	7	8	9	10
Local currency (DOP)	59 279	83 553	102 549	123 912	146 895	172 401	201 375	260 713	376 255	754 652
USD[1]	1 418	1 999	2 453	2 964	3 514	4 124	4 817	6 236	9 000	18 051
Dollars in PPP[2]	2 941	4 146	5 088	6 148	7 289	8 554	9 992	12 936	18 669	37 444
Ratio to the minimum wage[3]	0.6	0.8	1.0	1.2	1.4	1.7	1.9	2.5	3.6	7.3

1. Average official exchange rates published by the central bank.
2. Calculated using the implied conversion rate (National currency per current international dollar in purchasing power parity) published by the IMF in the World Economic Outlook dataset.
3. Ratio of the income decile to the official minimum wage of the country.

1. Personal income tax system

The fiscal year is the calendar year.

1.1. *Central government income tax*

The personal income tax is levied on income from all sources (domestic and global), including those obtained by performing personal work (salaried or independent). Employment income includes salaries, bonuses, premiums, commissions and allowances (housing and education) and in-kind benefits.

The main exemptions for the personal income tax are:

- Compensation paid due to work injury.
- Amounts paid in compliance with life insurance contracts.
- All severance and job termination compensation received in accordance with the Labour Code.
- Compensation paid due to disability or illness.
- Alimonies determined by law.

1.1.1. *Tax unit*

Members of the family are taxed separately

Resident individuals are subject to the income tax on their domestic and global income. Non-residents are subject to the tax on their income derived from Dominican Republic sources.

1.1.2. *Tax allowances and tax credits*

1.1.2.1. Standard tax allowances and tax credits

- Contributions to approved social security plans that benefit the employee up to 5% of the taxable income during a fiscal year.

1.1.2.2. Main non-standard tax allowances and tax credits

- Expenses incurred to maintain a source of income.

1.1.3. *Tax schedule*

The annual income tax liability is calculated on the taxable income according to the following schedule in 2013:

Income (DOP)up to	Marginal rate (%)
399 923	0
599 884	15
833 171	20
above	25

*There is an additional tax of 29% on the value of fringe benefits provided by employers to their employees. Such benefits are in addition to the wages received by the employee.

1.2. *State and local taxes*

No state or local taxes are levied on wages.

2. Compulsory social security contribution to schemes operated within the government sector

2.1. *Employee contributions*

Program	Marginal rate (%)
Old age, disability and survivors program	2.87
Healthcare program	3.04
Professional Training Institute – INFOTEP	0.05

Employees pay social security contributions on their gross wages. The lower earnings threshold is the minimum wage (DOP 8 648 per month and DOP 103 776 annually in 2013). The upper earnings ceilings for contributions vary between programs. The old age, disability and survivor's program has a ceiling of 20 times the minimum wage; the ceilings for the health care program and the professional training institute contributions are 10 times the minimum wage.

2.2. *Employer contributions*

Employers are required to contribute to the following public programs.

Program	Marginal rate (%)
Old age, retirement and disability program	7.10
Healthcare	7.09
Work injury	1.20
Professional Training Institute – INFOTEP	1.00

The employer social security contribution rates are applied to the payroll. The upper earnings ceiling for the old age, disability and survivor's program is set at 20 times the minimum wage. The corresponding ceilings for the Healthcare program, Professional Training Institute and Work injury programs are 10 times the minimum wage.

3. Universal cash transfer

3.1. *Amount for spouse and for dependent children*

None.

4. Main changes in tax/benefit since 2013

The new income tax legislation specifies that from the beginning of 2016, the personal income tax thresholds will be adjusted annually for inflation.

5. Memorandum items

5.1. *Identification of an AW*

The data refer to the earnings of workers within the formal sector. The average worker's wage was calculated using microdata from the national household surveys.

Ecuador

The country profile includes data on the income taxes paid by workers, their social security contributions, the family benefits they receive in the form of cash transfers as well as the social security contributions and payroll taxes paid by the employers. Results reported include the average and marginal tax burdens for eight different family types.

It also describes the personal income tax systems, all compulsory social security contribution schemes and universal cash transfers as well as recent changes in the tax/benefit system.

Ecuador 2013

Tax / benefit of single persons

	Wage level (% of average wage)	67	100	167	67
	Number of children	0	0	0	2
1.	**Gross wage earnings**	5 365	8 007	13 372	5 365
2.	**Standard tax allowances**	1 389	2 073	3 462	1 389
	Basic allowance	0	0	0	0
	Married or head of family	0	0	0	0
	Dependent children	0	0	0	0
	Deduction for social security contributions and income taxes	507	757	1 264	507
	Work-related expenses	0	0	0	0
	Other	882	1 316	2 198	882
3.	**Tax credits or cash transfers included in taxable income**	0	0	0	0
4.	**Central government taxable income (1-2+3)**	3 976	5 934	9 911	3 976
5.	**Central government income tax liability (exclusive of tax credits)**	0	0	0	0
6.	**Tax credits**	0	0	0	0
	Basic credit	0	0	0	0
	Married or head of family	0	0	0	0
	Children	0	0	0	0
	Other	0	0	0	0
7.	**Central government income tax finally paid (5-6)**	0	0	0	0
8.	**State and local taxes**	0	0	0	0
9.	**Employees' compulsory social security contributions**				
	Gross earnings	507	757	1 264	507
10.	**Total payments to general government (7+8+9)**	507	757	1 264	507
11.	**Cash transfers from general government**	0	0	0	0
	For head of family	0	0	0	0
	For two children	0	0	0	0
12.	**Take-home pay (1-10+11)**	4 858	7 251	12 109	4 858
13.	**Employer's compulsory social security contributions**	593	886	1 479	593
14.	**Average rates**				
	Income tax (7 / 1)	0.0%	0.0%	0.0%	0.0%
	Employees' social security contributions (9 / 1)	9.5%	9.5%	9.5%	9.5%
	Total payments less cash transfers [(10-11) / 1]	9.5%	9.5%	9.5%	9.5%
	Total tax wedge including employer's social security contributions [(10+13-11) / (1+13)]	18.5%	18.5%	18.5%	18.5%
15.	**Marginal rates**				
	Total payments less cash transfers: principal earner	9.5%	9.5%	9.5%	9.5%
	Total payments less cash transfers: spouse	N.A.	N.A.	N.A.	N.A.
	Total tax wedge: principal earner	18.5%	18.5%	18.5%	18.5%
	Total tax wedge: spouse	N.A.	N.A.	N.A.	N.A.

Ecuador

Tax / benefit of married couples

Wage level (% of average wage)	100-0	100-33	100-67	100-33
Number of children	2	2	2	0
Gross wage earnings	8 007	10 650	13 372	10 650
Standard tax allowances	2 073	2 507	3 462	2 507
Basic allowance	0	0	0	0
Married or head of family	0	0	0	0
Dependent children	0	0	0	0
Deduction for social security contributions and income taxes	757	757	1 264	757
Work-related expenses	0	0	0	0
Other	1 316	1 751	2 198	1 751
Tax credits or cash transfers included in taxable income	0	0	0	0
Central government taxable income (1-2+3)	5 934	8 143	9 911	8 143
Central government income tax liability (exclusive of tax credits)	0	0	0	0
Tax credits	0	0	0	0
Basic credit	0	0	0	0
Married or head of family	0	0	0	0
Children	0	0	0	0
Other	0	0	0	0
Central government income tax finally paid (5-6)	0	0	0	0
State and local taxes	0	0	0	0
Employees' compulsory social security contributions				
Gross earnings	757	757	1 264	757
Total payments to general government (7+8+9)	757	757	1 264	757
Cash transfers from general government	0	0	0	0
For head of family	0	0	0	0
For two children	0	0	0	0
Take-home pay (1-10+11)	7 251	9 893	12 109	9 893
Employer's compulsory social security contributions	886	886	1 479	886
Average rates				
Income tax (7 / 1)	0.0%	0.0%	0.0%	0.0%
Employees' social security contributions (9 / 1)	9.5%	7.1%	9.5%	7.1%
Total payments less cash transfers [(10-11) / 1]	9.5%	7.1%	9.5%	7.1%
Total tax wedge including employer's social security contributions [(10+13-11) / (1+13)]	18.5%	14.2%	18.5%	14.2%
Marginal rates				
Total payments less cash transfers: principal earner	9.5%	9.4%	9.5%	9.4%
Total payments less cash transfers: spouse	0.0%	0.0%	9.5%	0.0%
Total tax wedge: principal earner	18.5%	18.5%	18.5%	18.5%
Total tax wedge: spouse	0.0%	0.0%	18.5%	0.0%

The national currency is the USD. In 2013, the average worker earned USD 8007.43.

The Report includes estimates of the tax wedge over the whole of the income distribution ordered by deciles of total labour income of formal wage earners derived from the household surveys.

	Deciles of Incomes									
	1	2	3	4	5	6	7	8	9	10
Local currency (USD)	3 361	4 037	4 243	4 758	5 519	6 387	7 541	9 394	12 003	23 021
Dollars in PPP[1]	6 110	7 341	7 714	8 651	10 034	11 612	13 711	17 080	21 823	41 857
Ratio to the minimum wage[2]	0.9	1.1	1.1	1.2	1.4	1.7	2.0	2.5	3.1	6.0

1. Calculated using the implied conversion rate (National currency per current international dollar in purchasing power parity) published by the IMF in the World Economic Outlook dataset.
2. Ratio of the income decile to the official minimum wage of the country.

1. Personal income tax system

The fiscal year is the calendar year.

1.1. *Central government income tax*

The personal income tax in Ecuador is applied to employment, self-employment and investment income. Employment income encompasses all wages, compensation or benefits in-kind received under a written or verbal contract.

The main exemptions are:

- Severance payments
- Christmas bonus
- Education bonus
- Domestic interest paid on savings' deposits
- Payments due to illness and disability

1.1.1. *Tax unit*

Members of the family are taxed separately.

Ecuadorians are liable to personal income tax on their worldwide income. Non-residents however, are only liable on the Ecuadorian-source income. For tax purposes, an individual will be considered as a resident if their stay in Ecuador exceeds 183 days in the year.

1.1.2. *Tax allowances and tax credits*

1.1.2.1. Standard tax allowances and tax credits

- Compulsory social security contributions.
- Contributions to pension plans.

1.1.2.2. Main non-standard tax allowances and tax credits

- Up to 50% of the taxpayer's income due to personal expenses on housing, nutrition, education, clothing and health. The expenses are limited to 1.3 times the minimum exempt income established by the personal income tax schedule. The taxpayer is required to furnish invoices for the claimed expenses.

1.1.3. *Tax schedule*

The annual income tax liability was calculated on the taxable income according to the following schedule in 2013:

Income (USD) up to	Marginal rate (%)
10 180	0
12 970	5
16 220	10
19 470	12
38 930	15
58 390	20
77 870	25
103 810	30
above	35

1.2. *State and local taxes*

No state or local taxes are levied on wages.

2. Compulsory social security contribution to schemes operated within the government sector

2.1. *Employee contributions*

Program	Marginal rate (%)
Old age, disability and death program	6.64
Unemployment insurance	2.00
Farmer's social insurance	0.35
Organic law for the disabled	0.10
Administration expenses	0.36

Employee social security contributions are levied on gross wages. The lower earnings threshold is the minimum wage (USD3 816 in 2013). There are no upper ceilings to the contributions.

2.2. *Employer contributions*

Employers are required to contribute to the following public programs.

Program	Marginal rate (%)
Old age, retirement and disability program	3.10
Healthcare	5.71
Work injury	0.55
Unemployment insurance	1.00
Farmer's social insurance	0.35
Administration expenses	0.44

The contribution rates for the employer are applied to the payroll.

3. Universal cash transfer

3.1. *Amount for spouse and for dependent children*

None.

4. Main changes in tax/benefit since 2013

The thresholds to the personal income tax schedule are uprated each year. The 2016 schedule is shown below. The tax rates remained unchanged.

Annual personal income tax schedule for 2016	
Income (USD) up to	Marginal rate (%)
11 170	0
14 240	5
17 800	10
21 370	12
42 740	15
64 090	20
85 470	25
113 940	30
above	35

5. Memorandum items

5.1. *Identification of an AW*

The data refer to the earnings of workers within the formal sector. The average worker's wage was calculated using microdata from the national household surveys.

El Salvador

The country profile includes data on the income taxes paid by workers, their social security contributions, the family benefits they receive in the form of cash transfers as well as the social security contributions and payroll taxes paid by the employers. Results reported include the average and marginal tax burdens for eight different family types.

It also describes the personal income tax systems, all compulsory social security contribution schemes and universal cash transfers as well as recent changes in the tax/benefit system.

El Salvador 2013

Tax / benefit of single persons

	Wage level (% of average wage)	67	100	167	67
	Number of children	0	0	0	2
1.	**Gross wage earnings**	3 556	5 308	8 864	3 556
2.	**Standard tax allowances**	1 915	2071	2 378	1 915
	Basic allowance	0	0	0	0
	Married or head of family	0	0	0	0
	Dependent children	0	0	0	0
	Deduction for social security contributions and income taxes	315	471	778	315
	Work-related expenses	0	0	0	0
	Other	1 600	1 600	1 600	1 600
3.	**Tax credits or cash transfers included in taxable income**	0	0	0	0
4.	**Central government taxable income (1-2+3)**	1 641	3 237	6 486	1 641
5.	**Central government income tax liability (exclusive of tax credits)**	0	0	454	0
6.	**Tax credits**	0	0	0	0
	Basic credit	0	0	0	0
	Married or head of family	0	0	0	0
	Children	0	0	0	0
	Other	0	0	0	0
7.	**Central government income tax finally paid (5-6)**	0	0	454	0
8.	**State and local taxes**	0	0	0	0
9.	**Employees' compulsory social security contributions**				
	Gross earnings	315	471	778	315
10.	**Total payments to general government (7+8+9)**	315	471	1 232	315
11.	**Cash transfers from general government**	0	0	0	0
	For head of family	0	0	0	0
	For two children	0	0	0	0
12.	**Take-home pay (1-10+11)**	3 241	4 837	7 632	3 241
13.	**Employer's compulsory social security contributions**	520	776	1 276	520
14.	**Average rates**				
	Income tax (7 / 1)	0.0%	0.0%	5.1%	0.0%
	Employees' social security contributions (9 / 1)	8.9%	8.9%	8.8%	8.9%
	Total payments less cash transfers [(10-11) / 1]	8.9%	8.9%	13.9%	8.9%
	Total tax wedge including employer's social security contributions [(10+13-11) / (1+13)]	20.5%	20.5%	24.7%	20.5%
15.	**Marginal rates**				
	Total payments less cash transfers: principal earner	8.9%	8.9%	15.4%	8.9%
	Total payments less cash transfers: spouse	N.A.	N.A.	N.A.	N.A.
	Total tax wedge: principal earner	20.5%	20.5%	21.2%	20.5%
	Total tax wedge: spouse	N.A.	N.A.	N.A.	N.A.

El Salvador 2013

Tax / benefit of married couples

		100-0	100-33	100-67	100-33
	Wage level (% of average wage)	100-0	100-33	100-67	100-33
	Number of children	2	2	2	0
1.	**Gross wage earnings**	5 308	7 059	8 864	7 059
2.	**Standard tax allowances**	2 071	3 671	3 986	3 671
	Basic allowance	0	0	0	0
	Married or head of family	0	0	0	0
	Dependent children	0	0	0	0
	Deduction for social security contributions and income taxes	471	471	786	471
	Work-related expenses	0	0	0	0
	Other	1 600	3 200	3 200	3 200
3.	**Tax credits or cash transfers included in taxable income**	0	0	0	0
4.	**Central government taxable income (1-2+3)**	3 237	3 388	4 878	3 388
5.	**Central government income tax liability (exclusive of tax credits)**	0	0	0	0
6.	**Tax credits**	0	0	0	0
	Basic credit	0	0	0	0
	Married or head of family	0	0	0	0
	Children	0	0	0	0
	Other	0	0	0	0
7.	**Central government income tax finally paid (5-6)**	0	0	0	0
8.	**State and local taxes**	0	0	0	0
9.	**Employees' compulsory social security contributions**				
	Gross earnings	471	471	786	471
10.	**Total payments to general government (7+8+9)**	471	471	786	471
11.	**Cash transfers from general government**	0	0	0	0
	For head of family	0	0	0	0
	For two children	0	0	0	0
12.	**Take-home pay (1-10+11)**	4 837	6 588	8 078	6 588
13.	**Employer's compulsory social security contributions**	776	793	1 296	793
14.	**Average rates**				
	Income tax (7 / 1)	0.0%	0.0%	0.0%	0.0%
	Employees' social security contributions (9 / 1)	8.9%	6.7%	8.9%	6.7%
	Total payments less cash transfers [(10-11) / 1]	8.9%	6.7%	8.9%	6.7%
	Total tax wedge including employer's social security contributions [(10+13-11) / (1+13)]	20.5%	16.1%	20.5%	16.1%
15.	**Marginal rates**				
	Total payments less cash transfers: principal earner	8.9%	8.9%	8.9%	8.9%
	Total payments less cash transfers: spouse	0.0%	0.0%	8.9%	0.0%
	Total tax wedge: principal earner	20.5%	20.5%	20.5%	20.5%
	Total tax wedge: spouse	0.9%	0.9%	20.5%	0.9%

The national currency is the USD. In 2013, the average worker earned USD 5 307.72.

The Report includes estimates of the tax wedge over the whole of the income distribution ordered by deciles of total labour income of formal wage earners derived from the household surveys.

	Deciles of Incomes									
	1	2	3	4	5	6	7	8	9	10
Local currency (USD)	2 130	2 526	2 802	3 039	3 491	4 242	5 296	6 247	7 877	15 657
Dollars in PPP[1]	4 321	5 124	5 683	6 164	7 080	8 605	10 743	12 671	15 978	31 759
Ratio to the minimum wage[2]	0.9	1.1	1.2	1.3	1.5	1.9	2.3	2.8	3.5	6.9

1. Calculated using the implied conversion rate (National currency per current international dollar in purchasing parity power) published by the IMF in the World Economic Outlook dataset.
2. Ratio of the income decile to the official minimum wage of the country.

1. Personal income tax system

The fiscal year is the calendar year.

1.1. *Central government income tax*

The income tax law of El Salvador establishes that all income (cash or in-kind) received in the national territory and all foreign investments that produce gains within the country are subject to the income tax.

The personal income tax is calculated on the taxable income which is derived after applying the tax allowances to the gross income.

1.1.1. *Tax unit*

Members of the family are taxed separately.

1.1.2. *Tax allowances and tax credits*

1.1.2.1. Standard tax allowances and tax credits

- Employee contributions to the old age pension program and those paid to the ISSS.
- Resident individuals may deduct USD 1 600 if their annual income is less than USD 9 100. Otherwise, taxpayer's are entitled to a USD 800 deduction.

1.1.2.2. Main non-standard tax allowances and tax credits

None.

1.1.3. *Tax schedule*

The annual income tax liability was calculated on the taxable income according to the following schedule in 2013:

Income (USD) up to	Marginal rate (%)
4 064.00	0
9 142.86	10
22 857.14	20
above	30

1.2. *State and local taxes*

There is no state or local tax levied on wages.

2. Compulsory social security contribution to schemes operated within the government sector

2.1. *Employee contributions*

Employee contributions are levied on the gross earnings under two headings.

Individuals contribute 3% of their wages to the government sponsored National Institute of Social Security (ISSS). The annual lower earnings threshold is the minimum wage, USD 2 265.96 in 2013. The upper ceiling was USD 8 228.52.

Resident individuals also contribute 6.25% of their wages to a privately managed old age pension program (AFP). The lower earnings threshold is the minimum wage and the upper ceiling was USD 65 608.56. The annual bonus (Aguinaldo) is exempt from the contributions.

2.2. *Employer contributions*

Employers are required to contribute to the following public programs.

Program	Marginal rate (%)
National Institute of Social Security (ISSS)	7.5
Old age pension (AFP)*	6.75
Salvadorian Institute for Professional Formation (INSAFORP)**	1.0

*Privately managed.
**Levied on companies with more than 10 employees.

The employer contribution rates are levied on the payroll. The contribution to the AFP has a lower earnings threshold of the minimum wage and an upper ceiling of USD 65 608.56. The annual bonus (Aguinaldo) is exempt from contributions.

3. Universal cash transfer

3.1. *Amount for spouse and for dependent children*

None.

4. Main changes in tax/benefit since 2013

None.

5. Memorandum items

5.1. *Identification of an AW*

The data refer to the earnings of workers within the formal sector. The average worker's wage was calculated using microdata from the national household surveys.

Guatemala

The country profile includes data on the income taxes paid by workers, their social security contributions, the family benefits they receive in the form of cash transfers as well as the social security contributions and payroll taxes paid by the employers. Results reported include the average and marginal tax burdens for eight different family types.

It also describes the personal income tax systems, all compulsory social security contribution schemes and universal cash transfers as well as recent changes in the tax/benefit system.

Guatemala

Tax / benefit of single persons

	Wage level (% of average wage)	67	100	167	67
	Number of children	0	0	0	2
1.	**Gross wage earnings**	31 197	46 563	77 760	31 197
2.	**Standard tax allowances**	53 389	57 533	63 921	53 389
	Basic allowance	48 000	48 000	48 000	48 000
	Married or head of family	0	0	0	0
	Dependent children	0	0	0	0
	Deduction for social security contributions and income taxes	261	1 879	3 138	261
	Work-related expenses	0	0	0	0
	Other	5 128	7 654	12 782	5 128
3.	**Tax credits or cash transfers included in taxable income**	0	0	0	0
4.	**Central government taxable income (1-2+3)**	0	0	13 839	0
5.	**Central government income tax liability (exclusive of tax credits)**	0	0	692	0
6.	**Tax credits**	0	0	0	0
	Basic credit	0	0	0	0
	Married or head of family	0	0	0	0
	Children	0	0	0	0
	Other	0	0	0	0
7.	**Central government income tax finally paid (5-6)**	0	0	692	0
8.	**State and local taxes**	0	0	0	0
9.	**Employees' compulsory social security contributions**				
	Gross earnings	261	1 879	3 138	261
10.	**Total payments to general government (7+8+9)**	261	1 879	3 830	261
11.	**Cash transfers from general government**	0	0	0	0
	For head of family	0	0	0	0
	For two children	0	0	0	0
12.	**Take-home pay (1-10+11)**	30 936	44 684	73 930	30 936
13.	**Employer's compulsory social security contributions**	1 303	4 930	8 233	1 303
14.	**Average rates**				
	Income tax (7 / 1)	0.0%	0.0%	0.9%	0.0%
	Employees' social security contributions (9 / 1)	0.8%	4.0%	4.0%	0.8%
	Total payments less cash transfers [(10-11) / 1]	0.8%	4.0%	4.9%	0.8%
	Total tax wedge including employer's social security contributions [(10+13-11) / (1+ 3)]	4.8%	13.2%	14.0%	4.8%
15.	**Marginal rates**				
	Total payments less cash transfers: principal earner	0.8%	4.0%	8.0%	0.8%
	Total payments less cash transfers: spouse	N.A.	N.A.	N.A.	N.A.
	Total tax wedge: principal earner	4.8%	13.2%	16.8%	4.8%
	Total tax wedge: spouse	N.A.	N.A.	N.A.	N.A.

Guatemala

Tax / benefit of married couples

		100-0	100-33	100-67	100-33
	Wage level (% of average wage)	100-0	100-33	100-67	100-33
	Number of children	2	2	2	0
1.	**Gross wage earnings**	46 563	61 929	77 760	61 929
2.	**Standard tax allowances**	57 533	108 188	110 922	108 188
	Basic allowance	48 000	96 000	96 000	96 000
	Married or head of family	0	0	0	0
	Dependent children	0	0	0	0
	Deduction for social security contributions and income taxes	1 879	2 008	2 140	2 008
	Work-related expenses	0	0	0	0
	Other	7 654	10 180	12 782	10 180
3.	**Tax credits or cash transfers included in taxable income**	0	0	0	0
4.	**Central government taxable income (1-2+3)**	0	0	0	0
5.	**Central government income tax liability (exclusive of tax credits)**	0	0	0	0
6.	**Tax credits**	0	0	0	0
	Basic credit	0	0	0	0
	Married or head of family	0	0	0	0
	Children	0	0	0	0
	Other	0	0	0	0
7.	**Central government income tax finally paid (5-6)**	0	0	0	0
8.	**State and local taxes**	0	0	0	0
9.	**Employees' compulsory social security contributions**				
	Gross earnings	1 879	2 008	2 140	2 008
10.	**Total payments to general government (7+8+9)**	1 879	2 008	2 140	2 008
11.	**Cash transfers from general government**	0	0	0	0
	For head of family	0	0	0	0
	For two children	0	0	0	0
12.	**Take-home pay (1-10+11)**	44 684	59 921	75 620	59 921
13.	**Employer's compulsory social security contributions**	4 930	5 572	6 233	5 572
14.	**Average rates**				
	Income tax (7 / 1)	0.0%	0.0%	0.0%	0.0%
	Employees' social security contributions (9 / 1)	4.0%	3.2%	2.8%	3.2%
	Total payments less cash transfers [(10-11) / 1]	4.0%	3.2%	2.8%	3.2%
	Total tax wedge including employer's social security contributions [(10+13-11) / (1+13)]	13.2%	11.2%	10.0%	11.2%
15.	**Marginal rates**				
	Total payments less cash transfers: principal earner	4.0%	4.0%	4.0%	4.0%
	Total payments less cash transfers: spouse	0.8%	0.8%	0.8%	0.8%
	Total tax wedge: principal earner	13.2%	13.2%	13.2%	13.2%
	Total tax wedge: spouse	4.8%	4.8%	4.8%	4.8%

The national currency is the Quetzal (GTQ). In 2013, the average exchange rate was GTQ 7.86 to USD 1. In that year, the average worker earned GTQ 46 562.97.

The Report includes estimates of the tax wedge over the whole of the income distribution ordered by deciles of total labour income of formal wage earners derived from the household surveys.

	Deciles of Incomes									
	1	2	3	4	5	6	7	8	9	10
Local currency (GTQ)	20 619	28 537	31 674	34 366	37 209	41 208	45 036	51 409	62 054	115 061
USD[1]	2 624	3 631	4 030	4 373	4 735	5 243	5 731	6 542	7 896	14 641
Dollars in PPP[2]	5 510	7 626	8 464	9 184	9 944	11 012	12 035	13 738	16 583	30 749
Ratio to the minimum wage[3]	0.7	1.0	1.1	1.2	1.3	1.5	1.6	1.8	2.2	4.1

1. Average official exchange rates published by the central bank.
2. Calculated using the implied conversion rate (National currency per current international dollar in purchasing power parity) published by the IMF in the World Economic Outlook dataset.
3. Ratio of the income decile to the official minimum wage of the country.

1. Personal income tax system

The fiscal year is the calendar year.

1.1. *Central government income tax*

The personal income tax is applicable to all labour and capital income. Labour income arises from any fee or income derived from personal work carried out under a dependency relationship with the employer either within or outside of Guatemala (Decree 10-2012, Art. 4). When such activities take place within Guatemala, the tax is withheld and treated as an advance on the total amount of the tax liability for the individual taxpayer.

An individual's tax liability is calculated on his/her total income less the allowable deductions and income exemptions.

Exempt income provisions include:

- The annual bonus paid to workers up to 100% of the ordinary monthly salary or wage.
- Single or periodic payments of indemnities or pensions relating to death or disability caused by accident or illness.
- Severance payments received by workers in both the public and private sector.

1.1.1. *Tax unit*

Members of the family are taxed separately.

1.1.2. *Tax allowances and tax credits*

1.1.1.1. Standard tax allowances and tax credits

- A basic allowance of GTQ 48 000.00.
- Employee social security contributions paid to the IGSS.

1.1.1.2. Main non-standard tax allowances and tax credits

- Donations to charitable institutions for which proof can be provided.
- Insurance premiums covering the accidental death of a worker.
- Verified amounts granted to cover travel and expenses both inside and outside the country.

1.1.3. *Tax schedule*

The annual personal income tax liability was calculated according to the following schedule in 2013:

Income (GTQ) up to	Marginal rate (%)
300 000	5.0
above	7.0

1.2. *State and local taxes*

There is no state or local tax levied on wages.

2. Compulsory social security contribution to schemes operated within the government sector

2.1. *Employee contributions*

Program	Marginal rate (%)
Old age pensions (IGSS)	1.83
Healthcare (IGSS)	2.0
Work injury (IGSS)	1.0

Employee social security contributions are levied on the gross wage. The lower threshold is the national minimum wage, which was equal to GTQ 2 363.25 in 2013. The bonus that acts as an incentive to workers in the private sector (GTQ 250) is exempt from contributions. The annual bonus paid to workers at the end of year is also exempt from contributions.

2.2. *Employer contributions*

Employers are required to contribute to the following public programs.

Program	Marginal rate (%)
Institute of Guatemala of Social Security (IGSS)	10.67
Technical Institute for Training and Productivity – INTECAP	1.0
Recreation Institute for Private Sector Workers – IRTRA	1.0

The employer social security contribution rates are applied to the payroll.

3. Universal cash transfer

3.1. *Amount for spouse and for dependent children*

None.

4. Main changes in tax/benefit since 2013

None.

5. Memorandum items

5.1. *Identification of an AW*

The data refer to the earnings of workers within the formal sector. The average worker's wage was calculated using microdata from the national household surveys.

Honduras

The country profile includes data on the income taxes paid by workers, their social security contributions, the family benefits they receive in the form of cash transfers as well as the social security contributions and payroll taxes paid by the employers. Results reported include the average and marginal tax burdens for eight different family types.

It also describes the personal income tax systems, all compulsory social security contribution schemes and universal cash transfers as well as recent changes in the tax/benefit system.

Honduras 2013

Tax / benefit of single persons

	Wage level (% of average wage)	67	100	167	67
	Number of children	0	0	0	2
1.	**Gross wage earnings**	77 362	115 465	192 827	77 362
2.	**Standard tax allowances**	52 717	58 981	71 698	52 717
	Basic allowance	40 000	40 000	40 000	40 000
	Married or head of family	0	0	0	0
	Dependent children	0	0	0	0
	Deduction for social security contributions and income taxes	0	0	0	0
	Work-related expenses	0	0	0	0
	Other	12 717	18 981	31 698	12 717
3.	**Tax credits or cash transfers included in taxable income**	0	0	0	0
4.	**Central government taxable income (1-2+3)**	24 645	56 484	121 129	24 645
5.	**Central government income tax liability (exclusive of tax credits)**	0	0	1 669	0
6.	**Tax credits**	0	0	0	0
	Basic credit	0	0	0	0
	Married or head of family	0	0	0	0
	Children	0	0	0	0
	Other	0	0	0	0
7.	**Central government income tax finally paid (5-6)**	0	0	1 669	0
8.	**State and local taxes**	0	0	0	0
9.	**Employees' compulsory social security contributions**				
	Gross income	0	4 200	4 200	0
10.	**Total payments to general government (7+8+9)**	0	4 200	5 869	0
11.	**Cash transfers from general government**	0	0	0	0
	For head of family	0	0	0	0
	For two children	0	0	0	0
12.	**Take-home pay (1-10+11)**	77 362	111 265	186 957	77 362
13.	**Employer's compulsory social security contributions**	0	8 148	8 148	0
14.	**Average rates**				
	Income tax (7 / 1)	0.0%	0.0%	0.9%	0.0%
	Employees' social security contributions (9 / 1)	0.0%	3.6%	2.2%	0.0%
	Total payments less cash transfers [(10-11) / 1]	0.0%	3.6%	3.0%	0.0%
	Total tax wedge including employer's social security contributions [(10+13-11) / (1+13)]	0.0%	10.0%	7.0%	0.0%
15.	**Marginal rates**				
	Total payments less cash transfers: principal earner	0.0%	0.0%	12.5%	0.0%
	Total payments less cash transfers: spouse	N.A.	N.A.	N.A.	N.A.
	Total tax wedge: principal earner	0.0%	0.0%	12.5%	0.0%
	Total tax wedge: spouse	N.A.	N.A.	N.A.	N.A.

Honduras 2013

Tax / benefit of married couples

		100-0	100-33	100-67	100-33
	Wage level (% of average wage)	100-0	100-33	100-67	100-33
	Number of children	2	2	2	0
1.	**Gross wage earnings**	115 465	153 568	192 827	153 568
2.	**Standard tax allowances**	58 981	105 244	111 698	105 244
	Basic allowance	40 000	80 000	80 000	80 000
	Married or head of family	0	0	0	0
	Dependent children	0	0	0	0
	Deduction for social security contributions and income taxes	0	0	0	0
	Work-related expenses	0	0	0	0
	Other	18 981	25 244	31 698	25 244
3.	**Tax credits or cash transfers included in taxable income**	0	0	0	0
4.	**Central government taxable income (1-2+3)**	56 484	56 484	81 129	56 484
5.	**Central government income tax liability (exclusive of tax credits)**	0	0	0	0
6.	**Tax credits**	0	0	0	0
	Basic credit	0	0	0	0
	Married or head of family	0	0	0	0
	Children	0	0	0	0
	Other	0	0	0	0
7.	**Central government income tax finally paid (5-6)**	0	0	0	0
8.	**State and local taxes**	0	0	0	0
9.	**Employees' compulsory social security contributions**				
	Gross income	4 200	4 200	4 200	4 200
10.	**Total payments to general government (7+8+9)**	4 200	4 200	4 200	4 200
11.	**Cash transfers from general government**	0	0	0	0
	For head of family	0	0	0	0
	For two children	0	0	0	0
12.	**Take-home pay (1-10+11)**	111 265	149 368	188 627	149 368
13.	**Employer's compulsory social security contributions**	8 148	8 148	8 148	8 148
14.	**Average rates**				
	Income tax (7 / 1)	0.0%	0.0%	0.0%	0.0%
	Employees' social security contributions (9 / 1)	3.6%	2.7%	2.2%	2.7%
	Total payments less cash transfers [(10-11) / 1]	3.6%	2.7%	2.2%	2.7%
	Total tax wedge including employer's social security contributions [(10+13-11) / (1+13)]	10.0%	7.6%	6.1%	7.6%
15.	**Marginal rates**				
	Total payments less cash transfers: principal earner	0.0%	0.0%	0.0%	0.0%
	Total payments less cash transfers: spouse	0.0%	0.0%	0.0%	0.0%
	Total tax wedge: principal earner	0.0%	0.0%	0.0%	0.0%
	Total tax wedge: spouse	0.0%	0.0%	0.0%	0.0%

The national currency is the Lempira (HNL). In 2013, the average exchange rate was HNL 19.73 to USD 1. In that year, the average worker earned HNL 115 465.02.

The Report includes estimates of the tax wedge over the whole of the income distribution ordered by deciles of total labour income of formal wage earners derived from the household surveys.

	Deciles of Incomes									
	1	2	3	4	5	6	7	8	9	10
Local currency (HNL)	47 014	68 493	76 957	83 682	88 106	95 396	113 091	138 634	177 428	302 226
USD[1]	2 382	3 471	3 900	4 241	4 465	4 834	5 731	7 025	8 991	15 316
Dollars in PPP[2]	4 674	6 810	7 651	8 320	8 760	9 485	11 244	13 783	17 640	30 048
Ratio to the minimum wage[3]	0.6	0.9	1.0	1.0	1.1	1.2	1.4	1.7	2.2	3.8

1. Average official exchange rates published by the central bank.
2. Calculated using the implied conversion rate (National currency per current international dollar in purchasing power parity) published by the IMF in the World Economic Outlook dataset.
3. Ratio of the income decile to the official minimum wage of the country.

1. Personal income tax system

The fiscal year is the calendar year.

1.1. *Central government income tax*

Law decree No. 25-63 establishes the income tax in Honduras. This tax applies to employment income, self-employment, business income and investment income. It covers all kinds of profits, rents, gains, utilities, dividends, salaries, wages, and fees.

Employment income refers to salaries, pensions, bonuses, commissions and benefits in kind paid to an employee in exchange for his work.

Exempt income – the most notable types of income relating to employment are:

- Vacation bonus of up to thirty days paid in accordance with the Labour Code.
- The thirteenth and fourteenth months' bonuses up to ten times the average minimum wage, in each case.

1.1.1. *Tax unit*

Members of the family are taxed separately.

The personal income tax is applied to residents and other persons residing in Honduras for more than 3 consecutive months, regardless of their nationality.

1.1.2. *Tax allowances and tax credits*

1.1.2.1. Standard tax allowances and tax credits

- A basic allowance of HNL 40 000.

1.1.2.2. Main non-standard tax allowances and tax credits

- Donations and bequests to the state, municipalities, education institutions, sports or charitable institutions up to10% of the taxable income.

1.1.3. *Tax schedule*

The personal income tax liability was calculated on the taxable income according to the following schedule in 2013:

Income (HNL) up to	Marginal rate (%)
110 000	0.0
200 000	15.0
500 000	20.0
above	25.0

1.2. *State and local taxes*

No state or local taxes are levied on wages.

2. Compulsory social security contribution to schemes operated within the government sector

2.1. *Employee contributions*

Program	Marginal rate (%)
Old age, disability and death program (IHSS)	1.0
Healthcare and Maternity Insurance (IHSS)	2.50
Social Housing Fund – FOSOVI	1.5

The employee contributions are levied on gross wages. The lower threshold is the monthly minimum national wage, which was equal to HNL 6 670.85 in 2013.The upper ceiling is HNL 7 000 according to the SOJD Resolution No.02-29-02-2011 that applied for that year. The thirteenth and fourteenth month bonuses are exempt from social security contributions.

2.2. *Employer contributions*

Employers are required to contribute to the following public programs.

Program	Marginal rate (%)
Old age, disability and death program (IVM)	2.0
Healthcare and Maternity Insurance (SEM)	5.0
Work Injury	0.2
Social Housing Fund – FOSOVI	1.5
Professional Formation National Institute – INFOP	1.0

The employer contribution rates are applied to the payroll.

3. Universal cash transfer

3.1. *Amount for spouse and for dependent children*

None.

4. Main changes in tax/benefit since 2013

In July 2015, a social security law was passed introducing a new multi-pillar social security scheme. The program is structured with a collective capitalization pillar and a complementary pillar with individual accounts. The most important development is that employers will make a new payment of 4% of the payroll in respect of labour insurance. Companies with less than 10 workers are exempt from this contribution until January 2018.

5. Memorandum items

5.1. *Identification of an AW*

The data refer to the earnings of workers within the formal sector. The average worker's wage was calculated using microdata from the national household surveys.

Taxing Wages in Latin America and the Caribbean

Jamaica

The country profile includes data on the income taxes paid by workers, their social security contributions, the family benefits they receive in the form of cash transfers as well as the social security contributions and payroll taxes paid by the employers. Results reported include the average and marginal tax burdens for eight different family types.

It also describes the personal income tax systems, all compulsory social security contribution schemes and universal cash transfers as well as recent changes in the tax/benefit system.

Jamaica 2013

Tax / benefit of single persons

	Wage level (% of average wage)	67	100	167	67
	Number of children	0	0	0	2
1.	**Gross wage earnings**	240 525	358 993	599 519	240 525
2.	**Standard tax allowances**	513 325	516 287	522 300	513 325
	Basic allowance	507 312	507 312	507 312	507 312
	Married or head of family	0	0	0	0
	Dependent children	0	0	0	0
	Deduction for social security contributions and income taxes	6 013	8 975	14 988	6 013
	Work-related expenses	0	0	0	0
	Other	0	0	0	0
3.	**Tax credits or cash transfers included in taxable income**	0	0	0	0
4.	**Central government taxable income (1-2+3)**	0	0	77 219	0
5.	**Central government income tax liability (exclusive of tax credits)**	0	0	19 305	0
6.	**Tax credits**	0	0	0	0
	Basic credit	0	0	0	0
	Married or head of family	0	0	0	0
	Children	0	0	0	0
	Other	0	0	0	0
7.	**Central government income tax finally paid (5-6)**	0	0	19 305	0
8.	**State and local taxes**	0	0	0	0
9.	**Employees' compulsory social security contributions**				
	Gross earnings	10 824	16 155	26 978	10 824
	Taxable income	5 277	7 875	13 152	5 277
10.	**Total payments to general government (7+8+9)**	16 100	24 030	59 435	16 100
11.	**Cash transfers from general government**	0	0	0	0
	For head of family	0	0	0	0
	For two children	0	0	0	0
12.	**Take-home pay (1-10+11)**	224 425	334 963	540 084	224 425
13.	**Employer's compulsory social security contributions**	28 683	42 810	71 493	28 683
14.	**Average rates**				
	Income tax (7 / 1)	0.0%	0.0%	3.2%	0.0%
	Employees' social security contributions (9 / 1)	6.7%	6.7%	6.7%	6.7%
	Total payments less cash transfers [(10-11) / 1]	6.7%	6.7%	9.9%	6.7%
	Total tax wedge including employer's social security contributions [(10+13-11) / (1+13)]	16.6%	16.6%	19.5%	16.6%
15.	**Marginal rates**				
	Total payments less cash transfers: principal earner	6.7%	6.7%	31.1%	6.7%
	Total payments less cash transfers: spouse	N.A.	N.A.	N.A.	N.A.
	Total tax wedge: principal earner	16.6%	16.6%	38.4%	16.6%
	Total tax wedge: spouse	N.A.	N.A.	N.A.	N.A.

Jamaica 2013

Tax / benefit of married couples

	Wage level (% of average wage)	100-0	100-33	100-67	100-33
	Number of children	2	2	2	0
1.	**Gross wage earnings**	358 993	477 461	599 519	477 461
2.	**Standard tax allowances**	516 287	1 026 561	1 029 612	1 026 561
	Basic allowance	507 312	1 014 624	1 014 624	1 014 624
	Married or head of family	0	0	0	0
	Dependent children	0	0	0	0
	Deduction for social security contributions and income taxes	8 975	11 937	14 988	11 937
	Work-related expenses	0	0	0	0
	Other	0	0	0	0
3.	**Tax credits or cash transfers included in taxable income**	0	0	0	0
4.	**Central government taxable income (1-2+3)**	0	0	0	0
5.	**Central government income tax liability (exclusive of tax credits)**	0	0	0	0
6.	**Tax credits**	0	0	0	0
	Basic credit	0	0	0	0
	Married or head of family	0	0	0	0
	Children	0	0	0	0
	Other	0	0	0	0
7.	**Central government income tax finally paid (5-6)**	0	0	0	0
8.	**State and local taxes**	0	0	0	0
9.	**Employees' compulsory social security contributions**				
	Gross earnings	16 155	21 486	26 978	21 486
	Taxable income	7 875	10 474	13 152	10 474
10.	**Total payments to general government (7+8+9)**	24 030	31 960	40 130	31 960
11.	**Cash transfers from general government**	0	0	0	0
	For head of family	0	0	0	0
	For two children	0	0	0	0
12.	**Take-home pay (1-10+11)**	334 963	445 501	559 388	445 501
13.	**Employer's compulsory social security contributions**	42 810	56 937	71 493	56 937
14.	**Average rates**				
	Income tax (7 / 1)	0.0%	0.0%	0.0%	0.0%
	Employees' social security contributions (9 / 1)	6.7%	6.7%	6.7%	6.7%
	Total payments less cash transfers [(10-11) / 1]	6.7%	6.7%	6.7%	6.7%
	Total tax wedge including employer's social security contributions [(10+13-11) / (1+13)]	16.6%	16.6%	16.6%	16.6%
15.	**Marginal rates**				
	Total payments less cash transfers: principal earner	6.7%	6.7%	6.7%	6.7%
	Total payments less cash transfers: spouse	6.7%	6.7%	6.7%	6.7%
	Total tax wedge: principal earner	16.6%	16.6%	16.6%	16.6%
	Total tax wedge: spouse	16.6%	16.6%	16.6%	16.6%

The national currency is the Jamaican dollar. In 2013, the average exchange rate was JMD 98.28 to USD 1. In that year, the average worker earned JMD 358 993.22.

The Report includes estimates of the tax wedge throughout over the whole of the income distribution ordered by deciles of total labour income of formal wage earners derived from the household surveys.

	Deciles of Incomes									
	1	2	3	4	5	6	7	8	9	10
Local currency (JMD)	58 903	61 500	77 400	193 555	206 334	266 227	385 740	409 530	670 184	1 500 617
USD[1]	599	626	788	1 969	2 099	2 709	3 925	4 167	6 819	15 268
Dollars in PPP[2]	973	1 016	1 279	3 198	3 409	4 399	6 374	6 767	11 074	24 795
Ratio to the minimum wage[3]	0.2	0.2	0.3	0.7	0.8	1.0	1.4	1.5	2.5	5.6

1. Average official exchange rates published by the central bank.
2. Calculated using the implied conversion rate (National currency per current international dollar in purchasing parity power) published by the IMF in the World Economic Outlook dataset.
3. Ratio of the income decile to the official minimum wage of the country.

1. Personal income tax system

The fiscal year for the income tax is the calendar year.

1.1. Central government income tax

The personal income tax is applied to any income for the individual arising from employment or self-employment, pensions, superannuation or other allowances, deferred pay and compensation for loss of office.

Income from employment includes all salaries, fees, wages, plus all provisions or payments in respect of living or other accommodation, entertainment and other benefits in kind.

1.1.1. Tax unit

Members of the family are taxed separately.

Individuals who are residents and domiciled in Jamaica are taxed on their world-wide income. Individuals not domiciled are taxed only on their Jamaican-source income and any other income that is remitted to Jamaica. Non-residents are taxed only on their Jamaican-source income and on remittances of foreign income to Jamaica. Individuals are considered as residents if they remain in Jamaica for six months of the tax year or more.

1.1.2. Tax allowances and tax credits

1.1.2.1. Standard tax allowances and tax credits

- A standard deduction of JMD 507 312.
- Social security contributions up to 10% of gross income.

1.1.2.2. Main non-standard tax allowances and tax credits

- The amounts of any donations not exceeding one twentieth of the statutory taxable income.

1.1.3. *Tax schedule*

A flat rate tax of 25% was applied to the taxable income in 2013.

1.2. *State and local taxes*

No state or local taxes are levied on wages.

2. Compulsory social security contribution to schemes operated within the government sector

2.1. *Employee contributions*

Program	Marginal rate (%)
National Insurance Scheme (NIS)	2.50
National Housing Trust (NHT)	2.00
Education tax	2.25

The employee contributions for the NIS and NHT programs are levied on gross wages. The education tax is levied on the statutory income which provides an allowance for the NIS contributions.

2.2. *Employer contributions*

Employers are required to contribute to the following public programs.

Program	Marginal rate (%)
National Insurance Scheme (NIS)	2.50
National Housing Trust (NHT)	3.00
Human Employment and Resource Training Program (HEART)	3.00
Education tax	3.50

The employer contributions to the NIS and NHT programs are levied on the payroll. The HEART is also levied on the payroll, where total payroll costs exceed JMD 173 328 per year. The education tax is levied on the employees' statutory income which provides an allowance for the employees' NIS contributions.

3. Universal cash transfer

3.1. *Amount for spouse and for dependent children*

None.

4. Main changes in tax/benefit since 2013

The annual income tax allowance is adjusted each year. For 2015, the threshold was equal to JMD 557 232.

5. Memorandum items

5.1. *Identification of an AW*

The data refer to the earnings of workers within the formal sector. The average worker's wage was calculated using microdata from the national household surveys.

Mexico

The country profile includes data on the income taxes paid by workers, their social security contributions, the family benefits they receive in the form of cash transfers as well as the social security contributions and payroll taxes paid by the employers. Results reported include the average and marginal tax burdens for eight different family types.

It also describes the personal income tax systems, all compulsory social security contribution schemes and universal cash transfers as well as recent changes in the tax/benefit system.

Mexico 2013

Tax / benefit of single persons

	Wage level (% of average wage)	67	100	167	67
	Number of children	0	0	0	2
1.	**Gross wage earnings**	66 278	98 922	165 200	66 278
2.	**Standard tax allowances**	2 166	2 300	2 573	2 166
	Basic allowance	0	0	0	0
	Married or head of family	0	0	0	0
	Dependent children	0	0	0	0
	Deduction for social security contributions and income taxes	0	0	0	0
	Work-related expenses	0	0	0	0
	Other	2 166	2 300	2 573	2 166
3.	**Tax credits or cash transfers included in taxable income**	0	0	0	0
4.	**Central government taxable income (1-2+3)**	64 112	96 622	162 627	64 112
5.	**Central government income tax liability (exclusive of tax credits)**	4 445	8 383	21 428	4 445
6.	**Tax credits**	3 536	0	0	3 536
	Basic credit	0	0	0	0
	Married or head of family	0	0	0	0
	Children	0	0	0	0
	Other	3 536	0	0	3 536
7.	**Central government income tax finally paid (5-6)**	909	8 383	21 428	909
8.	**State and local taxes**	0	0	0	0
9.	**Employees' compulsory social security contributions**				
	Gross earnings	1 574	2 461	4 301	1 574
10.	**Total payments to general government (7+8+9)**	2 484	10 845	25 728	2 484
11.	**Cash transfers from general government**	0	0	0	0
	For head of family	0	0	0	0
	For two children	0	0	0	0
12.	**Take-home pay (1-10+11)**	63 794	88 077	139 471	63 794
13.	**Employer's compulsory social security contributions**	15 844	21 581	33 332	15 844
14.	**Average rates**				
	Income tax (7 / 1)	1.4%	8.5%	13.0%	1.4%
	Employees' social security contributions (9 / 1)	2.4%	2.5%	2.6%	2.4%
	Total payments less cash transfers [(10-11) / 1]	3.7%	11.0%	15.6%	3.7%
	Total tax wedge including employer's social security contributions [(10+13-11) / (1+13)]	22.3%	26.9%	29.7%	22.3%
15.	**Marginal rates**				
	Total payments less cash transfers: principal earner	13.2%	18.7%	24.0%	13.2%
	Total payments less cash transfers: spouse	N.A.	N.A.	N.A.	N.A.
	Total tax wedge: principal earner	25.6%	31.0%	35.5%	25.6%
	Total tax wedge: spouse	N.A.	N.A.	N.A.	N.A.

Mexico 2013

Tax / benefit of married couples

	Wage level (% of average wage)	100-0	100-33	100-67	100-33
	Number of children	2	2	2	0
1.	**Gross wage earnings**	98 922	131 566	165 200	131 566
2.	**Standard tax allowances**	2 300	3 776	4 466	3 776
	Basic allowance	0	0	0	0
	Married or head of family	0	0	0	0
	Dependent children	0	0	0	0
	Deduction for social security contributions and income taxes	0	0	0	0
	Work-related expenses	0	0	0	0
	Other	2 300	3 776	4 466	3 776
3.	**Tax credits or cash transfers included in taxable income**	0	0	0	0
4.	**Central government taxable income (1-2+3)**	96 622	127 790	160 733	127 790
5.	**Central government income tax liability (exclusive of tax credits)**	8 383	10 112	12 828	10 112
6.	**Tax credits**	0	4 882	3 536	4 882
	Basic credit	0	0	0	0
	Married or head of family	0	0	0	0
	Children	0	0	0	0
	Other	0	4 882	3 536	4 882
7.	**Central government income tax finally paid (5-6)**	8 383	5 230	9 293	5 230
8.	**State and local taxes**	0	0	0	0
9.	**Employees' compulsory social security contributions**				
	Gross earnings	2 461	3 237	4 036	3 237
10.	**Total payments to general government (7+8+9)**	10 845	8 466	13 328	8 466
11.	**Cash transfers from general government**	0	0	0	0
	For head of family	0	0	0	0
	For two children	0	0	0	0
12.	**Take-home pay (1-10+11)**	88 077	123 100	151 871	123 100
13.	**Employer's compulsory social security contributions**	21 581	31 832	37 425	31 832
14.	**Average rates**				
	Income tax (7 / 1)	8.5%	4.0%	5.6%	4.0%
	Employees' social security contributions (9 / 1)	2.5%	2.5%	2.4%	2.5%
	Total payments less cash transfers [(10-11) / 1]	11.0%	6.4%	8.1%	6.4%
	Total tax wedge including employer's social security contributions [(10+13-11) / (1+13)]	26.9%	24.7%	25.0%	24.7%
15.	**Marginal rates**				
	Total payments less cash transfers: principal earner	18.7%	18.7%	18.7%	18.7%
	Total payments less cash transfers: spouse	-7.3%	8.5%	13.2%	8.5%
	Total tax wedge: principal earner	31.0%	31.0%	31.0%	31.0%
	Total tax wedge: spouse	18.4%	21.5%	25.6%	21.5%

The national currency is the Mexican Peso (MXN). In 2013, the average exchange rate was MXN 12.77 to USD 1. In the same year, the average worker in Mexico earned MXN 98 921.91.

The Report includes estimates of the tax wedge over the whole of the income distribution ordered by deciles of total labour income of formal wage earners derived from the household surveys.

	Deciles of Incomes									
	1	2	3	4	5	6	7	8	9	10
Local currency (MXN)	20 208	39 193	48 496	58 156	67 907	80 081	96 719	120 798	161 584	335 537
USD[1]	1 583	3 070	3 798	4 555	5 319	6 272	7 575	9 461	12 656	26 281
Dollars in PPP[2]	2 595	5 034	6 229	7 469	8 722	10 285	12 422	15 515	20 753	43 095
Ratio to the minimum wage[3]	0.9	1.7	2.1	2.5	2.9	3.4	4.1	5.1	6.8	14.2

1. Average official exchange rates published by the central bank.
2. Calculated using the implied conversion rate (National currency per current international dollar in purchasing parity power) published by the IMF in the World Economic Outlook dataset.
3. Ratio of the income decile to the official minimum wage of the country.

1. Personal income tax system

The fiscal year for the income tax is the calendar year.

1.1. *Central government income tax*

The personal income tax is levied on income attained from employment by individuals as wages, salaries, allowances, gratuities, fees and bonuses. Some specific fringe benefits are also taxed in addition to statutory employee profit sharing distributions.

1.1.1. *Tax unit*

Members of the family are taxed separately.

Mexican resident individuals are taxed on their worldwide income, while non-residents are taxed only on their Mexican-sourced income.

1.1.2. *Tax allowances and tax credits*

1.1.2.1. Standard tax allowances and tax credits

- Mexico's labour law establishes a minimum holiday bonus. This bonus amounts to 25% of six days of the worker's wage with an upper limit equivalent to 15 days of the minimum wage (the minimum wage for the entire country).[1]
- End of year bonuses up to 30 days of the minimum wage.

1.1.2.2. Main non-standard tax allowances and tax credits

- Compulsory transportation costs.
- Taxpayers can deduct an unlimited amount of medical expenses. Taxpayers may also claim these deductions on behalf of their spouses or dependents if they earn less than the minimum wage of the area in which they reside.
- Complementary contributions to retirement plans are eligible as long as they do not exceed 10% of the taxable income and 5 times the annual minimum wage (MXN 115 194).
- Taxpayers may deduct funeral expenses for the spouse and close relatives up to a maximum of the annual minimum wage of the geographical area where the taxpayer resides.
- Charitable donations to federal, state and municipal governments and non-profit organisations involved in the field of social beneficence, education, culture, research and technology.
- Deposits on special savings accounts and insurance premiums to pension plans for the acquisition of shares of investment societies, as long as they do not exceed MXN 152 000.
- Health insurance premiums for the individual if the beneficiary is the taxpayer, and/or his/her family.
- Deductions of the taxpayer's personal educational expenses or those of his/her spouse, parents, children, and other close relatives, according to the following table:

Education level	Maximum annual deduction (MXN)
Kinder garden	14 200
Primary education	12 900
Secondary education	19 900
Technical profession	17 100
High school	24 500

1.1.3. *Tax schedule*

The personal income tax liability was calculated on the taxable income according to the following schedule in 2013:

Income up to (MXN)	Marginal rate (%)
5 952.84	1.92
50 524.92	6.40
88 793.04	10.88
103 218.00	16.00
123 580.20	17.92
249 243.48	21.36
392 841.96	23.52
above	30.00

1.1.4. *Employment subsidy credit*

An employment subsidy credit is assigned according to the following schedule. It is paid by employers who can credit it against their tax liabilities. This credit is thus a fiscal expense for the government. The amount of the subsidy decreases as earnings increase. No employment subsidy credit was given to workers with annual earnings of over MXN 88 587.97. Employees with an income tax liability that is less than the amount of the credit they are entitled to receive the credit along with their salary. Other workers receiving the credit are entitled to credit it against the calculated income tax.

Income (MXN) up to	Amount of the subsidy (MXN)
21 227.52	4 884.24
31 840.56	4 881.96
41 674.08	4 879.44
42 454.44	4 713.24
53 353.80	4 589.52
56 606.16	4 250.76
64 025.04	3 898.44
74 696.04	3 535.56
85 366.80	3 042.48
88 587.96	2 611.32
above	0

1.2. *State and local taxes*

No state or local taxes are levied on wages.

2. Compulsory social security contribution to schemes operated within the government sector

2.1. *Employee contributions*

Program	Marginal rate (%)
Old age, disability and survivors programs*	1.75
Sickness and maternity, disability and life insurance	0.625
Sickness and maternity**	0.4

*1.125% of the contribution is paid to privately managed funds.
**0.40% is paid in addition to 0.625% when the individual's income exceeds 3 times the monthly minimum wage for the Federal District of Mexico.

Employee social security contributions are levied on gross wages. The upper ceiling for social security contributions was 25 times the minimum legal wage (MXN 70 912.20 per year in 2013) applying in the Federal District of Mexico (MWFD).

2.2. *Employer contributions*

Employers are required to contribute to the following public programs.

Program	Marginal rate (%)
Pensions, old age and survivors program*	6.9
Disability and life insurance	1.75
Work injury	0.25 – 1.98
Nursery and social services	1.0
Sickness and maternity (in kind and monetary benefits)	1.75
Housing Fund**	5.0

Program *(cont.)*	Marginal rate (%) *(cont.)*
Sickness and maternity (regular)	20.4
Sickness and maternity	1.1

*2.0% and 3.15% are paid to privately managed funds in respect of retirement and discharge and old age insurance.
**Paid to privately managed funds.

Employer contributions are levied on the payroll. In 2013, there was an upper ceiling of 25 times the MWFD on the wages used to calculate the contributions. The 1.1% contribution for sickness and maternity was levied on wages in excess of 3 times the MWDF.

3. Universal cash transfer

3.1. *Amount for spouse and for dependent children*

There are no universal cash transfers.

4. Main changes in tax/benefit since 2013

The tax schedule was amended at the upper end of the earnings distribution in 2015 as follows

Income (MXN) up to	Marginal rate (%)
5 952.84	1.92
50 524.92	6.40
88 793.04	10.88
103 218.00	16.00
123 580.20	17.92
249 243.48	21.36
392 841.96	23.52
750 000.00	30.00
999 999.96	32.00
3 000 000.00	34.00
above	35.00

5. Memorandum items

5.1. *Identification of an AW*

The data refer to the earnings of workers within the formal sector. The average worker's wage was calculated using microdata from the national household surveys as well as the average income deciles.

Note

1. There are two minimum wages in Mexico: Zone A which is equal to MXN 64.76 per day, which is the minimum wage of the Federal District of Mexico; and Zone B which is equal to MXN 61.38 on a daily basis.

Nicaragua

The country profile includes data on the income taxes paid by workers, their social security contributions, the family benefits they receive in the form of cash transfers as well as the social security contributions and payroll taxes paid by the employers. Results reported include the average and marginal tax burdens for eight different family types.

It also describes the personal income tax systems, all compulsory social security contribution schemes and universal cash transfers as well as recent changes in the tax/benefit system.

Nicaragua 2013

Tax / benefit of single persons

	Wage level (% of average wage)	67	100	167	67
	Number of children	0	0	0	2
1.	**Gross wage earnings**	53 085	79 231	132 316	53 085
2.	**Standard tax allowances**	7 408	11 057	18 465	7 408
	Basic allowance	0	0	0	0
	Married or head of family	0	0	0	0
	Dependent children	0	0	0	0
	Deduction for social security contributions and income taxes	3 045	4 545	7 590	3 045
	Work-related expenses	0	0	0	0
	Other	4 363	6 512	10 875	4 363
3.	**Tax credits or cash transfers included in taxable income**	0	0	0	0
4.	**Central government taxable income (1-2+3)**	45 677	68 174	113 851	45 677
5.	**Central government income tax liability (exclusive of tax credits)**	0	0	4 578	0
6.	**Tax credits**	0	0	0	0
	Basic credit	0	0	0	0
	Married or head of family	0	0	0	0
	Children	0	0	0	0
	Other	0	0	0	0
7.	**Central government income tax finally paid (5-6)**	0	0	4 578	0
8.	**State and local taxes**	0	0	0	0
9.	**Employees' compulsory social security contributions**				
	Gross income	3 045	4 545	7 590	3 045
10.	**Total payments to general government (7+8+9)**	3 045	4 545	12 168	3 045
11.	**Cash transfers from general government**	0	0	0	0
	For head of family	0	0	0	0
	For two children	0	0	0	0
12.	**Take-home pay (1-10+11)**	50 040	74 686	120 148	50 040
13.	**Employer's compulsory social security contributions**	8 857	13 220	22 077	8 857
14.	**Average rates**				
	Income tax (7 / 1)	0.0%	0.0%	3.5%	0.0%
	Employees' social security contributions (9 / 1)	5.7%	5.7%	5.7%	5.7%
	Total payments less cash transfers [(10-11) / 1]	5.7%	5.7%	9.2%	5.7%
	Total tax wedge including employer's social security contributions [(10+13-11) / (1+13)]	19.2%	19.2%	22.2%	19.2%
15.	**Marginal rates**				
	Total payments less cash transfers: principal earner	5.7%	5.7%	18.6%	5.7%
	Total payments less cash transfers: spouse	N.A.	N.A.	N.A.	N.A.
	Total tax wedge: principal earner	19.2%	19.2%	30.3%	19.2%
	Total tax wedge: spouse	N.A.	N.A.	N.A.	N.A.

Nicaragua 2013

Tax / benefit of married couples

		100-0	100-33	100-67	100-33
	Wage level (% of average wage)	100-0	100-33	100-67	100-33
	Number of children	2	2	2	0
1.	**Gross wage earnings**	79 231	105 377	132 316	105 377
2.	**Standard tax Allowances**	11 057	13 206	18 465	13 206
	Basic allowance	0	0	0	0
	Married or head of family	0	0	0	0
	Dependent children	0	0	0	0
	Deduction for social security contributions and income taxes	4 545	4 545	7 590	4 545
	Work-related expenses	0	0	0	0
	Other	6 512	8 661	10 875	8 661
3.	**Tax credits or cash transfers included in taxable income**	0	0	0	0
4.	**Central government taxable income (1-2+3)**	68 174	92 171	113 851	92 171
5.	**Central government income tax liability (exclusive of tax credits)**	0	0	0	0
6.	**Tax credits**	0	0	0	0
	Basic credit	0	0	0	0
	Married or head of family	0	0	0	0
	Children	0	0	0	0
	Other	0	0	0	0
7.	**Central government income tax finally paid (5-6)**	0	0	0	0
8.	**State and local taxes**	0	0	0	0
9.	**Employees' compulsory social security contributions**				
	Gross income	4 545	4 545	7 590	4 545
10.	**Total payments to general government (7+8+9)**	4 545	4 545	7 590	4 545
11.	**Cash transfers from general government**	0	0	0	0
	For head of family	0	0	0	0
	For two children	0	0	0	0
12.	**Take-home pay (1-10+11)**	74 686	100 833	124 726	100 833
13.	**Employer's compulsory social security contributions**	13 220	13 220	22 077	13 220
14.	**Average rates**				
	Income tax (7 / 1)	0.0%	0.0%	0.0%	0.0%
	Employees' social security contributions (9 / 1)	5.7%	4.3%	5.7%	4.3%
	Total payments less cash transfers [(10-11) / 1]	5.7%	4.3%	5.7%	4.3%
	Total tax wedge including employer's social security contributions [(10+13-11) / (1+13)]	19.2%	15.0%	19.2%	15.0%
15.	**Marginal rates**				
	Total payments less cash transfers: principal earner	5.7%	5.7%	5.7%	5.7%
	Total payments less cash transfers: spouse	0.0%	0.0%	5.7%	0.0%
	Total tax wedge: principal earner	19.2%	19.2%	19.2%	19.2%
	Total tax wedge: spouse	0.0%	0.0%	19.2%	0.0%

The national currency is the Cordoba (NIO). In 2013, the average exchange rate was NIO 24.72 to USD 1. In that year, the average worker earned NIO 79 231.20 on an annual basis.

The Report includes estimates of the tax wedge over the whole of the income distribution ordered by deciles of total labour income of formal wage earners derived from the household surveys.

	Deciles of Incomes									
	1	2	3	4	5	6	7	8	9	10
Local currency (NIO)	31 287	40 320	46 884	51 881	58 574	65 930	73 350	85 253	110 888	230 139
USD[1]	1 265	1 631	1 896	2 098	2 369	2 667	2 967	3 448	4 485	9 309
Dollars in PPP[2]	3 253	4 193	4 875	5 395	6091	6 856	7 627	8 865	11 530	23 930
Ratio to the minimum wage[3]	0.7	0.9	1.0	1.1	1.3	1.4	1.6	1.9	2.4	5.0

1. Average official exchange rates published by the central bank.
2. Calculated using the implied conversion rate (National currency per current international dollar in purchasing parity power) published by the IMF in the World Economic Outlook dataset.
3. Ratio of the income decile to the official minimum wage of the country.

1. Personal income tax system

The fiscal year is the calendar year.

1.1. *Central government income tax*

Equity Law No. 453 establishes that all income received within the Nicaraguan territory is liable to income tax. This includes employment income consisting of salaries, wages, pensions, bonuses, premiums and allowances, self-employment and business income and investment income.

Exempt income:

The most noteworthy types of exempt income relating to employment include:

- Compensations and indemnifications for the worker and his/her beneficiaries.
- The thirteenth month bonus component of wages.

1.1.1. *Tax unit*

Members of the family are taxed separately.

Personal income tax applies to all residents and non-residents receiving income in the country.

1.1.2. *Tax allowances and tax credits*

1.1.2.1. Standard tax allowances and tax credits

- Social security contributions paid to the Nicaraguan Institute for Social Security (INSS).

1.1.2.2. Main non-standard tax allowances and tax credits

- Contributions of employed individuals to approved retirement accounts that are not part of the social security scheme.

1.1.3. *Tax schedule*

The annual personal income tax liability was calculated according to the following schedule in 2013:

Income (NIO) up to	Marginal rate (%)
75 000	0
100 000	10
200 000	15
300 000	20
500 000	25
Above	30

1.2. *State and local taxes*

No state or local taxes are levied on wages.

2. Compulsory social security contribution to schemes operated within the government sector

2.1. *Employee contributions*

Program	Marginal rate (%)
Old age, disability and death program	4.0
Healthcare and Maternity program	2.25

The employee contributions are levied on the gross wage. The lower earnings threshold of earnings is the monthly minimum national wage, NIO 3 801.83 in 2013. The upper ceiling for contributions was NIO 37 518. The annual yearly thirteen month bonus is exempt from social security contributions.

2.1. *Employer contributions*

Employers are required to contribute to the following public programs.

Program	Marginal rate (%)
Old age, disability and death program	7.0
Healthcare and Maternity program	6.0
Work Injury	1.5
War victims	1.5
Technological National Institute – INATEC	2.0

The employer contribution rates are levied on the payroll.

3. Universal cash transfer

3.1. *Amount for spouse and for dependent children*

None.

4. Main changes in tax/benefit since 2013

Through decree 37-2013, the social security contribution rates paid by the employer to the old age program are being gradually increased from 2014. The schedule of the increases is:

2014: 8%

2015: 9%

2016: 9.5%

2017: 10%.

5. Memorandum items

5.1. *Identification of an AW*

The data refer to the earnings of workers within the formal sector. The average worker's wage was calculated using microdata from the national household surveys.

Panama

The country profile includes data on the income taxes paid by workers, their social security contributions, the family benefits they receive in the form of cash transfers as well as the social security contributions and payroll taxes paid by the employers. Results reported include the average and marginal tax burdens for eight different family types.

It also describes the personal income tax systems, all compulsory social security contribution schemes and universal cash transfers as well as recent changes in the tax/benefit system.

Panama 2013

Tax / benefit of single persons

	Wage level (% of average wage)	67	100	167	67
	Number of children	0	0	0	2
1.	**Gross wage earnings**	6 166	9 202	15 368	6 166
2.	**Standard tax allowances**	0	0	0	0
	Basic allowance	0	0	0	0
	Married or head of family	0	0	0	0
	Dependent children	0	0	0	0
	Deduction for social security contributions and income taxes	0	0	0	0
	Work-related expenses	0	0	0	0
	Other	0	0	0	0
3.	**Tax credits or cash transfers included in taxable income**	0	0	0	0
4.	**Central government taxable income (1-2+3)**	6 166	9 202	15 368	6 166
5.	**Central government income tax liability (exclusive of tax credits)**	0	0	655	0
6.	**Tax credits**	0	0	0	0
	Basic credit	0	0	0	0
	Married or head of family	0	0	0	0
	Children	0	0	0	0
	Other	0	0	0	0
7.	**Central government income tax finally paid (5-6)**	0	0	655	0
8.	**State and local taxes**	0	0	0	0
9.	**Employees' compulsory social security contributions**				
	Gross earnings	702	1 048	1 750	702
10.	**Total payments to general government (7+8+9)**	702	1 048	2 406	702
11.	**Cash transfers from general government**	0	0	0	0
	For head of family	0	0	0	0
	For two children	0	0	0	0
12.	**Take-home pay (1-10+11)**	5 463	8 154	12 962	5 463
13.	**Employer's compulsory social security contributions**	918	1 371	2 289	918
14.	**Average rates**				
	Income tax (7 / 1)	0.0%	0.0%	4.3%	0.0%
	Employees' social security contributions (9 / 1)	11.4%	11.4%	11.4%	11.4%
	Total payments less cash transfers [(10-11) / 1]	11.4%	11.4%	15.7%	11.4%
	Total tax wedge including employer's social security contributions [(10+13-11) / (1+13)]	22.9%	22.9%	26.6%	22.9%
15.	**Marginal rates**				
	Total payments less cash transfers: principal earner	11.4%	11.4%	26.4%	11.4%
	Total payments less cash transfers: spouse	N.A.	N.A.	N.A.	N.A.
	Total tax wedge: principal earner	22.9%	22.9%	35.9%	22.9%
	Total tax wedge: spouse	N.A.	N.A.	N.A.	N.A.

Panama 2013

Tax / benefit of married couples

	Wage level (% of average wage)	100-0	100-33	100-67	100-33
	Number of children	2	2	2	0
1.	**Gross wage earnings**	9 202	12 239	15 368	12 239
2.	**Standard tax allowances**	800	800	800	800
	Basic allowance	0	0	0	0
	Married or head of family	800	800	800	800
	Dependent children	0	0	0	0
	Deduction for social security contributions and income taxes	0	0	0	0
	Work-related expenses	0	0	0	0
	Other	0	0	0	0
3.	**Tax credits or cash transfers included in taxable income**	0	0	0	0
4.	**Central government taxable income (1-2+3)**	8 402	11 439	14 568	11 439
5.	**Central government income tax liability (exclusive of tax credits)**	0	0	0	0
6.	**Tax credits**	0	0	0	0
	Basic credit	0	0	0	0
	Married or head of family	0	0	0	0
	Children	0	0	0	0
	Other	0	0	0	0
7.	**Central government income tax finally paid (5-6)**	0	0	0	0
8.	**State and local taxes**	0	0	0	0
9.	**Employees' compulsory social security contributions**				
	Gross earnings	1 048	1 394	1 750	1 394
10.	**Total payments to general government (7+8+9)**	1 048	1 394	1 750	1 394
11.	**Cash transfers from general government**	0	0	0	0
	For head of family	0	0	0	0
	For two children	0	0	0	0
12.	**Take-home pay (1-10+11)**	8 154	10 845	13 618	10 845
13.	**Employer's compulsory social security contributions**	1 371	1 823	2 289	1 823
14.	**Average rates**				
	Income tax (7 / 1)	0.0%	0.0%	0.0%	0.0%
	Employees' social security contributions (9 / 1)	11.4%	11.4%	11.4%	11.4%
	Total payments less cash transfers [(10-11) / 1]	11.4%	11.4%	11.4%	11.4%
	Total tax wedge including employer's social security contributions [(10+13-11) / (1+13)]	22.9%	22.9%	22.9%	22.9%
15.	**Marginal rates**				
	Total payments less cash transfers: principal earner	11.4%	11.4%	11.4%	11.4%
	Total payments less cash transfers: spouse	11.4%	11.4%	11.4%	11.4%
	Total tax wedge: principal earner	22.9%	22.9%	22.9%	22.9%
	Total tax wedge: spouse	22.9%	22.9%	22.9%	22.9%

The national currency is the Balboa (PAB) which is equivalent to the USD. In 2013, the average worker earned PAB 9 202.49.

The Report includes estimates of the tax wedge over the whole of the income distribution ordered by deciles of total labour income of formal wage earners derived from the household surveys.

	Deciles of Incomes									
	1	2	3	4	5	6	7	8	9	10
Local currency (PAB)	3 557	4 782	5 267	5 903	6 438	7 142	8 306	10 001	12 920	29 279
USD[1]	3 557	4 782	5 267	5 903	6 438	7 142	8 306	10 001	12 920	29 279
Dollars in PPP[2]	6 262	8 420	9 274	10 393	11 335	12 574	14 623	17 607	22 747	51 547
Ratio to the minimum wage[3]	0.6	0.9	1.0	1.1	1.2	1.3	1.5	1.8	2.3	5.3

1. Average official exchange rates published by the central bank.
2. Calculated using the implied conversion rate (National currency per current international dollar in purchasing parity power) published by the IMF in the World Economic Outlook dataset.
3. Ratio of the income decile to the official minimum wage of the country.

1. Personal income tax system

The fiscal year is the calendar year.

1.1. *Central government income tax*

The sources of income liable to income tax include employment income consisting of wages, salaries, bonuses, pensions, fees and other payments in exchange for services. Education allowances plus, self-employment, business and investment income are also liable.

Exempt income:

The most noteworthy types of exempt income relating to employment include:

- Sums received as compensation or indemnification for accidents or injuries at work and benefits paid by the Social Security Fund.
- Money donated to charitable institutions.
- Bonuses paid to public sector workers adhering to a voluntary retirement plan.
- Severance pay and other bonuses up to PAB 5 000.

1.1.1. *Tax unit*

Members of the family are taxed separately.

Personal income tax applies to all residents and non-residents receiving income in the country, regardless of the nationality of the individual and the origin of the payment. A legal resident for tax purposes is a person who has resided or remained in the country for 183 days during the calendar year.

1.1.2. *Tax allowances and tax credits*

1.1.2.1. Standard tax allowances and tax credits

- When filing jointly, a married couple may deduct PAB 800.00

1.1.2.2. Main non-standard tax allowances and tax credits

- Interest paid on mortgages on the purchase or improvement of a taxpayer's main residence in Panama up to PAB 15 000.
- Interest paid on loans to finance the education of the taxpayer.
- Interest paid on loans granted by the Human Resources Training and Formation Institute (IFARHU).
- Medical expenses paid within the country subject to documentation being provided.

1.1.3. *Tax schedule*

The annual personal income tax liability schedule was calculated on the taxable income according to the following schedule in 2013:

Income (PAB) up to	Marginal rate (%)
11 000	0
50 000	15
above	25

1.2. *State and local taxes*

No state or local taxes are levied on wages.

2. Compulsory social security contribution to schemes operated within the government sector

2.1. *Employee contributions*

Program	Marginal rate (%)
Old age, disability and death program	9.25
Healthcare program	0.50
Education insurance	1.25

The employee contributions are levied on gross wages. The monthly lower earnings threshold for the old age and healthcare programs was PAB 1 200 in 2013. There was no lower earnings threshold for the education insurance. The contribution rate to the old age, disability and death program was reduced to 7.25% for the annual 13th month bonus for the old age program.

2.2. *Employer contributions*

Employers are required to contribute to the following public programs.

Program	Marginal rate (%)
Old age, disability and death program	4.25
Healthcare and Maternity program	8.00
Work Injury	0.42
Education insurance	1.50

The employer contributions are levied on the payroll. A 10.75% contribution rate for the old age, disability and death program is levied on bonuses paid to the employees.

The work injury contribution rate corresponds to a grade 6 risk activity.

3. Universal cash transfer

3.1. *Amount for spouse and for dependent children*

None.

4. Main changes in tax/benefit since 2013

None.

5. Memorandum items

5.1. *Identification of an AW*

The data refer to the earnings of workers within the formal sector. The average worker's wage was calculated using microdata from the national household surveys.

Paraguay

The country profile includes data on the income taxes paid by workers, their social security contributions, the family benefits they receive in the form of cash transfers as well as the social security contributions and payroll taxes paid by the employers. Results reported include the average and marginal tax burdens for eight different family types.

It also describes the personal income tax systems, all compulsory social security contribution schemes and universal cash transfers as well as recent changes in the tax/benefit system.

Paraguay 2013

Tax / benefit of single persons

	Wage level (% of average wage)	67	100	167	67
	Number of children	0	0	0	2
1.	**Gross wage earnings**	23 666 005	35 322 396	58 988 401	23 666 005
2.	**Standard tax allowances**	2 129 940	3 179016	5 308 956	2 129 940
	Basic allowance	0	0	0	0
	Married or head of family	0	0	0	0
	Dependent children	0	0	0	0
	Deduction for social security contributions and income taxes	2 129 940	3 179016	5 308 956	2 129 940
	Work-related expenses	0	0	0	0
	Other	0	0	0	0
3.	**Tax credits or cash transfers included in taxable income**	0	0	0	0
4.	**Central government taxable income (1-2+3)**	21 536 065	32 143 380	53 679 445	21 536 065
5.	**Central government income tax liability (exclusive of tax credits)**	0	0	0	0
6.	**Tax credits**	0	0	0	0
	Basic credit	0	0	0	0
	Married or head of family	0	0	0	0
	Children	0	0	0	0
	Other	0	0	0	0
7.	**Central government income tax finally paid (5-6)**	0	0	0	0
8.	**State and local taxes**	0	0	0	0
9.	**Employees' compulsory social security contributions**				
	Gross earnings	2 129 940	3 179 016	5 308 956	2 129 940
10.	**Total payments to general government (7+8+9)**	2 129 940	3 179 016	5 308 956	2 129 940
11.	**Cash transfers from general government**	0	0	0	0
	For head of family	0	0	0	0
	For two children	0	0	0	0
12.	**Take-home pay (1-10+11)**	21 536 065	32 143 380	53 679 445	21 536 065
13.	**Employer's compulsory social security contributions**	3 549 901	5 298 359	8 848 260	3 549 901
14.	**Average rates**				
	Income tax (7 / 1)	0.0%	0.0%	0.0%	0.0%
	Employees' social security contributions (9 / 1)	9.0%	9.0%	9.0%	9.0%
	Total payments less cash transfers [(10-11) / 1]	9.0%	9.0%	9.0%	9.0%
	Total tax wedge including employer's social security contributions [(10+13-11) / (1+13)]	20.9%	20.9%	20.9%	20.9%
15.	**Marginal rates**				
	Total payments less cash transfers: principal earner	9.0%	9.0%	9.0%	9.0%
	Total payments less cash transfers: spouse	N.A.	N.A.	N.A.	N.A.
	Total tax wedge: principal earner	20.9%	20.9%	20.9%	20.9%
	Total tax wedge: spouse	N.A.	N.A.	N.A.	N.A.

Paraguay 2013

Tax / benefit of married couples

		Wage level (% of average wage)	100-0	100-33	100-67	100-33
		Number of children	2	2	2	0
1.	**Gross wage earnings**		35 322 396	46 978 787	58 988 401	46 978 787
2.	**Standard tax allowances**		3 179 016	3 179 016	5 308 956	3 179 016
	Basic allowance		0	0	0	0
	Married or head of family		0	0	0	0
	Dependent children		0	0	0	0
	Deduction for social security contributions and income taxes		3 179 016	3 179 016	5 308 956	3 179 016
	Work-related expenses		0	0	0	0
	Other		0	0	0	0
3.	**Tax credits or cash transfers included in taxable income**		0	0	0	0
4.	**Central government taxable income (1 - 2 + 3)**		32 143 380	43 799 771	53 679 445	43 799 771
5.	**Central government income tax liability (exclusive of tax credits)**		0	0	0	0
6.	**Tax credits**		0	0	0	0
	Basic credit		0	0	0	0
	Married or head of family		0	0	0	0
	Children		0	0	0	0
	Other		0	0	0	0
7.	**Central government income tax finally paid (5-6)**		0	0	0	0
8.	**State and local taxes**		0	0	0	0
9.	**Employees' compulsory social security contributions**					
	Gross earnings		3 179 016	3 179 016	5 308 956	3 179 016
10.	**Total payments to general government (7 + 8 + 9)**		3 179 016	3 179 016	5 308 956	3 179 016
11.	**Cash transfers from general government**		0	0	0	0
	For head of family		0	0	0	0
	For two children		0	0	0	0
12.	**Take-home pay (1-10+11)**		32 143 380	43 799 771	53 679 445	43 799 771
13.	**Employer's compulsory social security contributions**		5 298 359	5 414 923	8 848 260	5 414 923
14.	**Average rates**					
	Income tax (7 / 1)		0.0%	0.0%	0.0%	0.0%
	Employees' social security contributions (9 / 1)		9.0%	6.8%	9.0%	6.8%
	Total payments less cash transfers [(10-11) / 1]		9.0%	6.8%	9.0%	6.8%
	Total tax wedge including employer's social security contributions [(10+13-11) / (1+ 13)]		20.9%	16.4%	20.9%	16.4%
15.	**Marginal rates**					
	Total payments less cash transfers: principal earner		9.0%	9.0%	9.0%	9.0%
	Total payments less cash transfers: spouse		0.0%	0.0%	9.0%	0.0%
	Total tax wedge: principal earner		20.9%	20.9%	20.9%	20.9%
	Total tax wedge: spouse		1.0%	1.0%	20.9%	1.0%

The national currency is the Guarani (PYG). In 2013, the average exchange rate was PYG 4 357.61 to USD 1. In that year, the average worker earned PYG 35 322 396.

The Report includes estimates of the tax wedge over the whole of the income distribution ordered by deciles of total labour income of formal wage earners derived from the household surveys.

	Deciles of Incomes									
	1	2	3	4	5	6	7	8	9	10
Local currency (thousands of PYG)	14 355	18 818	20 211	22 811	25 232	29 543	34 394	40 611	52 385	96 048
USD[1]	3 294	4 318	4 638	5 235	5 790	6 780	7 893	9 320	12 021	22 041
Dollars in PPP[2]	6 341	8 312	8 927	10 076	11 145	13 050	15 192	17 938	23 139	42 426
Ratio to the minimum wage[3]	0.7	0.9	1.0	1.1	1.3	1.5	1.7	2.0	2.6	4.8

1. Average official exchange rates published by the central bank.
2. Calculated using the implied conversion rate (National currency per current international dollar in purchasing power parity) published by the IMF in the World Economic Outlook dataset.
3. Ratio of the income decile to the official minimum wage of the country.

1. Personal income tax system

The fiscal year is the calendar year.

1.1. Central government income tax

The personal income tax in Paraguay dates from a law enacted in 2004 that was enforced in 2012. The tax is applied to all income from employment or self-employment earned in Paraguay by both residents and non-residents. It also applies to dividends, interest, profits and capital gains.

1.1.1. Tax unit

Members of the family are taxed separately.

1.1.2. Tax allowances and tax credits

1.1.2.1. Standard tax allowances and tax credits

- Social security contributions.

1.1.2.2. Main non-standard tax allowances and tax credits

- Personal and family expenses in the country relating to food, drink and household goods, education, health, housing or leisure activities of the taxpayer or her dependents.
- Donations to the state, municipalities and religious institutions that are properly recognized by the competent authorities.
- Contributions to pension plans.

1.1.3. *Tax schedule*

The annual personal income tax liability was calculated on the taxable income according to the following schedule in 2013:

Income (PYG) up to	Marginal rate (%)
179 089 056	0.0
198 987 840	8.0
above	10.0

The minimum wage in Paraguay for 2013 was PYG 1 658 232 per month.

1.2. *State and local taxes*

No state or local taxes are levied on wages.

2. Compulsory social security contribution to schemes operated within the government sector

2.1. *Employee contributions*

Program	Marginal rate (%)
Old age, disability and death program	9.0

The employee contributions are levied on gross wages. The lower earnings threshold is the minimum wage, PYG 19 898 784 in 2013, and there is no upper ceiling on the contributions.

2.2. *Employer contributions*

Employers are required to contribute to the following public programs.

Program	Marginal rate (%)
Old age program	14.0
National System for Labour Training	1.0

The employer contributions are levied on the payroll.

3. Universal cash transfer

3.1. *Amount for spouse and for dependent children*

None.

4. Main changes in tax/benefit since 2013

From 2014, the threshold for paying personal income tax is being reduced by an amount of 12 times the minimum wage each year until it reaches 36 times the minimum wage. In 2016, the minimum threshold was PYG 131 331 960 (72 times the minimum wage).

5. Memorandum items

5.1. *Identification of an AW*

The data refer to the earnings of workers within the formal sector. The average worker's wage was calculated using microdata from the national household surveys.

Peru

The country profile includes data on the income taxes paid by workers, their social security contributions, the family benefits they receive in the form of cash transfers as well as the social security contributions and payroll taxes paid by the employers. Results reported include the average and marginal tax burdens for eight different family types.

It also describes the personal income tax systems, all compulsory social security contribution schemes and universal cash transfers as well as recent changes in the tax/benefit system.

Peru 2013

Tax / benefit of single persons

	Wage level (% of average wage)	67	100	167	67
	Number of children	0	0	0	2
1.	**Gross wage earnings**	11 413	17 034	28 447	11 413
2.	**Standard tax allowances**	25 900	25 900	25 900	25 900
	Basic allowance	25 900	25 900	25 900	25 900
	Married or head of family	0	0	0	0
	Dependent children	0	0	0	0
	Deduction for social security contributions and income taxes	0	0	0	0
	Work-related expenses	0	0	0	0
	Other	0	0	0	0
3.	**Tax credits or cash transfers included in taxable income**	0	0	0	0
4.	**Central government taxable income (1-2+3)**	0	0	2 547	0
5.	**Central government income tax liability (exclusive of tax credits)**	0	0	382	0
6.	**Tax credits**	0	0	0	0
	Basic credit	0	0	0	0
	Married or head of family	0	0	0	0
	Children	0	0	0	0
	Other	0	0	0	0
7.	**Central government income tax finally paid (5-6)**	0	0	382	0
8.	**State and local taxes**	0	0	0	0
9.	**Employees' compulsory social security contributions**				
	Gross earnings	1 240	1 850	3 090	1 240
10.	**Total payments to general government (7+8+9)**	1 240	1 850	3 472	1 240
11.	**Cash transfers from general government**	0	0	0	0
	For head of family	0	0	0	0
	For two children	0	0	0	0
12.	**Take-home pay (1-10+11)**	10 173	15 184	24 975	10 173
13.	**Employer's compulsory social security contributions**	918	1 371	2 289	918
14.	**Average rates**				
	Income tax (7 / 1)	0.0%	0.0%	1.3%	0.0%
	Employees' social security contributions (9 / 1)	10.9%	10.9%	10.9%	10.9%
	Total payments less cash transfers [(10-11) / 1]	10.9%	10.9%	12.2%	10.9%
	Total tax wedge including employer's social security contributions [(10+13-11) / (1+13)]	17.5%	17.5%	18.7%	17.5%
15.	**Marginal rates**				
	Total payments less cash transfers: principal earner	10.9%	10.9%	25.9%	10.9%
	Total payments less cash transfers: spouse	N.A.	N.A.	N.A.	N.A.
	Total tax wedge: principal earner	17.5%	17.5%	31.4%	17.5%
	Total tax wedge: spouse	N.A.	N.A.	N.A.	N.A.

Peru 2013

Tax / benefit of married couples

	Wage level (% of average wage)	100-0	100-33	100-67	100-33
	Number of children	2	2	2	0
1.	**Gross wage earnings**	17 034	22 655	28 447	22 655
2.	**Standard tax allowances**	25 900	51 800	51 800	51 800
	Basic allowance	25 900	51 800	51 800	51 800
	Married or head of family	0	0	0	0
	Dependent children	0	0	0	0
	Deduction for social security contributions and income taxes	0	0	0	0
	Work-related expenses	0	0	0	0
	Other	0	0	0	0
3.	**Tax credits or cash transfers included in taxable income**	0	0	0	0
4.	**Central government taxable income (1-2+3)**	0	0	0	0
5.	**Central government income tax liability (exclusive of tax credits)**	0	0	0	0
6.	**Tax credits**	0	0	0	0
	Basic credit	0	0	0	0
	Married or head of family	0	0	0	0
	Children	0	0	0	0
	Other	0	0	0	0
7.	**Central government income tax finally paid (5-6)**	0	0	0	0
8.	**State and local taxes**	0	0	0	0
9.	**Employees' compulsory social security contributions**				
	Gross earnings	1 850	1 850	3 090	1 850
10.	**Total payments to general government (7+8+9)**	1 850	1 850	3 090	1 850
11.	**Cash transfers from general government**	0	0	0	0
	For head of family	0	0	0	0
	For two children	0	0	0	0
12.	**Take-home pay (1-10+11)**	15 184	20 805	25 357	20 805
13.	**Employer's compulsory social security contributions**	1 371	1 371	2 289	1 371
14.	**Average rates**				
	Income tax (7 / 1)	0.0%	0.0%	0.0%	0.0%
	Employees' social security contributions (9 / 1)	10.9%	8.2%	10.9%	8.2%
	Total payments less cash transfers [(10-11) / 1]	10.9%	8.2%	10.9%	8.2%
	Total tax wedge including employer's social security contributions [(10+13-11) / (1+13)]	17.5%	13.4%	17.5%	13.4%
15.	**Marginal rates**				
	Total payments less cash transfers: principal earner	10.9%	10.9%	10.9%	10.9%
	Total payments less cash transfers: spouse	0.0%	0.0%	10.9%	0.0%
	Total tax wedge: principal earner	17.5%	17.5%	17.5%	17.5%
	Total tax wedge: spouse	0.0%	0.0%	17.5%	0.0%

The national currency is the Sol (PEN). In 2013, the average exchange rate was PEN 2.72 to USD 1. In that year, the average worker earned PEN 17 034.11.

The Report includes estimates of the tax wedge over the whole of the income distribution ordered by deciles of total labour income of formal wage earners derived from the household surveys.

	Deciles of Incomes									
	1	2	3	4	5	6	7	8	9	10
Local currency (PEN)	6 377	8 516	9 710	10 904	12 503	14 224	16 228	19 606	25 246	48 230
USD[1]	2 346	3 133	3 573	4 012	4 600	5 233	5 970	7 213	9 288	17 744
Dollars in PPP[2]	4 187	5 591	6 376	7 160	8 210	9 339	10 655	12 873	16 576	31 668
Ratio to the minimum wage[3]	0.7	0.9	1.1	1.2	1.4	1.6	1.8	2.2	2.8	5.4

1. Average official exchange rates published by the central bank.
2. Calculated using the implied conversion rate (National currency per current international dollar in purchasing parity power) published by the IMF in the World Economic Outlook dataset.
3. Ratio of the income decile to the official minimum wage of the country.

1. Personal income tax system

The fiscal year is the calendar year.

1.1. *Central government income tax*

The income tax is levied on income of any source. It is comprised by five categories: i) income produced by the exploitation of capital goods; ii) other capital gains; iii) corporate income; iv) income from self-employment and v) income from employment.

Income from employment includes: wages, salaries, premiums, bonuses and commissions.

The main exemptions relating to income from employment are:

- Compensation paid due to illness, or work injuries.
- Subsidies for illness and maternity.
- Interest and gains from public notes or bonds issued by the government of Peru.

1.1.1. *Tax unit*

Members of the family are taxed separately.

The personal income tax is applied to all residents and non-residents receiving income in the country. For the purposes of the tax code, a person who resides in the country for more than 183 days in the year is considered to be a Peruvian resident.

1.1.2. *Tax allowances and tax credits*

1.1.2.1. Standard tax allowances and tax credits

- 7 tax units (PEN 25 900). A tax unit was equivalent to PEN 3 700 in 2013.

1.1.2.2. Main non-standard tax allowances and tax credits

None.

1.1.3. Tax schedule

The annual personal income tax liability was calculated on the taxable income according to the following schedule in 2013:

Income (PEN) up to	Marginal rate (%)
99 900 (27 tax units)	15.0
199 800 (54 tax units)	21.0
above	30.0

1.2. State and local taxes

No state or local taxes are levied on wages.

2. Compulsory social security contribution to schemes operated within the government sector

2.1. Employee contributions

Program	Marginal rate (%)
Old age, disability and death program	13.0

The employee contributions are levied on gross wages. The lower earnings threshold is the minimum wage (PEN 9 000 per year). There is no upper ceiling on the contributions. Mid and end year bonuses are exempt from social security contributions.

2.2. Employer contributions

Employers are required to contribute to the following public programs.

Program	Marginal rate (%)
Healthcare programs	9.0
Work Injury	0.6

The employer contributions are levied on the payroll. Mid and end year bonuses paid to employees are exempt from social security contributions.

3. Universal cash transfer

3.1. Amount for spouse and for dependent children

None.

4. Main changes in tax/benefit since 2013

The income tax schedule for the fifth category was updated as follows for 2015:

Tax units up to	Marginal rate (%)
5	8.0
20	14.0
35	17.0
45	20.0
above	30.0

The taxable unit in 2015 was PEN 3 850.

5. Memorandum items

5.1. *Identification of an AW*

The data refer to the earnings of workers within the formal sector. The average worker's wage was calculated using microdata from the national household surveys.

Trinidad and Tobago

The country profile includes data on the income taxes paid by workers, their social security contributions, the family benefits they receive in the form of cash transfers as well as the social security contributions and payroll taxes paid by the employers. Results reported include the average and marginal tax burdens for eight different family types.

It also describes the personal income tax systems, all compulsory social security contribution schemes and universal cash transfers as well as recent changes in the tax/benefit system.

Trinidad and Tobago 2013

Tax / benefit of single persons

		67	100	167	67
	Wage level (% of average wage)	67	100	167	67
	Number of children	0	0	0	2
1.	**Gross wage earnings**	33 034	49 305	82 339	33 034
2.	**Standard tax allowances**	61 558	62 105	63 667	61 558
	Basic allowance	60 000	60 000	60 000	60 000
	Married or head of family	0	0	0	0
	Dependent children	0	0	0	0
	Deduction for social security contributions and income taxes	1 558	2 105	3 667	1 558
	Work-related expenses	0	0	0	0
	Other	0	0	0	0
3.	**Tax credits or cash transfers included in taxable income**	0	0	0	0
4.	**Central government taxable income (1-2+3)**	0	0	18 672	0
5.	**Central government income tax liability (exclusive of tax credits)**	0	0	4 668	0
6.	**Tax credits**	0	0	0	0
	Basic credit	0	0	0	0
	Married or head of family	0	0	0	0
	Children	0	0	0	0
	Other	0	0	0	0
7.	**Central government income tax finally paid (5-6)**	0	0	4 668	0
8.	**State and local taxes**	0	0	0	0
9.	**Employees' compulsory social security contributions**				
	Gross earnings	1 686	2 234	3 795	1 686
10.	**Total payments to general government (7+8+9)**	1 686	2 234	8 464	1 686
11.	**Cash transfers from general government**	0	0	0	0
	For head of family	0	0	0	0
	For two children	0	0	0	0
12.	**Take-home pay (1-10+11)**	31 348	47071	73 875	31 348
13.	**Employer's compulsory social security contributions**	2 515	3 610	6 733	2 515
14.	**Average rates**				
	Income tax (7 / 1)	0%	0%	6%	0%
	Employees' social security contributions (9 / 1)	5%	5%	5%	5%
	Total payments less cash transfers [(10-11) / 1]	5%	5%	10%	5%
	Total tax wedge including employer's social security contributions [(10+13-11) / (1+13)]	12%	11%	17%	12%
15.	**Marginal rates**				
	Total payments less cash transfers: principal earner	0%	0%	25%	0%
	Total payments less cash transfers: spouse	N.A.	N.A.	N.A.	N.A.
	Total tax wedge: principal earner	0%	0%	25%	0%
	Total tax wedge: spouse	N.A.	N.A.	N.A.	N.A.

Trinidad and Tobago 2013

Tax / benefit of married couples

	Wage level (% of average wage)	100-0	100-33	100-67	100-33
	Number of children	2	2	2	0
1.	**Gross wage earnings**	49 305	65 575	82 339	65 575
2.	**Standard tax allowances**	62 105	122 994	123 663	122 994
	Basic allowance	60 000	120 000	120 000	120 000
	Married or head of family	0	0	0	0
	Dependent children	0	0	0	0
	Deduction for social security contributions and income taxes	2 105	2 994	3 663	2 994
	Work-related expenses	0	0	0	0
	Other	0	0	0	0
3.	**Tax credits or cash transfers included in taxable income**	0	0	0	0
4.	**Central government taxable income (1-2+3)**	0	0	0	0
5.	**Central government income tax liability (exclusive of tax credits)**	0	0	0	0
6.	**Tax credits**	0	0	0	0
	Basic credit	0	0	0	0
	Married or head of family	0	0	0	0
	Children	0	0	0	0
	Other	0	0	0	0
7.	**Central government income tax finally paid (5-6)**	0	0	0	0
8.	**State and local taxes**	0	0	0	0
9.	**Employees' compulsory social security contributions**				
	Gross earnings	2 234	3 251	3 920	3 251
10.	**Total payments to general government (7+8+9)**	2 234	3 251	3 920	3 251
11.	**Cash transfers from general government**	0	0	0	0
	For head of family	0	0	0	0
	For two children	0	0	0	0
12.	**Take-home pay (1-10+11)**	47 071	62 324	78 419	62 324
13.	**Employer's compulsory social security contributions**	3 610	4 786	6 125	4 786
14.	**Average rates**				
	Income tax (7 / 1)	0.0%	0.0%	0.0%	0.0%
	Employees' social security contributions (9 / 1)	4.5%	5.0%	4.8%	5.0%
	Total payments less cash transfers [(10-11) / 1]	4.5%	5.0%	4.8%	5.0%
	Total tax wedge including employer's social security contributions [(10+13-11) / (1+13)]	11.0%	11.4%	11.4%	11.4%
15.	**Marginal rates**				
	Total payments less cash transfers: principal earner	0.0%	0.0%	0.0%	0.0%
	Total payments less cash transfers: spouse	6.3%	0.0%	0.0%	0.0%
	Total tax wedge: principal earner	0.0%	0.0%	0.0%	0.0%
	Total tax wedge: spouse	12.6%	0.0%	0.0%	0.0%

The national currency is the Trinidad and Tobago dollar (TTD). In 2013, the average official exchange rate was TTD 6.39 to USD 1. In that year, the average worker earned TTD 49 304.75.

The Report includes estimates of the tax wedge over the whole of the income distribution ordered by deciles of total labour income of formal wage earners derived from the household surveys.

	Deciles of Incomes									
	1	2	3	4	5	6	7	8	9	10
Local currency (TTD)	9 385	18 396	24 558	30 361	36 477	43 334	51 561	62 455	79 871	136 649
USD[1]	1 469	2 880	3 844	4 752	5 710	6 783	8 071	9 776	12 502	21 390
Dollars in PPP[2]	2 266	4 442	5 930	7 332	8 809	10 465	12 451	15 082	19 288	32 999
Ratio to the minimum wage[3]	0.4	0.7	0.9	1.2	1.4	1.7	2.0	2.4	3.1	5.3

1. Average official exchange rates published by the central bank.
2. Calculated using the implied conversion rate (National currency per current international dollar in purchasing parity power) published by the IMF in the World Economic Outlook dataset.
3. Ratio of the income decile to the official minimum wage of the country.

1. Personal income tax system

The tax year for the personal income tax is the calendar year.

1.1. *Central government income tax*

The Income Tax Act Ch:75:01 and the Income Tax Employment Regulations Act 77/57, together with subsequent updates, represent the legislation governing the income tax in Trinidad and Tobago.

The taxable income of employees includes salaries, wages, bonuses, overtime, the value of board or lodging, stipend, commission or other payments for services, directors fees, retirement allowances or pensions accruing or received in Trinidad and Tobago. It does not include any salary or share of profits arising from a trade, profession or vocation carried on by an individual either as a sole trader or in partnership.

1.1.1. *Tax unit*

Members of the family are taxed separately

Individuals residing in Trinidad and Tobago are liable to personal tax on their worldwide income.

1.1.2. *Tax allowances and tax credits*

1.1 2.1. Standard tax allowances and tax credits

- A personal allowance of TTD 60 000.
- 70% of employee social security contributions up to TTD 30 000.

1.1.2.2. Main non-standard tax allowances and tax credits

- Foreign tertiary education expenses up to TTD 60 000 subject to an acceptance letter, proof of payment and statement of expenses being provided.
- A deduction for first-time home owners limited to TTD 18 000.
- Deferred annuities, tax savings and pension fund plans up to TTD 30 000.
- Alimony or maintenance paid in accordance with a court ruling.
- Travelling expenses, for official purposes, up to two thirds of the total.
- A tax credit for purchases of solar water heating equipment.
- A tax credit for venture capital investments up to 25% of the total investment.
- A tax credit for purchases of CNG kits and cylinders (equipment to adjust cars to run on natural gas).

The annual income tax liability was a flat rate 25% of taxable income in 2013.

1.3. State and local taxes

No state or local taxes are levied on wages.

2. Compulsory social security contributions

2.1. Employee and employer contributions

Employees and employers are required to pay contributions, levied on gross wages, for old age, disability and survivors programs to the National Insurance Board. Payments were in accordance with the following schedule in 2013.

Wage Class	Income (TTD) up to	Employee Contribution	Employer Contribution
1	12 995.88	405.6	811.20
2	17 159.88	588.12	1 176.24
3	23 399.88	790.92	1 581.84
4	29 123.88	1 024.40	2 048.80
5	35 399.88	1 257.36	2 514.72
6	42 635.88	1 521.00	3 042.00
7	49 919.88	1 804.92	3 609.84
8	57 203.88	2 088.84	4 177.68
9	65 519.88	2 393.04	4 786.08
10	73 319.88	2 707.64	5 415.28
11	81 635.88	3 021.72	6 043.44
12	90 995.88	3 366.48	6 732.96
13	100 355.88	3 731.52	7 463.04
14	111 803.88	4 137.12	8 274.24
15	119 999.88	4 520.36	9 040.72
16	above	4 680.52	9 361.04

In addition, employees, and other individuals also pay a health surcharge, levied on gross income to cover the provisions of health services in Trinidad and Tobago. The schedule of contributions is as follows:

Wage level class	Income (TTD) up to	Employee contribution (TTD)
1	5 639.88	249.60
2	above	429.00

3. Universal cash transfer

3.1. Amount for spouse and for dependent children

None.

4. Main changes in tax/benefit since 2013

The personal income tax allowance was increased to TTD 72 000 in 2015.

5. Memorandum items

5.1. Identification of an AW

The average worker's wage and average deciles of income have been estimated from data collected in the Household Budget Survey 2008/2009, adjusted for inflation.

Uruguay

The country profile includes data on the income taxes paid by workers, their social security contributions, the family benefits they receive in the form of cash transfers as well as the social security contributions and payroll taxes paid by the employers. Results reported include the average and marginal tax burdens for eight different family types.

It also describes the personal income tax systems, all compulsory social security contribution schemes and universal cash transfers as well as recent changes in the tax/benefit system.

Uruguay 2013

Tax / benefit of single persons

	Wage level (% of average wage)	67	100	167	67
	Number of children	0	0	0	2
1.	**Gross wage earnings**	168 880	252 060	420 940	168 880
2.	**Standard tax allowances**	0	0	0	0
	Basic allowance	0	0	0	0
	Married or head of family	0	0	0	0
	Dependent children	0	0	0	0
	Deduction for social security contributions and income taxes	0	0	0	0
	Work-related expenses	0	0	0	0
	Other	0	0	0	0
3.	**Tax credits or cash transfers included in taxable income**	0	0	0	0
4.	**Central government taxable income (1-2+3)**	168 880	252 060	420 940	168 880
5.	**Central government income tax liability (exclusive of tax credits)**	0	3 383	25 730	0
6.	**Tax credits**	3 042	4 540	7 582	10 367
	Basic credit	0	0	0	0
	Married or head of family	0	0	0	0
	Children	0	0	0	0
	Other	3 042	4 540	7 582	10 367
7.	**Central government income tax finally paid (5-6)**	0	0	18 148	0
8.	**State and local taxes**	0	0	0	0
9.	**Employees' compulsory social security contributions**				
	Gross earnings	30 419	45 401	75 820	32 744
10.	**Total payments to general government (7+8+9)**	30 419	45 401	93 967	32 744
11.	**Cash transfers from general government**	0	0	0	10 824
	For head of family	0	0	0	0
	For two children	0	0	0	10 824
12.	**Take-home pay (1-10+11)**	138 461	206 659	326 972	146 960
13.	**Employer's compulsory social security contributions**	30 264	45 170	75 433	30 264
14.	**Average rates**				
	Income tax (7 / 1)	0.0%	0.0%	4.3%	0.0%
	Employees' social security contributions (9 / 1)	18.0%	18.0%	18.0%	19.4%
	Total payments less cash transfers [(10-11) / 1]	18.0%	18.0%	22.3%	13.0%
	Total tax wedge including employer's social security contributions [(10+13-11) / (1+13)]	30.5%	30.5%	34.1%	26.2%
15.	**Marginal rates**				
	Total payments less cash transfers: principal earner	18.0%	18.0%	31.2%	19.4%
	Total payments less cash transfers: spouse	N.A.	N.A.	N.A.	N.A.
	Total tax wedge: principal earner	30.5%	30.5%	41.7%	31.6%
	Total tax wedge: spouse	N.A.	N.A.	N.A.	N.A.

Uruguay 2013

Tax / benefit of married couples

		100-0	100-33	100-67	100-33
	Wage level (% of average wage)	100-0	100-33	100-67	100-33
	Number of children	2	2	2	0
1.	**Gross wage earnings**	252 060	335 239	420 940	335 239
2.	**Standard tax allowances**	0	0	0	0
	Basic allowance	0	0	0	0
	Married or head of family	0	0	0	0
	Dependent children	0	0	0	0
	Deduction for social security contributions and income taxes	0	0	0	0
	Work-related expenses	0	0	0	0
	Other	0	0	0	0
3.	**Tax credits or cash transfers included in taxable income**	0	0	0	0
4.	**Central government taxable income (1-2+3)**	252 060	335 239	420 940	335 239
5.	**Central government income tax liability (exclusive of tax credits)**	3 383	3 383	3 383	3 383
6.	**Tax credits**	12 786	20 925	23 154	5 924
	Basic credit	0	0	0	0
	Married or head of family	0	0	0	0
	Children	0	0	0	0
	Other	12 786	20 925	23 154	5 924
7.	**Central government income tax finally paid (5-6)**	0	0	0	0
8.	**State and local taxes**	0	0	0	0
9.	**Employees' compulsory social security contributions**				
	Gross earnings	48 871	62 708	81 615	59 238
10.	**Total payments to general government (7+8+9)**	48 871	62 708	81 615	59 238
11.	**Cash transfers from general government**	5 400	5 400	5 400	0
	For head of family	0	0	0	0
	For two children	5 400	5 400	5 400	0
12.	**Take-home pay (1-10+11)**	208 589	277 931	344 725	276 001
13.	**Employer's compulsory social security contributions**	45 170	60 076	75 433	60 076
14.	**Average rates**				
	Income tax (7 / 1)	0.0%	0.0%	0.0%	0.0%
	Employees' social security contributions (9 / 1)	19.4%	18.7%	19.4%	17.7%
	Total payments less cash transfers [(10-11) / 1]	17.2%	17.1%	18.1%	17.7%
	Total tax wedge including employer's social security contributions [(10+13-11) / (1+13)]	29.8%	29.7%	30.6%	30.2%
15.	**Marginal rates**				
	Total payments less cash transfers: principal earner	19.4%	19.4%	19.4%	18.0%
	Total payments less cash transfers: spouse	16.6%	16.6%	19.4%	16.6%
	Total tax wedge: principal earner	31.6%	31.6%	31.6%	30.5%
	Total tax wedge: spouse	29.3%	29.3%	31.6%	29.3%

The national currency is the Uruguayan Peso (UYU). In 2013, the average exchange rate was UYU 19.98 to USD 1. In that year, the average worker earned UYU 252 059.77. Uruguay also has a Base for Benefits and Contributions (Base de Prestaciones y Contribuciones – BPC) which was UYU 2 598 in 2013.

The Report includes estimates of the tax wedge over the whole of the income distribution ordered by deciles of total labour income of formal wage earners derived from the household surveys.

	Deciles of Incomes									
	1	2	3	4	5	6	7	8	9	10
Local currency (UYU)	72 683	113 038	137 576	160 878	183 553	213 336	248 077	301 959	385 284	690 033
USD[1]	3 638	5 658	6 886	8 053	9 187	10 678	12 417	15 114	19 285	34 539
Dollars in PPP[2]	4 203	6 537	7 956	9 303	10 614	12 337	14 345	17 461	22 280	39 902
Ratio to the minimum wage[3]	0.8	1.2	1.4	1.7	1.9	2.2	2.6	3.2	4.1	7.3

1. Average official exchange rates published by the central bank.
2. Calculated using the implied conversion rate (National currency per current international dollar in purchasing parity power) published by the IMF in the World Economic Outlook dataset.
3. Ratio of the income decile to the official minimum wage of the country.

1. Personal income tax system

The tax year for the personal income tax is the calendar year.

1.1. *Central government income tax*

The income tax is levied on Uruguayan-sourced income. In addition, some foreign sources of income, such as capital gains and labour income are also liable. The personal income tax is divided into two categories. The first applies to capital gains which are subject to a tax rate of 12%. The second applies to all sources of labour income.

Labour income includes all income, such as wages, commissions, overtime, bonuses, holiday pay, etc. It does not include amounts paid in respect of family allowances, subsidies (for sickness, unemployment and maternity) and temporary compensation due to layoffs.

1.1.1. *Tax unit*

In this Report, it is assumed that members of the family are taxed separately. In practice, spouses may opt to file a joint tax return for the household.

1.1.2. *Tax allowances and tax credits*

1.1.2.1. Standard tax credits

- Social security contributions paid to the Social Prevision Bank (Banco de Previsión Social – BPS).

- An annual allowance of 13 BPCs for each child in the care of the taxpayer.
- An annual allowance of 6.5 BPCs for each child in respect of medical expenses for children or other dependents.

The total of the tax credits is calculated by applying a marginal rate to the allowances according to the following schedule. The tax credits are then deducted from the liable personal income tax.

Allowances (BPC) up to	Allowances (UYU) up to	Marginal rate (%)
36	93 528	10
96	249 408	15
516	1 340 568	20
816	2 119 968	22
1 296	3 367 008	25
above	above	30

1.1.3. *Tax schedule*

The annual income tax liability was calculated on the taxable income according to the following schedule in 2013:

Income (BPC) up to	Income (UYU) up to	Marginal rate (%)
84	218 232	0
120	311 760	10
180	467 640	15
600	1 558 800	20
900	2 338 200	22
1 380	3 585 240	25
onward	above	30

1.2. *State and local taxes*

No state or local taxes are levied on wages.

2. Compulsory social security contributions

2.1. *Employee contributions*

Employees are required to pay contributions for the following:

- Old age, disability and survivors program. Employees paid 15% of their gross wages excluding the annual bonus. There is an upper ceiling to these contributions (UYU 569 124 in 2013).
- Healthcare services. Employees without children earning up to UYU 84 570 (30 BPC) per year paid 3% of their gross wage. The contribution rate was raised to 4.5% if earnings were higher. There was also an additional 1.5% for employees with children.
- Labour reconversion fund (FRL). Employees paid a contribution of 0.125% of the gross wages excluding the annual bonus.

2.2. *Employer contributions*

Employers are required to make the following contributions on behalf of their employees:

- Old age, disability and survivors program -7.5% of the payroll subject to an upper ceiling of UYU 1 278 588 in 2013.

- Healthcare insurance -5% of the payroll.
- Work injury insurance -6.9% of the payroll.
- Labour reconversion fund (FRL) -0.125% of the payroll.

3. Universal cash transfer

3.1. *Amount for spouse and for dependent children*

There are cash transfers for children paid on a monthly basis. In 2013, the annual amounts paid are described in the following schedule.

Income (BPC) up to	Income (UYU) up to	Transfer per child (UYU)
78	202 644	5 412
120	311 760	2 700
above	above	0

4. Main changes in tax/benefit since 2013

The BPC varies in accordance to the consumer price index. This directly affects the income tax schedule, monetary transfers and social security contributions. In 2015 the BPC was UYU 3 052.

5. Memorandum items

5.1. *Identification of an AW*

The data refer to the earnings of workers within the formal sector. The average worker's wage was calculated using microdata from the national household surveys.

Venezuela

The country profile includes data on the income taxes paid by workers, their social security contributions, the family benefits they receive in the form of cash transfers as well as the social security contributions and payroll taxes paid by the employers. Results reported include the average and marginal tax burdens for eight different family types.

It also describes the personal income tax systems, all compulsory social security contribution schemes and universal cash transfers as well as recent changes in the tax/benefit system.

Venezuela 2013

Tax / benefit of single persons

	Wage level (% of average wage)	67	100	167	67
	Number of children	0	0	0	2
1.	**Gross wage earnings**	36 508	54 490	90 998	36 508
2.	**Standard tax allowances**	82 818	82 818	82 818	82 818
	Basic allowance	82 818	82 818	82 818	82 818
	Married or head of family	0	0	0	0
	Dependent children	0	0	0	0
	Deduction for social security contributions and income taxes	0	0	0	0
	Work-related expenses	0	0	0	0
	Other	0	0	0	0
3.	**Tax credits or cash transfers included in taxable income**	0	0	0	0
4.	**Central government taxable income (1-2+3)**	0	0	8 180	0
5.	**Central government income tax liability (exclusive of tax credits)**	0	0	491	0
6.	**Tax credits**	1 070	1 070	1 070	3 210
	Basic credit	0	0	0	0
	Married or head of family	0	0	0	0
	Children	0	0	0	2 140
	Other	1 070	1 070	1 070	1 070
7.	**Central government income tax finally paid (5-6)**	0	0	0	0
8.	**State and local taxes**	0	0	0	0
9.	**Employees' compulsory social security contributions**				
	Gross earnings	2 010	3 001	5 011	2 010
10.	**Total payments to general government (7+8+9)**	2 010	3 001	5 011	2 010
11.	**Cash transfers from general government**	0	0	0	0
	For head of family	0	0	0	0
	For two children	0	0	0	0
12.	**Take-home pay (1-10+11)**	34 498	51 489	85 987	34 498
13.	**Employer's compulsory social security contributions**	5 278	7 878	13 156	5 278
14.	**Average rates**				
	Income tax (7 / 1)	0.0%	0.0%	0.0%	0.0%
	Employees' social security contributions (9 / 1)	5.5%	5.5%	5.5%	5.5%
	Total payments less cash transfers [(10-11) / 1]	5.5%	5.5%	5.5%	5.5%
	Total tax wedge including employer's social security contributions [(10+13-11) / (1+13)]	17.4%	17.4%	17.4%	17.4%
15.	**Marginal rates**				
	Total payments less cash transfers: principal earner	5.5%	5.5%	5.5%	5.5%
	Total payments less cash transfers: spouse	N.A.	N.A.	N.A.	N.A.
	Total tax wedge: principal earner	17.4%	17.4%	17.4%	17.4%
	Total tax wedge: spouse	N.A.	N.A.	N.A.	N.A.

Venezuela 2013

Tax / benefit of married couples

		100-0	100-33	100-67	100-33
	Wage level (% of average wage)	100-0	100-33	100-67	100-33
	Number of children	2	2	2	0
1.	**Gross wage earnings**	54 490	72 471	90 998	72 471
2.	**Standard tax allowances**	82 818	165 636	165 636	165 636
	Basic allowance	82 818	165 636	165 636	165 636
	Married or head of family	0	0	0	0
	Dependent children	0	0	0	0
	Deduction for social security contributions and income taxes	0	0	0	0
	Work-related expenses	0	0	0	0
	Other	0	0	0	0
3.	**Tax credits or cash transfers included in taxable income**	0	0	0	0
4.	**Central government taxable income (1-2+3)**	0	0	0	0
5.	**Central government income tax liability (exclusive of tax credits)**	0	0	0	0
6.	**Tax credits**	4 280	4 280	4 280	2 140
	Basic credit	0	0	0	0
	Married or head of family	1 070	1 070	1 070	1 070
	Children	2 140	2 140	2 140	0
	Other	1 070	1 070	1 070	1 070
7.	**Central government income tax finally paid (5-6)**	0	0	0	0
8.	**State and local taxes**	0	0	0	0
9.	**Employees' compulsory social security contributions**				
	Gross earnings	3 001	3 991	5 011	3 991
10.	**Total payments to general government (7+8+9)**	3 001	3 991	5 011	3 991
11.	**Cash transfers from general government**	0	0	0	0
	For head of family	0	0	0	0
	For two children	0	0	0	0
12.	**Take-home pay (1-10+11)**	51 489	68 480	85 987	68 480
13.	**Employer's compulsory social security contributions**	7 878	10 478	13 156	10 478
14.	**Average rates**				
	Income tax (7 / 1)	0.0%	0.0%	0.0%	0.0%
	Employees' social security contributions (9 / 1)	5.5%	5.5%	5.5%	5.5%
	Total payments less cash transfers [(10-11) / 1]	5.5%	5.5%	5.5%	5.5%
	Total tax wedge including employer's social security contributions [(10+13-11) / (1+13)]	17.4%	17.4%	17.4%	17.4%
15.	**Marginal rates**				
	Total payments less cash transfers: principal earner	5.5%	5.5%	5.5%	5.5%
	Total payments less cash transfers: spouse	5.5%	5.5%	5.5%	5.5%
	Total tax wedge: principal earner	17.4%	17.4%	17.4%	17.4%
	Total tax wedge: spouse	17.4%	17.4%	17.4%	17.4%

The national currency is the Bolivar. In 2013, the average exchange rate was VEF 6.28 to USD 1. In that year, the average worker earned VEF 54 489.74 and the Tax Unit (Unidad Tributaria – UT) was VEF 107.

The Report includes estimates of the tax wedge over the whole of the income distribution ordered by deciles of total labour income of formal wage earners derived from the household surveys.

	Deciles of Incomes									
	1	2	3	4	5	6	7	8	9	10
Local currency (VEN)	29 289	35 075	38 300	41 892	45 342	48 664	53 738	59 857	73 294	131 171
USD[1]	4 661	5 581	6 095	6 666	7 215	7 744	8 551	9 525	11 663	20 873
Dollars in PPP[2]	7 365	8 819	9 630	10 534	11 401	12 236	13 512	15 051	18 430	32 982
Ratio to the minimum wage[3]	0.9	1.1	1.2	1.3	1.4	1.5	1.7	1.8	2.3	4.0

1. Average official exchange rates published by the central bank.
2. Calculated using the implied conversion rate (National currency per current international dollar in purchasing power parity) published by the IMF in the World Economic Outlook dataset.
3. Ratio of the income decile to the official minimum wage of the country.

1. Personal income tax system

The fiscal year for the income tax is the calendar year.

1.1. *Central government income tax*

The personal income tax is levied on wages, salaries or compensation for work received from employment plus income and gains received from self-employment or from professional activities. It is also levied on any investment income or capital gains.

The main exemptions for the income tax are:

- Compensations and indemnities relating to work injuries that are paid to the worker or his/her beneficiaries.
- Pensions or retirement income.
- Interest received on fixed income deposits, bonds, savings certificates or any other savings instruments specified by the laws relating to banks and other financial institutions.
- Interest paid on national bonds and any other debt instruments issued by the national government.

1.1.1. *Tax unit*

Members of the family are taxed separately.

Individuals who are residents of Venezuela are liable for personal income tax on their worldwide income. Non-residents are taxed on their Venezuelan-sourced income.

1.1.2. *Tax allowances and tax credits*

1.1.2.1. Standard tax allowances and tax credits

- A standard allowance of 774 tax units.[1]
- An allowance for each child aged 25 or less of 10 tax units.
- A tax rebate of 10 tax units when couples file separately. Only one of the spouses can claim this credit.

1.1.2.2. Main non-standard tax allowances and tax credits

- The amounts paid to training institutes in the country in respect of the education of taxpayers and their dependents aged 25 or less.
- Insurance premiums paid to resident companies to cover hospitalisation, surgery and maternity.
- Medical, dental and hospital service expenses incurred by the taxpayer, spouse, and children.
- Interest paid on loans to purchase the main residence, up to 1 000 tax units per year.
- Payments of rent on the taxpayer's main residence up to 800 tax units per year.

1.1.3. *Tax schedule*

The annual income tax liability was calculated on the taxable income according to the following schedule in 2013:

Income (tax units) up to	Income (VEF) up to	Marginal rate (%)
1 000	107 000.00	6
1 500	160 500.00	9
2 000	214 000.00	12
2 500	267 500.00	16
3 000	321 000.00	20
4 000	428 000.00	24
6 000	642 000.00	29
above	above	34

1.2. *State and local taxes*

No state or local taxes are levied on wages.

2. Compulsory social security contributions

2.1. *Employee contributions*

Program	Marginal rate (%)
Pensions, old age and survivor's program	4.0
Unemployment insurance	0.5
Housing and Habitat Subsystem	1.0
National Institute for Educational Cooperation*	0.5

The employee contributions are levied on gross wages excluding the end-year bonus (equivalent to a month's wage). There is an upper ceiling on the contributions of 5 times the annual minimum wage (VEF 162 665 in 2013).

The contributions to the national institute for educational co-operation are paid on profits distributed by companies. For this exercise the assumption is that the distributed profits amount to 30 days of the employee's wage, which equals the minimum set by the Organic Law of the Workers (LOTTT due to its initials in Spanish) in Articles 131 and 132.

2.2. *Employer contributions*

Employers are required to contribute to the following public programs.

Program	Marginal rate (%)
Pensions, old age and survivor's program	9.0
Work injury	0.75
Unemployment insurance	2.0
Housing and Habitat Subsystem	2.0
National Institute for Educational Cooperation	2.0

The employers' contributions are levied on the payroll.

3. Universal cash transfer

3.1. *Amount for spouse and for dependent children*

None.

4. Main changes in tax/benefit since 2013

The value of the tax units is adjusted each year. In 2015, the tax unit was VEF 150.

5. Memorandum items

5.1. *Identification of an AW*

The data refer to the earnings of workers within the formal sector. The average worker's wage was calculated using microdata from the national household surveys.

Note

1. Taxpayers are entitled either to itemise the main non-standard allowances described or opt for the 774 tax unit standard allowance. This Report uses the latter.

ANNEX

Methodology and limitations

I. Methodology

1. *Introduction*

The personal circumstances of taxpayers vary greatly throughout the countries covered in the Report. A specific methodology has been adopted to produce comparative statistics covering taxes, benefits and labour costs across Latin American and Caribbean countries which is based on the compulsory payments methodology for OECD economies.

- The Report focuses on eight different family types which vary by household composition and level of earnings. The Report also showcases results throughout the income distribution of labour income.
- Each household contains a full-time adult employee working in one of a broad range of productive sectors within each Latin American and Caribbean economy. Some of the family profiles include a second working spouse.
- The annual income from employment is assumed to be equal to a given fraction of the average gross wage earnings of these workers.
- In case of deciles of income, employment earnings are equal to the average earnings per decile.
- Additional assumptions are also made regarding other relevant personal circumstances of these wage earners in order to calculate their tax/benefit position.

Under the compulsory payments methodology:

- The deductions from labour income (referred to in this Report as taxes) are defined as personal income tax, employee and employer social security contributions (paid either to general government or privately managed funds) and payroll taxes less cash transfers.
- Labour costs are defined as the sum of gross wage earnings, employer's social security contributions (paid either to general government or privately managed funds) and payroll taxes.

The guidelines described in the following paragraphs form the basis for the calculations shown throughout the Report. Table A.1 sets out the terminology that is used. Where a country has had to depart from the guidelines, this is noted in the text and/or in the country details contained in Part II of the Report. The number of taxpayers with the defined characteristics and the wage level of the average workers vary between both Latin American and Caribbean economies and OECD economies.

2. *Taxpayer characteristics*

The eight household types identified in the Report are set out in Table A.2. Any children in the household are assumed to be aged 15 or under. The family is assumed to have no income source other than employment and cash benefits.

3. *The range of industries covered*

The standard assumption for calculating average wage earnings is based on the weighted labour income average derived from income household surveys for Latin American and Caribbean countries.

In the cases of Argentina, Brazil, Chile, Colombia and Mexico, the standard assumption for calculating average wages is based on the Sectors B-N of the International Standard Industrial Classification of all Economic Activities (ISIC Revision 4, United Nations).

Table A.1. **Terminology**

	General terms
Average worker (AW)	An adult full-time worker in any of the productive sectors classifications of income household surveys.
Single persons	Unmarried men and women.
Couple with children	Married couples with two dependent children.
Labour costs	The sum of gross wage earnings, employer social security contributions (paid either to general government or privately managed funds) and payroll taxes.
Net take-home pay	Gross wage earnings minus the sum of personal income taxes and social security contributions paid by the employee (either to general government or privately managed funds), plus any cash transfers received from the general government.
Personal average tax rate (tax burden)	The sum of the personal income tax and social security contributions paid by the employee (either to general government or privately managed funds) expressed as a percentage of the gross wage earnings.
Tax wedge	The sum of personal income tax, employee and employer social security contributions (paid either to general government or privately managed funds) and payroll taxes, less cash transfers, expressed as a percentage of total labour costs.
Marginal rate	The percentage of an additional unit of currency that is paid in taxes or social security contributions.
Elasticity of income after-tax	Percentage change in "after-tax" income following an increase in one currency unit of income before tax (defined more precisely as 1 minus a marginal tax rate divided by 1 minus the corresponding average tax rate).
	Terms used under income tax
Tax reliefs	A generic term used to cover the ways of giving favourable income tax treatment to potential taxpayers.
Tax allowances or tax deductions	Amounts deducted from gross earnings to arrive at taxable income.
Tax credits	Amounts which a taxpayer may deduct from his/her tax liability. They are described as payable if they can exceed the tax liability. They may also be referred to as refundable tax credits.
Standard tax reliefs or standard tax deductions	Reliefs unrelated to the actual expenses incurred by taxpayers and automatically available to all taxpayers who satisfy eligibility criteria established by the legislation. These include deductions for compulsory social security contributions and end-year bonuses.
Basic relief or basic deduction	Any standard tax deduction available irrespective of marital and family status.
Marriage allowance	Additional tax relief given to married couples. (In some countries, this is not distinguished from basic deductions, which may be doubled on marriage).
Non-standard tax reliefs or deductions	Reliefs or deductions wholly determined by reference to actual expenses incurred.
Average rate of income tax	Amount of income tax payable after accounting for any reliefs calculated on the basis of the tax provisions covered in this Report, divided by gross wage earnings.
Schedule rate	The rate which appears in the schedules of the income tax or social security contributions.
	Terms used under cash transfers
Cash transfers	Cash payments made by the general government, through specific agencies, paid to the household, usually in respect of dependent children or spouse.

Table A.2. **Characteristics of taxpayers**

Marital status	Children	Principal earner	Secondary earner
Single individual	No children	67% of average wage	
Single individual	No children	100% of average wage	
Single individual	No children	167% of average wage	
Single individual	2 children	67% of average wage	
Married couple	2 children	100% of average wage	
Married couple	2 children	100% of average wage	33% of average wage
Married couple	2 children	100% of average wage	67% of average wage
Married couple	No children	100% of average wage	33% of average wage

Table A.3. **International standard industrial classification of all economic activities**

Revision 4 (ISIC Rev 4.)	
A	Agriculture, forestry and fishing
B	Mining and quarrying
C	Manufacturing
D	Electricity, gas, steam and air conditioning supply
E	Water supply; sewerage, waste management and remediation activities
F	Construction
G	Wholesale and retail trade, repair of motor vehicles and motorcycles
H	Transportation and storage
I	Accommodation and food service activities
J	Information and communication
K	Financial and insurance activities
L	Real estate activities
M	Professional, scientific and technical activities
N	Administrative and support service activities
O	Public administration and defence; compulsory social security
P	Education
Q	Human health and social work activities
R	Arts, entertainment and recreation
S	Other service activities
T	Activities of households as employers; undifferentiated goods – and services – producing activities of households for own use
U	Activities of extraterritorial organisations and bodies

4. *Defining gross wage earnings*

This section sets out the assumptions underlying the calculation of the average earnings figures for the "average worker". The gross wage earnings data have been established using statistical data from the sources set out for each country in Table A.4. Further information on the calculation of the earnings figure is provided in Part II.

- The data relate to the average earnings in the industry sectors included in the national household surveys for the country as a whole.
- The calculations are based on the earnings of a formal salaried full-time adult worker (including both manual and non-manual). They relate to the average earnings of all workers in the industry sectors covered. No account is taken of variation between males and females or due to age or region.
- The worker is assumed to be full-time employed during the entire year without breaks for sickness or unemployment.

- Two of the household types include a second earner at 33% of average earnings. Such individuals are more likely to be working part-time rather than full-time.
- The earnings calculation includes all cash remuneration paid to workers in the industries covered taking into account average amounts of overtime, cash supplements (e.g. Christmas bonuses, thirteenth month) and vacation payments typically paid to them.
- The earnings figures include supervisory and/or management employees.
- Fringe benefits – which include, for example, provision of food, housing or clothing by the employer either free of charge or at below market-price – are excluded from the calculation of average earnings. Fringe benefits have not been taken into account mainly due to:
  - These types of benefits are difficult to price in a consistent manner. For instance, they may be valued at the actual cost to the employer, their value to the employee or their fair market value.
  - In most countries, they are of minimal importance for the great majority of workers, especially for those at the average wage level.
  - Tax calculations would require additional assumptions and would be more complex if the tax treatment of fringe benefits were incorporated.

Table A.4. **Source of earnings data, 2013**

Country	Source
Argentina	Encuesta Permanente de Hogares – Continua (EPHC) 2003 – 2014 – Instituto Nacional de Estadísticas y Censos (INDEC) and Sistema Integrado Previsional Argentino (SIPA).
Bolivia	Encuesta Continua de Hogares (ECH) – Instituto Nacional de Estadística (INE)
Brazil	Pesquisa Nacional por Amostra de Domicilio (PNAD) – Instituto Brasileiro de Geografía e Estadística (IBGE)
Chile	Encuesta de Caracterización Socioeconómica Nacional (CASEN) – Ministerio de Desarrollo Social (MIDEPLAN) for the labour income decile distribution and the monthly simple of business with +10 employees from the National Institute of Statistics (INE) for the average wage.
Colombia	Gran Encuesta Integrada de Hogares (GEIH) – Departamento Administrativo Nacional de Estadística (DANE)
Costa Rica	Encuesta Nacional de Hogares (ENAHO) – Instituto Nacional de Estadísticas y Censos (INEC)
Dominican Republic	Encuesta Nacional de Fuerza de Trabajo (ENFT) – Banco Central de la República Dominicana (BCDR)
Ecuador	Encuesta Nacional de Empleo, Desempleo y Subempleo (ENEMDU) – Instituto Nacional de Estadística y Censos (INEC)
El Salvador	Encuesta de Hogares de Propósitos Múltiples (EHPM) – Dirección General de Estadística y Censos (DIGESTYC)
Guatemala	Encuesta Nacional de Empleo e Ingresos (ENEI) – Instituto Nacional de Estadística (INE)
Honduras	Encuesta Permanente de Hogares de Propósitos Múltiples (EPHPM) – Instituto Nacional de Estadísticas (INE)
Jamaica	Labour Force Survey (LFS) – Statistical Institute of Jamaica (STATIN)
Mexico	Encuesta Nacional de Ingresos y Gastos de Hogares (ENIGH) – Instituto Nacional de Estadística y Geografía (INEGI) and administrative data from the Mexican Social Security Institute and the National Minimum Wage Commission (CONASAMI)
Nicaragua	Encuesta Continua de Hogares (ECH) – Instituto Nacional de Información de Desarrollo (INIDE)
Panama	Encuesta de Hogares de Propósitos Múltiples (EHPM) – Instituto Nacional de Estadística y Censo (INEC)
Paraguay	Encuesta Permanente de Hogares (EPH) – Dirección General de Estadística y Censos (DGEEC)
Peru	Encuesta Nacional de Hogares (EPH) – Instituto Nacional de Estadística e Informática (INEI).
Trinidad and Tobago	Continuous Sample Survey of Population (CSSP) – Central Statistical Office, Office of the Prime Minister (CSO)
Uruguay	Encuesta Continua de Hogares (ECH) – Instituto Nacional de Estadística (INE)
Venezuela	Encuesta de Hogares por Muestreo (EHM) – Instituto Nacional de Estadística (INE)

5. *Calculating average gross wages and wage earnings by decile of income*

Table A.5 describes the average gross wage and corresponding decile figures calculated for each country. Since statistical data on average gross wage earnings are not generally available in Latin American and Caribbean countries, the process adopted to make appropriate estimates differs from the traditional methodology followed in OECD (2016) Taxing Wages for OECD countries. In this Report, earnings are generally estimated from reported earnings of formal salaried workers on a monthly basis. These estimates are then multiplied by 12 to produce an annual estimate. In the cases of Bolivia and Chile, the data has been adjusted to reflect the real wage increases in 2012 and 2013.

Table A.5. **Estimated gross wage earnings, 2013 (in thousands of national currency)**

Country	Average wage	D1	D2	D3	D4	D5	D6	D7	D8	D9	D10
Argentina	72.91	22.89	38.19	47.22	53.95	59.96	69.65	81.72	94.09	113.12	176.51
Bolivia	40.42	13.79	19.57	23.75	27.29	31.38	36.00	41.42	49.22	62.12	112.20
Brazil	22.69	7.76	8.39	9.45	10.78	12.36	14.73	17.40	22.20	31.10	75.53
Chile	6 604	1 686	2 504	2 563	2 746	3 154	3 635	4 449	5 747	8 035	19 322
Colombia	17 636	6 869	8 279	8 776	9 533	10 750	12 370	14 998	18 785	26 245	59 217
Costa Rica	5 607	1 363	2 362	2 834	3 204	3 631	4 210	5 057	6 473	9 193	17 181.09
Dominican Republic	225.96	59.28	83.55	102.55	123.91	146.90	172.40	201.38	260.71	376.25	754.65
Ecuador	8.01	3.36	4.04	4.24	4.76	5.52	6.39	7.54	9.39	12.00	23.02
El Salvador	5.31	2.13	2.53	2.80	3.04	3.49	4.24	5.30	6.25	7.88	15.66
Guatemala	46.56	20.62	28.54	31.67	34.37	37.21	41.21	45.04	51.41	62.05	115.06
Honduras	115.47	47.01	68.49	76.96	83.68	88.11	95.40	113.09	138.63	177.43	302.23
Jamaica	358.99	58.90	61.50	77.40	193.55	206.33	266.23	385.74	409.53	670.18	1 500.62
Mexico	98.92	20.21	39.19	48.50	58.16	67.91	80.08	96.72	120.80	161.58	335.54
Nicaragua	79.23	31.29	40.32	46.88	51.88	58.57	65.93	73.35	85.25	110.89	230.14
Panama	9.20	3.56	4.78	5.27	5.90	6.44	7.14	8.31	10.00	12.92	29.28
Paraguay	35 322	14 355	18 818	20 211	22 811	25 232	29 543	34 394	40 611	52 385	96 048.16
Peru	17.03	6.38	8.52	9.71	10.90	12.50	14.22	16.23	19.61	25.25	48.23
Trinidad and Tobago	49.30	9.38	18.40	24.56	30.36	36.48	43.33	51.56	62.46	79.87	136.65
Uruguay	252.06	72.68	113.04	137.58	160.88	183.55	213.34	248.08	301.96	385.28	690.03
Venezuela	54.49	29.29	35.08	38.30	41.89	45.34	48.66	53.74	59.86	73.29	131.17

The traditional methodology is for countries to calculate annual average earnings from the average of hourly earnings in each week, month or quarter, weighted by the hours worked during each period, and multiplied by the average number of hours worked during the year, assuming that the worker is neither unemployed nor sick and including periods of paid vacation.

Table A.6. **Purchasing power parities and exchange rates for 2013**

Country	International currency symbol	Exchange rates[1]	Implied purchasing power parities[2]
Argentina	ARS	5.50	3.66
Bolivia	BOB	6.98	3.23
Brazil	BRL	2.16	1.60
Chile	CLP	495.31	345.29
Colombia	COP	1 869.10	1 174.83
Costa Rica	CRC	490.67	363.41
Dominican Republic	DOP	41.81	20.15
Ecuador	USD	1.00	0.55
El Salvador	USD	1.00	0.49
Guatemala	GTQ	7.86	3.74
Honduras	HNL	19.73	10.06
Jamaica	JMD	98.28	60.52
Mexico	MXN	12.77	7.79
Nicaragua	NIO	24.72	9.62
Panama	PAB	1.00	0.57
Paraguay	PYG	4 357.61	2 263.92
Peru	PEN	2.72	1.52
Trinidad and Tobago	TTD	6.39	4.14
Uruguay	UYU	19.98	17.29
Venezuela	VEF	6.28	3.98

1. Average of 12 month daily rates in terms of one USD.
2. National currency per current international dollar in purchasing power parity. Published by the IMF in the World Economic Outlook dataset.

6. *Coverage of taxes and benefits*

The Report is concerned with personal income tax plus employee and employer social security contributions payable on wage earnings. In addition, payroll taxes (see Section 9) are included in the calculation of the total wedge between labour costs to the employer and the corresponding net take-home pay of the employee.

The calculation of the net income after allowing for payments of tax and compulsory social security contributions includes family benefits paid by general government as cash transfers (see Section 10). Income tax due on capital income and non-wage labour income, direct taxes, other than the personal income tax (net wealth tax, corporate income tax) and all indirect taxes are not considered in this Report.

In this study, all compulsory social security contributions are included regardless of whether they are paid to general government or privately managed funds. Social security contributions paid to general government clearly resemble taxes. They may, however, differ from taxes in that the receipt of social security benefits depends upon appropriate contributions having been made, although the size of the benefits is not necessarily related to the amount of the contributions. Compulsory social security contributions to privately managed funds are also included given that they are compulsory payments and that several countries in the region have adopted some kind of privately managed social security program. Countries finance compulsory public social security programmes to a varying degree from general tax and non-tax revenue together with earmarked contributions. Better comparability between countries is obtained by treating social security contributions as taxes, but they are listed under a separate heading so that their amounts can be identified in any analysis.

7. Calculation of personal income taxes

The specific methods by which income tax payments are calculated for each country are described in Part II of this Report. First, the tax allowances applicable to a taxpayer with the characteristics and income level related to gross annual wage earnings of an average worker are determined. Next, the schedule of tax rates is applied and the resulting tax liability is reduced by any relevant tax credits. An important issue arising in the calculation of the personal income tax liability involves determining which tax reliefs or tax deductions should be taken into account. Two broad categories of reliefs may be distinguished:

- *Standard tax reliefs*: deductions which are unrelated to actual expenditures incurred by the taxpayer and are automatically available to all taxpayers who satisfy the eligibility rules specified in the legislation. Standard tax reliefs are usually fixed amounts or fixed percentages of income and are typically the most important set of reliefs in the determination of the income tax paid by workers. These reliefs are taken into account in the calculations – they include:
  - the *basic relief* which is fixed and is available to all taxpayers or all wage earners, irrespective of their marital or family status;
  - the *standard relief* which is available to taxpayers depending on their *marital status*;
  - the *standard child relief* granted to a family with children aged fifteen or under;
  - the *standard relief* in respect of *work expenses*, which is usually a fixed amount or fixed percentage of (gross) wage earnings; and,
  - tax reliefs/deductions allowed for *mandatory social security contributions* and other (sub-central government) *income taxes* are also considered as standard reliefs since they apply to all wage earners and represent relate to compulsory payments.
- *Non-standard tax reliefs*: These are reliefs which are wholly determined by reference to actual expenses incurred. They are therefore neither fixed amounts nor fixed percentages of income. Examples of non-standard tax reliefs include reliefs for interest on qualifying loans (e.g. for the purchase of a house), private insurance premiums, and charitable donations. These are not taken into account in calculating the tax position of employees.

Standard reliefs are separately identified and their impact on average tax rates is calculated in the results tables shown in Part II of this Report. The latter includes a brief description of the main non-standard reliefs for the majority of the countries.

8. Social security contributions

Compulsory social security contributions paid by employees and employers to general government, to social security funds under the effective control of government or to privately managed funds are included in the coverage of this Report. In most countries, contributions are levied on gross earnings and earmarked to provide social security benefits.

9. Payroll taxes

The tax base of a payroll tax is either a proportion of the payroll or a fixed amount per employee.

Payroll taxes are included in total tax wedges described in this Report, given that they increase the gap between gross labour costs and net take-home pay in the same way as income tax and social security contributions do. The main difference compared with the latter is that the payment of payroll taxes does not confer an entitlement to social security benefits.

Also, the tax base of payroll taxes may differ from the tax base of employer social security contributions. For example, certain fringe benefits may only be liable to payroll tax. Because this Report presents the standard case, the payroll tax base is – depending on the relevant legislation – gross wages (excluding fringe benefits and other items of compensation that vary per employee), gross wages plus employer social security contributions, or a fixed amount per employee.

10. *Family and cash benefits from the general government*

Tax reliefs and family cash transfers universally paid in respect of dependent children aged 15 years or under who are attending school are included in the scope of the study. Where tax reliefs or cash transfers vary within this age range, the most generous provisions are adopted.

Relevant cash payments are those received from general government. In some cases, for example in Colombia, the cash benefits include amounts that are paid without consideration of the number of children.

11. *Payable tax credits*

Payable (non-wastable) tax credits are tax credits that can exceed tax liability, where the excess, if any, can be paid as a cash transfer to the taxpayer. In principle, these credits can be treated in different ways according to whether they are regarded as tax provisions or cash transfers or a combination of these.

OECD (2015a) Revenue Statistics publication[1] requires that

- Only the portion of a payable tax credit that is claimed to reduce or eliminate a taxpayer's liability (the "tax expenditure" component) should be deducted in the reporting of tax revenues;
- The part of the tax credit that exceeds a taxpayer's tax liability and is paid to him/her (the "cash transfer" component) should be treated as an expenditure item and not deducted in the reporting of tax revenues.

In OECD (2016) Taxing Wages publication and in this Report, the full amount of any payable tax credit is taken into account in the income tax calculation. Strict consistency with OECD/ECLAC/CIAT/IDB (2016) Revenue Statistics in Latin American and Caribbean publication would require that only the tax expenditure component be offset against derived income tax, with the excess (if any) treated as a cash transfer. However, this approach would diminish rather than strengthen the informational content of the derived results in this Report. In particular, limiting tax credit claims to tax expenditure amounts would yield a zero income tax liability and zero average income tax rate where cash refunds are provided. Where tax credits claims are not constrained in this way, negative income tax liabilities and negative average income tax rates would result where cash transfers are provided. Arguably, these negative amounts more clearly convey the taxpayer's position (which is improved relative to the no-tax situation). Also, not including the cash transfer portion of payable tax credits in the "cash transfers from general government" item of the country tables permits greater transparency of the latter which focuses on "pure" cash transfers only.

12. *The calculation of the marginal tax rates*

In most cases, the marginal tax rates are calculated by considering the impact of a small increase (one unit of local currency) in gross earnings on personal income tax, social security contributions and cash benefits. However, in the case of a non-working spouse, the move from a zero to a small positive income is unrepresentative of income changes and therefore of little interest. So, for this case, the marginal rates for the spouse are calculated by considering the impact of an income increase from zero to 33% of the average wage.

II. Limitations

1. *General limitations*

The simple approach of comparing the tax/benefit position of example families avoids many of the conceptual and definitional problems involved in more complex international comparisons of tax burdens and general government cash transfer programmes. However, a drawback of this methodology is that the earnings of an average worker will usually occupy a different position in the overall income distribution in different economies, although the earnings relate to workers in similar jobs in various OECD member countries.

Because of the limitations on the taxes and benefits covered in the Report, the data cannot be taken as an indication of the overall impact of the government sector on the welfare of taxpayers and their families. Complete coverage would require studies of the impact of indirect taxes, the treatment of non-wage labour income and other income components under personal income taxes and the effect of other tax allowances and cash benefits. Complete coverage would also require that consideration be given to the effect on welfare of services provided by the state, either free or below cost, and the incidence of corporate and other direct taxes on earnings and prices. Such a broad coverage is not possible in an international comparison of all OECD and Latin American and Caribbean countries. The differences between the results shown here and those of a full study of the overall impact on employees of government interventions in the economy would vary from one country to another. They would depend on the relative shares of different kinds of taxes in government revenues and on the scope and nature of government social expenditures.[2]

The Report shows only the formal incidence of taxes and social security contributions on employees and employers. The final, economic incidence of these deductions may be quite different, because the burden may be shifted from employers onto employees and vice versa by market adjustments to gross wages.

The income left at the disposal of a taxpayer may represent different standards of living in various countries because the range of goods and services on which the income is spent and their relative prices differ as between countries. In those countries where the general government sector provides a wide range of goods and services (generous basic old age pension, free health services, public housing, university education, etc.), the taxpayer may be left with less cash income but may enjoy the same living standards as a taxpayer receiving a higher cash income but living in a country where there are fewer publicly provided goods and services.

Finally, it should be noted that the results presented for Brazil, Chile and Mexico in this Report differ from those presented in OECD (2015b) in the annual OECD Taxing Wages publication. The figures presented in this report have been calculated under the Compulsory Payments methodology which includes all mandatory social security contributions irrespective of whether they are paid to general government or privately managed funds.

2. Some specific limitations on the income tax calculation

The exclusion of non-wage income and the limited number of tax reliefs covered imply that the average rates of income tax in the tables in this publication will not necessarily reflect the actual rates confronting taxpayers at these levels of earnings. Actual rates may be lower than the calculated rates because the latter do not take into account non-standard expense-related reliefs. On the other hand, actual rates may be higher than calculated rates because the latter do not take into account tax on non-wage income received by employees.

The decision not to calculate separately average rates of income tax taking into account the effect of non-standard tax reliefs was taken because:

- Expense-related deductions are substitutes for direct cash subsidies, in many cases. To take into account these reliefs while ignoring any corresponding direct subsidies would distort comparisons of take-home pay plus cash transfers;
- The special tax treatment of certain expenses may be linked to special treatment of any income associated with these expenses (e.g. the tax treatment voluntary social security contributions and pension income) which is beyond the scope of this study.

Notes

1. A Special Feature in the 2001 edition discusses the alternative treatments and the conceptual and practical difficulties that arise in deciding which is the most appropriate approach for the purpose of reporting internationally comparable tax revenue figures.
2. For an analysis on tax and social spending incidence, consult: Lustig, N. (2016), "El impacto del sistema tributario y el gasto social en la distribución del ingreso y la pobreza en América Latina: Argentina, Bolivia, Brasil, Chile, Colombia, Costa Rica, Ecuador, El Salvador, Guatemala, Honduras, México, Perú y Uruguay", CEQ *Working paper* No. 47, Commitment to Equity Institute, Tulane University.

References

OECD (2016a), *Taxing Wages 2016*, OECD Publishing, Paris, *http://dx.doi.org/10.1787/tax_wages-2016-en*

OECD/CIAT/IDB (2016), *Revenue Statistics in Latin America and the Caribbean 2016*, OECD Publishing, Paris, *http://dx.doi.org/10.1787/rev_lat_car-2016-en-fr*

OECD (2015a), *Revenue Statistics 2015*, OECD Publishing, Paris, *http://dx.doi.org/10.1787/rev_stats-2015-en-fr*

OECD (2015b), *Taxing Wages 2015*, OECD Publishing, Paris, *http://dx.doi.org/10.1787/tax_wages-2015-en*

OECD PUBLISHING, 2, rue André-Pascal, 75775 PARIS CEDEX 16
(23 2016 32 1P1) ISBN 978-92-64-26256-0 – 2016

www.ingramcontent.com/pod-product-compliance
Lightning Source LLC
Chambersburg PA
CBHW061203240926
51846CB00006B/1105
* 9 7 8 9 2 6 4 2 6 2 5 6 0 *